DEVON, CORNWALL
& SOUTHWEST
ENGLAND

OLIVER BERRY
BELINDA DIXON

DEVON, CORNWALL & SOUTHWEST ENGLAND

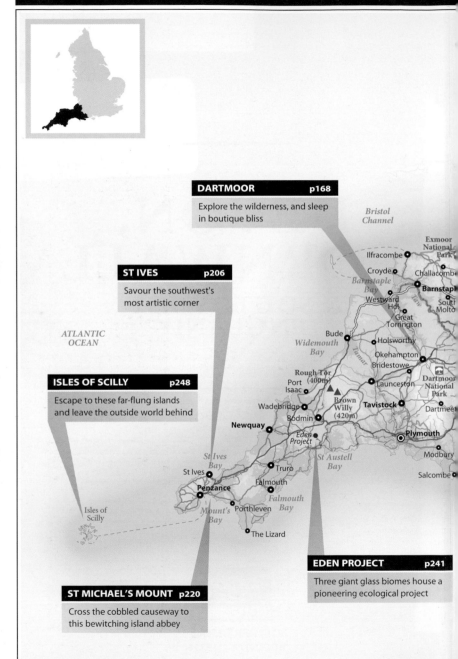

DARTMOOR p168

Explore the wilderness, and sleep in boutique bliss

ST IVES p206

Savour the southwest's most artistic corner

ISLES OF SCILLY p248

Escape to these far-flung islands and leave the outside world behind

EDEN PROJECT p241

Three giant glass biomes house a pioneering ecological project

ST MICHAEL'S MOUNT p220

Cross the cobbled causeway to this bewitching island abbey

Bristol Channel

Exmoor National Park

Ilfracombe
Croyde
Challacombe
Barnstaple Bay
Barnstaple
Westward Ho!
South Molton
Great Torrington

Bude
Widemouth Bay
Holsworthy
Okehampton
Bridestowe

ATLANTIC OCEAN

Rough Tor (400m)
Port Isaac
Launceston
Dartmoor National Park
Wadebridge
Brown Willy (420m)
Tavistock
Dartmeet
Newquay
Bodmin
Eden Project
Plymouth
Modbury
St Ives Bay
St Austell Bay
St Ives
Truro
Salcombe
Falmouth
Penzance
Falmouth Bay
Isles of Scilly
Mount's Bay
Porthleven
The Lizard

Taw
Tamar

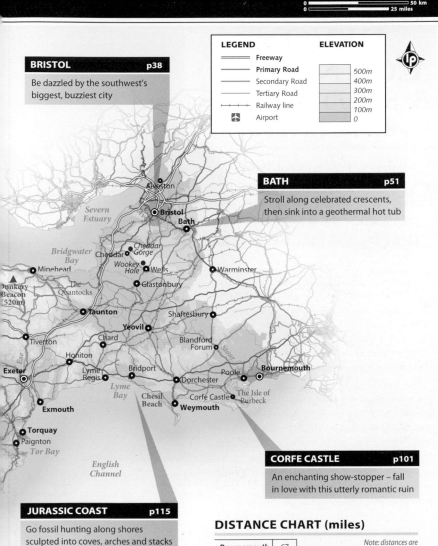

LEGEND

══════ Freeway
────── Primary Road
────── Secondary Road
────── Tertiary Road
+−+−+−+ Railway line
✈ Airport

ELEVATION

500m
400m
300m
200m
100m
0

BRISTOL p38

Be dazzled by the southwest's biggest, buzziest city

BATH p51

Stroll along celebrated crescents, then sink into a geothermal hot tub

Severn Estuary

Alveston

Bristol
Bath

Bridgwater Bay

Cheddar Gorge
Cheddar
Wookey Hole
Wells

Minehead

Warminster

Dunkery Beacon (520m)

The Quantocks

Glastonbury

Taunton

Shaftesbury

Tiverton

Yeovil

Chard

Blandford Forum

Honiton

Exeter

Lyme Regis

Bridport

Poole

Bournemouth

Exmouth

Lyme Bay

Chesil Beach

Dorchester

Corfe Castle

The Isle of Purbeck

Weymouth

Torquay
Paignton
Tor Bay

English Channel

CORFE CASTLE p101

An enchanting show-stopper – fall in love with this utterly romantic ruin

JURASSIC COAST p115

Go fossil hunting along shores sculpted into coves, arches and stacks

DISTANCE CHART (miles)

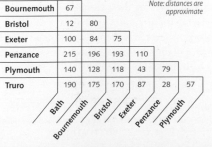

Note: distances are approximate

	Bath	Bournemouth	Bristol	Exeter	Penzance	Plymouth
Bournemouth	67					
Bristol	12	80				
Exeter	100	84	75			
Penzance	215	196	193	110		
Plymouth	140	128	118	43	79	
Truro	190	175	170	87	28	57

INTRODUCING
DEVON, CORNWALL & SOUTHWEST ENGLAND

WHEN THE REST OF THE NATION WANTS TO ESCAPE, IT'S THIS FAR-FLUNG CORNER OF ENGLAND, THE WESTCOUNTRY, THEY INVARIABLY HEAD FOR.

DAVID TOMLINSON

JURASSIC COAST

Every year millions of visitors flock to the region's shores to feel the sand between their toes and paddle in the briny blue, and with over 650 miles of coastline and clifftops to explore, not to mention some of England's greenest, grandest countryside, it's not really surprising.

But while the stirring scenery is undoubtedly one of the main attractions, there's much more to this region than just shimmering sands and grandstand views. After decades of economic underinvestment and industrial decline, things are really changing out west. Run-down harbours are being renovated. Celebrity chefs are setting up shop along the coastline. Old fishing harbours, derelict mining towns and faded seaside resorts are reinventing themselves as cultural centres, artistic havens and gastronomic hubs. Whichever way you look at it, there seems to be something special in the air, and it's not just the salty tang of sea breeze. Everyone seems to want their own little slice of the southwest lifestyle these days, and it's high time you found out why.

EDEN PROJECT

TOP Bathers bask in the sun by the limestone rock arch, Durdle Door (p102) **BOTTOM LEFT** The space-age biomes of the Eden Project (p241) **BOTTOM RIGHT** Bristol's famous landmark, the Clifton Suspension Bridge (p41)

BRISTOL

DARTMOOR

BATH

TONY WHEELER

HOLGER LEUE

CORFE CASTLE

TOP LEFT View from Haytor, Dartmoor National Park (p168) **TOP RIGHT** The ruins of Corfe Castle (p101) loom behind the village pub **BOTTOM LEFT** Bath's Coloseum-inspired terrace, the Circus (p53) **BOTTOM CENTRE** Boats line the harbour of artists' haven St Ives (p206) **BOTTOM RIGHT** A prehistoric burial mound on St Mary's, Isles of Scilly (p250)

DAVID TIPLING

ST IVES

ISLES OF SCILLY

GETTING STARTED

WHAT'S NEW?

★ A mining World Heritage Site for Cornwall and west Devon (p205)

★ Public access to Agatha Christie's house at Greenway (p152)

★ A boutique hotel overlooking Mawgan Porth (p302)

★ New sections of the Cornish Way cycling trail (p242)

★ Europe's first artificial surf reef near Bournemouth (p90)

CLIMATE: EXETER

Average Max/Min

Temp °C / °F

Rainfall in / mm

PRICE GUIDE

	BUDGET	MIDRANGE	TOP END
SLEEPING	<£80	£80-130	>£130
MEALS	<£10	£10-20	>£20
ATTRACTIONS	<£5	£5-10	>£10

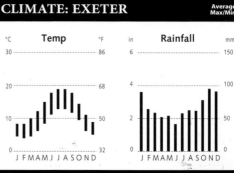

TOP LEFT Summer's in bloom, Lanhydrock (p249) **LEFT** Great British staple: fish and chips **CENTRE LEFT** The terraced cobbled lanes of Clovelly (p181) **RIGHT** Hiking along the South West Coast Path (p271)

ACCOMMODATION

Whether you're after a budget campsite, a boutique B&B or a supremely comfy country hotel, you'll be spoilt for choice in the Westcountry. There's an enormous range of accommodation to suit all budgets, but the most popular spots are often booked out in summer, so it's worth planning as far ahead as you can. Many visitors opt for self-catering to keep costs in check; with a bit of digging you'll turn up some wonderfully quirky properties, from converted barns to landmark lighthouses and retro caravans. For more on accommodation, see p287.

MAIN POINTS OF ENTRY

BRISTOL AIRPORT (BRS; ☎ 0871 33 44 344; www.bristolairport.co.uk) The region's largest airport. Serves mainly UK and European destinations.

EXETER AIRPORT (EXT; ☎ 01392-367433; www.exeter-airport.co.uk) Budget flights covering the UK and some continental destinations.

NEWQUAY AIRPORT (NQY; ☎ 01637-860600; www.newquaycornwallairport.com) Cornwall's only airport, with regular links to London Stansted, Gatwick and a few other UK airports, as well as flights to the Isles of Scilly.

THINGS TO TAKE

ANDREW MARSHALL & LEANNE WALKER

* Swimwear, beach towel, snorkel and sunscreen

* A good raincoat – waterproof and breathable is best

* Comfy shoes for the coast paths

* Flip-flops or sandals for the beach

* Picnic gear – thermos, corkscrew, crockery, cool bag

WEBLINKS

VISIT SOUTHWEST (www.visitsouthwest.co.uk) Comprehensive tourist site.

TRAVELINE SW (www.travelinesw.org.uk) Public transport info.

SIMPLY SCILLY (www.simplyscilly.co.uk) The lowdown on the Isles of Scilly.

ADVENTURE SOUTHWEST (www.itsadventuresouthwest.co.uk) Outdoor pursuits.

SEIZE THE DAYS (www.lonelyplanet.com/132days) Weekly update on UK activities/events.

LEE PENKELLY / ALAMY

MARCH

ST PIRAN'S DAY

CORNWALL
Processions and events on 5 March in honour of Cornwall's patron saint, culminating in a big march across the sands of Perranporth.

MAY

'OBBY 'OSS

PADSTOW
Padstow's colourful 'osses whirl round the harbour in this ancient fertility rite on 1 May (p197).

FLORA DAY

HELSTON
Townsfolk take to Helston's streets in early May to celebrate the coming of spring (p222; www.helstonfloraday.org.uk). The day's main event is the Furry Dance.

BATH INTERNATIONAL MUSIC FESTIVAL

BATH
Bath's celebration of classical, opera, jazz and world music, some of which is outdoors and free, runs from late May to early June (www.bathmusicfest.org.uk).

JUNE

BATH FRINGE FESTIVAL

BATH
Britain's largest fringe theatre festival after Edinburgh, spanning May and June (www.bathfringe.co.uk).

GLASTONBURY FESTIVAL

PILTON
The mother of all music festivals. A mad, mud-soaked rite of passage for every self-respecting British teenager. Held in late June (www.glastonburyfestivals.co.uk).

JULY

EDEN SESSIONS

EDEN PROJECT, BODELVA
Big-name gigs in the shadow of Eden's biomes, held over successive weeks in July and August (p241; www.edensessions. com).

PORT ELIOT FESTIVAL

ST GERMANS, CORNWALL
Blending literature, arts, dance, poetry and live music, this magical festival takes place in the sweeping grounds of a Cornish country house (p245; www.porteliot litfest.com).

TOP LEFT Starbursts explode behind Smeaton's Tower during the Fireworks Championships in Plymouth (p162) **RIGHT** A man feels the weight of the flaming world on his shoulders, Ottery St Mary

AUGUST

RIP CURL BOARDMASTERS

NEWQUAY
The largest surf, skate and music festival in Europe. Surfing and extreme sports on Fistral, bands on Mawgan Porth (www. ripcurlboardmasters.com).

BRITISH FIREWORKS CHAMPIONSHIPS

PLYMOUTH
Plymouth's skies are filled with bursts of colour for this two-night contest in mid-August. Fantastic fun and completely free (www.britishfireworks.co.uk).

INTERNATIONAL BALLOON FIESTA

BRISTOL
Hot-air balloons from across the world soar above the grounds of Ashton Court (p44; www.bristolballoonfiesta.co.uk).

BRISTOL HARBOUR FESTIVAL

BRISTOL
Music, dance, circus acts and lots of ships hit the harbourside for this big Bristol knees-up (p46; www.bristolhar bourfestival.co.uk).

OCTOBER

FALMOUTH OYSTER FESTIVAL

FALMOUTH
Mass oyster eating on Falmouth's quayside, plus cookery demos, boat races and concerts. Held in late October (www. falmouthoysterfestival.co.uk).

NOVEMBER

BLAZING TAR BARRELS

OTTERY ST MARY
Unhinged locals carry flaming tar barrels through packed-out streets on 5 November each year, while paramedics and health-and-safety officials look on in horror.

DECEMBER

CHRISTMAS LIGHTS

MOUSEHOLE
This tiny Cornish fishing village lights up the festive season in truly stunning style.

DOUG MCKINLAY

CULTURE

NATIONAL TRUST

TYNTESFIELD (p51) A grand Victorian mansion just outside Bristol that offers a fascinating chance to see a restoration work in progress.

LANHYDROCK (p249) A glimpse of Cornish aristocratic life in Victorian England, complete with enormous kitchens, drawing rooms and period bedrooms.

MONTACUTE (p79) This rosy-bricked Somerset mansion boasts the longest Long Gallery in England, lined with Elizabethan portraits on loan from the National Gallery.

KNIGHTSHAYES COURT (p134) Devon's grandest slice of Gothic Revival was designed by the eccentric architect William Burges and is packed with mock-medieval drama.

COTEHELE (p245) A Tudor beauty in southeast Cornwall, with a restored quay and a working watermill.

WORLD HERITAGE SITES

Mining in Cornwall and west Devon (p205) has a heritage stretching back well over 3000 years that has left a lasting mark on the region's landscape and culture. So it seems entirely fitting that many of the most important mining areas now form part of the region's newest Unesco World Heritage Site, the Cornwall and West Devon Mining Landscape (p205; www.cornish-mining.org.uk), designed to promote understanding of this powerhouse industry and protect its heritage. But the mining landscape certainly isn't the only thing to make it onto Unesco's radar. Bath's unique Georgian architecture (p51) has been protected under World Heritage status since 1987, and in 2001 the entire Jurassic Coast (p115) became the UK's second natural landscape to qualify as a World Heritage Site after the Giant's Causeway in Northern Ireland.

TOP LEFT An ancient Cornish grave, Lanyon Quoit (p213) **LEFT** The grand manor of Montacute House (p79) **CENTRE RIGHT** The fabled coastline of Tintagel (p192) **FAR RIGHT** Botallack Mine clings to the cliffs (p212)

CLASSIC CASTLES

CORFE CASTLE Wander among the romantic ruins of this tumbledown Dorset fortress (p101).

TINTAGEL Clifftop castle rumoured to be the birthplace of King Arthur (p192).

ST MAWES One of Henry VIII's best-preserved Tudor keeps (p238).

POWDERHAM CASTLE Half fortress, half stately home (p135).

RESTORMEL CASTLE Classic circular medieval keep built by Edward the Black Prince (p241).

DAVID LICHTNEKER / ALAMY

ANDREW MARSHALL & LEANNE WALKER

DON'T MISS EXPERIENCES

⋆ Unforgettable theatre – Catch a play at the clifftop Minack Theatre (p215)

⋆ SS *Great Britain* – Climb aboard Brunel's landmark steamship on Bristol's harbourside (p38)

⋆ Eden Project – Marvel at the ecological ambition of Cornwall's world-famous biomes (p241)

⋆ Hot baths – Take a soothing dip in the rooftop pool at the Thermae Bath Spa (p57)

⋆ Maritime history – View the shipshape collection in Falmouth's National Maritime Museum (p228)

⋆ Agatha Christie – Wander around her inspirational house, Greenway (p152)

⋆ Tin mines – Descend into the depths of one of Cornwall's deepest mines, at Geevor (p211)

RESOURCES

WWW.VENUE.CO.UK Latest listings for Bristol & Bath.

WWW.SOMERSETARTS .COM Lively arts site for Somerset.

WWW.THEATREBRISTOL .NET Plays and theatrical happenings in Bristol.

WWW.CORNWALLCUL TURE.CO.UK Cultural listings.

WWW.KNEEHIGH.CO .UK Cornwall's much-lauded theatre company.

CULTURE

DENNIS JOHNSON

ARTY EXPERIENCES

ARNOLFINI (p44) Browse the work at Bristol's warehouse gallery.

NEWLYN ART GALLERY & THE EXCHANGE (p217) Cutting-edge arts institutions in Penzance.

BARBARA HEPWORTH MUSEUM (p207) Visit the studio of St Ives' celebrated sculptor.

RUSSELL-COTES ART GALLERY (p92) Huge arts repository amassed by a 19th-century collector.

TOP GARDENS

The southwest is famous for its glorious gardens. Here are a few of our favourites.

LOST GARDENS OF HELIGAN Forgotten garden restored in spectacular style (p239).

TREBAH & GLENDURGAN Side-by-side estates developed by the Fox family (p232).

ABBEY GARDEN Scilly's subtropical wonder (p252).

BARRINGTON COURT Historic garden designed by Gertrude Jekyll (p79).

ROSEMOOR Sixty-five acres of RHS splendour (p181).

HESTERCOMBE Three stunning gardens for the price of one (p75).

THE GARDEN HOUSE Wild botanical adventure near Yelverton (p171).

LITERARY LOCATIONS

The southwest is littered with literary locations. For many, Dorset is synonymous with Thomas Hardy (p105), while Bath provides the quintessential Jane Austen setting (p56). Mystery supremo Agatha Christie lived near Dartmouth (p152) and wove countless local places into her novels, while thriller writer Daphne du Maurier was based in Fowey and often employed Cornish locations in her books. Then there's John Betjeman, who holidayed in north Cornwall throughout his life and was buried in St Endellion Church near Port Isaac (p192). But the literary links don't stop there – for more ideas, check out our itinerary on p32.

TOP LEFT Bath's Pulteney Bridge, one of the few in the world lined with shops (p62) **RIGHT** The clifftop Minack Theatre overlooks the Atlantic at Porthcurno (p215)

ANCIENT REMAINS

The southwest has an astonishingly rich concentration of prehistoric sites. Most of the region's ancient remains were erected by neolithic settlers, including the stone circles at Stanton Drew in Somerset (p69), the Merry Maidens near Penzance (p213), the Hurlers on Bodmin Moor (p247) and Merrivale on Dartmoor (p171). Quite what these stone circles were used for is a matter of great debate – some people think they were used as celestial timepieces, while others think they served some ritual or magical purpose. Other structures have more obvious functions: quoits (pillars topped by a capstone) mark ancient burial sites, while menhirs (standing stones) were usually used as way markers or to commemorate important figures.

QUIRKY MUSEUMS

* Maritime history in a landmark lighthouse on the Lizard (p224)

----

* Tales of smugglers and shipwrecks in Charlestown (p240)

----

* Explore the history of fossil hunting on the Jurassic Coast (p117)

----

* The UK's top collection of classic cars in Yeovil (p79)

----

* Exeter's eccentric celebration of celluloid (p129)

----

* Witchy memorabilia collected by an ex–MI6 spy in Boscastle (p191)

GLENN BEANLAND

FOOD & DRINK

FOODIE HUBS

DARTMOUTH One of Devon's prettiest ports is awash with great food – from fine dining to kiosk fare (p157).

BATH Packed with exquisite eateries from gourmet vegetarian to bistros laced with Gallic charm (p59).

PADSTOW The port that kick-started the region's culinary renaissance is a food fan's delight (p197).

BRISTOL From Michelin-starred restaurants to gourmet sausage and pie shops (don't forget the mash; p46).

TORQUAY The English Riviera's foodie central – superb seafood, stunning views (p147).

BOURNEMOUTH Choose from beachside bistros or French-style brasseries (p98).

ST IVES Cornwall's quaintest port serves some of its most imaginative food; expect seafood treats galore (p209).

A GOURMET REGION

The southwest is one of Britain's happening foodie hot spots. Take a superb array of local, seasonal and organic produce, mix in a range of atmospheric eateries and finish with a sizable scattering of celebrity chefs. The result? A region whipping up a perfect culinary storm – and a series of very satisfied stomachs. But the southwest's food does more than just fill bellies. It also helps bridge that disconnect between producer and consumer. It's a magic added-ingredient, because a dish eaten on a farm, in a vineyard or beside a fish quay is different. You can see where it comes from; you can taste where it comes from. It's something no amount of added flavourings and fancy cooking can replicate. For more on the region's cuisine, see p281.

TOP LEFT The serious business of the Cornish pasty (p282) **LEFT** 'Catch of the Day' equals zero food miles at this village pub **CENTRE RIGHT** Harvesting at Sharpham Vineyard (p150) **FAR RIGHT** When in Devonshire…

TOP RESTAURANTS

GIDLEIGH PARK The southwest's best, set in a luxurious country pile (p176).

BORDEAUX QUAY Provincial European flavours infuse meals at Bristol's most stylish eatery (p46).

SIENNA This sleek Dorchester venue is a favourite with the foodie crowd (p110).

RIVERFORD FIELD KITCHEN A pioneering eco-eatery dishing up superb meals in a Devon farm canteen (p151).

PAUL AINSWORTH AT NO 6 The Mediterranean in the heart of Padstow (p198).

DON'T MISS EXPERIENCES

* ★ Wine – Perfect your palate just yards from the vines at the region's beguiling wineries

---

* ★ Picnics – Watch from picturesque cliffs as the sun sets over the sea, surfers and your starter

---

* ★ Chefs – See how those celebrity chefs cope with your very own taste test

---

* ★ Rustic pubs – Drink in centuries of history, culture and top cider and beer

---

* ★ Seafood – Watch fish being landed, then dine on gourmet delights, or a supertasty crab roll

---

* ★ Cream teas – Just-baked scones, homemade jam and so-thick-you-can-stand-your-spoon-up-in-it clotted cream

TOP DROPS

CAMEL VALLEY Acclaimed Cornish wines including dry whites, sparkling reds and an elegant brut (p247).

SHARPHAM Expect oaked whites, ripe rosés and robust reds from this vineyard beside the River Dart (p150).

BURROW HILL Traditional Somerset cider, and an apple-based brandy that's aged for 15 years.

PLYMOUTH GIN Smooth spirit from the world's oldest gin distillery (p165).

BRISTOL BEER FACTORY Citrusy pale ale and a creamy dark stout (p49).

IMAGEBROKER / ALAMY

FOOD & DRINK

LOCALS' TIPS

SEAHORSE Superb seafood roasted over a charcoal fire – within sight of Dartmouth's fishing boats (p158).

KOTA Cornish organic meats and veg transformed by delicate Asian flavours (p227).

LORD POULETT ARMS Food fit for a duke served amid baronial-pile chic deep in rural Somerset (p80).

BILLY THE FISH Seafood fresh from the boats at a funky eatery run by a fisherman turned chef (p110).

COOKERY COURSES

RIVER COTTAGE At Hugh Fearnley-Whittingstall's east Devon HQ learn butchery, baking or allotment gardening (p126).

FAT HEN The ultimate no-miles food: wild food foraging in Cornwall's rugged far-western tip (p215).

BORDEAUX QUAY Move from basic to advanced in this slow-food haven. Or focus on cheese, steak, risotto or puds (p46).

SEAFOOD SCHOOL Spend one to four days mastering the basics at Rick Stein's Padstow kitchen classroom (p195).

ASHBURTON COOKERY Choose from 40 courses at an award-winning school on Dartmoor's southern fringe (www.ashburtoncookery school.co.uk).

FAMOUS CHEFS

Sometimes in the southwest it seems you can't go far without falling over a celebrity chef. Their restaurants pop up regularly, their presence raises the culinary bar and the profile of the region as somewhere to eat well. Their number includes Hugh Fearnley-Whittingstall on the Devon–Dorset border (p139), Jamie Oliver near Newquay (p201), Rick Stein in Padstow (p198), Garry Rhodes near Bournemouth (p99) and John Burton-Race at Dartmouth (p158). Some have proved powerful campaigners on ethical, sustainable, local and organic produce (see p281) – arguably one of the region's most important food exports.

TOP LEFT Traditionally brewed cider, or scrumpy, is renowned in the Westcountry (p284) **RIGHT** Enjoying a pint in the sunshine: another much-loved British tradition

FOOD HISTORY & CULTURE

The region's speciality foods and drinks speak eloquently of its past, and shape present cultural identity. The Cornish pasty is a miner's lunch turned cultural icon; its legacy is found in towns and cities around the world. The fish-filled stargazy pie evokes days when a failure to land the catch meant people went hungry. Cider conjures up a subsistence economy – a time when most people worked the land and this 'wine of wild orchards' helped bolster their pay. And Plymouth Gin speaks volumes about a county, and a country's, role in conquests that secured the British Empire – an entity that reshaped the world, and a legacy that lingers (sometimes painfully) in our modern world. In the southwest, the region's past and present combine on your plate. For more, see p282.

PUBS

Pop in for a pint at these favourites, or track down your own.

★ Turk's Head – Britain's most southerly ale house, on the Isles of Scilly (p255)

★ Queen's Arms – Sip draught farm cider or 10-year-old port at this gem (p80)

★ Warren House Inn – Real fires and great beer in the Dartmoor wilderness (p176)

★ Pandora Inn – Sink your drink on a pontoon at this waterside smugglers inn (p234)

★ Cove House Inn – Real ales, astounding sunsets and views down a 17-mile beach (p116)

OUTDOORS

GREAT ESCAPES

ADVENTURE PLAYGROUND

DARTMOOR Southern England's wildest, biggest, highest wilderness, perfect for hiking, cycling, climbing, white-water rafting – or stone-circle sitting (p168).

EXMOOR Hike or cycle amid more than 260 sq miles of gorse-covered hills fringed by precipitous cliffs and dotted with wild red deer (p80).

SOUTH WEST COAST PATH Britain's longest national trail winds for 630 miles from Poole in Dorset to Minehead in Somerset (p271).

BODMIN MOOR A myth-rich landscape peppered with stone circles and the iconic, crumbling ruins of tin mines (p247).

MENDIPS A 198-sq-mile Area of Outstanding Natural Beauty (AONB) that stretches across Somerset, just south of Bristol and Bath (p64).

The southwestern corner of England is a natural break-free zone with a checklist of charms. It boasts two national parks, hundreds of miles of coast and oodles of stunningly beautiful bits in between – here you can be as adventurous (or not) as you wish.

Hike the iconic South West Coast Path or wander intimate hills and desolate moors. Surfing and its sister sports exert a magnetic pull on people drawn by the biggest and best waves in England. Tempting cycling routes range from leg-testing gradients to hundreds of miles of level path.

Trot sedately on a horse, escape on a yacht, paddle around tranquil coves, clamber up a rock face, dive the UK's most exciting sites or test your mettle in a frenzy of adrenaline sports. Your break could signal the start of a new passion or the rediscovery of an old. See p271.

TOP CYCLE ROUTES

WEST COUNTRY WAY A 250-mile epic from Bath, via Bristol, Exmoor and Bodmin, to Padstow in north Cornwall (p273).

DEVON COAST TO COAST Ilfracombe to Plymouth, 102 glorious miles (p273).

CAMEL TRAIL A 17-mile, car-free trip from Bodmin Moor to the north Cornwall coast (p194).

RAILWAY PATH Glide from Bristol to Bath on a 16-mile ride (p45).

GRANITE WAY A spectacular 11 miles on a former Dartmoor railway line (p175).

DON'T MISS EXPERIENCES

* Sunsets – For cracking evening colours, try Cape Cornwall (p213), the Isles of Scilly (p248) and Hartland Point (p182)

* Cold swim – Experience sheer exhilaration by plunging off a hot sandy beach into far-from-warm seas

* Wildlife watching – Spot red deer on Exmoor, ponies on Dartmoor and basking sharks off Cornwall

* Climb the tors – Clamber up Dartmoor's and Bodmin's summits for buzzard's-eye views of gorse-smothered hills

* Wave riding – Hang ten, or hang on, in England's best surf spots

* Fossil hunting – Rummage for a piece of pre-history on Dorset's Jurassic Coast (p117)

CHILLING OUT

STARGAZING Fewer towns mean more stars; head for high ground for dazzling, unforgettable displays.

BEACHCOMBING Aka: 'reading the seaweed': escape into a soothing world of shells, pebbles and small discoveries.

SANDCASTLE BUILDING Rediscover the gentle thrill of building moat-rimmed forts; or go all arty and make a mermaid.

ROCKPOOLING Perch on a ledge, peer into a pool and watch tiny creatures emerge.

HOLGER LEUE

OUTDOORS

BEST BEACHES

SAUNTON SANDS A 3-mile undeveloped shore backed by the UK's biggest dune system (p180).

PORTHCURNO Near Land's End, this is one of Cornwall's most atmospheric beaches: a sand-filled cove framed by dramatic cliffs (p215).

DURDLE DOOR Your chance to soak up the sun, then swim beside a 150-million-year-old towering stone arch (p102).

BOURNEMOUTH Seven miles of sandy, kiss-me-quick, family friendly, seaside nostalgia (p90).

COAST PATH DAY WALKS

Superb, shorter clifftop hikes abound; here are some local favourites:

LYNMOUTH–COMBE MARTIN (13 miles) The realm of the red deer, where vertiginous cliffs meet open moor.

SALCOMBE–HOPE COVE (8 miles) Happy wanderings from a chic sailing port to an enchanting Devon fishing village.

LYME REGIS–WEST BAY (10 miles) Fossil-filled beaches and England's south-coast cliffs.

PENDEEN WATCH–SENNEN COVE (9 miles) Cracking views and the still-steaming Levant Mine.

SENNEN COVE–PORTHCURNO (6 miles) From surfing beaches to a cliffside theatre, via Land's End.

WALKING

The South West Coast Path is billed as the 630-mile adventure – and it lives up to the hype. Britain's longest national trail, it snakes from Poole in Dorset around Land's End to Minehead in Somerset. En route it passes cliffs crowned by tin mines, dazzling bays, pretty fishing villages and swaths of rural charm. It's so gorgeous you'll forgive it the combined climbs that are the equivalent of three Everests. Inland, Dartmoor, Exmoor and Bodmin Moor deliver hundreds of miles of wilderness walks that are rich in archaeology and laced with myth, while the Cotswold Way winds north for 102 enchanting miles out of Bath. See p271.

TOP LEFT Limestone stalactites and stalacmites adorn Cox's Cave in Cheddar Gorge (p65) **RIGHT** View from the coastal path along the Roseland Peninsula (p238)

WATER SPORTS

Few regions are so rich in idyllic places to get on, and in, the water. Again, geography plays its part: there are hundreds of miles of beautiful beaches, scores of historic sailing ports and an array of sheltered estuaries. Wind and wave patterns help too – Cornwall has the most consistent quality surf in the UK. The result of this embarrassment of natural riches is endless opportunities to surf, bodyboard, sail, kayak and dive.

As well as providing thrills, these experiences take you away from the crowds, offering an insider's view of the shore: secret coves, seal's-eye views of soaring cliffs and wildlife watching galore. See p273.

WATER-SPORTS SPOTS

★ Newquay – Learn to surf at buzzing Fistral Beach or nearby Watergate Bay (p199)

★ Widemouth Bay – Another beautiful Cornish surfing hot spot, 3 miles south of Bude (p190)

★ Sandbanks – Home to ranks of water-sport providers (p95)

★ Weymouth and Portland – World-class facilities at the home of the 2012 Olympics sailing events (p113)

★ Croyde – North Devon's chilled-out surfing hub, fringed by quaint thatched cottages (p179)

WAYNE WALTON

DOUG MCKINLAY

FAMILY TRAVEL

RESOURCES

FAMILY HOLIDAY SOUTH-WEST (www.family holidaysouthwest.com) Your first port of call for all things family-friendly.

CORNWALL BEACH GUIDE (www.cornwallbeachguide.co.uk) Useful guide to help choose your sands.

WHAT'S ON BRISTOL (www.whatsonbristol.co.uk) Click on 'Kids Zone' for ideas for kids in the big city.

DAY OUT WITH THE KIDS (www.dayoutwiththekids.co.uk) Online activity directory, searchable by region.

DON'T MISS EXPERIENCES

THE EDEN PROJECT Cornwall's lunar landing station goes down a treat with the kids, and it's educational too (p241).

NATIONAL MARINE AQUARIUM Play spot-the-shark around the tanks of Plymouth's aquarium (p166).

BRISTOL ZOO The southwest's biggest zoo is ideal for entertaining your wild things (p46).

FOSSIL HUNTING Take home your own archaeological souvenir after a fossil walk (p117).

AT-BRISTOL Everything's 100% hands-on at Bristol's science centre (p46).

ADVENTURE SPORTS Learn to surf, coasteer or kite-buggy on Newquay's beaches (p199).

TRAVEL WITH CHILDREN

The southwest is a fabulous destination for kids, with loads of attractions and activities aimed specifically at young and enquiring minds. Many hotels, pubs and restaurants are well geared for younger travellers, but others only accept children over a certain age – check before you book. Travel times can be a major cause of tantrums – stock up with in-car entertainment before you leave. Lifeguard cover is usually seasonal and only available on larger beaches; be extra wary of rip currents and fast-rising tides. Lastly, British weather can play havoc with even the best-laid plans, so it's worth keeping a few indoor attractions up your sleeve in case the skies take a turn for the worse.

TOP Young girls catch the wind in their plastic windmills on the beach at St Ives (p206)

CONTENTS

THE AUTHORS

OLIVER BERRY

Coordinating Author, Bristol, Bath & Somerset, Cornwall, History, Cornwall & the Arts, Gardens
Oliver graduated from University College London and works as a writer and photographer. Proud to call Kernow home, he's always looking for excuses to explore it further; writing a guidebook's the best one yet. For this book he braved icy seawater and hot springs, conquered hummocks and tors, ate 16 types of seafood and spent far too long messing about on clifftops. He'd do it all again tomorrow, given half a chance.

BELINDA DIXON

Dorset, Devon, Outdoors, Food & Drink, Directory, Transport
Belinda came to the southwest for her postgrad, having been drawn there by the palm tree on campus. Like the best Westcountry limpets she's proved hard to shift since and now writes and broadcasts in the region. Research highlights include seeing the Durdle Door emerge from thick fog, touring TE Lawrence's home and rigorously testing local food and drink. Purely for research, you understand.

LONELY PLANET AUTHORS

Why is our travel information the best in the world? It's simple: our authors are passionate, dedicated travellers. They don't take freebies in exchange for positive coverage so you can be sure the advice you're given is impartial. They travel widely to all the popular spots, and off the beaten track. They don't research using just the internet or phone. They discover new places not included in any other guidebook. They personally visit thousands of hotels, restaurants, palaces, trails, galleries, temples and more. They speak with dozens of locals every day to make sure you get the kind of insider knowledge only a local could tell you. They take pride in getting all the details right, and in telling it how it is. Think you can do it? Find out how at lonelyplanet.com.

ITINERARIES

SOUTHWEST ESSENTIALS

THREE WEEKS // BRISTOL TO BOURNEMOUTH // 450 TO 500 MILES

This grand tour takes in the region's unmissable sights. Begin in big-city **Bristol** (p38) before heading for England's Georgian gem, **Bath** (p51). Detour via the tiny cathedral city of **Wells** (p62) en route to hippie central **Glastonbury** (p69) and its celebrated tor

and abbey. Cross **Exmoor** (p80) to cliffside **Clovelly** (p179) and Cornwall's culinary centre, **Padstow** (p194). Stop off at artistic **St Ives** (p206) before rounding **Land's End** (p215) en route to **the Lizard** (p222) and the harbours of **Falmouth** (p228) and **Fowey** (p242). Marvel at the domes of the **Eden Project** (p241), dine in **Dartmouth** (152), explore **Exeter** (p123) and hunt for fossils in **Lyme Regis** (p117), then finish up by the seaside in **Poole** (p94) and **Bournemouth** (p90).

ITINERARIES

ARCHITECTURAL TREASURES

TWO WEEKS // TYNTESFIELD TO MOUNT EDGCUMBE // 230 TO 250 MILES

Start near Bristol with restoration work-in-progress **Tyntesfield** (p51). Nearby **Prior Park** (p58) offers a glorious view of the Bath skyline. In Dorset, **Kingston Lacy** (p98) was designed by the architect of the Houses of Parliament, while **Sherborne New**

Castle (p109) was originally built for Sir Walter Raleigh. In Somerset, red-brick **Montacute** (p79) is famous for its gardens and long gallery, while **Dunster Castle** (p82) offers sweeping coastal views. For architecture showiness you can't top Devon's **Arlington Court** (p179) and **Knightshayes Court** (p134). You'll also find Agatha Christie's house at **Greenway** (p152) and Francis Drake's former seat at **Buckland Abbey** (p171). Across the Cornish border are the sculptures and topiary of **Antony** (p244) and the majestic edifice of **Mount Edgcumbe** (p244).

WILD VIEWS

TWO WEEKS // PORTLAND TO THE LIZARD // 240 TO 280 MILES

This one's for people who like their landscapes big, wild and empty. Begin with wide-angle views on the **Jurassic Coast** (p115), factoring in the rock arch at **Durdle Door** (p102), shell-shaped **Lulworth Cove** (p102), the lighthouse at **Portland Bill** (p113)

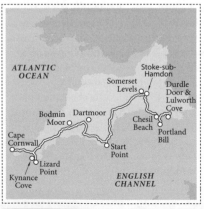

and the pebbly expanse of **Chesil Beach** (p114). Drink in the panorama from **Ham Hill** (p79) near Stoke-sub-Hamdon before crossing the flat **Somerset Levels** (p72) and detouring to the lighthouse at **Start Point** (p157). Swing northwest onto **Dartmoor** (p168) to explore wild tors and prehistoric ruins before traversing **Bodmin Moor** (p247) to **the Lizard** (p222), home to some of Cornwall's craggiest clifftop scenery, best seen around **Lizard Point** (p224) and **Kynance Cove** (p225). Finish on the headland of **Cape Cornwall** (p213).

HILLTOP HIKES

10 DAYS // CLEVEDON TO EXMOOR // 120 TO 150 MILES

This itinerary strings together some of the southwest's best hilltop walks. Start with coastal vistas on the **Poet's Walk** (p68) near Clevedon, followed by a hike along England's deepest ravine, **Cheddar Gorge** (p65). Move on to the Mendips' highest hill,

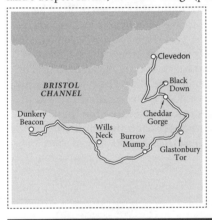

Black Down (p65), before getting up early to catch the sunrise from **Glastonbury Tor** (p69). To the south, **Burrow Mump** (p72) is the best place for surveying the Somerset Levels, while to the west sits **Wills Neck** (p77), the highest hump in the Quantocks. Further west, Exmoor has a wealth of lofty peaks, including Bossington Hill, Selworthy Beacon and the tallest of all, **Dunkery Beacon** (p82), from where the stunning views stretch all the way along the Somerset coast.

CLASSIC CASTLES

10 DAYS // CORFE TO TINTAGEL // 200 TO 250 MILES

Fortresses abound in the southwest. Most romantic of all is crumbling **Corfe Castle** (p101), blown to bits by a Roundhead cannon during the Civil War. **Maiden Castle** (p106) was once the largest Iron Age hillfort in Britain, and **Sherborne** (p109) boasts

not one but two impressive fortresses, but it's Devon that really tops the castle count. **Powderham** (p135) and **Okehampton** (p175) are classic medieval castles, and **Castle Drogo** (p175) is officially the last castle to be built in England. **Restormel Castle** (p241), high above Lostwithiel, is a fine example of a medieval keep, while Henry VII built the twin Tudor castles of **Pendennis** (p228) and **St Mawes** (p238). Clifftop **Tintagel** (p192) is the legendary birthplace of King Arthur.

ITINERARIES

EAT SOUTHWEST

FOUR DAYS // DARTMOUTH TO DORCHESTER // 120 TO 150 MILES

This itinerary strings together some of Dorset and Devon's best foodie experiences. Begin with breakfast in **Dartmouth** (p152) before sampling award-winning vintages at **Sharpham Vineyard** (p150), followed by home-grown produce from the fantastic

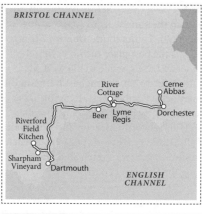

Riverford Field Kitchen (p151). Stop for fresh crab in **Beer** (p137) en route to celeb chef Hugh Fearnley-Whittingstall's HQ at **River Cottage** (p139) for tips on sustainable cooking, bread-making and allotment-tending. Finish with some slap-up seafood at **Hix** (p120) in Lyme Regis, gastro grub at the **New Inn** (p110) in Cerne Abbas or a Michelin-starred meal at **Sienna** (p110) in Dorchester.

A LITERARY LANDSCAPE

TWO WEEKS // BATH TO WAREHAM // 400 TO 450 MILES

The southwest landscape has inspired countless writers. Jane Austen set two novels in **Bath** (p56), while Coleridge penned poetry in **Nether Stowey** (p77). Henry Williamson set *Tarka the Otter* in north Devon (p180) and Charles Kingsley wrote *The*

Water Babies in **Clovelly** (p181). The cliffs around **Trebetherick** (p192) inspired John Betjeman, while Virginia Woolf immortalised **Godrevy** (p209) in *To the Lighthouse*. Two thrillmeisters have southwest connections: Daphne du Maurier lived in **Fowey** (p242), and Agatha Christie lived near **Dartmouth** (p152). **Lyme Regis** (p120) features in books by John Fowles and Tracey Chevalier, while you can visit houses belonging to Thomas Hardy in **Dorchester** (p104) and TE Lawrence near **Wareham** (p100).

BRISTOL, BATH & SOMERSET

3 PERFECT DAYS

☙ DAY 1 // BATH ESSENTIALS

Bath marks the start of your Somerset adventure. Begin with a (very) early-morning peek round the Roman Baths (p52) followed by a guided tour of the city's landmarks (p56). Pick up lunch at Chandos Deli or the Boston Tea Party (p59) for some alfresco eating in Royal Victoria Park (p53). Visit No 1 Royal Crescent (p53), then wander via the Circus (p53), the Georgian Garden (p53) and Queen Square (p53) for a browse around the city-centre shops (p62). Have supper at The Circus (p59) or Hudson Steakhouse (p60).

☙ DAY 2 // OVER TO WELLS

Squeeze in an early-morning dip at the delightful Thermae Bath Spa (p57) before a visit to the grand estate of Prior Park (p58). Then it's a leisurely drive southwest to the miniature cathedral city of Wells (p62) for a mosey around the cathedral (p63) and the Bishop's Palace (p63). Dine at Goodfellows (p64) or Old Spot (p64), or if you're feeling flush, an evening at Millers at Glencot House (p68).

☙ DAY 3 // COUNTRY PURSUITS

Set out early for a jaunt to the top of Glastonbury Tor (p69) – the earlier you get there, the better the views. Detour via the abbey (p70) and savour lunch at Glastonbury classics, the Rainbow's End (p71) or the Who'd A Thought It Inn (p72). Drive across the Levels (p72) for an afternoon at the Willowcraft and Wetlands Centre (p73), a walk around a nature reserve (p72) or a tipple at a cider brewer (p73). Finish in style at Farmer's Inn (p75) or the Willow Tree (p76).

SOMERSET

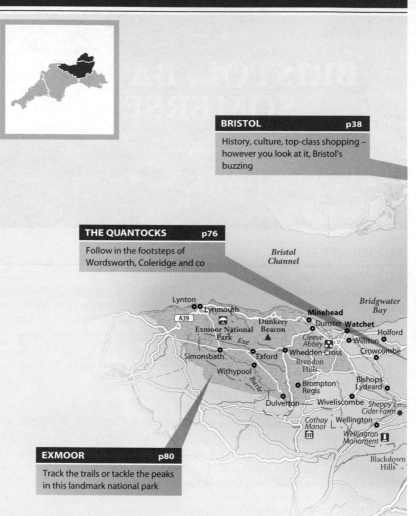

BRISTOL   p38

History, culture, top-class shopping –
however you look at it, Bristol's
buzzing

THE QUANTOCKS   p76

Follow in the footsteps of
Wordsworth, Coleridge and co

EXMOOR   p80

Track the trails or tackle the peaks
in this landmark national park

GETTING AROUND

Bristol is a major transport hub, with easy access both to the M4 east to London, and the M5 and A38, which both run roughly in tandem in a northeast–southwest direction across the county. Train and bus links between the main towns are excellent, but anywhere off the beaten track – including the Mendips, the Quantocks, Exmoor and the Levels – you'll really need your own wheels to get around. Cycling is well worth considering, with plenty of disused railway lines, canal paths and country lanes to explore.

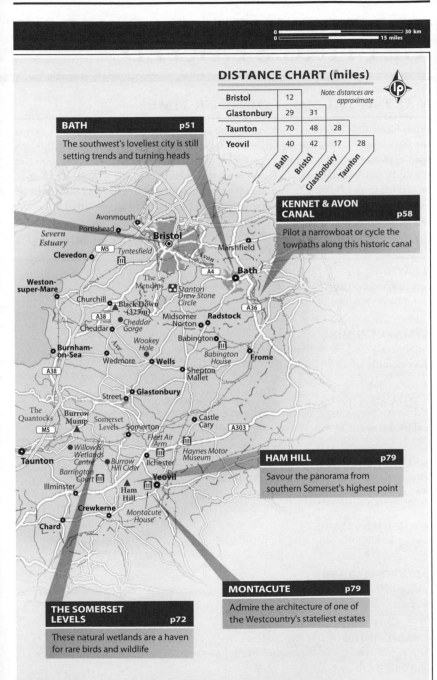

DISTANCE CHART (miles)

	Bath	Bristol	Glastonbury	Taunton
Bristol	12			
Glastonbury	29	31		
Taunton	70	48	28	
Yeovil	40	42	17	28

Note: distances are approximate

BATH p51

The southwest's loveliest city is still setting trends and turning heads

KENNET & AVON CANAL p58

Pilot a narrowboat or cycle the towpaths along this historic canal

HAM HILL p79

Savour the panorama from southern Somerset's highest point

MONTACUTE p79

Admire the architecture of one of the Westcountry's stateliest estates

THE SOMERSET LEVELS p72

These natural wetlands are a haven for rare birds and wildlife

BRISTOL, BATH & SOMERSET

BRISTOL, BATH & SOMERSET GETTING STARTED

MAKING THE MOST OF YOUR TIME

From buzzy big cities to sweeping coastline and forgotten moors, Somerset's a treat for the senses. Outside the big cities of Bristol and Bath, it's one of the southwest's least-explored corners, and makes a fabulous place to give the crowds the slip. But it's much more than just a place to mooch the rural back roads – there are trails to be tackled in the Quantocks and Mendips, birds to be spotted around the Somerset Levels, gardens and country houses galore and sunrises to be savoured from the top of Glastonbury Tor.

TOP TOURS & COURSES

❦ BATH
Few British cities have as much history per square inch, so what better way to learn about Bath than on a guided tour (p56)?

❦ CANAL CRUISING
Putter along the Kennet & Avon Canal aboard a narrowboat (p58), or learn the art of river-punting (p56).

❦ WILLOW
Willow has been a staple Somerset industry for centuries. Learn about this ancient crop and try your hand at some willow craft at the Willows & Wetlands Visitor Centre (p73).

❦ CIDER
Somerset is the spiritual home of scrumpy, and several local breweries will let you peek at their vats before sampling the goods (p73).

❦ WILDLIFE SAFARIS
Brace yourself for a bone-jarring 4WD adventure on the wilds of Exmoor (p80).

❦ COOKING CLASSES
Several of the region's top chefs hold culinary masterclasses – our favourites are at Bordeaux Quay (p46), Bertinet Kitchen (p57) and Andrews on the Weir (p84).

❦ BALLOONING
Bath's pretty enough on the ground, but it looks even better from a few hundred feet up (p58).

GETTING AWAY FROM IT ALL

* **Ashton Court Estate** Minutes from the big city, this sprawling country estate is a favourite retreat for Bristolians looking to leave the urban grind behind (p44).

* **Somerset Levels** This enormous natural wetland sits bang in the heart of Somerset, but receives far fewer visitors than the nearby national parks. Nature reserves provide a haven for all kinds of unusual flora and fauna (p72).

* **The Quantocks** Where hikers in the know go when they want the trails all to themselves (p76).

* **Kennet & Avon Canal** Once a busy industrial thoroughfare, this tranquil 19th-century waterway is now the preserve of kayaks and canal boats (p58).

ADVANCE PLANNING

* **Bath** (p51) One thing you won't be able to escape in Bath is other people, especially in July and August. Book well ahead for restaurants, hotels, accommodation and the Thermae Bath Spa.

* **Glastonbury** (p69) The festival kicks off in mid- to late June, selling out months in advance. Local roads are gridlocked: steer clear unless you've got a ticket.

* **Crowds** Cheddar Gorge, Wookey Hole and the Exmoor coast get busy in summer. Be prepared for traffic jams.

* **Driving** Pricey parking, traffic and complicated one-way systems make driving in Bristol and Bath a headache. Consider making alternative plans.

TOP RESTAURANTS

BORDEAUX QUAY
Warehouse dining with a sustainable slant on the Bristol waterfront (p46).

BATH PRIORY
Michael Caines' Michelin-starred country house (p59).

MILLER'S AT GLENCOT HOUSE
Fantastically over-the-top dining amongst antiques and oils (p68).

THE OLIVE TREE
Bath's classiest table is at the Queensberry Hotel (p60).

THE QUEEN'S ARMS
Award-winning pub hidden away in the Corton Denham countryside (p80).

RESOURCES

* **Visit Somerset** (www.visitsomerset.co.uk) First port of call for Somerset

* **Heart of Somerset** (www.heartofsomerset.com) Covers the Blackdowns, Quantocks and Somerset Levels

* **Visit South Somerset** (www.visitsouthsomerset.com) Yeovil and south Somerset

* **Exmoor National Park** (www.exmoor-nationalpark.gov.uk) Official site for the National Park Authority

* **Mendips** (www.mendiphillsaonb.org.uk) Packed with info on the Mendips Area of Outstanding Natural Beauty (AONB)

BRISTOL
······

pop 380,615

The southwest's biggest city has been through a wardrobe of outfits down the centuries – river village, mercantile city, slave port, shipbuilding centre, industrial powerhouse and aeronautical hub – but somehow she's never quite received the respect she deserves.

But there's a new sense of energy in Bristol these days. Massive investment has resulted in the revitalisation of the harbourside, the construction of one of the southwest's largest shopping centres at Cabot Circus, and the multimillion-pound redevelopment of a new Museum for Bristol on the city's docks (due for completion in 2011). Throw in a bevy of top-class restaurants, a buzzing artistic sector and a crackling cultural scene, and you have a city that's crying out for exploration.

Strategically sited at the confluence of the Frome and Avon, Bristol began life as the small river port of Brigstow, and by the mid-14th century had blossomed into Britain's third-largest harbour. The city later grew rich as a transatlantic trading hub, earning much of its profits from the so-called 'Triangle Trade' in guns, New World goods and slaves (see p260). Bristol later became a centre for shipbuilding and aviation, and was badly bombed during WWII; postwar reconstruction left the city with its share of concrete carbuncles, but recent redevelopment has breathed life back into many of its more neglected areas.

ESSENTIAL INFORMATION

EMERGENCIES // Bristol Royal Infirmary (Map p40; ☎ 0117-923 0000; Marlborough St; ☼ 24hr) **Police Station** (☎ 0845 456 7000) New Bridewell

(Map p42; Rupert St; ☼ 9.30am-5pm Mon-Fri); Trinity Rd (Map p42; Trinity Rd; ☼ 24hr)

TOURIST INFORMATION // Bristol Visitor Information Centre (Map p42; ☎ 0333-321 0101; www.visitbristol.co.uk; E Shed, 1 Canon's Rd; ☼ 10am-6pm) In a new purpose-built location on the harbour.

ORIENTATION

The city centre, north of the river, is compact but hilly. The central area revolves around St Nicholas Market. Park St is lined with shops and cafes up to the university, while the restaurant and bar scene of Whiteladies Rd stretches north. The hilltop suburb of Clifton, with its Georgian terraces, cafes and boutique shops, is west of the centre. The Clifton Suspension Bridge spans the Avon from Clifton to Leigh Woods in north Somerset.

As in any big city, it's worth taking care at night, especially around Cheltenham Rd, Gloucester Rd, St Paul's, Easton and Montpelier, which all have a reputation for street crime. Grab a cab after dark.

The main station is Bristol Temple Meads, which is a mile southeast of the centre. Some trains use Bristol Parkway, 5 miles to the north. The bus station is on Marlborough St, northeast of the city centre.

EXPLORING BRISTOL

♥ SS GREAT BRITAIN // STEP ABOARD BRUNEL'S LANDMARK LINER

Moored alongside Bristol's historic floating harbour is the **SS Great Britain** (Map p40; ☎ 0117-929 1843; www.ssgreatbritain.org; Great Western Dock, Gas Ferry Rd; adult/child £11.95/9.50; ☼ 10am-5.30pm Apr-Oct, 10am-4.30pm Nov-Mar; ⓖ), one of the great monuments of the city's industrial past. The second of

BRISTOL & BRUNEL

Bristol's most famous son is **Isambard Kingdom Brunel** (1806–59) – the industrial genius and pioneering engineer responsible for the Clifton Suspension Bridge, the SS *Great Britain* and the Great Western Railway, amongst many other things.

Precocious young Isambard was picked out for greatness from an early age. Educated at the Lycée Henri-Quatre in Paris and the University of Caen, Brunel was barely 20 when he was appointed chief engineer of the Thames Tunnel between Rotherhithe and Wapping, designed by his father Marc. The project was fraught with difficulties; foul-smelling river water and explosive gases were a constant threat, and the tunnel was flooded twice in 1827 and 1828 (Brunel was almost drowned while trying to rescue trapped workers). While convalescing, he entered a competition to design a new bridge over the Avon at Clifton. His first submission was rejected, but the competition was run again in 1831 and Brunel's design was awarded first prize. The foundation stone was laid in June the same year, but Brunel sadly died before his first major commission was completed.

Thankfully he had time to see other schemes to fruition. During his 30-year career Brunel built the Tamar Rail Bridge, founded the Great Western Railway Line and designed three of the world's greatest ships (see p38). He also built 1000 miles of railway lines, modernised the docks at Bristol, Plymouth and Cardiff, designed the world's first prefabricated field hospital and worked on railway projects everywhere from India to Italy.

Despite surviving on a daily diet of four hours' sleep and 40 cigars, Brunel's closest shave came when he nearly choked to death having accidentally swallowed a coin while performing a conjuring trick for his children. His eventual end was more prosaic; he suffered a stroke in 1859, just before the *Great Eastern* made its first voyage to New York, and died 10 days later at the age of 53.

Brunel's groundbreaking transatlantic steamers, completed in 1843 between the *Great Western* in 1837 and the *Great Eastern* in 1852, the *Great Britain* was the first iron-hulled transatlantic liner to be powered by a revolutionary screw propeller. Unfortunately, huge construction and running costs meant the ship ran at a massive loss, and she only served as a liner for a few years before being sold off to serve as a transport vessel, troopship and coal-hulk. By 1937 she had been abandoned near Port Stanley in the Falklands, an ignominious fate for such a majestic vessel.

Happily, that wasn't the end of the *Great Britain*. After being towed back to Bristol in 1970 aboard a floating pontoon, a 30-year, £11.3 million restoration project has restored the ship in splendid fashion. Refurbished rooms include the galley, surgeon's quarters, mess hall and the engine room, but the highlight is the 'glass sea' on which the ship sits, enclosing an airtight dry dock that preserves the delicate hull.

Moored nearby is a replica of John Cabot's ship **Matthew** (Map p40; ☎ 0117-927 6868; www.matthew.co.uk), built in 1997 to coincide with the quincentenary celebrations of the explorer's original voyage. Consult the website for forthcoming sailings. There's also a small **maritime heritage centre**. Tickets for the SS *Great Britain* cover entry to all three sites.

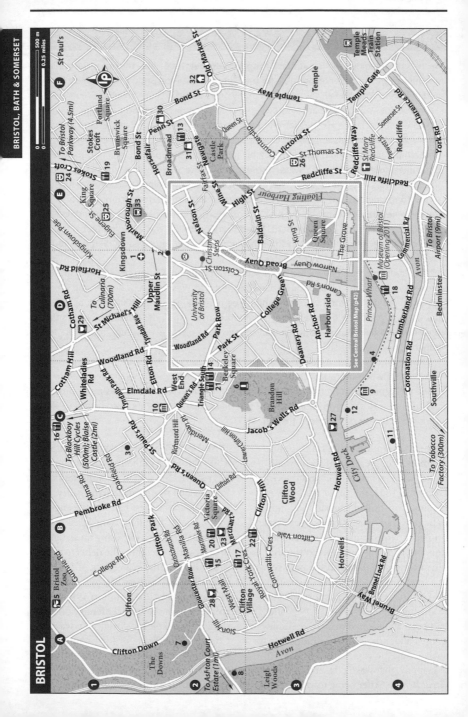

East along the river are the grey iron cranes of **Prince's Wharf**, where the new Museum of Bristol is under construction in a riverside warehouse that formerly housed the city's industrial museum.

❧ CLIFTON & THE SUSPENSION BRIDGE // THE CITY'S POSHEST POSTCODE

During the 18th and 19th centuries the spa resort of Clifton was transformed into an elegant suburb where the city's well-heeled businessmen could live far from the squalor and smells of the city docks. Clifton sits on a hilltop overlooking the Avon Gorge, stretching from Whiteladies Rd to the river; the further west you go, the grander the houses become, especially around the galleried mansions and orderly terraces of **Cornwallis Crescent** and **Royal York Crescent**. These days Clifton is still Bristol's most desirable (and expensive) address, with a villagelike mix of cafes, boutiques and designer shops.

Just to the west is Bristol's most famous (and photographed) landmark, the **Clifton Suspension Bridge** (www.cliftonbridge.org.uk; toll for cars 50p), which spans the 214m gap over Avon Gorge to Leigh Woods in Somerset. It's another Brunel masterpiece; construction work began in 1836, although Brunel died before the bridge's completion in 1864. It was designed to carry light horse-drawn traffic and foot passengers, but these days around 12,000 motor vehicles trundle across daily. At 245ft (74m) above the river, it's also a magnet for stunts and suicides; in 1885 Sarah Ann Hedley famously jumped from the bridge after a lovers' tiff, but her voluminous petticoats parachuted her to earth and she lived to be 85.

There's a **visitor information point** (Map p40; ☎ 0117-0974 4665; visitinfo@cliftonbridge. org; ☺ 10am-5pm) near the tower on the Leigh Woods side. Free guided tours leave at 3pm on Saturdays and Sundays from May to October.

❧ WALKING TOURS // GET UNDER THE CITY'S SKIN

A guided tour is a good way to get your Bristol bearings. The best is the **Bristol Highlights Walk** (☎ 0117-968 4638; ☺ 11am Sat Apr-Sep), taking in the old town, city centre and harbourside. Themed tours exploring Clifton, the slave trade and Bristol's wine merchants are also available. All tours leave from outside the tourist office and are completely free.

Mp3 tours can be downloaded from **Visit Bristol** (http://visitbristol.co.uk/site/visitor -information/multimedia/mp3-audio-tours): options are Bristol's Quayside, the Brunel Mile

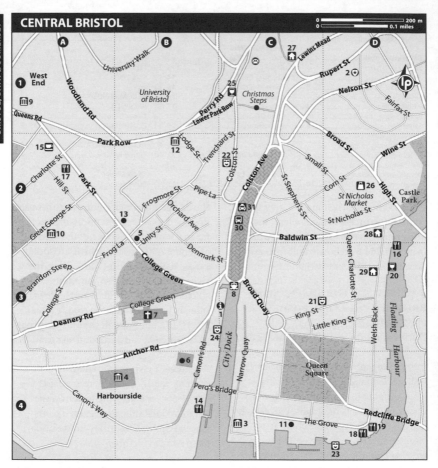

CENTRAL BRISTOL

and City Docks, Bristol's heritage and the Slave Trade.

♥ AVON CRUISES // HOP ON A RIVER BOAT

Bristol still looks at its best seen from the water. **Bristol Packet** (Map p40; ☎ 0117-926 8157; www.bristolpacket.co.uk; adult/child £5.25/4.75; ☺ every 45min 11am-4.15pm Sat & Sun & daily during school holidays) runs a fleet of wooden-hulled boats that chug around the Floating Harbour from Wapping Wharf near SS *Great Britain* and Bristol Packet Pontoon near the Watershed. There are also weekly cruises along the Avon from May to October (adult/child £14/12), plus less frequent trips to Bath, Beese's Tea Garden and the Lock & Weir pub.

Bristol Ferry Boat Co (Map p42; ☎ 0117-927 3416; www.bristolferry.com; adult/child return £3.30/2.70, day-pass £7/5) runs two hourly commuter routes from the city centre dock, near the tourist office. The blue route goes east to Temple Meads via Millennium Sq, Welsh Back and Castle Park (for Broadmead and Cabot Circus); the red route goes west to Hotwells via Millennium Sq and the SS *Great Britain*.

🍂 PICNIC ON THE DOWNS // PANORAMIC PARKLAND

The grassy parks of **Clifton Down** and **Durdham Down** (locally known simply as The Downs) provide one of the city's best green spaces, offering an awesome vista over the river and the suspension bridge. Just above the bridge is an observatory housing a **camera obscura** (Map p40; ☎ 0117-974 1242; adult/child £2/1, for Giant's Cave £1.50/50p; ☽ 10.30am-5.30pm), one of only two in England; and a tunnel leading down to the **Giant's Cave**, a natural cavern that emerges halfway down the cliff with dizzying views down towards the Avon.

🍂 HISTORIC BRISTOL // HOUSES, TOWERS, CASTLES AND CATHEDRALS

For a taste of the life once enjoyed by Bristol's wealthy merchants, head for the 18th-century **Georgian House** (Map p42; ☎ 0117-921 1362; 7 Great George St; admission free; ☽ 10am-5pm Sat-Wed). This six-storeyed mansion belonged to the West India merchant John Pinney, along with his slave Pero (after whom Pero's Bridge across the harbour is named). The house has survived the centuries largely intact, with sitting parlours, period bedrooms, a book-lined library and basement kitchen, stocked with jelly moulds, spice boxes and a roasting spit big enough to roast an ox.

Even earlier is the **Red Lodge** (Map p42; ☎ 0117-921 1360; Park Row; admission free; ☽ 10am-5pm Sat-Wed), built in 1590 but remodelled in 1730. Built to accompany a great house that stood on the site of the Colston Hall, the house bears Elizabethan, Stuart and Georgian features, including a Tudor 'knot' garden and the lavishly panelled oak room.

THE BRISTOL LIDO

Bath isn't the only southwest city with its own outdoor hot tub. The **Bristol Lido** (Map p40; ☎ 0117-933 9530; www.lidobristol.com; Oakfield Pl; adult/child pool ticket £15/7.50; ☽ 7am-10pm) was built as the Clifton Lido in 1849 by Richard Shackleton Pope, one of the city's most notable Victorian architects. The lido closed in 1990 but has been lavishly redeveloped by the owners of the Glassboat (p48), who have supplemented the original outdoor heated pool with spa rooms, a sauna, a sundeck and a swish restaurant. It even has its own cafe-bar – and there can't be many places where you indulge in a glass of cold prosecco and a cream tea at a Grade II–listed swimming pool, now can there?

On the top of Brandon Hill stands the 105m-high **Cabot Tower**, built in 1897 to commemorate 400 years since John Cabot's pioneering voyage sailed from Bristol to Newfoundland. It's been closed to the public since some alarming cracks appeared near the viewing platform, but is scheduled for repair soon, and Brandon Park still provides a good viewpoint over downtown Bristol.

Over on College Green is **Bristol Cathedral** (Map p42; ☎ 0117-926 4879; www. bristol-cathedral.co.uk; College Green; ☑ 8am-6pm), a Grade I–listed 'Hall Church' (meaning the aisles, choir and nave are the same height). It's mainly 19th century, apart from the Norman chapter house and a rare Saxon carving in the south transept.

Five miles north of Bristol in the suburb of Henbury is **Blaise Castle** (off Map p40; ☎ 0117-903 9818; general.museum@bristol. gov.uk; Henbury Rd; admission free; ☑ 10am-5pm Sat-Wed), a manor built for merchant banker John Harford between 1796 and 1798, surrounded by 650 acres of Humphry Repton–designed parkland. Now owned by the city council, it takes a journey through the city's past, with a costume gallery, vintage toy collection and Victorian schoolroom, as well as a 'Bristol at Home Gallery' stocked with antiquated vacuum cleaners, tin baths and other cutting-edge household appliances. Buses 1 and 40/40A run from the city centre.

✤ ARTY BRISTOL // FROM OLD MASTERS TO ABSTRACT ART

The **Bristol City Museum & Art Gallery** (Map p42; ☎ 0117-922 3571; Queen's Rd; admission free; ☑ 10am-5pm) makes a good place for a cultural stop, with a decent collection of old masters on the first floor, and galleries dedicated to ceramics, decorative arts, archaeology, geology and natural history.

More classical art can be found in the grandiose surroundings of the **Royal West of England Academy** (Map p40; ☎ 0117-973 5129; www.rwa.org.uk; Queen's Rd; adult/ child £4/free; ☑ 10am-5.30pm Mon-Sat, 2-5.30pm Sun), whose permanent collection includes artists from the Newlyn, St Ives and Bloomsbury Schools.

Modern work is the focus at the open-plan **Arnolfini** (Map p42; ☎ 0117-929 9191; www.arnolfini.org.uk; 16 Narrow Quay; admission free), a cutting-edge exhibition space for contemporary arts, photography, dance and other cultural happenings. Entry to exhibitions is free, but you'll have to pay for music events, screenings or dance performances.

On the south side of the river is **Spike Island** (Map p40; ☎ 0117-929 2266; www.spike island.org.uk; 133 Cumberland Rd; ☑ 11am-5pm Tue-Sun, cafe 9am-5pm Mon-Fri, 11am-4pm Sat & Sun), a contemporary arts centre that's reopened after a £2.25 million revamp, with artists' studios, galleries and a super cafe.

✤ ASHTON COURT ESTATE // OPEN COUNTRY ON BRISTOL'S DOORSTEP

Two miles from the city centre, this huge **estate** (off Map p40; admission free; ☑ 8am-9.15pm May-Aug, earlier closing rest of year) is Bristol's 'green lung', with 850 sprawling acres of oak woodland, trails and public park. Originally established for the Smyth family, and partly landscaped by Humphry Repton, the estate is now the nation's third most-visited park, and on hot days half of Bristol hightails it out of the city in search of some of Ashton's grassy spaces. It hosts many of Bristol's keynote events, including the balloon and kite festivals, and also contains the Avon Timberland Trail, the UK's only urban mountain bike trail.

Free estate maps are available from the **visitor centre** (☎ 0117-963 9174; for enquiries

BANKSY

Bristol's best-known artistic export is **Banksy** (www.banksy.co.uk), a guerrilla graffitist, political prankster and street stenciller whose provocative works have been gracing the city's walls for more than a decade. Banksy's true identity is a closely guarded secret, but rumour has it that his real name is either Robert or Robin Banks, he was born in 1974 in Yate, 12 miles from Bristol, and cut his teeth in a Bristol graffiti outfit. Some people are convinced Banksy isn't one person, but a collective of artists working under a single name: the truth is, no one has the foggiest idea, and the man himself certainly doesn't seem intent on revealing his identity any time soon.

Taking a wry, witty and protest-laced look at modern life, Banksy's notorious stunts include spraying 'fat lane' on a Venice Beach sidewalk, smuggling inflatable Guantanamo Bay prisoners into Disneyland and building a Stonehenge made of Portaloos at the Glastonbury festival. Ironically for such an anti-establishment figure, Banksy is almost mainstream these days – his work has even been sold at Sotheby's. His first film, *Exit Through the Gift Shop*, premiered at Sundance Film Festival in 2010.

Despite opposition from the city's conservative quarters, Bristol has taken Banksy firmly into its bosom: his 2009 exhibition at the City Museum & Art Gallery had Bristolians queuing round the block. There are still a few Banksy originals dotted round the city too:

★ The 'love triangle' stencil (featuring an angry husband, a two-timing wife and a naked man dangling from a window) on the wall of a sexual-health clinic on Frogmore St (although sadly it's recently been splashed with paint).

★ A SWAT marksman taking aim on Upper Maudlin St, above the Fireworks Gallery & Studio.

★ Charion, the River Styx boatman on the side of the Thekla (p50).

★ 'Mild Mild West' featuring a Molotov cocktail-wielding teddy bear on Stokes Croft.

★ 'Take the Money and Run', a multicoloured mural located near St Andrews Rd in Montpelier.

doreen.pastor@bristol.gov.uk; ⏱ 8.30am–4.30pm Mon-Thu, 8am-4.30pm Fri).

☙ ON YOUR BIKE // PEDAL FROM BRISTOL TO BATH

The **Bristol and Bath Railway Path** (www.bristolbathrailwaypath.org.uk) is a 13-mile trail along a disused train track formerly operated by the Midland Railway, passing through lovely Somerset and Gloucestershire countryside before joining up with the Avon Canal into Bath. The official starting point in Bristol is on St Philips Rd, just off Midland Rd, but there are access points all along the route.

Bikes can be hired in Bristol from **Ferry Station** (Map p42; ☎ 0117-376 3942; www.ferrystation.co.uk; Narrow Quay) and **Blackboy Hill Cycles** (☎ 0117-973 1420; www.blackboy cycles.co.uk; 180 Whiteladies Rd; ⏱ 9am-5.30pm Mon-Sat, 11am-4pm Sun), while the popular cycle cafe and workshop **Mud Dock** (Map p42; ☎ 0117-934 9734; www.mud-dock.com; 40 The Grove; ⏱ 8.30am-6pm Mon-Fri, 9am-6pm Sat) provides secure bike parking, lockers and shower (£2 per day). For bike hire at the Bath end, see p62.

BRISTOL FOR KIDS // THE BIG CITY FOR LITTLE PEOPLE

Top spot on Bristol's harbourside goes to the city's science museum, **At-Bristol** (Map p42; ☎ 0845 345 1235; www.at-bristol. uk; Harbourside; adult/child £10.80/7; ⏰ 10am-5pm Mon-Fri, 10am-6pm Sat & Sun). Interactivity is the watchword – no dusty museum cases here. Instead you'll find yourself inside a tornado, creating a giant bubble, investigating the mechanics of flight or creating an animated TV show.

Across the square is Bristol's **Blue Reef Aquarium** (Map p42; ☎ 0117-929 8929; www.bluereefaquarium.co.uk; Harbourside; adult/child £13.50/9.20; ⏰ 10am-5pm Mon-Fri, 10am-6pm Sat & Sun), with tanks re-creating 40 underwater environments from tropical seas to mangrove forests and coral reefs, complete with underwater viewing tunnel. The 3D IMAX cinema shows marine-themed films.

In a lovely spot on Clifton Hill, **Bristol Zoo** (Map p40; ☎ 0117-973 8951; www.bristolzoo. org.uk; Clifton; adult/child £11.81/7.27; ⏰ summer 9am-5.30pm, winter 9am-5pm) is one of the country's finest. Highlights include gorilla and gibbon islands, a reptile and bug house, a butterfly forest, a lion enclosure, a monkey jungle and the Twilight World, populated by two-toed sloths and naked mole rats. The new Zooropia (adult/child £7.50/6) experience lets your little monkeys go wild on net ramps, rope bridges, hanging logs and a zip-line.

FESTIVALS & EVENTS

St Paul's Carnival (www.stpaulscarnival.co.uk) Multicultural street party on the first Saturday in July.
Bristol Harbour Festival (www.bristol harbourfestival.co.uk) Bands, DJs and big ships on the dockside in late July.
International Balloon Fiesta (www.bristol balloonfiesta.co.uk) Ashton Court hosts a major hot-air balloonfest in August.

Bristol Pride (www.bristolpride.org) Bristol's gay community is out and proud in August.
International Kite Festival (www.kite -festival.org) Flies at Ashton Court in September.
Encounters (www.encounters-festival.org.uk) The city's main film fest hosts features, docos and short films in November.
Christmas Market Late November and December.

GASTRONOMIC HIGHLIGHTS

BORDEAUX QUAY ££

Map p42; ☎ 0117-943 1200; www.bordeaux-quay. co.uk; V-Shed, Canon's Way; 2-course lunch menu £16.50, brasserie mains £8.50-11, restaurant mains £13.50-18.50; ⏰ lunch & dinner
Housed in a wonderful dock warehouse, this is the first restaurant to attain a gold rating from the Soil Association, so your conscience can rest easy while you tuck into some of the city's best food, blending seasonal southwest ingredients with the flavours of provincial European cuisine. The industrial-chic building is a stunner, and there's also a bakery, deli, wine bar and much-trumpeted cookery school.

BRASSERIE BLANC ££

Map p40; ☎ 01179-102 410; bristol@brasserieblanc. com; The Friary Bldg, Cabot Circus; mains £9.75-27.50; ⏰ lunch & dinner
Celeb chef Raymond Blanc has opened the Bristol outpost of his bistro chain in a former Quaker meeting hall, overlooking a square in the Quakers Friars shopping district. With its mezzanine gallery, candelabra and soaring pillars, it's a graceful setting in which to sample Blanc's trademark French cuisine.

CLIFTON SAUSAGE ££

Map p40; ☎ 0117-973 1192; 7-9 Portland St; mains £8.50-16.50; ⏰ lunch & dinner

48 HOURS IN BRISTOL

A couple of days isn't really enough to get under Bristol's skin, but you can make a start. Begin with a wander around the harbourside, factoring in stops at the **Arnolfini Arts Centre** (p44) and Brunel's landmark steamer, the **SS Great Britain** (p38), or, if you're travelling with kids, a visit to **At-Bristol** (p46). Have lunch at **Bordeaux Quay** (p46), and then embark on a leisurely **river trip** (p42) or some shopping around **St Nick's Market** and **Cabot Circus** (p50). Round things off at **Brasserie Blanc** (p46).

Day two's reserved for **Clifton** (p41), including a stroll across the **suspension bridge**, a wander around the **Downs** (p43), lunch at **Primrose Café** (below) and an afternoon at either **Bristol Zoo** (p46), the **Bristol City Museum** (p44) or **Ashton Court** (p44). Finish with supper at **Fishers** (below) or the **Cowshed** (below).

At least six different bangers grace the menu at Clifton's premier gastropub, from pork, plum and ginger to lamb, mint and apricot, plus the house special 'Clifton' (pork, mustard and Somerset cider). It's a favourite hang-out for Clifton's trendy set, with a feel more brasserie than boozer.

❤ COWSHED ££

Map p40; ☎ 0117-973 3550; www.thecowshed bristol.com; 46 Whiteladies Rd; 3-course lunch £10, dinner mains £13.95-21.95; ✆ lunch & dinner

A new arrival on the Whiteladies scene. The Cowshed's modus operandi is to bring 'the taste of the countryside to the city': chunky portions of steak, pork and lamb served on rustic wooden trays are accompanied by a choice of minty potatoes, creamy mash or fat chips. The house special is the 'hot stone', which allows you to cook your own steak on a stone slab. Sunday lunch is a standout – bookings essential.

❤ FISHERS ££

Map p40; ☎ 0117-974 7044; www.fishers-restaurant. com; 35 Princess Victoria St; 2-course lunch £8.50, mains £14.25-18.95; ✆ lunch & dinner

Ceiling sails, porthole windows and storm lanterns conjure a shipshape atmosphere at this Clifton seafooderie,

which prides itself on the freshness of its fish deliveries. The seafood is simple and superb, from bream fillets to full-blown bouillabaisse, while the hot shellfish platter (£21.50 to £36) is ideal for sharing.

❤ GOLDBRICK HOUSE ££

Map p42; ☎ 0117-945 1950; www.goldbrickhouse. co.uk; 69 Park St; mains £11.95-18.50; ✆ 9am-11pm Mon-Sat, 10am-6pm Sun

A fave among Bristol's moneyed-up media crowd, this place combines the ambience of a private gentleman's club (squeaky leather sofas, armchairs, chandeliers) with the champagne-and-cocktails feel of a Soho bar. Light bites downstairs, sophisticated Brit suppers upstairs.

❤ PRIMROSE CAFÉ ££

Map p40; ☎ 0117-946 6577; www.primrosecafe. co.uk; 1-2 Boyce's Ave; dinner á la carte £12.50-16.50, 2-/3-course menu £15.95/18.95; ✆ 9am-5pm Mon-Sat, 9am-3pm Sun

The classic Clifton cafe is as popular for coffee with the Sunday papers as for a late-night meal with chums. Pavement tables are dotted around Parisian-style, while the dining room is a cosy grotto of fairy lights, white linen and church candles. Expect British food with a French accent; it's popular, so dinner bookings are a good idea.

♥ RIVERSTATION ££

Map p42; ☎ 0117-914 4434; www.riverstation.co.uk; The Grove; 2-/3-course lunch £12/14.75, dinner mains £13-19; ☯ lunch & dinner

A decade on and Bristol's original riverside diner is still setting the pace. It's split over two levels (downstairs, a lively bar-kitchen; upstairs, a barrel-roofed brasserie) and still commands a big following for its impressive continental cuisine. Still the city's top place for waterfront dining.

♥ SEVERNSHED ££

Map p42; ☎ 0117-925 1212; www.shedrestaurants. co.uk; The Grove; mains from £12, menus £18.95-22.95; ☯ lunch & dinner

Occupying a Brunel-designed boatshed, the Severnshed boasts one of the city's most exciting settings, replete with a riverside patio, A-frame dining room and six-tonne hovering bar that spins and zips around the restaurant. The food is British bistro-style, while bartenders mix bespoke cocktails such as Green Goblin, Royal Raspberry Doily and Wild Goose Chase.

♥ THALI CAFÉ £

Map p40; ☎ 0117-942 6687; www.thethalicafe.co.uk; 1 Regent St; set meal £6.95; ☯ lunch & dinner Tue-Sun, dinner Mon

Authentic street food and bright Bollywood-style decor has underpinned the success of this popular Indian cafe, which now has four locations around the city. The most convenient is the Clifton branch, where traditional thalis (multi-course dishes served on a steel plate) feature *paneer* (Indian cheese), fish, lentil dhal and a veg curry, all for £6.95.

ALSO RECOMMENDED

Boston Tea Party (www.bostonteaparty.co.uk) Cafe chain with branches including Princess Victoria St, Park St and Whiteladies Rd.

Chandos Deli (www.chandosdeli.com) Ideal for a quick lunch stop; branches include Whiteladies Rd, Princess Victoria St and Quakers Friars.

Culinaria (off Map p40; ☎ 0117-973 7999; www. culinariabristol.co.uk; 1 Chandos Rd; mains £13-17.50; ☯ lunch & dinner Thu-Sat) French dining near Whiteladies Rd.

Glassboat (Map p42; ☎ 0117-929 0704; Welsh Back; lunch £7-8, mains £14-21; ☯ closed Sun) Romantic setting on a converted riverboat.

Olive Shed (Map p40; ☎ 0117-929 1960; www. theoliveshed.com; Princes Wharf; ☯ 6.30-10pm Wed, noon-10pm Thu-Sat, noon-4pm Sun) Another popular waterside restaurant, serving mainly tapas and Med food.

Pieminister (Map p40; ☎ 0117-942 9500; www. pieminister.co.uk; 24 Stokes Croft; pies £3.50; ☯ 11am-7pm Sat, 11am-5pm Sun) Bristol's deluxe pie emporium is based on Stokes Croft but has a concession in St Nick's market.

Rocotillo's (Map p40; ☎ 0117-929 7207; 1 Queens Row; mains from £4; ☯ breakfast & lunch) American diner serving slap-up burgers and thick shakes.

NIGHTLIFE

Bristol has plenty of places to wet your whistle, with new bars opening up practically every week (and often closing as quickly). The fortnightly magazine *Venue* (www.venue.co.uk) details the latest tips (£1.20). Freebie *Folio* is published monthly. The centre of Bristol's gay scene extends around Frogmore St and the surrounding streets.

PUBS & BARS

♥ APPLE

Map p42; ☎ 0117-925 3500; www.applecider.co.uk; Welsh Back

Stocking more ciders than you could possibly hope to imbibe, this refurbished Dutch riverboat is a temple to the art of scrumpy-drinking. Alongside traditional tipples sourced from Somerset farms, look out for six perries (pear ciders), raspberry and strawberry ciders, and brands from South Africa and Sweden. Big glass windows look out onto the water from the barge, or you could bag a table by the quayside.

ALBION

Map p40; ☎ 0117-973 3522; www.thealbionclifton. co.uk; Boyces Ave

If you're after a good Clifton pint, there's nowhere better than the Albion. Flag-stones, oak tables and leather chairs con-jure a welcoming village-pub feel, and on the pumps you'll find Butcombe Bitter, Otter Bright and Doom Bar.

THE GRAIN BARGE

Map p40; ☎ 0117-902 6317; www.grainbarge.com; Mardyke Wharf, Hotwell Rd; ⌚ noon-11pm Tue-Thu & Sun, noon-11.30pm Fri & Sat

Built in 1936, overhauled in 2007, this tow-barge near the SS *Great Britain* is owned by the city's microbrewery, the Bristol Beer Factory. River views unfurl through the windows of the shipshape bar, or there's an upstairs deck for sunny days. Boutique beers include traditional No 7 Bitter, creamy Milk Stout, pale Sun-rise Ale and dark Exhibition Ale.

THE GRAPES

Map p40; ☎ 0117-914 9109; 2 Sion Pl; ⌚ from 6pm Tue-Sat, 1-5pm & 7pm-midnight Sun

Owned by ex-pop-video director Bill Butt and managed by Sean Cook, bassist from cult '90s band Spiritualised, this ubercool Clifton hang-out is unsurpris-ingly a fave for Bristol's actors, musos and TV types. Inside, the pub's dotted with original artwork (look out for a hu-man skeleton dangling from the ceiling and a croc's skull behind the bar), but it's the great gig line-up that packs in the punters.

THE HIGHBURY VAULTS

Map p40; ☎ 0117-973 3203; 164 St Michaels Hill

A scruffy boozer on the university's door-step, often crammed with academic types. The long corridor bar leads through a series of rooms, crammed with snug corners and wood-panelled benches, and there's a choice of at least eight ales.

ZERODEGREES

Map p42; ☎ 0117-925 2706; www.zerodegrees. co.uk; 53 Colston St

Plentiful glass, chrome and steel lend this microbrewery an atmosphere that's closer to the feel of a boutique bar than a spit-and-sawdust pub. Options range from fruit beers and pale wheat ale to Czech-style black and Pilsner lagers.

LIVE MUSIC

COLSTON HALL

Map p42; ☎ 0117-922 3686; www.colstonhall.org; Colston St

Bristol's venerable city concert hall has gone all gold and shiny thanks to the re-cent multimillion-pound redevelopment of its foyer; shame they couldn't have spared some cash for the auditorium. Still, it's the place for touring bands and big-name comedy.

CROFT

Map p40; ☎ 0117-987 4144; www.the-croft.com; 117-119 Stokes Croft

Chilled venue with a policy of supporting breaking acts and Bristol-based artists. Cover charge depends on who's playing in the band room, but it's usually free to hang out in the front bar.

FLEECE & FIRKIN

Map p40; ☎ 0117-945 0996; www.fleecegigs.co.uk; 12 St Thomas St

A small, intimate pub venue, favoured by indie artists and breaking names on the local scene.

❦ **THEKLA**

Map p42; ☎ 0117-929 3301; www.theklabristol.co.uk;
The Grove

Bristol's famous club-pub-boat has nights to cater for all tastes: electro-punk, indie, disco and new wave, plus live gigs and legendary leftfield night Blowpop once a month.

THEATRES & CINEMAS

❦ **CUBE**

Map p40; ☎ 0117-907 4190; www.cubecinema.com;
4 Princess Row

This offbeat arts cinema is the antithesis of a big multiplex (it calls itself a 'micro-plex' to underline the point). Indie and art-house films are its bread and butter, but exhibitions, debates and live talks feature too.

❦ **BRISTOL OLD VIC**

Map p42; ☎ 0117-987 7877; www.bristololdvic.org.uk; 103 The Cut

Now under the creative control of maverick theatre director Tom Morris (brother of satirist Chris Morris), the UK's oldest theatre (built in 1766) has been pulled back from the brink and is once again at the heart of the city's thespian scene. Fundraising and reconstruction are ongoing; check the website for the latest news.

❦ **TOBACCO FACTORY**

off Map p40; ☎ 0117-902 0344; www.tobaccofactory.com; Raleigh Rd

Smaller-scale work heads across the river to this theatre in Southville. Catch bus 24 or 25 from Broadmead to the Raleigh Rd stop.

❦ **WATERSHED**

Map p42; ☎ 0117-927 5100; www.watershed.co.uk; 1 Canon's Rd

Waterfront arts venue, cinema and media centre that hosts a regular film programme and the **Encounters Film Festival** (www.encounters-festival.org.uk).

RECOMMENDED SHOPS

Shop-o-philes will find plenty to feed their habit, whether it's a designer hand-me-down in a retro clothes shop or a choice cheese in a local market. Top stop is the **St Nicholas Market** (Map p42; Corn St; ⏱ 9.30am-5pm Mon-Sat), a chaotic melee of wobbly stalls selling everything from handmade jewellery to artisan bread.

Outside, Corn St is the venue for regular markets, including a **farmer's market** every Wednesday, and a **slow food market** on the first Sunday of every month. There's also the **Nails Market** every Friday and Saturday, stocked with handmade cards, craftwork and quirky clothing.

The city's big shopping centres are **Broadmead** and the spanking-new **Cabot Circus** (Map p40; www.cabotscircus.co.uk), both crammed with high street names. Luxury brands tend to favour the more exclusive area around **Quakers Friars**.

For clothes, records and retro furniture, the scruffy neighbourhoods around Gloucester Rd, North St and Easton are all good areas to explore, while the chi-chi boutiques of **Clifton** are good for antiques, gifts and designer furniture.

TRANSPORT

TO/FROM THE AIRPORT

AIRPORT // Bristol International Airport (☎ 0870 121 2747; www.bristolairport.co.uk) is 8 miles southwest of town.

BUS // Bristol International Flyer (http://flyer.bristolairport.co.uk) runs shuttle buses (one way/return £6/9, 30 minutes, every 10 minutes at peak times) from the bus station and Temple Meads.

~ WORTH A TRIP ~

Formerly the aristocratic home of the Gibbs family, **Tyntesfield** (NT; ☎ 01275-461900; tyntesfield@nationaltrust.org.uk; Wraxall; adult/child £10/5; ☻ 11am-5pm Sat-Wed Mar-Oct) is an ornate Victorian pile that was acquired by the National Trust in 2002. Prickling with spiky turrets, the house was built in grand Gothic Revival style by the architect John Norton, and is crammed with decorative arts, a working kitchen garden and a magnificent private chapel. The house is currently undergoing extensive renovation, so it's still a work in progress – you can even climb up to see the roof being restored. Wraxall is about 8 miles east of Bristol.

GETTING AROUND

BIKE // For bike rental, see p45.

BUS // The main bus station on Marlborough St has an **enquiry office** (Map p40; ☻ 7.30am-6pm Mon-Fri, 10am-6pm Sat). Bus 8/9 goes to Clifton (10 minutes), Whiteladies Rd and Bristol Zoo; the 48/49 runs via Eastville; and the 76/77 travels to Gloucester Rd. The X39/339 (four per hour Monday to Saturday, two per hour Sunday) and the 332 (hourly Monday to Saturday, seven on Sunday) are the quickest to Bath. The 376 goes to Wells and Glastonbury every half-hour Monday to Friday.

CAR & MOTORCYCLE // Traffic and expensive parking makes driving in Bristol a headache, so you're better off using the **park-and-ride buses** (☎ 0117-922 2910; return before 10am Mon-Fri £3.50, after 10am Mon-Fri £2.50, Sat £2.50; ☻ every 10min Mon-Sat) from Portway, Bath Rd and Long Ashton.

TAXI // There are central taxi ranks on St Augustine's Pde, Baldwin St and Colston Ave. Official taxis have lights on top and stick to council-set rates; beware unscrupulous minicabs. Reputable companies: **Bristol Brunel Taxis** (☎ 0117-947 7153), **Bristol Hackney Cabs** (☎ 0117-953 8638) and **Bristol Streamline Taxis** (☎ 0117-926 4001).

TRAIN // Bristol is an important rail hub, with the main routes operated by **First Great Western** (www.firstgreatwestern.co.uk), **Crosscountry** (www.crosscountrytrains.co.uk) and **South West Trains** (www.southwesttrains.co.uk). The city's central station is Temple Meads, although many trains stop at Bristol Parkway in the northern suburb of Stoke Gifford. Frequent connections serve London (£19.50 to £34, 1¾ hours) and the southwest, including Exeter (£22 to £39.50, one hour), Plymouth (£32 to £54, 2½ hours) and Penzance (£37 to £70, 4¼ hours), plus local services to Bath (£5.80, 11 minutes, four per hour).

SOMERSET
· · · · · ·

Somerset's a county that neatly splits between town and country. While the flush and fashionable flock to Bristol and Bath, rural Somerset ambles along in its own sleepy way, seemingly unflustered by the onward march of the modern world. This is still a deeply agricultural corner of England, where cider's brewed in the time-honoured fashion and thatch still graces many a rooftop, and outside the main towns you'll be treated to a largely unsullied landscape, from the lofty hills of the Quantocks and the Mendips down to one of the nation's last great wetlands on the Somerset Levels.

BATH

pop 90,144

If ever there was a city that needs no introduction, it's Bath. For nigh-on three centuries this sophisticated, stately, ever-so-slightly snooty city has been setting trends (architectural, cultural, fashionable) for the rest of the nation to follow. Its streets are graced with some

ACCOMMODATION

Accommodation in Somerset ranges from bargain B&Bs to plush country hotels. Bristol's hotel scene is dominated by the big business chains, and demand always outstrips supply in Bath, so book well ahead for both. As always, prices tend to skyrocket in summer.

Check out our Accommodation chapter (p288) for full reviews, or take your pick from one of these recommended options.

* **Hotel du Vin** (p288) Sugar factory turned sexy city sleep

* **Queensberry Hotel** (p289) Boutique Bath with a price tag to match

* **Farmer's Inn** (p290) As cosy as country inns come

* **The Farmyard** (p290) Self-catering, 21st-century style

of the finest Georgian architecture anywhere in Britain; in fact, the entire place has been placed on the World Heritage list by Unesco. It's not without its drawbacks, though – it's posh, pricey and the rush-hour traffic will have you weeping into your steering wheel – but despite its problems, it's simply impossible not to be dazzled by this radiant pearl of a city.

The Celts were the first to establish a temple near Bath's natural hot springs, but it was the Romans who put the place on the map, founding the spa town of Aquae Sulis in AD 44. The city later became an important religious centre, beginning with an early Saxon monastery, followed several centuries later by the completion of Bath Abbey in 1616. But it was during the 17th and 18th centuries that Bath really hit its stride. Under the auspices of philanthropist Ralph Allen, architects John Wood (Elder and Younger) and bon viveur extraordinaire Beau Nash, the city became the toast of British high society and witnessed the construction of a slew of ambitious architectural projects, including the Royal Crescent, the Circus (p53) and the great estate of Prior Park (p58).

More recently, there's been considerable kerfuffle about two other controversial building projects – the futuristic Thermae Bath Spa (p57) and the redevelopment of the SouthGate shopping centre (p62).

ESSENTIAL INFORMATION

TOURIST INFORMATION // Bath tourist office (☎ enquiries 0906-711-2000, accommodation 0844 847 5256; www.visitbath.co.uk; Abbey Churchyard; ⏰ 9.30am-6pm Mon-Sat & 10-4pm Sun Jun-Sep, 9.30am-5pm Mon-Sat & 10am-4pm Sun Oct-May) Phone enquiries are charged at 50p per minute.

ORIENTATION

The city sits in a bowl-shaped valley ringed by seven hills. Right in the city centre are the Abbey, Pump Rooms, Roman Baths and the tourist office; the Royal Crescent overlooks the city's north side above Royal Victoria Park. The Bath Spa train station sits at the southern end of Manvers St, while the bus station is just to the west along Dorchester St.

EXPLORING BATH

❦ THE ROMAN BATHS // BATH'S HISTORIC HOT TUB

Without its baths, well, Bath just wouldn't be Bath. Roman generals,

Regency dandies and regal monarchs have all taken a dip in the city's hot springs, which bubble up from deep underground at a constant temperature of 46°C. Various fanciful claims have been applied to the cure-all waters – they're meant to be good for everything from an ingrown toenail to a foul temper, and even supposedly a herd of leprous pigs belonging to Bath's legendary founder, King Bladud.

The **Roman Baths** (☎ 01225-477785; www.romanbaths.co.uk; Abbey Churchyard; adult/child £11.50/7.50, Jul & Aug £12.25/6.50; ⊗ 9am-8pm Jul & Aug, 9am-6pm Mar-Jun, Sep & Oct, 9.30am-5.30pm Jan, Feb, Nov & Dec, last admission 1hr before closing) comprise one of the best-preserved ancient Roman spas in the world. While taking a dip in the waters may no longer be on the agenda, you can still wander around most of the complex. Unfortunately, crowds reach titanic proportions at peak times – to avoid the worst crush, visit early or late in the day, and steer clear of July and August.

You can choose to take one of the hourly guided tours, or borrow a free multilingual audioguide (including one featuring a typically wry commentary by bestselling author Bill Bryson). The centrepiece of the complex is the **Great Bath**, a huge 1.6m-deep hot pool, lined with lead and encircled by pillars that once supported an enclosing roof. Excavated passages lead to the **East** and **West Baths**, which still has its original hypocaust *pilae* (tile stacks allowing the circulation of hot air).

The **King's Bath** was built in the 12th century around the original sacred spring; 1.5 million litres of hot water still pour into the pool every day. Elsewhere you can see the Roman version of a sauna in the **Laconicum**, as well as the cold-water **Circular Bath**. There's also a small **museum** displaying fascinating archaeological finds, including a huge collection of votive coins thrown into the spring, as well as stone fragments from the lost Roman temple.

Near the main entrance is the **Pump Room**, chandelier-clad and serving up the city's fanciest afternoon tea (although at an eye-watering £17.50, it doesn't come cheap).

🌱 BATH ABBEY // GOTHIC GRANDEUR IN THE CITY CENTRE

The last great Gothic church to be built in England, **Bath Abbey** (☎ 01225-422462; www.bathabbey.org; requested donation £2.50; ⊗ 9am-6pm Mon-Sat Easter-Oct, 9am-4.30pm Nov-Easter, afternoons only Sun year-round) was built between 1499 and 1616 on the site of two former churches: an 8th-century abbey and a Norman cathedral built around 1090. Alongside the usual Gothic glass and flying buttresses, the cathedral's most notable features are its fan-vaulted ceiling and its west facade, where angels climb up and down stone ladders, commemorating the dream that inspired Bishop Oliver King to construct the cathedral in the first place. Inside are memorials to Isaac Pitman, (the inventor of shorthand), James Montague (Bishop of Bath and Wells 1608–16) and dandy Beau Nash, who is buried beneath the nave. On the southern side of the abbey, the **Vaults Heritage Museum** (⊗ 10am-4pm Mon-Sat) contains stone bosses, statuary and other archaeological artefacts.

🌱 ROYAL CRESCENT & THE CIRCUS // THE CITY'S ARCHITECTURAL GEMS

The crowning glory of Georgian Bath is the **Royal Crescent**, a semicircular

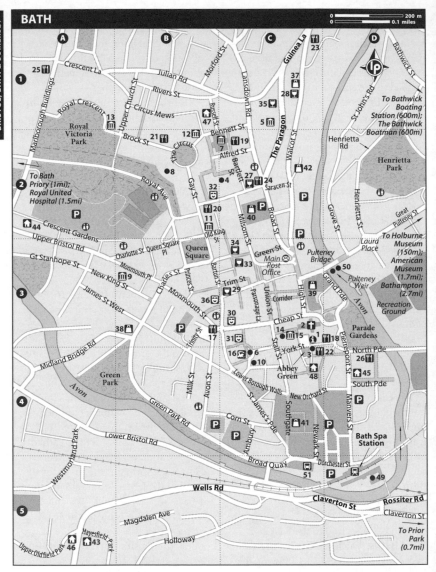

BATH

0 _____ 200 m
0 _____ 0.1 miles

terrace of 30 houses overlooking the green sweep of Royal Victoria Park. Designed by John Wood the Younger (1728–82) between 1767 and 1775, the Grade I–listed terrace is the most important Georgian street in Britain. Despite the symmetry of Ionic columns and Palladian porticos, inside no two houses are the same; purchasers were allowed to redesign the interior as long they preserved the Crescent's uniform exterior. Most were let out to socially suitable families visiting Bath for the summer season; these days they're mostly split

ESSENTIAL INFORMATION		GASTRONOMIC HIGHLIGHTS 🍴		RECOMMENDED SHOPS 🛍	
Tourist Office	1 C3	Boston Tea Party	17 B3	Bath Aqua Glass	37 C1
		Café Retro	18 D3	Bath Farmer's	
EXPLORING BATH		Casani's	19 C2	Market	(see 38)
Assembly Rooms	(see 7)	Chandos Deli	20 B2	Green Park Station	38 B3
Bath Abbey	2 C3	Circus	21 B2	Guild Hall Market	39 C3
Bath Festivals Box		Demuth's	22 C4	Milsom St	40 C2
Office	3 C4	Hudson Steakhouse	23 C1	Southgate Shopping	
Bertinet Kitchen	4 C2	Jika Jika	24 C2	Centre	41 C4
Building of Bath		Marlborough Tavern	25 A1	Thoughtful Bread	
Museum	5 C1	Moon & Sixpence	(see 40)	Co.	(see 38)
Cross Bath	6 C4	Olive Tree Restaurant	(see 47)	Walcot St Flea	
Fashion Museum	7 C2	Onefishtwofish	26 D4	Market	42 C2
Georgian Garden	8 B2				
Herschel Museum of		NIGHTLIFE 🍷 🎭		ACCOMMODATION 🏠	p288
Astronomy	9 B3	Adventure Café	27 C2	139 Bath	43 A5
Hot Bath	10 C4	Bell	28 C1	Brooks	44 A2
Jane Austen Centre	11 B2	Gascoyne Place	29 C3	Halcyon	45 D4
Museum of East Asian		Komedia	30 C3	Oldfields	46 A5
Art	12 B2	Little Theatre Cinema	31 C3	Queensberry Hotel	47 B1
No 1 Royal Crescent	13 A1	Moles	32 B2	Three Abbey Green	48 C4
Pump Room	14 C3	Porter Cellar Bar	(see 32)		
Roman Baths & Museum	15 C3	Raven	33 C3	TRANSPORT	
Thermae Bath Spa	16 C4	Salamander	34 C3	Avon Valley Cyclery	49 D5
Vaults Heritage		Star Inn	35 C1	Boat Trip Departures	50 D3
Museum	(see 2)	Theatre Royal	36 B3	Bus & Coach Station	51 C5

into flats that command a quite staggering price tag. Look out for the acorns on the rooftops, a sly nod to the legend of King Bladud's pigs.

At the eastern end of the terrace, **No 1 Royal Crescent** (☎ 01225-428126; www. bath-preservation-trust.org.uk; adult/child £6/2.50; 🕑 10.30am-5pm Tue-Sun mid-Feb–mid-Oct, 10.30am-4pm mid-Oct–Dec) was given to the Bath Preservation Trust in 1968 by the shipping magnate Major Bernard Cayzer, and has since been restored using only 18th-century materials. Rooms on show include the gentleman's study, dining room, a lady's bedroom and basement kitchen.

East along Brock St is another of the city's Georgian masterworks, the **Circus**, supposedly inspired by the Roman Colosseum. The circus was conceived by John Wood the Elder, but he died soon after the first stone was laid, and the project was subsequently completed by his son between 1754 and 1768. Arranged over three uniform terraces, the 33 houses overlook a circular garden

populated by plane trees; each of the three storeys showcases a different style of classical column (Ionic, Doric and Corinthian), and there are supposedly secret Masonic symbols hidden away amongst the exterior carvings. A German bomb demolished several houses in 1942, although they've since been rebuilt in seamless style. Look out for plaques to Thomas Gainsborough (no 17), Lord Clive of India (no 14) and David Livingstone (no 13), all former residents.

Along Gravel Walk between Royal Crescent and Queen Square is the **Georgian Garden** (admission free; 🕑 9.30am-4.30pm Mon-Fri May-Oct), restored to resemble a typical town-house garden of the 18th century, with formal flowerbeds, stone-flagged paths and gravel walkways (no lawns – gravel was easier to rake over when it became discoloured by chimney fumes).

Further into the city is **Queen Square**, John Wood the Elder's first major architectural commission, built between 1729 and 1736.

MESSING ABOUT ON THE RIVER

One of the best ways to appreciate Bath's skyline is from the water. Cruise boats depart from the quay under Pulteney Bridge and putter upriver on an hour-long trip to nearby **Bathampton**. Companies include **Pulteney Cruisers** (☎ 01225-312900; www.bathboating.com; adult/child £8/4), the **Pulteney Princess** (☎ 07791-910650; www.pulteneypriness.co.uk; adult/child £7/3) and **Bath City Boat Trips** (☎ 07974-560197; www.bathcityboattrips.com; adult/child £6.95/4.95). Trips run Easter to October.

If you prefer exploring under your own steam, the delightful **Bathwick Boating Station** (☎ 01225-312900; www.bathboating.co.uk; Forrester Rd, Bathwick; adult/child first hr £7/3.50, subsequent hr £3/1.50; ☺ 10am-6pm Easter-Oct) has been hiring out skiffs (row boats), flat-bottomed punts and Canadian canoes from its riverside station in Bathwick since 1833. Skiffs and canoes are easier to master, while punting is an acquired art; which-ever you choose, note the sign that sagely advises 'It is unwise to indulge in alcohol when boating'. You have been warned…

❦ WALKING TOURS // BRUSH UP ON CITY HISTORY

The best Bath tour is completely free: the **Mayor's Guides Tour** (☎ 01225-477411; www.thecityofbath.co.uk) leaves from outside the Pump Room at 10.30am and 2pm Sunday to Friday, and 10.30am on Saturday. From May to September there are extra tours at 7pm on Tuesday, Friday and Saturday.

Bibliophiles might prefer **Jane Austen's Bath** (☎ 01225-443000; adult/child £6/5), conducted by bonneted guides dressed in suitably frilly fashion. You can download your own free MP3 tour at www.visitbath.co.uk/janeausten/audio-tour.

Ask at the tourist office about Bath's many other tours.

❦ ASSEMBLY ROOMS // WHERE GEORGIAN BATH WENT OUT TO PLAY

Built in 1771 under the supervision of Beau Nash, the city's **Assembly Rooms** (☎ 01225-477785; Bennett St; ☺ 10.30am-5pm Mar-Oct, 10.30am-4pm Nov-Feb) were the centre of Bath's busy social scene. Chamber concerts, card games and balls welcomed many famous visitors including Jane Austen, Charles Dickens, Haydn and Strauss. You can wander around the card room, tearoom and ballroom, all lit by their original spectacular 18th-century chandeliers (one of which nearly crushed the artist Thomas Gainsborough in 1771). Astonishingly, the Assembly Rooms were almost entirely gutted by fire during WWII, but have since been painstakingly restored.

In the basement is the **Fashion Museum** (www.museumofcostume.co.uk; adult/child £5/5, joint ticket with Roman Baths £15/9), which houses a huge wardrobe of outfits including lavish 18th-century embroi-dered waistcoats, a collection of 500 handbags and a display of terrifying whalebone corsets.

❦ JANE AUSTEN CENTRE // BATH'S LITERARY CONNECTIONS

Though Bath only features in two Jane Austen novels (*Persuasion* and *North-anger Abbey*), for many people the city provides the quintessential backdrop for her novels. Austen lived in Bath from 1801 to 1806, and the **Jane Austen Cen-tre** (☎ 01225-443000; www.janeausten.co.uk; 40 Gay St; adult/child £6.50/3.50; ☺ 9.45am-5.30pm Apr-Sep,

11am-4.30pm Oct-Mar) explores the author's connections with the city through costumed guides, pictorial prints and Austen-themed exhibits. There's even a Regency tearoom and a gift shop stocked with lace parasols.

❦ OTHER MUSEUMS // ART, ARCHITECTURE AND AMERICANA

The **Building of Bath Museum** (☎ 01225-333895; www.bath-preservation-trust. org.uk; The Vineyards, The Paragon; adult/child £4/2; 🕙 10.30am-5pm Tue-Sun mid-Feb–Nov) traces the city's architectural evolution, with displays detailing everything from how to build a sash window to the most fashionable wallpapers of 18th-century society.

Across town is the **Herschel Museum of Astronomy** (☎ 01225-311342; 19 New King St; adult/child £4.50/2.50; 🕙 1-5pm Mon, Tue, Thu & Fri, 11am-5pm Sat & Sun Feb-Nov), the former home of classical composer, astronomer and telescope-maker William Herschel, whose achievements included the discovery of Uranus in 1781 and the construction of several pioneering telescopes.

The city's main art repository, the **Holburne Museum** (☎ 01225-466669; Great Pulteney St) is currently undergoing a huge refurbishment programme and will be shrouded in scaffold until 2012.

Till then, you'll have to fulfil your artistic leanings at the **Museum of East Asian Art** (☎ 01225-464640; www.meaa.org. uk; 12 Bennett St; adult/13-18yr/2-12yr £5/3.50/2; 🕙 10am-5pm Tue-Sat, noon-5pm Sun), which has a collection of over 2000 decorative artefacts from China, Japan, Korea and Southeast Asia, or the **American Museum in Britain** (☎ 01225-460503; www. americanmuseum.org; Claverton Manor; adult/child £8/4.50; 🕙 noon-5pm),which houses Britain's largest collection of American folk art, including Native American textiles, patchwork quilts and historic maps. The museum is 4 miles from the city centre; catch buses 18/418/U18 from the bus station.

❦ BATH'S BATH // SINK INTO THE CITY'S SWISH NEW SPA

The waters of the Roman Baths might be off the agenda, but you can still sample Bath's curative waters at the **Thermae Bath Spa** (☎ 01225-331234; www. thermaebathspa.com; Hot Bath St; spa sessions Cross Bath adult/child £12/9, New Royal Bath per 2hr/4hr/ day £20/30/50, spa packages from £65; 🕙 Cross Bath 10am-8pm, New Royal Bath 9am-10pm). Controversially incorporating the old **Cross Bath** into a shell of Georgian stone, steel and glass, the complex incorporates heated pools with a range of ominous-sounding treatments including peat baths, body cocoons, Vichy showers and the 'Kraxen Stove'. Best of all is the open-air rooftop pool, where you can admire the cityscape dressed in nowt but a bathrobe and slippers.

The baths get very busy, especially at weekends. Bookings are a very good idea.

❦ BERTINET KITCHEN // TIPS FROM A MASTER BAKER

If you've always wanted to learn the secrets of the perfect loaf, the **Bertinet Kitchen Cookery School** (☎ 01225-445531; www.thebertinetkitchen.com; 12 St Andrew's Terrace) is for you. Run by Richard Bertinet, the school specialises in masterclasses in bread-baking, pastry-making and classic patisseries, as well as more general cookery courses (there's even a hands-on pudding-making class for the kids). Lessons fill up fast; if the school is fully booked, pastries, croissants and breads are available from the shop on weekend mornings.

❦ PRIOR PARK // RALPH ALLEN'S SHOWPIECE ESTATE

Capability Brown and the poet Alexander Pope both had a hand in the design of **Prior Park** (NT; ☎ 01225-833422; www.priorpark@nationaltrust.org.uk; Ralph Allen Dr; adult/child £5/2.80; ⊙ 11am-5.30pm Wed-Mon mid-Feb–Nov, 11am-5.30pm Sat & Sun Nov-Jan). This 18th-century landscaped garden on the city's southern fringe was built by the entrepreneur Ralph Allen, who made his fortune founding Britain's postal service, and owned many of the quarries from which the city's celebrated Bath stone was mined.

Allen conceived Prior Park as an architectural showpiece to demonstrate what could be achieved with his versatile amber-hued stone. Although the magnificent house is now occupied by a private school, you can wander around the estate's cascading lakes and winding walkways. At the bottom of the gardens is a famous Palladian bridge, one of only four such structures in the world – some of the graffiti dates back to the early 1800s.

UP, UP & AWAY

For a truly unforgettable view of Bath, you can't beat sailing skywards in a **hot-air balloon**. Operators launch from Royal Victoria Park: the most experienced are **Bath Balloons** (☎ 0844 391 0404; www.bathballoons.co.uk; standard flights £95-135, sundowner flights £115, family ticket £390) and **Bailey Balloons** (☎ 01275-375300; www.baileybaloons.co.uk; standard flights £99-135). Note that flights aren't exclusive – you'll need to book the whole balloon (around £500 to £550) if you want it to yourself – and that trips are entirely dependent on the British weather playing ball.

Unsurprisingly, the views of Bath are inspiring, and if you feel like a longer walk, you can follow the Bath Skyline, a 6-mile circular trail taking in pretty woodland and blustery hilltops around the estate.

Prior Park is a mile south of the River Avon. It's a steep walk up on foot, or you can catch bus 2 from the bus station. Parking is reserved for disabled visitors.

❦ THE KENNET & AVON CANAL // PUTTER ALONG AN IDYLLIC WATERWAY

Constructed as an industrial link joining the River Avon and Thames, the **Kennet & Avon Canal** twists and turns from the southwest side of Bath for 87 miles east to Newbury, travelling past the Grade I–listed Dundas Aqueduct, the valley of Stoke Limpley and various picturesque bits of Wiltshire and Berkshire en route. The canal's commercial viability was eclipsed by the advent of the railway in the mid-18th century, but holiday barges and houseboats still putter along the peaceful waterways; the towpath is also very popular with local joggers, anglers and cyclists.

The canal is notable for its elaborate system of over a hundred **locks**, many of which are now listed monuments. Five miles outside Bath off the A36, you can visit the **Claverton Pumping Station** (☎ 01225-483001; www.claverton.org; ⊙ 10am-4pm Wed, 10am-5pm Sat & Sun Apr-Oct), one of several pumping stations designed to maintain water levels in the canal. The station's giant waterwheel was built in 1810, and is capable of raising up to 100,000 gallons of water every hour.

The **Kennet & Avon Canal Trust** (☎ 01380-721279; www.katrust.org) operates four vintage narrowboats from several locations, including Bradford-on-Avon,

Devizes and Hungerford. Nearest to Bath is the **Jubilee** (☎ 0800 121 4682; jubilee@katrust-ent.org.uk; ⏱ trips noon-2pm & 2.30-6pm Sun & bank holidays Apr-Oct, also 2.30-6pm Tue Jul & Aug), a 50ft narrowboat built in 1976, which runs cruises from Brassknocker Basin, just outside Bath.

With more time, you could even rent your own live-aboard from **Moonraker Boats** (☎ 07973-876891; www.moonboats.co.uk; per week £950-2475) and **Bath Canal Boats** (☎ 01225-312935; www.bathcanalboats.co.uk; per week £895-1800).

FESTIVALS & EVENTS

Bookings are handled by the **Bath Festivals Box Office** (☎ 01225-463362; www.bath festivals.org.uk; 2 Church St).
Bath Literature Festival (www.bathlitfes.org) Book readings, signings and major authors. Early March.
Bath International Music Festival (www.bathmusicfest.org.uk) Held from mid-May to June, spanning everything from classical to jazz, world and folk.
Bath Fringe Festival (www.bathfringe.co.uk) Major theatre fringefest, second only in size to Edinburgh. Early June.
Jane Austen Festival (www.janeausten.co.uk) September sees Bath celebrate its Austen connections with readings and costume parades.
Bath Film Festival (www.bathfilmfestival.org. uk) Small celluloid celebration in September.
Christmas Markets Held beside the Abbey.

GASTRONOMIC HIGHLIGHTS

Celeb chefs Jamie Oliver and Hugh Fearnley-Whittingstall have both recently set up shop in Bath, adding to the city's already packed scene.

❧ BATH PRIORY £££
☎ 01225-331922; www.thebathpriory.co.uk; lunch menu £24-30, dinner menu £65; ⏱ lunch & dinner
It's a little way out of Bath proper, but for full-blown fine-dining, nowhere tops Michael Caines' country house stunner.

This is high-end dining at its fussiest: truffle-buttered turbot, roast venison loin and crab ravioli served up in a formal setting, with tall windows overlooking grassy lawns. Little wonder it's bagged a Michelin star.

❧ THE BATHWICK BOATMAN ££
☎ 01225-428844; www.bathwickboatman.com; Bathwick; mains £12.50-15.50, Sun lunch 2/3 courses £15.50/18.50; ⏱ lunch Tue-Sun, dinner Tue-Sat
For romantic dining, the Boatman is the place. Lodged inside a timber boathouse beside the boating station, it's run by husband-and-wife team Ben and Rosy Hall, who've brought several years in Italy to their latest venture. Inside, pine tables and upside-down canoes; outside, a divine waterfront terrace for alfresco dining.

❧ CASANI'S £££
☎ 01225-780055; www.casanis.co.uk; 4 Saville Row; dinner mains £16-24; ⏱ lunch & dinner Tue-Sat
The French address in Bath, along a pedestrian alley off George St. Crisp white cloths and chandeliers in the upstairs-downstairs dining rooms, partnered by a menu of classic French dishes: *tournedos de boeuf* (beef fillet), *pavé d'agneau* (thick-cut lamb steak), *magret de canard* (duck steak).

❧ THE CIRCUS ££
☎ 01225-466020; www.thecircuscafeandrestaurant. co.uk; 34 Brock St; lunch £5.50-9.70, dinner mains £11-13.90; ⏱ lunch & dinner
Just off the Royal Crescent, this accomplished city diner deserves its reputation as one of Bath's best places to eat. It's sophisticated but not remotely snobby; moody lighting, fireplaces and modern art provide an intimate town-house setting for chef-proprietor Ali Golden's impeccable Brit food. At these prices, it's a steal.

☙ DEMUTH'S ££

☎ 01125-446059; www.demuths.co.uk; 2 North Pde Passage; mains £9.75-12.50; ☺ lunch & dinner

Veggie dishes are all very well, but they're about as tasty as cold pudding, right? Wrong. This place dispels all the myths about vegetarian food – it is one of Bath's most innovative eateries and has scooped a host of awards for its exciting, all-veg dishes, from spiced sweet potato and pea pilaf to fennel, apricot and chickpea tagine.

☙ HUDSON STEAKHOUSE £££

☎ 01225-332323; www.hudsonbars.com; 14 London St; mains £15-30; ☺ dinner Mon-Sat

Steak, steak and more steak is pretty much what's on offer at this much-garlanded place at the top of Walcot St, but for committed carnivores there's nowhere better. Top-quality cuts take in everything from delicate filet mignon to cowboy rib steak, all sourced from a Staffordshire farmers' co-op.

☙ MARLBOROUGH TAVERN ££

☎ 01225-423731; www.marlborough-tavern.com; 35 Marlborough Bldgs; mains £10.95-15.95; ☺ lunch & dinner

Gastropubs come and go, but the Marlborough's as reliable as ever. Chef Richard Whiting is passionate about big country flavours – pork with bean casserole, chestnut-and-thyme stuffed chicken – and the interior is a contemporary combo of wood, leather and off-white tones. Unlike most pubs, you can make reservations. Do.

☙ MOON & SIXPENCE ££

☎ 01225-320088; www.moonandsixpence.co.uk; 27 Milsom Pl; 2-course lunch £11.95, dinner mains £15.50-21.95; ☺ lunch & dinner

Fresh from an expensive refit, this restaurant in upmarket Milsom Place has two guises: the relaxed New Moon bar-

brasserie upstairs, and a more formal restaurant below. Food throughout is 'modern international' (think wood pigeon with puy lentils, or sea bass with chive mash), but for proper eats you'll be happiest downstairs amongst the box hedges and courtyard tables.

☙ ONEFISHTWOFISH ££

☎ 01225-330236; 10a North Pde; mains £13-18; ☺ dinner Tue-Sun

Lights twinkle beneath a barrel-brick roof at this cellar seafood restaurant, which ships fish from southwest ports and cooks up everything from wonton salmon to Marseillaise bouillabaisse. There's a 'no fish' option for non-piscatarians.

☙ OLIVE TREE RESTAURANT £££

☎ 01225-447928; Queensbury Hotel, Russell St; dinner mains £21.75-27.75; ☺ lunch Tue-Sun, dinner Mon-Sun

For a treat, the Queensberry Hotel's posh, pricey restaurant is tough to top. Studiously minimalist and sparkling with boutique British cuisine, you'll need a gastronomic glossary to decipher the menu – monkfish with slow-cooked Jacob's Ladder, or pork with cox apple and crackling pencil.

ALSO RECOMMENDED

Boston Tea Party (☎ 01225-313901; 19 Kingsmead Sq; ☺ 7.30am-7pm Mon-Sat, 9am-7pm Sun) Chunky sandwiches, veggie wraps and homemade cakes.
Café Retro (☎ 01225-339347; www.caferetro. co.uk; 18 York St; mains £5-12; ☺ 9am-5pm Mon-Sat, 10am-5pm Sun; ☞) Quirky cafe popular for its laidback vibe and hearty comfort food.
Jika Jika (☎ 01225-429903; www.jikajika.co.uk; 4a Princes Bldgs, George St; ☺ 7.30am-8pm Mon-Thu, 7.30am-9pm Fri, 8.30am-9pm Sat, 10.30am-4pm Sun; ☞) Boutique coffeehouse serving Bath's finest espresso.
Sally Lunn's (☎ 01225-461634; www.sallylunns. co.uk; 4 North Pde Passage; ☺ breakfast, lunch & din-

ner) Historic teashop serving Sally Lunn's buns, trencherman's plates and cream teas.

NIGHTLIFE

PUBS & CAFES

☙ ADVENTURE CAFÉ

☎ 01225-462038; 5 Princes Bldgs; ☜

Californian bohemia meets urban chic at this cafe-cum-hangout, all picture windows, distressed wood and deep sofas. Cappuccinos by morning, ciabattas at noon, cocktails after dark. Nice patio too.

☙ THE BELL

☎ 01225-460426; www.walcotstreet.com; 103 Walcot St; ☜

Scruffily stylish pub on boho Walcot St, with a cavernous central bar and a beer garden out back which hosts visiting bands. Nine ales on tap plus two guests from visiting breweries.

☙ GASCOYNE PLACE

☎ 01225-445854; www.gascoyneplace.co.uk; 1 Sawclose; mains £10.95-16.95; ☯ lunch & dinner

A good gastropub in a central spot on Sawclose. There's a choice of settings – cosy snug, candlelit bar, cellar room – backed by a solid British menu.

☙ PORTER CELLAR BAR & MOLES

☎ 01225-424104; www.theporter.co.uk; George St

Bath's only 100% veggie pub is a reliable fave with local students, who squeeze onto benches for cheap beer and wholefood grub. The owners also run Bath's main gig venue, **Moles** (☎ 01225-404445; www.moles.co.uk; 14 George St), underneath the street.

☙ THE RAVEN

☎ 01225-425045; www.theravenofbath.co.uk; Queen St; ☜

This pint-sized pub serves one of the city's best ale selections, earning it the nod from the ale aficionados at CAMRA. Inside, the feel is classic Brit boozer: bench booths, beer mats on the tables and lines of long-handled pumps along the bar. House brews are Raven and Raven's Gold.

☙ THE SALAMANDER

☎ 01225-428889; www.bathales.com; 3 John St

The Salamander is owned by the city's main microbrewer, Bath Ales. Scuffed floors, bar stools and plenty of nooks and crannies conjure a traditional feel in the long main bar, and there are plenty of Bath Ales brews on the pumps. At the lighter end are amber-coloured Gem and Golden Hare, while strongest of all is dark Rare Hare at a punchy 5.2%. If something tickles your taste buds, you can buy your chosen ale in 5L casks.

☙ STAR INN

☎ 01225-425072; www.star-inn-bath.co.uk; 23 The Vineyards off the Paragon; ☜

Not many pubs can claim to be a registered relic, but the Star can – it's listed on the National Inventory of Historic Pubs, and boasts many of its original 19th-century bar fittings. It's the brewery tap for Bath-based Abbey Ales; beer is served in traditional jugs, and you can ask for a complimentary pinch of snuff in the 'smaller bar'.

THEATRES & CINEMAS

☙ KOMEDIA

☎ 0845 293 8480; www.komedia.co.uk; 22-23 Westgate St

The Brighton-based comedy and cabaret venue has extended its reach west to Bath. Big-name comedy acts, burlesque shows and club nights all make a showing. The busiest night is Saturday for the Krater comedy club.

☙ LITTLE THEATRE CINEMA

☎ 01225-466822; www.picturehouses.co.uk/cinema/The_Little; St Michael's Pl

Bath's beloved art-house cinema, screening mostly fringe and foreign-language films. For mainstream offerings, there's an Odeon down the road on James St West.

♥ THEATRE ROYAL
☎ 01225-448844; www.theatreroyal.org.uk; Sawclose

The city's theatre features comedy, drama, opera, ballet and world music in the main auditorium, and more experimental productions in the Ustinov Studio.

RECOMMENDED SHOPS

Bath's oldest shopping landmark is **Pulteney Bridge**, one of only a handful in the world to be lined by shops (the most famous other example is the Ponte Vecchio in Florence). It was built in 1773 and is now Grade I listed.

After much comment and controversy, Bath's multimillion-pound shopping centre **SouthGate** (www.southgatebath.com) has finally been finished. It's been deliberately designed to fit in with Bath's existing Georgian architecture, and the developers have generally done an admirable job – sadly the same can't always be said for the high street shopfronts.

Elsewhere in the city, designer boutiques cluster around **Milsom Street**, while the **Guild Hall** has small stalls made for browsing. For indie shopping, **Walcot Street** is the place, with a quirky mix of reclamation yards, cheese sellers, craft shops and secondhand clothing emporia – it even has its own glassblower, **Bath Aqua Glass** (☎ 01225-319606; www.bathaquaglass.com; 105-107 Walcot St).

The city's markets include a fantastic **farmer's market** (www.bathfarmersmarket.co.uk), held every Saturday in the former station at Green Park. There's also a **flea market** on Walcot St every Saturday.

TRANSPORT

BIKE // Avon Valley Cyclery (☎ 01225-461880; www.bikeshop.uk.com; Arch 37; half-/full day £10/15; 9.30am-5pm Mon-Sat, till 8pm Thu) is handy for both the train station and the Bristol and Bath Railway Path.

BUS // Bath's new bus and coach station (enquiries office 9am-5pm Mon-Sat) is on Dorchester St. Useful services are the X39/339 to Bristol (55 minutes, four per hour Monday to Saturday, half-hourly Sunday), the 173 (hourly Monday to Saturday, six on Sunday) to Wells, and the 174 to Frome (hourly Monday to Saturday).

CAR // Driving in Bath can be a nightmare thanks to rush-hour traffic, a bewildering one-way system and ludicrously expensive street parking. **Park-and-ride services** (☎ 01225-464446; return £2.50; every 10-15min, 6.15am-7.30pm) operate at Lansdown to the north, Newbridge to the west and Odd Down to the south (it's 10 minutes to the centre). If you brave the city, the best-value car park is underneath the Southgate shopping centre (two/three/four/five/eight hours £3/4/5/7/9.50, after 6.30pm £2).

TRAIN // Direct trains leave for London Paddington and London Waterloo (£22 to £39, 1½ hours, at least hourly), plus several per hour to Bristol (£5.80, 11 minutes). Less frequent local trains serve Frome, Weston-super-Mare, Dorchester and Weymouth.

WELLS

pop 10,406

Even by England's proportionally challenged standards, Wells is a minuscule city – it only qualifies for the title thanks to its cathedral, a seat of ecclesiastical power since the 12th century, and still the residence of the Bishop of Bath and Wells. The cathedral forms the centrepiece of one of the best-preserved medieval closes in Britain, an alluring collection of cobbled streets, cloistered walkways and a moat-fringed Bishop's Palace where the swans have been trained to order their supper by tinkling a bell. The cathedral close has featured in countless films and costume dramas, but despite its starry connections, Wells is a quiet, sleepy city, and a good base for further forays into northern Somerset.

ESSENTIAL INFORMATION

TOURIST INFORMATION // Wells tourist office (☎ 01749-672552; www.wells.gov.uk; Market Pl; ⏰ 9.30am-5.30pm Apr-Oct, 10am-4pm Nov-Mar)

EXPLORING WELLS

❦ WELLS CATHEDRAL // SOMERSET'S GOTHIC GLORY

Few churches can match the sheer wow factor of **Cathedral Church of St Andrew** (☎ 01749-674483; www.wellscathedral.org. uk; Chain Gate, Cathedral Green; requested donation adult/child £5.50/2.50; ⏰ 7am-7pm Apr-Sep, 7am-6pm Oct-Mar). Built in stages between 1180 and 1508, Wells bears the classic hallmarks of Gothic church-building, but is most famous for the **west front**, a sculpture gallery depicting various lords, notables and saintly characters, and its **scissor arches**, installed to counter subsidence caused by the central tower (the cathedral's original spire burned down in the 15th century). **Penniless Porch**, a corner gate leading onto Market Pl, was the preferred haunt for Wells' medieval beggars.

Other highlights are the Tolkienesque **Chapter House** (1306), the elegant **lady chapel** (1326) and a **mechanical clock** dating from 1390, the second-oldest in England after Salisbury Cathedral's. Free guided **tours** are available year-round, but you'll need a photography permit (£3) from the cathedral shop to take pictures.

❦ BISHOP'S PALACE // SOAK UP THE ECCLESIASTICAL ATMOSPHERE

A stroll from the cathedral brings you to the 13th-century **Bishop's Palace**

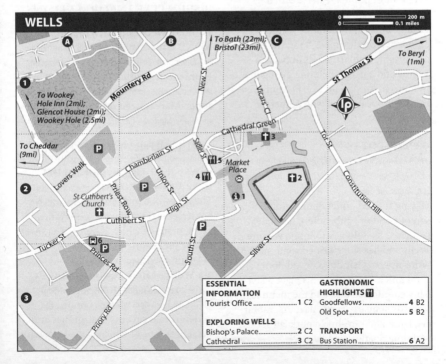

WELLS

To Bath (22mi); Bristol (23mi)

To Beryl (1mi)

To Wookey Hole Inn (2mi); Glencot House (2mi); Wookey Hole (2.5mi)

To Cheddar (9mi)

Mounitery Rd

New St

Vicars' Cl

St Thomas St

Cathedral Green

Sadler St

Market Place

Chamberlain St

Union St

Lovers' Walk

St Cuthbert's Church

Priest Row

High St

Cuthbert St

Tor St

Constitution Hill

Tucker St

Princes Rd

South St

Silver St

Priory Rd

ESSENTIAL INFORMATION		GASTRONOMIC HIGHLIGHTS 🍴	
Tourist Office	1 C2	Goodfellows	4 B2
		Old Spot	5 B2
EXPLORING WELLS			
Bishop's Palace	2 C2	**TRANSPORT**	
Cathedral	3 C2	Bus Station	6 A2

BRISTOL, BATH & SOMERSET

BRISTOL, BATH & SOMERSET

(☎ 01749-678691; www.bishopspalacewells.co.uk; adult/child £5/2; ☺ summer 10.30am-6pm, winter 10.30am-4pm), ringed by a moat spanned by a medieval drawbridge. Though the original Great Hall fell into ruin in the 16th century, you can still see the Gothic state rooms, the ceremonial Corona-tion Cape and the 'Glastonbury Chair', the prototype for a folding oak chair much-copied during the Middle Ages. The four natural wells after which the city is named bubble up in the palace's grounds. The palace gardener conducts tours on summer evenings.

GASTRONOMIC HIGHLIGHTS

🌱 GOODFELLOWS ££

☎ 01749-673866; www.goodfellowswells.co.uk; 5 Sadler St; mains £11.50-25, 3-course dinner menu £35; ☺ cafe 8.30am-5pm Mon-Sat & 6-10pm Wed-Sat, restaurant lunch Tue-Sat, dinner Wed-Sat
Wells' most popular eatery, with a continental cafe-brasserie-baker on the ground floor, and a swanky seafood emporium on the upper floor. It's light and bright, with artful bits of twisted willow and abstract painting giving it a modern metropolitan feel. Flavour-wise, think European laced with Somerset ingredients.

🌱 OLD SPOT £££

☎ 01749-689099; 12 Sadler St; 2-/3-course lunch £15/17.50, dinner menu £21.50/26.50; ☺ lunch Wed-Sun, dinner Tue-Sat
Having trained under Simon Hopkin-son of London's Bibendum, Ian Bates launched his solo gastronomic venture in Wells and has since earned some stellar write-ups. Big windows, wood floors and rural knick-knacks give his place a styl-ishly countrified feel, and the menu leans towards similarly rustic flavours: rabbit, eel, lamb and rare-breed pork, all served with imagination and flair.

TRANSPORT

BUS // Bus 375/376 goes to Bristol (one hour) at least hourly from Monday to Saturday, while the 29 travels to Glastonbury (20 minutes, five to seven daily) and Taunton (one hour). Bus 126 runs to Cheddar (25 min-utes) hourly Monday to Saturday and every two hours on Sunday.

THE MENDIPS

Stretching for 124 sq miles between Weston-super-Mare and Frome are the **Mendip Hills**, a range of limestone humps surveying the Somerset coast. Usually just known as the Mendips, the area was once an important area for mining and quarrying, but is now a heartland for rambling and mountain-biking, especially since it was made an Area of Outstanding Natural Beauty (AONB) in 1972.

ESSENTIAL INFORMATION

TOURIST INFORMATION // Mendips **AONB Office** (☎ 01761-462338; www.mendip hillsaonb.org.uk; Charterhouse Centre, near Blagdon), **Frome tourist office** (☎ 01373-467271; enquir ies@frometouristinfo.co.uk; 2 Bridge St) and **Weston-super-Mare tourist office** (☎ 01934-888800; westontouristinfo@n-somerset.gov.uk; Beach Lawns).

EXPLORING THE MENDIPS

🌱 WOOKEY HOLE // GOING DEEP, DEEP UNDERGROUND

The limestone rock around northern Somerset is riddled with subterranean caves, many of which were used as shel-ters by prehistoric people. Just north of Wells, the River Axe has carved out **Wookey Hole** (☎ 01749-672243; www. wookey.co.uk; adult/child £16/11; ☺ 10am-5pm Apr-Oct, 10.30am-4pm Nov-Mar), famous for its underground caverns, stalagmites and stalactites (one of which is the legendary witch of Wookey Hole, who was supposedly turned to stone by a Glastonbury monk). A guided tour takes in the main chambers, but because many of the caves are under water, no one knows how far they extend – the deepest cave dive ever recorded in Britain was made here in September 2004, when divers reached a depth of 45.5m.

Wookey's other touristy attractions include a mirror maze, an Edwardian penny arcade, a paper mill and a newly appointed witch, Carla Calamity (ex-estate agent Carole Bonahan beat 300 other applicants to the job after a series of gruelling witch auditions in mid-2009).

❦ CHEDDAR GORGE // BRAVE THE CROWDS IN A LIMESTONE VALLEY

Carved out during the last ice age, Cheddar Gorge is the largest ravine in England, in places towering over 138m above the twisting road. The gorge was extensively used by prehistoric settlers: the oldest complete skeleton found in Britain was discovered here in 1903. Tests suggest it dates from 7150 BC, and that the 'Cheddar Man' still has genetic descendants living in the area. Despite its natural attractions, Cheddar is a very touristy affair – expect legions of screaming schoolkids at busy times.

At the heart of the valley are the **Cheddar Caves** (☎ 01934-742343; www.cheddarcaves.co.uk; Explorer Ticket adult/child/family £17/11/44; ☺ 10am-5.30pm Jul & Aug, 10.30am-5pm Sep-Jun). **Gough's Cave** is the largest, stretching more than 1.3 miles through stalactite-draped 'rooms' including the Diamond Chamber, Aladdin's Cave and Solomon's Temple. Further down the valley is **Cox's Cave**, discovered in 1837 when a mill-worker fell through a hole in the roof.

The Explorer ticket includes the **Cheddar Man & Cannibals Museum** and the 274-step slog to the **Lookout Tower**, from where you can see to Exmoor on a clear day. A signposted 3-mile round walk follows the edge of the gorge, and makes a good place to escape the Cheddar crowds.

Caving and abseiling trips are also offered by **Rocksport** (☎ 01934-742343; caves@cheddarcaves.co.uk; adult/child £31/25 incl gorge admission).

❦ HILLS AND VALLEYS // PUFF YOUR WAY TO PANORAMIC VIEWS

Hikers and landscape junkies are spoilt for choice in the Mendips. Among the most popular hiking targets are **Black Down**, the Mendips' highest point at 325m, **Crook Peak** (near Axbridge) and **Bleadon Hill**, with great views over Weston-super-Mare and the north Somerset coast. The ditches and earthworks of the Iron Age hillfort at **Dolebury Warren** make another good target for an afternoon hike. For longer jaunts, the **Mendip Way** runs for 30 miles across the southern Mendips between Weston-super-Mare and Frome.

> ## TOP FIVE
>
> ### PUBS FOR SUNDAY LUNCH
> For a slap-up Sunday feed:
>
> - ★ **Clifton Sausage** (p46) Still our favourite Sunday lunch in Bristol
> - ★ **Marlborough Tavern** (p60) A Bath beauty
> - ★ **Queens Arms** (p80) Award-winning food in Corton Denham
> - ★ **Lord Poulett Arms** (p80) A boutique bolt-hole in Hinton St George
> - ★ **Wookey Hole Inn** (p68) Full of quirky character

CHEDDAR CHEESE

Cheddar's strong, crumbly, tangy **cheese** is the essential ingredient in any ploughman's sandwich, and has been produced in the area since at least the 12th century. Henry II proclaimed it 'the best cheese in Britain', and the king's accounts from 1170 record that he purchased 10,240lb (around 3650kg) of the stuff. In the days before refrigeration, the Cheddar caves made the ideal cool store for the cheese, with a constant temperature of around 7°C, but the powerful smell attracted rats and the practice was eventually abandoned.

These days most cheddar is made far from the village, but if you're interested in seeing how the genuine article is made, you can still head for the **Cheddar Gorge Cheese Company** (☎ 01934-742810; www.cheddargorgecheeseco.co.uk; Cheddar; admission £1.95; ☷ 10am-5.30pm). You can take a guided tour of the factory from April to October, and pick up cheesy souvenirs at the on-site shop.

Northwest of Wookey Hole about 4 miles from Wells is **Ebbor Gorge**, just as impressive as its neighbour in Cheddar but much less visited. A circular trail winds along the gorge edge, offering vertiginous views, and you can often spot birds of prey swooping around the valley walls. Further north is another famous lookout point at **Deer Leap**. Both can be reached along narrow minor roads off the A371.

For more outdoor ideas, including nature-craft, abseiling and caving trips, check out the comprehensive listings at **Active Mendip** (www.activemendipvenues.co.uk), or contact **Walk the Mendips** (☎ 01761-463356; www.walkthemendips.com), a Blagdon-based outfit run by ecologist Adrian Boots, who runs bushcraft courses and wild food walks.

❦ NATURE RESERVES // SAVOUR THE MENDIPS' WILDER SIDE

Many of the Mendips' former quarries and mining areas have become havens for wildlife. The lead mines and slag-heaps around **Blackmoor Reserve, Ubbley Warren** and the superbly named **Velvet Bottom** harbour a varied habitat of heath, wetland and woodland that

supports many rare birds and butterflies. Further east near Priddy, walking and cycling trails wind around the old leadworks at **Priddy Mineries** and **Stockhill Forest**.

Until the Middle Ages, large tracts of the Mendips lay beneath swampy meadows, and the remaining wetlands provide another important wildlife habitat. **Chew Valley Lake** is one of the best places for bird-spotting.

❦ MENDIP VILLAGES // A VISION OF OLDE ENGLAND

Much of the Mendips seems to have been stuck in a time warp for at least the last couple of centuries, and there are some gorgeous thatched villages to explore, including **Chewton Mendip** with its 15th-century church, the twin thatched villages of **East** and **West Harptree**, and little **Priddy**, famous for its annual **Folk Festival** (www.priddyfolk.org) and **Sheep Fair** (www.priddysheepfair.co.uk), held on the village green since 1348.

Flung out on the eastern edge of the Mendips, the small market town of **Frome** is known for its shopping, with a selection of jewellers, clothes shops, antique dealers and knick-knack boutiques scattered along its streets, especially the arty area around **Catherine Hill**. It's also the starting point for the **Colliers Way** (NCN 24; www.colliersway.co.uk), a 23-mile jaunt along the course of the old Somerset Coal Canal (later a railway), travelling via the Limpley Stoke Valley en route to Bath.

Just over 3 miles southwest off the A361 is **Nunney Castle** (admission free; ☾year-round), the only castle in England with its own original moat. Built in the 1370s by Sir John de la Mere, the castle was updated during the 16th century and became a Royalist stronghold during the Civil War. It's still in fairly good shape, despite being bombarded by Parliamentarian cannons and the collapse of one of its walls in 1910.

☙ WESTON-SUPER-MARE // A CLASSIC SLICE OF THE BRITISH SEASIDE

West of the Mendips lies **Weston-super-Mare**, a sprawling seaside resort that sprang up in the mid-19th century to cater for the huge swathes of Victorian tourists who were looking for a spot of sand and seaside within easy reach of Bristol. The town's most famous landmark is its turn-of-the-20th-century **Grand Pier** (www.grandpier.co.uk), originally planned to be almost 1.5 miles long, though it was eventually reined in to a more modest length of 400m. The pier's celebrated pavilion was razed by a massive fire in 2008; a £39 million restoration project is under way, due for completion in 2010.

Weston's candy-floss, kiss-me-quick atmosphere isn't to everyone's tastes, but the surrounding coastline is mightily impressive, especially along the **toll road** from the Weston seafront up to Sand Bay. From here, a path leads up to the National Trust–owned **Sand Point**, offering a fabulous view across the Bristol Channel to South Wales. The Bristol Channel has the world's second largest

---

▸ TOP FIVE

SOMERSET CAMPSITES

- ★ **Batcombe Vale** (☎ 01749-831207; www.batcombevale.co.uk; near Shepton Mallet; sites for 2 adults £16; ☾ Easter–Sep) Much-lauded site set amongst four private lakes, where you can fish for supper from one of the complementary rowing boats.

- ★ **Westermill Farm** (☎ 01643-831238; www.westermill.com; Exford; per adult/car £5/2.50) Five hundred acres of Exmoor hill farm, four peaceful camping fields and a farm shop where you can buy milk, bread and eggs.

- ★ **Burrowhayes Farm** (NT; ☎ 01643-862463; www.burrowhayes.co.uk; Porlock; sites from around £12; ☾ mid-Mar–Oct) Country camping on a working National Trust farm in the Horner Valley, with its own riding stables and Exmoor ponies.

- ★ **Old Oaks** (☎ 01458-831437; www.theoldoaks.co.uk; near Glastonbury; sites £13-26) Mendips views, a kids-free policy and comprehensive facilities (including ecofriendly recycling bins and a heated shower block) earn this Glastonbury site top marks.

- ★ **Newton Mill** (☎ 01225-333909; www.newtonmillpark.co.uk; near Bath; sites from £20) One of the top options near Bath, with a wooded tent meadow, an award-winning loo block and an excellent cafe-bar in a converted mill.

tidal range, and plans are afoot to build a huge electricity-generating tidal barrier across the mouth of the Severn Estuary. If completed, it could generate up to 5% of the UK's electricity.

For more blustery atmosphere, another fine coastal trail known as the **Poet's Walk** begins in nearby Clevedon, said to have inspired several writers including Tennyson, Thackeray and Coleridge. In the opposite direction are the gritty sands of **Burnham-on-Sea**, still a favourite spot for hardy British bathers, none of whom seem bothered by the dun-coloured water or the proximity of a nuclear power station at nearby Hinkley Point.

GASTRONOMIC HIGHLIGHTS

There are some cracking pubs dotted around the Mendips. Our favourites include the **Crown** (☎ 01934-852995) in Churchill and the **Hunters Lodge** (☎ 01749-672275) near Priddy, both proper old-time country affairs where the ale takes precedence over posh decor and fancy food.

❦ BARLEY WOOD WALLED GARDEN CAFÉ // WRINGTON £

☎ 01934-863713; www.walledgarden.co.uk; Long Lane; lunch £3-10; ❧ 10am-4pm
Sample rare-estate teas and homemade cakes in a restored Victorian greenhouse, all the while gazing out over the Mendip Hills. This heavenly wholefood cafe is part of the Barley Wood garden near Wrington; after eating you can enjoy strolling round the walled allotments or browsing studios that are home to local artists.

❦ THE COVE // WESTON-SUPER-MARE ££

☎ 01934-418217; www.the-cove.co.uk; Birnbeck Rd; mains £15.95-18.95; ❧ lunch & dinner

Forget fish and chips and bacon baps – this snazzy bistro has turned some heads since it opened on the Weston waterfront. Blond wood, white walls and glass doors create an atmosphere that's more West End than Weston, and chef Kieran Lenihan's menu is a proper, grown-up concern: pan-seared sea bass, spiced turbot, Old Spot pork belly.

❦ MILLER'S AT GLENCOT HOUSE // WOOKEY HOLE £££

☎ 01749-677160; www.glencothouse.co.uk; 2-/3-course lunch £14.75/17.95, 2-/3-course menu £29.50/34.50; ❧ lunch & dinner
For out-and-out theatricality, nowhere tops the Riverside Restaurant at Glencot House (p290). It's like stepping inside an Old Master canvas: chandeliers, animal heads, rugs and drapes adorn every inch of the house, while the menu brims with hefty hock of ham, rib of aged beef and sesame-crusted pheasant breast. Bonkers and brilliant.

❦ WOOKEY HOLE INN // WOOKEY HOLE ££

☎ 01749-676677; www.wookeyholeinn.com; mains £8-18; ❧ lunch & dinner
Terrifically quirky gastropub between Wells and Wookey Hole, with half-timbered heritage offset by an outdoor sculpture garden furnished with totem poles and Easter Island heads. The menu's really eclectic, mixing British goods with spicy Med flavours; Sunday lunch is particularly worthy of investigation.

TRANSPORT

BUS // The main bus hubs are Wells and Weston-super-Mare. Bus 126 runs to Cheddar (hourly Monday to Saturday, every two hours on Sunday), while the 162 (three daily) from Wells travels to Frome. The only Mendips bus is the 672/3 'Chew Valley Explorer' (three daily) from Bristol

∼ WORTH A TRIP ∼

While the crowds descend on Stonehenge and Avebury, the stone circles of **Stanton Drew** – the largest in Somerset – receive practically no visitors.

The complex consists of three stone circles ranging from 40m to 113m in diameter. The largest is the **Great Circle**, which probably once contained 30 stones, although only 27 survive today. Investigations by English Heritage in the late 1990s revealed an extensive network of pits and postholes within the circle, and suggested that the circles date from the same time as Woodhenge and Durrington Walls at Stonehenge, making them one of Somerset's oldest and most significant ancient monuments.

Near the village church and the Druid's Arms pub are three other stones (two standing, one lying down) known as the **Cove**; it's thought they may have once marked the entrance to a chamber tomb.

The stones are just off the B3130 to Chew Magna, 8 miles south of Bristol.

to Blagdon, with stops including Chew Magna, Stanton Drew, East and West Harptree, Compton Martin and Ubley. **TRAIN //** Weston-super-Mare's station has services to Bristol (£5.30 to £9.50, 25 to 35 minutes), Bath (£9.70, 45 minutes) and beyond.

GLASTONBURY

pop 8429
Ley lines converge, white witches convene, and every shop is filled with the aroma of smouldering joss sticks in good old Glastonbury. Famous for its annual musical mudfest, held on Michael Eavis' farm in nearby Pilton, Glastonbury was a centre for New Age culture long before the traveller buses and alternative types rolled in. The town's famous tor was an important pagan site and is rumoured by some to be the mythological Isle of Avalon, where King Arthur was entombed after his death. Whatever you make of the countless legends swirling around Glastonbury, one thing's for sure – if you need to knock your chakras into shape, this is definitely the right place.

ESSENTIAL INFORMATION

TOURIST INFORMATION // Glastonbury tourist office (☎ 01458-832954; www.glaston

burytic.co.uk; The Tribunal, 9 High St; ☺ 10am-4pm Mon-Fri, 10am-4.30pm Sat & Sun) Sells discount tickets.

EXPLORING GLASTONBURY

♥ GLASTONBURY TOR // HIKE TO THE TOP OF SOMERSET'S MOST SACRED HILL

There's a bewildering maze of myths associated with the emerald hump of Glastonbury Tor. To some it's the stronghold of Gwyn ap Nudd (ruler of Annwyn, the Faerie Kingdom), while to others it's the Celtic site of Ynys Witrin, the 'Isle of Glass'. Wearyall Hill, just below the tor, is supposedly where Joseph of Arimathea buried the Holy Grail following Christ's crucifixion. The most famous legend identifies the tor as Ynys yr Afalon, the 'Isle of Avalon', where King Arthur was taken after being mortally wounded by his nephew Mordred, and where Britain's 'once and future king' sleeps until his country calls again. Until the land was drained for agriculture in the 13th and 14th centuries, much of the surrounding countryside was surrounded by marshy wetland, and during times of high floods the area's hills would have appeared as islands – perhaps

BRISTOL, BATH & SOMERSET

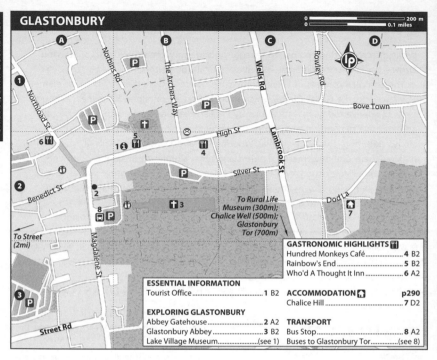

GLASTONBURY

ESSENTIAL INFORMATION
Tourist Office..................................... 1 B2

EXPLORING GLASTONBURY
Abbey Gatehouse................................ 2 A2
Glastonbury Abbey............................. 3 B2
Lake Village Museum.....................(see 1)

GASTRONOMIC HIGHLIGHTS 🍴
Hundred Monkeys Café...................... 4 B2
Rainbow's End 5 B2
Who'd A Thought It Inn 6 A2

ACCOMMODATION 🏠   **p290**
Chalice Hill 7 D2

TRANSPORT
Bus Stop... 8 A2
Buses to Glastonbury Tor...............(see 8)

explaining how some of the legends may have arisen.

The tor has been a site of pilgrimage since prehistoric times. A small fort existed here in the early 5th century, followed by a medieval church destroyed during a freak earthquake in 1275, and a second church built in the 1360s that survived until the Dissolution, when the last abbot of Glastonbury Abbey, Richard Whiting, was hanged, drawn and quartered on the tor. The last remaining section of the church, St Michael's Tower, still stands on top of the tor; it's Grade I listed and owned by the National Trust.

It's a short, steep 20-minute climb to the top. The main route starts just off Well House Lane, near the Chalice Well Gardens; concrete paths and steps help to prevent erosion. The Tor Bus (£1) from Dunstan's car park stops nearby.

One of the tor's most curious features is the series of seven terraces, which can be clearly seen winding their way around the hill's natural slope. Various theories have been put forward to explain them – including agricultural terracing, defensive ramparts and cattle tracks – but the most bizarre explanation is that they delineate a classical 'labyrinth', believed to have some ritual significance to ancient people. While no one's ever been able to conclusively prove the theory, one thing's for sure – the tor certainly makes a memorable spot to catch the sunrise.

❦ **GLASTONBURY ABBEY // ONE OF ENGLAND'S GREATEST MONASTERIES**
At the time of the Domesday Book, **Glastonbury Abbey** (☎ 01458-832267; www.glastonburyabbey.com; Magdalene St; adult/ child £5.50/3.50; ☼ 9am-6pm Jun-Aug, 9.30am-6pm Apr-May & Sep, 9.30am-5.30pm Mar & Oct,

9.30am-4.30pm Nov, 10am-4.30pm Dec-Feb) was the richest monastery in England, but it was destroyed by fire in 1184 and later rebuilt before being ransacked during the Dissolution.

While most of the abbey is in ruins, it's still possible to make out the nave walls, the remains of St Mary's chapel and the crossing arches. In the 13th century, monks uncovered a tomb inscribed *Hic iacet sepultus inclitus rex arturius in insula avalonia,* or 'Here lies buried the renowned King Arthur in the Isle of Avalon'. Inside the tomb were two skeletons, supposedly King Arthur and Queen Guinevere; the bones were buried beneath the altar in 1278, but were lost following the plundering of the abbey.

The **Holy Thorn** in the Abbey grounds is supposedly an offshoot of the thorn tree that sprang from Joseph of Arimathea's staff on Wearyall Hill. The tree blooms twice a year, at Christmas and Easter. The abbey also has a peaceful duck pond, pleasant cafe and a small historical museum.

♥ CHALICE WELL & GARDENS // FILL YOUR BOTTLE WITH HOLY H₂O

People have been dunking, drinking and paddling at the **Chalice Well & Gardens** (☎ 01458-831154; www.chalicewell.org.uk; Chikwell St; adult/child £3/1; ☺ 10am-5.30pm Apr-Oct, 10am-4pm Nov-Mar), a natural spring just below Glastonbury Tor, for at least 2000 years. The rust-red waters from this ancient well are rumoured to have healing properties, good for everything from eczema to smelly feet. Their distinctive crimson colour supposedly stems from the burial of the Holy Grail, although it's actually a result of iron deposits in the soil. The well is surrounded by gardens dotted with babbling pools and gnarled yew trees, and you can fill up your flasks with the sacred water from a lion's-head spout.

The Chalice Well is also known as the 'Red Spring' or 'Blood Spring'; its sister, **White Spring**, surfaces across Wellhouse Lane.

♥ MUSEUMS // FROM AGRICULTURE TO ANCIENT HISTORY

Glastonbury has a couple of intriguing museums. The **Rural Life Museum** (☎ 01458-831197; Abbey Farm, Chilkwell St; admission free; ☺ 10am-5pm Tue-Sat) contains tools and memorabilia relating to traditional Somerset industries such as willow-growing, peat-digging, cidermaking and cheesemaking.

On the main street above the tourist office is the **Lake Village Museum** (adult/child £2.50/1), which collects various artefacts recovered from the prehistoric swamp village discovered in nearby Godney in 1892. The village comprised five to seven groups of circular houses, built from reeds, hazel and willow, and was probably occupied by summer traders who lived the rest of the year around Glastonbury Tor.

GASTRONOMIC HIGHLIGHTS

♥ HUNDRED MONKEYS CAFÉ ££

☎ 01458-833386; 52 High St; mains £8-15; ☺ lunch & dinner Mon-Sat

Glastonbury is a bit short on restaurants, but the Hundred Monkeys fills the gap. No Indian throws or bean bags in sight; here it's all pine tables and blackboard menus stocked with decent bistro specials.

♥ RAINBOW'S END £

☎ 01458-833896; 17a High St; mains £4-10; ☺ 10am-4pm

The quintessential Glastonbury hippie cafe, decked out in rainbow shades, scuffed-up furniture and a profusion of potted plants. As you would expect, the food is wholefood and 100% homemade:

think bean chillies, quiches and homity pies that you chase down with big mugs of hot tea and hearty slabs of carrot cake.

♥ WHO'D A THOUGHT IT INN ££

☎ 01458-834460; www.whodathoughtit.co.uk; 17 Northload St; mains £8.25-16.95; ☺ lunch & dinner

In keeping with Glastonbury's outsider spirit, this town pub is brimming with wacky character, from the vintage signs and upside-down bike on the ceiling to the reclaimed red telephone box tucked in one corner. Locals pack in for its superior food and ales; Glastonbury king-pin Michael Eavis has even been known to pop in for a pint.

TRANSPORT

BUS // Bus 29 travels to Glastonbury from Taunton (50 minutes, five to seven daily), and to Wells in the opposite direction. The hourly 375/6 goes to Bristol (one hour 20 minutes) via Wells, and to Yeovil (one hour) in the opposite direction.

THE SOMERSET LEVELS

Covering 250 sq miles east and northeast of Taunton, the Somerset Levels is one of Britain's largest remaining native wetlands. Pan-flat and only just above sea level, it's an important haven for all kinds of wildlife, but it's actually not a natural landscape; the environment has been shaped by centuries of cultivation, and without human intervention would quickly return to peat bog, marsh and reed bed.

The fields and pastures are divided by drainage channels known as *rhynes* (pronounced 'reens') and traditional industries such as peat-cutting, reed-harvesting and willow-growing are still practised much as they were during the Middle Ages.

EXPLORING THE SOMERSET LEVELS

♥ BURROW MUMP & MUCHELNEY // CLIMB THE HOLY HILLS

Until the drainage of the Levels in the 14th century, the whole area was covered by shallow impassable marsh, interspersed by a few island humps. One of these is **Burrow Mump**, a 24m-high mound near Burrowbridge topped by a small chapel dedicated to St Michael; its curious name derives from two Old English words, both of which mean 'hill'. Nearby is the hill of **Athelney**, where King Alfred crisped his cakes before defeating the Danes and taking the English throne.

Alfred subsequently founded an abbey on Athelney in 888, which was torn down during the Dissolution along with **Muchelney** (EH; adult/child £4/2; ☺ 10am-6pm Jul-Aug, 10am-5pm Apr-Jun & Sep, 10am-4pm Oct), Somerset's second-oldest abbey after Glastonbury. Largely ruined, Muchelney still boasts the original abbot's house, cloister and a two-storeyed monk's lavatory – the only known monastic loo in England.

♥ NATURE RESERVES // BRING OUT YOUR INNER TWITCHER

The natural wetlands of the Levels provide a unique wildlife habitat. Three nature reserves have been established, the best-known of which is **Westhay Moor**, famous for the huge flocks of starlings (known as murmurations) that descend on the reserve during October and November. Slightly south are **Ham Wall** and **Shapwick Heath**, whose reed beds and waterways are home to otters, water voles, bitterns, grey heron and marsh harriers. All have public bird hides: dawn and dusk are the best times for birdwatching. For info on recent wildlife sightings contact the Glastonbury tourist office or visit www.somersetwildlife.org.

The area now occupied by Shapwick Heath is also crossed by the oldest man-made track in Britain, the **Sweet Track** (named after Ray Sweet, who discovered it in 1970). Constructed around 3806 BC using lines of planks, posts and angled stakes, the track was built to help prehistoric people cross the marshland during times of flood. Several sections now reside at the British Museum, but much of the track is still buried beneath the Somerset peat. A decked, wheelchair-accessible walkway traces its original course.

♣ PEDALLING THE LEVELS // CYCLE THE RIVER PARRETT TRAIL

Being as flat as a proverbial pancake, the Levels are ideal for some leisurely cycling. Several bike trails criss-cross the area, including the long-distance **River Parrett Trail** (www.riverparrett-trail.org.uk), a 50-mile route that starts in the Dorset hills and travels all the way to the Bristol Channel.

All the routes pass through the **Langport Visitor Centre** (☎ 01458-250350; ⏰ 10am-5pm Tue-Sun Apr-Sep, 10am-4pm Tue-Sun Oct-Mar), where you can hire bikes (adult/child £10/7 per day) and pick up information packs and trail maps.

♣ WILLOW WORKING // SOMERSET'S SUSTAINABLE WONDER CROP

Alongside cider-brewing and peat-digging, the most important local industry is **willow** (locally known as *withy*), a natural crop used for making everything

SOMERSET SCRUMPY

The classic Somerset tipple is **cider**, a traditional drink made from fermented apples that arrived in England with the Norman invasion. It comes in many varieties, ranging from dark and sweet to light and tart, but nearly all traditional cider has one thing in common – it's powerful stuff, often several times as strong as ale.

Scrumpy derives from the practice of using 'scrumped' apples; initially, the term referred to windfall apples, but later came to mean illicitly acquired fruit. Traditionally, brewers favoured varieties related to the wild crab apple (often with wonderful names such as Porter's Perfection, Brown Snout, Harry Masters Jersey and Red Streak) but other fruits are occasionally used (especially pears, used to make **perry**).

Once picked, apples are *scratted* (ground down) into a *pomace* (pulp) and pressed into a firm cake, rather confusingly called the *cheese*. Several cheeses are piled into the press and squeezed; the juice is left to ferment in oak casks for several weeks, et *voilà* – you've got your scrumpy.

Although most Somerset cider is made by industrial breweries (often using apples that aren't even grown in Somerset), there are still several small-scale brewers that make their cider in the time-honoured way. Julian Temperley's **Somerset Cider Brandy Company** (☎ 01460-240782; www.ciderbrandy.co.uk; Kingsbury Episcopi; ⏰ 9.30am-5.30pm Mon-Sat) brews a range of classic ciders, as well as premium cider brandies, sparkling apple juices and aperitifs.

Other brewers worth a visit include **Perry's Cider** (☎ 01460-55195; www.perryscider.co.uk; Dowlish Wake) near Ilminster, which has two vintage presses and a collection of antique cidermaking memorabilia, and the tiny family-run **Wilkins Cider Farm** (☎ 01934-712385; Land's End Farm, Mudgley) near Wedmore. Consult www.somersetcider.co.uk for more ideas.

from baskets to beehives, fish traps, pigeon panniers, canes and cricket bats. Willow harvesting dates back to the Iron Age, but it's an industry with one eye on the future – willow is a common biomass fuel in Nordic nations, and is being considered by several British councils as a future energy resource.

At the marvellous **Willows & Wetlands Visitor Centre** (☎ 01823-490249; adult/child £2.50/1.25; ☺ 9am-5pm Mon-Sat) in Stoke St Gregory, the Coates family have been harvesting and working willow since 1819. There's a fascinating exhibition of willowy artefacts and a shop where you can pick up souvenirs handcrafted by the centre's craftsmen (if you're after a new picnic basket, this is definitely the place). The centre also offers tours of its willow-beds, and holds willow workshops and demonstrations throughout the year.

GASTRONOMIC HIGHLIGHTS

❦ PUMPKIN DELICATESSEN £
☎ 01934-713289; www.pumpkinwedmore.co.uk; 1 The Borough Mall, Wedmore; mains £4-12; ☺ 8.30am-5pm Mon-Sat
Farm outlets and foodie shops are sprinkled liberally round little Wedmore, but top honours go to this sunny delicatessen just off the village's main street. Gourmet sandwiches, home-baked cakes and cheese plates are all worth the detour, and the shelves are overflowing with goodies from some of the southwest's finest suppliers.

❦ THE RUSTY AXE ££
☎ 01460-240109; www.therustyaxe.co.uk; Stembridge, near Martock; mains £9.50-13.95; ☺ lunch & dinner Tue-Sun
Cracking name, cracking pub, deep in the central Levels just outside Kingsbury Episcopi. Don't be tricked by the thatched exterior; inside the decor's light and continental, and outside there's a hedge-fringed patio shaded by umbrellas. The food's a cut above your average pub stuff too: warm wood pigeon salad, haddock battered in Potholer beer or pork-and-cider bangers with mash and gravy.

ALSO RECOMMENDED
King Alfred (☎ 01823-698379; Burrowbridge; mains £6-14) Classic village pub about a mile north of Stoke St Gregory, known for its food and live music.
Bird in Hand (☎ 01823-490248; North Curry; mains £8-15) Another reliable Sunday lunch stop on the Levels: slate-roofed, low-beamed and fire-lit.

TRANSPORT
BUS // Public transport on the Levels is limited. The most useful bus is the 54 (hourly, six on Sunday) between Taunton and Yeovil with stops at Curry Rivel, Langport, Pitney and Somerton.

TAUNTON & AROUND

Taunton is the heart of Somerset in more ways than one; it's bang in the middle of the county, and is also the area's county town and commercial centre. Originally founded by Saxon king Ine, the town became infamous during the 17th century Monmouth Rebellion, an uprising against ruling monarch James II. The rebellion was crushed at the Battle of Sedgemoor and its leaders were tried and condemned during the Bloody Assizes under Judge Jeffreys. These days it's a solid red-brick shopping town, and a useful gateway to the Quantocks.

ESSENTIAL INFORMATION
TOURIST INFORMATION // Taunton tourist office (☎ 01823 336344; tauntontic@taunton deane.gov.uk; Paul St; ☺ 9.30am-5.30pm Mon-Sat)

EXPLORING TAUNTON & AROUND

⚜ THE BLACKDOWN HILLS // GAZE OVER THE VALE OF TAUNTON DEANE

To the west of Taunton are the **Blackdown Hills** (www.blackdownhillsaonb.org.uk), a range of limestone peaks stretching across the Somerset–Devon border. The most famous feature on the Somerset side is the **Wellington Monument**, a 53m spire dedicated to the Duke of Wellington. Unsurprisingly, the Blackdowns offer fine views across the Vale of Taunton Deane and lots of hiking, biking and horse-riding opportunities. The tourist office stocks trail leaflets and cycling guides, and can put you in touch with the **Blackdown Hills Hedge Association** (www.blackdownhills-hedge.org. uk), which offers courses in rural skills such as hedge-laying, hurdling and coppicing.

⚜ GREEN FINGERS // GET SOME GARDENING INSPIRATION

Three miles north in Cheddon Fitzpaine is **Hestercombe** (☎ 01823-413923; www. hestercombe.com; adult/child £8.90/3.30; ⏱ 10am-6pm), which is really three garden designs rolled into one: a landscaped Georgian garden, a Victorian terrace and an Edwardian formal garden designed by the architect Sir Edmund Lutyens and the celebrated garden designer Gertrude Jekyll.

The gardens at **Cothay Manor** (☎ 01823-672283; www.cothaymanor.co.uk; adult/ child £6/3; ⏱ gardens 11am-4.30pm Tue-Thu & Sun Easter-Oct) are even older, thought to date from the 15th century. Several garden 'rooms' are accessible from the yew walk, including a delightful medieval cottage garden, although the house itself is only available for private tours.

⚜ WEST SOMERSET RAILWAY // CATCH A VINTAGE CHOO-CHOO

Chimneys chuff and wheels clatter on the **West Somerset Railway** (☎ 24hr talking timetable 01643-707650, other information 01643-704996; www.west-somerset-railway.co.uk), which has been chugging along the line from Bishops Lydeard (near Taunton) to Minehead since 1859. It is a real slice of bygone England, with vintage carriages, and time-warp stations dotted along the 20-mile route. There are several daily train services during the months of April to October, with a weekend-only service in winter; useful stops include Crowcombe Heathfield (for the Quantocks), Williton, Watchet and Dunster. A 24-hour rover ticket costs adult/child £14.80/7.40.

Bus 28 runs to Bishops Lydeard from Taunton (15 minutes, 11 daily Monday to Saturday), or you can catch the 50 'Steamlink' service to Taunton's town centre.

GASTRONOMIC HIGHLIGHTS

⚜ FARMER'S INN // WEST HATCH ££

☎ 01823-480480; www.farmersinnwesthatch.co.uk; mains £9.95-13.95; ⏱ lunch & dinner
Four miles east from Taunton in West Hatch, this boutique pub is mainly known for its lavish rooms (see p290), but it's worth a stop for some slap-up grub too. The menu is mainly gastropub standards – lamb rump, venison sausages, homemade fishcakes – and people travel for miles just to soak up the cosy, pint-by-the-fire feel.

⚜ GREYHOUND INN // STAPLE FITZPAINE ££

☎ 01823-480277; www.greyhoundinn.biz; mains £9.95-15.95; ⏱ lunch & dinner
Six miles south from Taunton in Staple Fitzpaine, this is a gem of a country pub –

TOP LOCAL SHOPS

Guilt-free grub that comes with zero food miles.

★ **Kilver Court** (☎ 01749-340417; www.kilvercourt.com; near Shepton Mallett; ☒ farm shop 8.30am-5.30pm Mon-Fri, 9.30-4pm Sun, till 7pm Thu) Seriously upmarket food complex, cafe and gardens run by Roger Saul, who founded the Mulberry fashion chain. Organic goods from his farm at Sharpham Park are available in the shop.

★ **Woody's Farm Shop** (☎ 01225-720006; www.woodysfarmshop.co.uk; Norton St Philip; ☒ 9am-6pm Mon-Sat, 10am-5pm Sun) No pretensions, just honest fish, meat, veg and bread.

★ **Whiterow Country Foods** (☎ 01373-830798; www.whiterowcountryfoods.co.uk; Beckington; ☒ 9am-6pm Mon-Fri, 9am-5pm Sat, 10am-2pm Sun) Veg, dairy and home-reared meats on a working pig and arable farm near Frome.

★ **Bath Sausage Shop** (☎ 01225-318300; www.sausage-shop.co.uk; 7 Green St, Bath) Award-winning bangers from traditional pork-and-cider to spicy Spanish chorizo.

★ **Thoughtful Bread Company** (☎ 01761-239074; www.thoughfulbreadcompany.com; Green Park Station, Bath; ☒ 9am-6pm Tue-Sat) Handmade artisan breads at Bath's eco-bakery.

★ **Brown & Forrest Smokery** (☎ 01458-250875; www.smokedeel.co.uk; Bowdens Farm, Hambridge, Langport; ☒ 10am-4pm Mon-Fri, 10am-4pm Sat) Smoked cheese, meat and eels done the traditional way.

fishing tackle and hunting prints carpet the walls, log fires roar in flagstoned hearths and creepers cover the 16th-century inn. The setting is a winner and the food and ales are ace.

☙ WILLOW TREE // TAUNTON £££

☎ 01823-352835; 3 Tower Lane; mains £15-22; ☒ dinner Tue-Sat

Run by ex-Roux brothers head chef, Darren Sherlock, this is Taunton's top table – it's tiny and tucked down an alley, so you'll need to book ahead. Sherlock is very much from the food-as-art school: portions are small, presentation is impeccable and flavours err towards the outlandish (ox-tongue tian, duck with fig and chervil, beetroot ice cream).

TRANSPORT

BUS // Taunton is a main bus hub. Useful lines include the regular 29 and 376 to Glastonbury, Wells and Bristol, the 28 (hourly Monday to Saturday, nine on Sunday) across the Quantocks to Minehead and the 54 (hourly, six on Sunday) across the Somerset Levels to Yeovil.

TRAINS // Regular trains from Taunton connect eastwards to Bristol and London, and westwards to Exeter, Plymouth and beyond.

THE QUANTOCKS

Running along a sharp 12-mile ridge between the Vale of Taunton Deane and the north Somerset coast, the rusty-red Quantocks (from the Celtic word *cantuc*, meaning 'circle') are 3 miles wide and just 384m at their highest point, Wills Neck. Much less well known than the neighbouring ranges of Exmoor and the Mendips, the Quantocks make a fantastic place for some solitary hiking. The high heathland is sprinkled with Bronze Age settlements and burial mounds, and literary buffs will be intrigued by the area's Coleridge connections: the poet lived for six years in Nether Stowey and penned some of his greatest poems there.

ESSENTIAL INFORMATION

**TOURIST INFORMATION // Quantocks
AONB Office** (☎ 01823-451884; www.quantock
hills.com; Fyne Court)

EXPLORING THE QUANTOCKS

❧ **COLERIDGE COTTAGE // VISIT
SAMUEL'S QUANTOCKS COTTAGE**
The Quantock villages feel like forgotten
corners of England, especially **Nether
Stowey**, Coleridge's former home village,
where the most eventful happening is
usually the daily postal delivery. Coleridge
moved to **Coleridge Cottage** (NT; ☎ 01278-
732662; 35 Lime St; adult £4/2; ⏰ 2-5pm Thu-Sun
Apr-Sep) in 1796 with his wife, Sarah, and
son Hartley. William Wordsworth and
his sister, Dorothy, followed a year later,
to nearby Alfoxden House in Holford. In

that year the two men worked on *Lyrical
Ballads* (1798), the poetic pamphlet that
kick-started the British romantic movement. It's impossible not to feel a shiver
standing in the place where Coleridge is
thought to have composed *The Rime of
the Ancient Mariner* and *Kubla Khan*.

❧ **STALK THE COUNTRYSIDE //
EXPLORE THE QUANTOCKS' QUIET
TRAILS**
The Quantocks is prime walking country, with public-access trails open to
walkers, mountain-bikers and horse
riders alike. The classic route is the
Coleridge Way (www.colerideway.co.uk), a
36-mile trail from Nether Stowey to
Porlock skirting the northern edge of
the Quantocks. The first section through
Holford Coombe was a favourite jaunt
of Coleridge and Wordsworth's.

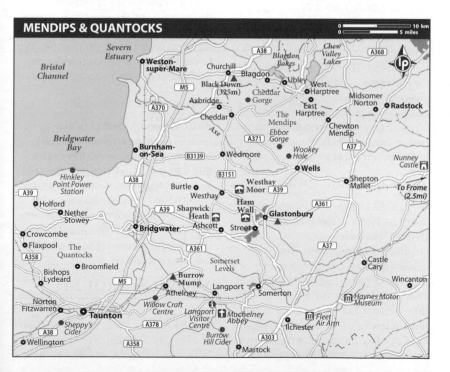

Other day targets include the accessible trails from Staple Plain to the top of **Beacon Hill** (310m) and Lydeard Hill or Triscombe to the high point of **Wills Neck** (384m). The **Great Wood** at the heart of the AONB is another beautiful walking area, carpeted with some of the oldest coppiced oaks in England. Nearby is the **Triscombe Stone**, a Bronze Age menhir, said to bring luck to those who sit on it.

Many of these sites fall along the **Quantock Greenway** (www.quantockonline.co.uk/tourism_leisure/activities/walks/greenway/greenway01.html), a figure-of-eight trail split into two sections: a northern loop (20 miles) from Crowcombe via Holford and Great Wood, and a southern loop (18 miles) from Broomfield/Fyne Court via the Triscombe Stone. It's still a work in progress; you'll need a good OS map.

Trail leaflets and advice can be picked up at the AONB office at **Fyne Court** (NT; ☎ 01823-652400; fynecourt@nationaltrust.org.uk; admission free; ⊙ 9am-5pm or dusk), a National Trust nature reserve at the Quantocks' southern end. The estate once belonged to the gentleman scientist, amateur poet and pioneering electrician Andrew Crosse, and although the house is in ruins, the fairy-tale grounds are spotted with nature trails, a 19th-century folly and a boathouse straight out of a story book.

GASTRONOMIC HIGHLIGHTS

☙ BLUE BALL INN // TRISCOMBE ££
☎ 0845 201 3319; www.blueballinn.co.uk; mains £12-18; ⊙ lunch & dinner
Originally an 18th-century barn, Triscombe's inn has undergone a change of owners, but the setting is as delightful as ever, surrounded by tiered gardens with the restaurant and bar squeezed under the A-frame rafters of the old hayloft. Local produce features heavily, and there are unusual ales including Exmoor Gold

and Stag, Cotleigh Tawny and Thatchers Cheddar Valley scrumpy.

☙ CAREW ARMS // CROWCOMBE ££
☎ 01984-618631; www.thecarewarms.co.uk; mains £8.95-14.95; ⊙ lunch & dinner
Plonked at the foot of the Quantocks in quaint Crowcombe, this red-brick hostelry has five centuries of experience and shows no signs of flagging. Classic character – inglenook fireplace, flagstone bar, grassy beer garden – plus an unusual menu of ploughman's plates and anti-pasti platters, washed down with Tawny Bitter, Otter Bright and Exmoor Ale.

☙ HOOD ARMS // KILVE ££
☎ 01278-741210; www.thehoodarms.com; mains £8.95-14.95; ⊙ lunch & dinner
The Hood has a reputation as one of the Quantocks' best grub pubs. Forget pints-of-prawns and scampi-in-a-basket – here the specials board is stocked with Exmoor trout, venison casserole and chomp of saltmarsh lamb. Hunting trophies, wooden beams and crimson carpets complete the upmarket country pub package.

TRANSPORT

BIKE // **Quantock Orchard Caravan Park** (☎ 01984-618618; www.quantock-orchard.co.uk; Crowcombe; per half-/full day £5/9) hires out bikes.
BUS // Bus 14 (four daily Monday to Saturday, six on Sunday) from Bridgwater to Minehead stops at Nether Stowey, Holford, Kilve and West Quantoxhead. The Sunday bus terminates at Watchet. The 28 (half-hourly Monday to Saturday, nine on Sunday) runs from Taunton to Minehead via Crowcombe and Bicknoller; Sunday buses only stop at Bicknoller.

YEOVIL & AROUND

pop 41,871
Named after the River Yeo, Yeovil grew up along the old Roman road, the Fosse Way, and during the Middle Ages be-

came a hub for glove-making (hence Yeovil Town Football Club's nickname, the Glovers). While far from the prettiest of Somerset towns, it's a useful launch pad for exploring the surrounding area.

ESSENTIAL INFORMATION

TOURIST INFORMATION // Yeovil tourist office (☎ 01963-462991; yeoviltic@southsomerset. gov.uk; Petter's Way)

EXPLORING YEOVIL & AROUND

❦ MUSEUMS FOR MOTORHEADS // AIRCRAFT AND AUTOMOBILES

Two museums near Yeovil house some pioneering petrol-powered machinery. Around 400 vintage motors are displayed at **Haynes Motor Museum** (☎ 01963-440804; www.haynesmotormuseum.com; adult/child £8.95/4.25; 9.30am-5.30pm Apr-Oct, 10am-4.30pm Nov-Mar) in Sparkford. The centrepiece is the 'Red Room', with 50 scarlet beauties ranging from a Ferrari 360 Spider to a 1980s Lamborghini Countach. Other halls cover the Dawn of Motoring, British Motorbikes, Motorsport, Speedway and International Cars, and in the British–American room you can contrast the relative merits of a Mini Cooper and a Cadillac.

Over in Yeovilton, the **Fleet Air Arm Museum** (☎ 01935-840565; www.fleetairarm. com; adult/child £10.50/7.50; 10am-5.30pm daily Apr-Oct, 10am-4.30pm Wed-Sun Nov-Mar) spans the history of naval aviation from Sopwiths to Phantom fighters. You can even walk onto the flight-deck of Concorde and take a simulated flight onto the aircraft carrier HMS *Ark Royal*.

❦ HISTORIC HOUSES // TWO NATIONAL TRUST GEMS

Few Somerset piles can outdo **Monta-cute House** (NT; ☎ 01935-823289; montacute@ nationaltrust.org.uk; adult/child house £8.90/4.20, garden only £6/3; house 11am-5pm Wed-Mon mid-Mar–mid-Oct, grounds 11am-5.30pm mid-Mar–Oct, 11am-4pm Wed-Sun Nov-Mar) for sheer scale and splendour. Built in the 1590s for Sir Edward Phelips, a Speaker of the House of Commons, the house is renowned for its plasterwork, paintings and tapestries, but the highlight is the enormous Long Gallery on the top floor, hung with over 60 Elizabethan-era portraits borrowed from the National Portrait Gallery (including a stunning portrait of Elizabeth I in full royal regalia, probably painted by George Gower). Beyond the house, formal grounds, woodland and park stretch to the highpoint of St Michael's Hill.

A short spin away is **Barrington Court** (NT; ☎ 01460-241938; Ilminster; adult/child £8.20/3.55; 11am-5pm Thu-Tue late Feb-Oct, 11am-4pm Sat & Sun Nov), built in the 16th century for a London merchant. Having endured fire damage and interior demolitions, the house was extensively restored in the 1920s by the Lyle family (of Tate & Lyle fame) with grounds designed by Gertrude Jekyll, who established a series of outside garden 'rooms', including a rose and lily garden and a wonderful arboretum.

❦ HAM HILL COUNTRY PARK // ANCIENT HISTORY AND EYE-POPPING VIEWS

Looming above the village of Stoke-sub-Hamdon, **Ham Hill** (☎ 01935-462462; hamhill@southsomerset.gov.uk; admission free) provides an unparalleled perspective over southern Somerset. Around 2500 years ago, this lofty hill was the site of one of the largest Iron Age hillforts in southwest Britain, and the earthworks, terraces, ditches and ramparts that defended the fort are still clearly visible.

In later centuries the site was occupied by the Romans before becoming a medieval village and Victorian stone quarry. Nowadays it's popular with hikers, dog-walkers and kite-flyers, with around 390 acres of open countryside to explore, and a thoroughly excellent pub, the **Prince of Wales** (☎ 01935-822848; www.princeofwaleshamhill.co.uk), for post-stroll sustenance. Bushcraft courses are run throughout the year; contact the **ranger's office** (☎ 01935-823617) for dates.

To the northeast you can wander around the remains of another Iron Age hillfort at **Cadbury Castle**, found 5 miles northeast of Yeovil, which, according to local legend was once the location of King Arthur's fabled castle, Camelot.

GASTRONOMIC HIGHLIGHTS

♥ LORD POULETT ARMS // HINTON ST GEORGE ££

☎ 01460-73149; www.lordpoulettarms.com; mains £10-19; ☺ lunch & dinner

This ritzy village pub blends medieval bits (rustic trusses, ham stone, hearths) with a keen eye for rustic-chic design. Ales are tapped from casks behind the bar, upstairs rooms are full of charm (see p290) and the food is touted as some of Somerset's finest – it scooped National Dining Pub of the Year in the 2009 *Good Pub Guide*.

♥ THE QUEEN'S ARMS // CORTON DENHAM ££

☎ 01963-220317; www.thequeensarms.com; mains £9.80-26

This backcountry beauty in tiny Corton Denham is equally heralded for its food; the AA named it their favourite pub in 2009, and it's graced the pages of most of the foodie guides. It's run by a pair of ex-pat Londoners: rugs, pew benches and scrubbed-up flagstones nod to its 18th-century heritage, but the gastro menu and rustic-chic rooms are altogether modern affairs.

EXMOOR NATIONAL PARK
· · · · · ·

Sandwiched between countryside and sea, straddling the Devon–Somerset border, Exmoor is a gentler (and greener) landscape than its unruly cousin Dartmoor to the south. A national park since 1954, Exmoor is a quintessential slice of the English countryside, with bottle-green fields and dry-stone walls that tumble down into densely wooded coombes. Curly horned sheep, red deer and stout Exmoor ponies can often be spotted wandering across the windy hilltops.

Most of the tourist action is found along around the national park's northern coast, which stretches from the brassy tourist resort of Minehead through the pretty villages of Porlock, Watchet, Dunster and Lynmouth, just across the Devon border.

ESSENTIAL INFORMATION

TOURIST INFORMATION // Exmoor National Park Authority (www.exmoor-nationalpark.gov.uk); Dulverton (☎ 01398-323841; 7-9 Fore St); Dunster (☎ 01643-821835); Lynmouth (☎ 01598-752509) **Porlock tourist office** (☎ 01643-863150; www.porlock.co.uk; High St; ☺ 10am-5pm Mon-Sat, 10am-1pm Sun Apr-Oct, 10.30am-1pm Tue-Fri, 10am-2pm Sat Nov-Mar) **Minehead tourist office** (☎ 01643-702624; 17 Friday St).

EXPLORING EXMOOR

♥ WILDLIFE SAFARIS // GO OFF-ROAD IN SEARCH OF RED DEER

Exmoor supports one of England's largest **wild deer** populations, best seen in autumn during the annual deer rut, when bellowing stags battle it out to try

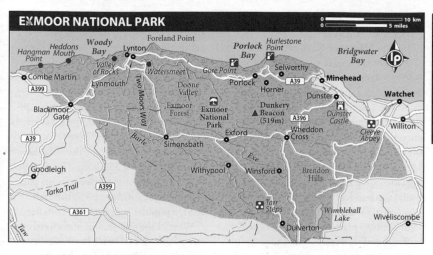

EXMOOR NATIONAL PARK

to win the favours of the choicest female. Despite their numbers, these skittish creatures are notoriously difficult to find without some local knowledge. The most reliable way to see them is on an organised **jeep safari**, which combines scenic sightseeing with a couple of hours of off-road wildlife-spotting action.

Trips start at around £30 for a half-day. All the operators favour slightly different areas of the moor, so ring around to see what's on offer.

Barle Valley Safaris (☎ 01643-851386; www. exmoorwildlifesafaris.co.uk; Dulverton & Dunster)

Discovery Safaris (☎ 01643-863080; www. discoverysafaris.com; Porlock)

Exmoor Safari (☎ 01643-831229; www.exmoor safari.co.uk; Exford)

Red Stag Safari (☎ 01643-841831; www.red stagsafari.co.uk)

🐾 ANIMAL CENTRES // PONIES AND PEREGRINES

Even with the best guide, you can't always bank on catching sight of Exmoor's more elusive residents, unless you head for the **Exmoor Owl & Hawk Centre** (☎ 01643-862816; www. exmoorfalconry.co.uk; Allerford near Porlock; adult/

child £7.50/5.50; ☉ 10am-5pm, owl show 11.45am, indoor flying display 2pm), which holds daily displays with its falcons, hawks, eagles and owls. You can even book your own private flying session if you're so inclined, or the kids could hitch a ride on the farm's Shetland ponies, donkeys and alpacas.

Exmoor's stubby ponies take centre stage at the **Exmoor Pony Centre** (☎ 01398-323093; www.exmoorponycentre.org. uk) near Ashwick. Like their Dartmoor cousins, Exmoor ponies were originally bred as beasts of burden, and despite their diminutive size they're notoriously hardy. Half-day pony experiences include a two-hour hack and cost £40 per person.

Another great way to explore the moor is on **horseback**. You'll find riding stables dotted all over the park.

Brendan Manor Stables (☎ 01598-741246) Near Lynton.

Burrowhayes Farm (☎ 01643-862463; www. burrowhayes.co.uk; Porlock)

Knowle Riding Centre (☎ 01643-841342; www.knowleridingcentre.co.uk; Dunster)

Outovercott Stables (☎ 01598-753341; www. outovercott.co.uk; Lynton)

♣ DUNSTER CASTLE // FALL FOR A FAIRY-TALE CASTLE

Rosy-hued **Dunster Castle** (NT; ☎ 01643-821314; castle adult/child £8.10/4, garden & park only £4.50/2; ☺ 11am-5pm Sat-Wed Mar-Oct, 11am-4pm Nov) sits atop a densely wooded hill on the moor's north coast. Constructed by the Luttrell family, whose manor once encompassed much of northern Exmoor, the castle's oldest sections date from the 13th century, although most of the building (including the turrets and exterior walls) were added during a 19th-century makeover. Inside are Tudor furnishings, 17th-century plasterwork and a ridiculously grand staircase, while the terraced gardens have views across the Exmoor coastline. Stay alert for spooks – the castle is supposedly one of England's most haunted.

Elsewhere around the village is a medieval **yarn market**, the red-brick **St George's Church** and a medieval **dovecote**, used for breeding edible squabs (young pigeons) for the castle dinner table. The village also has a working **watermill** (☎ 01643-821759; Mill Lane; admission £2.60; ☺ 11am-4.45pm Jul-Sep, 11am-5pm Sat-Thu Apr-Jun, Oct & Nov).

♣ PORLOCK // EXMOOR COAST AT ITS BEST

Thatched pubs, cob cottages and quiet shops line the main street of **Porlock**, one of the prettiest of Exmoor's coastal villages, and a favourite haunt of the Romantic poets: Coleridge was famously interrupted by 'a person from Porlock' while writing *Kubla Khan*, and never managed to finish it once he sat back down at his desk.

A mile or so further towards the coast is **Porlock Weir**, a stout granite quay curving around a shingly beach, backed by pubs, fishermen's storehouses and a few seasonal shops. The weir has been around for almost a thousand years (it's named in the Domesday Book as 'Portloc') and still makes a glorious place for a pub lunch and a stroll, with stirring views across the **Vale of Porlock** and easy access to the coast path. There's an especially scenic section leading west towards **Gore Point** and the pint-sized church at **Culbone**, reputed to be the smallest in England at just 35ft long. The shingle beach to the west of the weir forms part of the **Porlock Ridge** and **Saltmarsh SSSI**, a popular spot for local twitchers.

West of the village, the notoriously steep Porlock Hill reaches an engine-straining gradient of 1 in 4, but there's a more scenic route via the snaking **toll road** (cars/motorbikes/bicycles £2.50/1.50/1), which winds up through woodland en route to the Dunster Estate and Lynton and Lynmouth beyond.

♣ SELWORTHY BEACON & THE HOLNICOTE ESTATE // NATIONAL TRUST SPLENDOUR

To the east of Porlock, pebbly **Bossington Beach** and **Hurlestone Point** mark the northern edge of the huge 19 sq mile **Holnicote Estate** (☎ 01643-862452; holnicote@nationaltrust.org.uk), the largest NT-owned area of land on Exmoor. It formerly belonged to the local philanthropist and landowner Thomas Acland, who built the model village of **Selworthy** to provide accommodation for elderly workers on his estate. Although its cob-and-thatch cottages look ancient, in fact the oldest only dates back to 1828.

♣ DUNKERY BEACON // STRIKE OUT FOR THE SUMMIT

The highest point on Exmoor (and in Somerset) is **Dunkery Beacon** (519m). The hill can be tackled from several start-points, but the classic route begins in

Wheddon Cross. The trail to the summit leads through heather-clad countryside and the views from the top are unsurprisingly superb – if you're really lucky, you might even see Exmoor ponies and red deer on your way. The round trip is 8 miles, and steep in places; wear good boots and take a picnic.

Other popular Exmoor day hikes include the summit of **Selworthy Beacon** (308m) and the **Tarr Steps**, a clapper bridge thought to date back to 1000 BC. The bridge lies in woodland 4 miles northwest of Dulverton; the heaviest stones weigh up to 5 tonnes and span 55m of the fast-flowing River Barle.

OS maps and walking guides for these and other hikes can be picked up at any of the Exmoor NPA centres or the Porlock tourist office.

❧ BAKELITE MUSEUM // A BLAST FROM THE BRITISH PAST

This endearingly weird **museum** (☎ 01984-632133; adult £4; ☯ 10.30am-6pm) near Williton houses the nation's largest collection of **Bakelite** (otherwise known as *polyoxybenzylmethylenglycolanhydride*), one of the earliest plastics. This wonder material was used to make everything from telephones to radios, letter openers, eggcups, vacuum cleaners, toasters and even false teeth, and the museum has a treasure trove of pieces showcasing the material's myriad applications. The pièce de résistance has to be the full-size Bakelite coffin – pity the pall-bearers who had to lug that around…

❧ CLEEVE ABBEY // SAVOUR SOME CISTERCIAN TRANQUILLITY

Most visitors buzz straight past this tiny tumbledown **abbey** (adult/child £4/2; ☯ 10am-5pm), just outside Washford, but it's well worth investigating. It's one of the best examples of traditional Cistercian architecture in southwest England, and offers a fine glimpse into the life of the monks who lived here 800 years ago. Like all England's abbeys, it was largely torn down during the Dissolution, but you can still see the impressive cloister buildings, including the original gatehouse, refectory and the monks' dormitory, amongst the best preserved in England.

❧ LYNTON AND LYNMOUTH // TREK THROUGH RIVER GORGES

Across the border into Devon, the twin villages of **Lynmouth** and **Lynton** are set out across a steeply wooded slope that's traversed by a historic water-powered **cliff railway** (☎ 01598-753486; www.cliffrailway lynton.co.uk; one way/return £1.75/2.75; ☯ 8.45am-7pm Easter-Nov), designed by a pupil of Brunel in 1890.

Of the two, seasidey Lynmouth is the more popular, set around a small harbour ringed by fudge shops, ice-cream stalls and doily-clad tearooms, and crammed in the high season with coaches struggling to negotiate the village's hairpin bends. Clifftop Lynton is a quieter affair, perched on the bluffs and packed with grand Victorian piles left over from the town's 19th-century tourist heyday.

Several of the area's major rivers (including Hoar Oak Water and the East and West Lyn Rivers) congregate in the steeply walled coombes between Lynmouth and Lynton. In 1952 Lynmouth was devastated by a sudden flash flood caused by freak rainfall that swept most of the town into the sea and killed 34 people.

A good indication of this raw natural power can be seen at the **Glen Lyn Gorge** (☎ 01598-753207; adult/child £4/3; ☯ Easter-Oct), where the River West Lyn tumbles down the valley and feeds a miniature hydroelectric power station. Better still, follow the mile-long hike into the dramatic **Valley of the Rocks**, evocatively described by the poet Robert Southey as 'rock reeling upon rock, stone piled upon stone, a huge terrifying reeling mass'. Another gorgeous gorge walk leads 2 miles up the valley to **Watersmeet**, where the old fishing lodge turned National Trust teashop makes a restful place to recover after your uphill exertions.

GASTRONOMIC HIGHLIGHTS

✿ ANDREWS ON THE WEIR // PORLOCK £££

☎ 01643-863300; www.andrewsontheweir.co.uk; Porlock Weir; 2-/3-course menu £31.50/38.50

Exmoor's starriest and starchiest restaurant is nestled behind the Porlock breakwater. Chef Andrew Dixon sources all his produce from local farmers and fishing boats, so the menu is a riot of local flavours – Withycombe pork, Exmoor lamb and Devon scallops. Dinner can be pricey, but the £10 lunch menu is fab value. He also runs regular cooking courses.

✿ LEWIS'S TEA ROOMS // DULVERTON £

☎ 01398-323850; www.lewisexmoortearooms. co.uk; 13 High St; 2 scones & tea £5.25; ☺ breakfast & lunch Mon-Sat, dinner Thu-Sat

Is this the most perfect place for tea on Exmoor? According to the *Daily Telegraph* it is, and who are we to argue? Gooey cakes, spreads of sandwiches and piping-hot Welsh rarebits are the top choices; tables are pine, china's white and the waitresses are friendlier than Mary Poppins. Anyone for a cup of Elpitya Gunpowder?

✿ REEVE'S // DUNSTER ££

☎ 01643-821414; www.reevesrestaurantdunster. co.uk; lunch £4.95-14.25, dinner £12.95-24.95; ☺ lunch Thu-Sun, dinner Tue-Sat

Oak girders, worn-wood tables and twinkling candles create a bewitchingly cosy atmosphere at Reeve's, a reliable stalwart for dining in Dunster. Rich indulgent dishes are the watchword – guineafowl, lamb's liver, venison, slow-roasted partridge – but it's refreshingly unstuffy. Worth considering.

✿ TARR FARM INN // TARR STEPS ££

☎ 01643-851507; www.tarrfarm.co.uk; mains £15.95-22; ☺ lunch & dinner

You'll need a degree in map-reading to find it (don't rely on the satnav!), but you'll be glad you made the effort. Idyllically set on the rushing River Barle, this 16th-century restaurant-with-rooms welcomes all-comers; walkers and families come for a hearty lunch and cream teas, while after-dark diners sample more formal country fare.

✿ WOODS // DULVERTON ££

☎ 01398-324007; 4 Bank Sq; lunch £9.95-15, dinner £11-16.50; ☺ lunch & dinner

Despite the rustic tables, this splendid Dulverton restaurant has high culinary ambitions. It's well established as one of Exmoor's classiest eats, and locals and visitors alike cram in for its elegantly executed dishes – pork belly on champ, Red Ruby beef with Yorkshire pud. A real find.

TRANSPORT

BUS // The most useful buses are the coastal 28 (hourly, nine on Sunday) from Taunton, which stops at Crowcombe, Bicknoller, Williton, Watchet, Dunster and Minehead, and the inland 399 (three daily Monday to Saturday), which crosses the moor from Minehead to Tiverton via Dunster, Wheddon Cross, Exford and Dulverton. There are also two seasonal open-top services: the 39/300 'Coastal Link' from Minehead to Lynmouth via Selworthy and Porlock, and the 401 'Exmoor Explorer', which follows the coast from Porlock to Dunster and then circles inland via Wheddon Cross and Exford.

TRAIN // The West Somerset Railway (p75) stops at Williton, Watchet, Dunster and Minehead.

DORSET

3 PERFECT DAYS

☙ DAY 1 // HANDS-ON HISTORY

Start with the oldest – 150 million years to be exact. The waves have been shaping the stunning Durdle Door (p102) limestone rock arch for centuries; study it from the crescent beach alongside, then head to the water for an unforgettable swim. Next navigate winding lanes to Corfe Castle (p101), a shattered fortification that looms from the landscape in dramatic style. The battlement tour over, head to Clouds Hill (p100), the austere and deeply personal four-room home of Lawrence of Arabia.

☙ DAY 2 // HIGH-CLASS CUISINE, LOCAL LIFE

The sea has shaped life on Dorset's coast for centuries. Get a taste of it at bustling Mudeford Quay (p97), where gulls wheel as fishermen land a catch. Sample it fresh at their stall, then echo centuries of seafarers by navigating the surging water that is The Race – albeit by ferry. Your destination? Mudeford Sandbank, an idyllic spot to ease into easygoing beach life. Finally, head round the harbour to enjoy Dorset's incarnation as a foodie hot spot – at Gary Rhodes' sleek waterside eatery (p99).

☙ DAY 3 // A CLASSIC, JURASSIC DAY OUT

Some holiday souvenirs are special. Join a fossil-hunting trip (p117) near picturesque Lyme Regis and find your very own piece of prehistory to take home. Then, after savouring a quintessentially English afternoon tea (p120), study Lyme's literary links (think Jane Austen and Tracy Chevalier; p120) or discover the dinosaurs in local museums (p117). In the evening revel in the survival of that primitive but delectable life form – the oyster – at gourmets' favourite Hix Oyster & Fish House (p120).

DORSET

DORSET

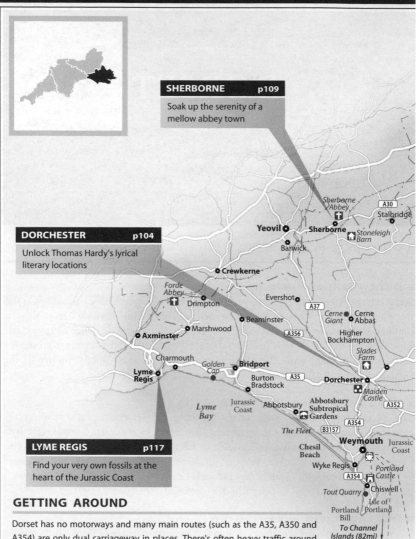

SHERBORNE   **p109**
Soak up the serenity of a mellow abbey town

DORCHESTER   **p104**
Unlock Thomas Hardy's lyrical literary locations

LYME REGIS   **p117**
Find your very own fossils at the heart of the Jurassic Coast

Sherborne Abbey   A30
Stalbridge
Yeovil   **Sherborne**   *Stoneleigh Barn*
Barwick
Crewkerne
Forde Abbey   Evershot   A37   *Cerne Giant*   Cerne Abbas
Drimpton   A356   Higher Bockhampton
Beaminster   *Slades Farm*
Marshwood
Axminster   Charmouth   **Bridport**   A35   **Dorchester**   *Maiden Castle*   A352
Lyme Regis   *Golden Cap*   Burton Bradstock
Lyme Bay   *Jurassic Coast*   Abbotsbury   **Abbotsbury Subtropical Gardens**   A354
The Fleet   B3157
Chesil Beach   **Weymouth**   *Jurassic Coast*
Wyke Regis   *Portland Castle*
A354
Tout Quarry   Chiswell
Isle of Portland
Portland Bill
To Channel Islands (82mi)

GETTING AROUND

Dorset has no motorways and many main routes (such as the A35, A350 and A354) are only dual carriageway in places. There's often heavy traffic around the main conurbations, while July and August bring congestion to villages and lanes, making parking scarce. Touring Bournemouth, Dorchester and Weymouth without a car is perfectly possible. Elsewhere, a sometimes-limited bus network prompts many to drive. Scenic routes include those from Swanage to Lyme Regis, and between Blandford Forum, Shaftesbury, Sherborne and Dorchester.

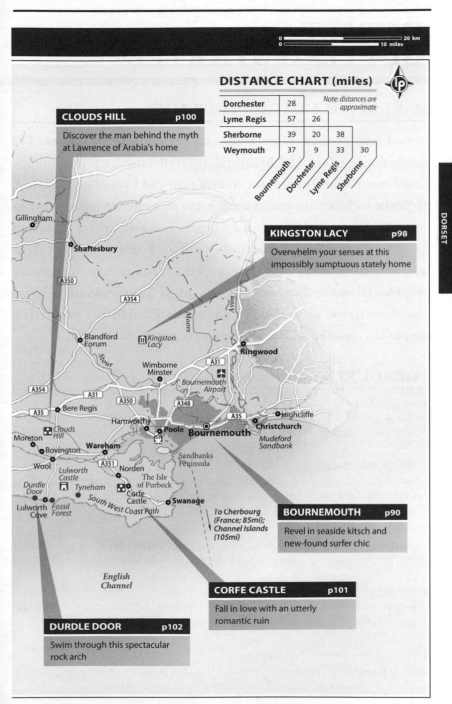

DORSET

DISTANCE CHART (miles)

Note: distances are approximate

	Bournemouth	Dorchester	Lyme Regis	Sherborne
Dorchester	28			
Lyme Regis	57	26		
Sherborne	39	20	38	
Weymouth	37	9	33	30

CLOUDS HILL p100

Discover the man behind the myth at Lawrence of Arabia's home

KINGSTON LACY p98

Overwhelm your senses at this impossibly sumptuous stately home

BOURNEMOUTH p90

Revel in seaside kitsch and new-found surfer chic

CORFE CASTLE p101

Fall in love with an utterly romantic ruin

DURDLE DOOR p102

Swim through this spectacular rock arch

To Cherbourg (France; 85mi); Channel Islands (105mi)

English Channel

DORSET GETTING STARTED

MAKING THE MOST OF YOUR TIME

Dorset inspires new discoveries and rekindles old passions. For astounding geology and breathtaking trails, focus on the Jurassic Coast around Lulworth Cove, Weymouth and Lyme Regis. Inland, exquisite architecture graces mellow towns such as Wimborne Minster, Sherborne and Blandford Forum. For history, try Kingston Lacy, Corfe Castle and Dorchester – once home to ancient Britons, Roman invaders and Thomas Hardy respectively. Weymouth provides Olympic-class water sports, while Bournemouth delivers seaside nostalgia by the bucket and spade. Even before you arrive, prepare to come back; Dorset tugs, very gently, at the soul.

TOP TOURS & COURSES

KAYAK THE JURASSIC COAST
Paddle past multimillion-year-old cliffs that soar from the waves, sculpted by the elements into exquisite coves, stacks and arches (p103).

INSPIRING HOLIDAY READING
Follow in the footsteps of Thomas Hardy (Dorchester; p105), TE Lawrence (Isle of Purbeck; p101) and Ian McEwan (Chesil Beach; p114), to name a few.

COOK WITH CONFIDENCE
TV chef **Lesley Waters** (☎ 0844 800 4633; www.lesleywaters.com; per day £250) stages workshops (Stress-Free Entertaining, anyone?) in a 17th-century west Dorset manor house.

SEE SCULPTURES IN SITU
More than 50 artworks carved from rock are still in Portland's Tout Quarry. Hunt out pieces by Antony Gormley and Dhruva Mistry amid the gullies and cliffs (p113).

TOUR A GEORGIAN TOWN
Strolling Blandford Forum's streets reveals a wealth of porticoes, colonnades and oriel windows; the whole town centre dates from the 18th century (p108).

GETTING AWAY FROM IT ALL

* **The Undercliffe** Just west of ever-popular Lyme Regis, a challenging cliff path enters this densely wooded nature reserve. Formed by massive landslips, it feels like an eerie lost world (p119).

* **Chesil Beach** Want to be alone? Head for this 17-mile-long, steep pebble ridge. Walk just a few hundred metres along and feel like a very small speck indeed (p114).

* **Wimborne Minster** Just 10 miles from Bournemouth's packed-out prom, climb up to this church's ancient chained library and escape to a world of medieval manuscripts written by monks (p97).

ADVANCE PLANNING

Fossil Hunting (p117) Ensure a trip to the beaches around Lyme Regis is in tune with the tides. The prime fossil-hunting sites are accessible only around low tide.

Restaurants Dorset's most popular eateries can fill up quickly – especially high-profile ones. If in doubt, it's best to book.

Army Firing Ranges Live firing restricts access to the South West Coast Path east of Lulworth Cove. Check times to ensure explorations of the lost village of Tyneham (p103) and Fossil Forrest (p103) are possible.

Clouds Hill (p100) The compelling home of Lawrence of Arabia is only open four afternoons a week.

TOP EATING EXPERIENCES

❦ SIENNA
Swish Dorchester eatery with a Michelin star (p110).

❦ RHODES SOUTH
Gary Rhodes' memorable waterside restaurant (p99).

❦ SHELLFISH BY THE SEA
Buy lunch from the fishermen at Lulworth Cove (p102), Weymouth Harbour (p112) and Mudeford Quay (p97).

❦ HIX OYSTER & FISH HOUSE
Inspired flavour combinations and one heck of a view (p120).

❦ NEW INN
Superb 13th-century gastropub in a beguiling village (p110).

RESOURCES

* **BBC Dorset** (www.bbc.co.uk/dorset) Local news, features, travel and weather

* **Jurassic Coast** (www.jurassiccoast.com) Official World Heritage Site guide

* **Rural Dorset** (www.ruraldorset.com) Tips on Dorset's inland spots

* **Swanage & Purbeck** (www.visitswanage andpurbeck.co.uk) Isle of Purbeck info

* **Visit Dorset** (www.visit-dorset.com) The county's official tourism website

DORSET

BOURNEMOUTH

· · · · · ·

pop 163,600

With its beaches and arcades, nightclubs and bars, Bournemouth embodies the modern British seaside. The conurbation draws them all: corporate delegates, coach tours, happy families and stag- and hen parties. Sometimes the edges rub – on weekend evenings parts of town are thick with L-plated angels and blokes in frocks, blonde wigs and slingbacks. But there's also a much sunnier side to the town. Bournemouth's seaside kitsch-rich, 7-mile sandy beach is perfect for promenading, sandcastle building and swimming. It's also home to another attraction: Europe's first artificial surf reef aims to bring bigger barrels and a wave of board-rider chic to town.

ESSENTIAL INFORMATION

TOURIST INFORMATION // Bournemouth tourist office (☎ 0845 051 1700; www.bournemouth.co.uk; Westover Rd; ☻ 10am-5pm Mon-Sat, plus 11am-4pm Sun Jun & Aug)

ORIENTATION

Bournemouth merges into Poole 5 miles to the west and Christchurch 5 miles to the east. Wimborne sits 10 miles north, with Kingston Lacy just a few miles away.

EXPLORING BOURNEMOUTH

Bournemouth was effectively born around 1810 when local landowner Lewis Tregonwell built a summer residence here. Initially the select settlement grew slowly; shops weren't allowed and tradesmen had to visit from neighbouring Poole. Then came the railway and within decades Bournemouth had grown into one of the largest resorts in Britain, noted for its chines (sharp-sided valleys) lined with holiday villas.

⚘ BEACH LIFE //REVEL IN GOLDEN SANDS AND RETRO CHARM

Bournemouth's 7-mile **beach** delivers a full-blooded blast of holiday nostalgia. Backed by 3000 deck chairs, this sandy strip regularly clocks up seaside awards and stretches from **Southborne** in the east to **Alum Chine** in the west, taking in two piers along the way.

Around **Bournemouth Pier** tap into decades of tradition and hire a **beach chalet** (☎ 0845 055 0968; per day/week from £17/55; ℗). The first resort to introduce these sandside homes from home in 1908, Bournemouth now has 1800 of them. Alternatively, invest in a deck chair (per day £2), windbreak (£2.50) or parasol (£4).

From Bournemouth Pier a 1.5-mile stroll east along the seafront leads to Boscombe Pier. En route is one of Bournemouth's 100-year-old cliff lifts, the **East Cliff Lift Railway** (☎ 01202-451781; Undercliff Dr; adult/child £1.20/80p; ☻ Easter-Oct). These cable-cars-on-rails take just minutes to whiz up the bracken-covered slopes, cutting out the short, steep hike up the zigzag paths.

At **Boscombe Pier** a stroll to the end of the boardwalk reveals wraparound views from the Isle of Wight in the east to the Isle of Purbeck in the west.

⚘ SURFING // GO ALL CALIFORNIAN BESIDE BOSCOMBE'S SOUPED-UP WAVES

Bournemouth is now the proud owner of Europe's first ever **artificial surf reef**. Made up of 55 immense sandbags (some 70m long), it sits submerged beneath the sea 220m offshore at **Boscombe Pier**. Despite initial teething problems, the aim remains to harness and increase existing waves, pushing them up and forming better breaks for surfers. The result is a faster, more challenging ride.

The reef isn't for beginners, but it's possible to learn nearby. The **Sorted Surf School** (☎ 01202-300668; www.bournemouth-surf school.co.uk; Undercliff Dr, Boscombe Beach), 300m west of Boscombe Pier, does lessons (per two hours £30) and hires out wetsuits (per four/eight hours £10/15), surfboards (four/eight hours £10/15), bodyboards (four/eight hours £5/10) and kayaks (one/two/four hours £10/15/25).

Boscombe's £11 million beachside redevelopment has also created the surfer cafe-bar **Urban Reef** (☎ 01202-443960; ⏰ 9am-11pm May-Dec, 9am-5pm Jan-Apr), as well as changing rooms and, a rare treat for British beachgoers, hot showers.

❦ **BEACH PODS // HIRE YOUR OWN ULTRAMODERN, DESIGNER CHALET**
The traditional British beach chalet just got funky. Boscombe's attempted rebirth as an oasis of surfer chic includes a range of hi-tech **beach pods** (☎ 0845 055 0968; per week winter/summer £85/250). Overlooking

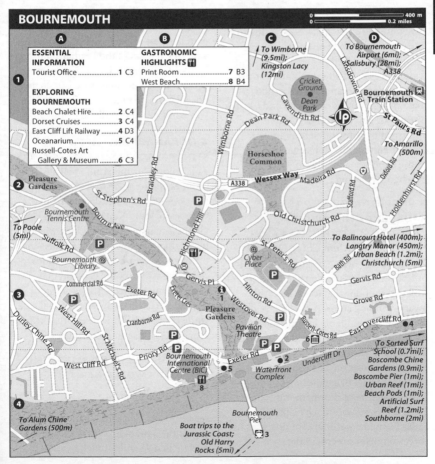

BOURNEMOUTH

0 ————— 400 m
0 ————— 0.2 miles

Ⓐ

ESSENTIAL INFORMATION
Tourist Office 1 C3

EXPLORING BOURNEMOUTH
Beach Chalet Hire..............2 C4
Dorset Cruises 3 C4
East Cliff Lift Railway 4 D3
Oceanarium.........................5 C4
Russell-Cotes Art
  Gallery & Museum 6 C3

Ⓑ

GASTRONOMIC HIGHLIGHTS 🍴
Print Room 7 B3
West Beach..........................8 B4

Ⓒ
To Wimborne (9.5mi);
Kingston Lacy (12mi)

Cricket Ground
Dean Park

Horseshoe Common

A338 Wessex Way

Dean Park Rd
Cavendish Rd
Wimborne Rd

Braidley Rd

Pleasure Gardens

St Stephen's Rd
Bournemouth Tennis Centre
Bourne Ave

To Poole (5mi)
Suffolk Rd

Bournemouth Library

Commercial Rd
West Hill Rd
Exeter Rd
Exeter Cres

St Michael's Rd

Durley Chine Rd

West Cliff Rd

Cranborne Rd
Priory Rd
Bournemouth International Centre (BIC)

Richmond Hill

Gervis Pl
Pleasure Gardens
Pavilion Theatre

Westover Rd
Hinton Rd
St Peter's Rd

@ Cyber Place

Old Christchurch Rd
Madeira Rd
Stafford Rd

Russell-Cotes Rd
East Overcliff Rd

Undercliff Dr
Waterfront Complex

Exeter Rd

To Alum Chine Gardens (500m)

Bournemouth Pier
Boat trips to the Jurassic Coast; Old Harry Rocks (5mi)

Ⓓ
To Bournemouth Airport (6mi); Salisbury (28mi); A338

Bournemouth 🚉 Train Station

Lansdowne Rd

St Paul's Rd

To Amarillo (500m)

Oxford Rd
Holdenhurst Rd

To Balincourt Hotel (400m); Langtry Manor (450m); Urban Beach (1.2mi); Christchurch (5mi)

Gervis Rd
Grove Rd

Bath Rd

To Sorted Surf School (0.7mi); Boscombe Chine Gardens (0.9mi); Boscombe Pier (1mi); Urban Reef (1mi); Beach Pods (1mi); Artificial Surf Reef (1.2mi); Southbourne (2mi)

DORSET

DORSET

Boscombe Pier, each has been individually designed by Wayne and Geraldine Hemingway (of Red or Dead fame), and feature oh-so-stylish murals and furnishings, microwaves and toasted sandwich makers. You can't sleep in the pods, but during the day you can head out onto your own balcony, settle back in your limited-edition director's chair, take in the panoramic views and watch the beachgoers playing in the waves below.

♥ PUBLIC GARDENS // TRACE BOURNEMOUTH'S ORIGINS THROUGH SUBTROPICAL PLANTS

Bournemouth's **Alum Chine Gardens** (Mountbatten Rd; ☺ open access) provide a taste of Bournemouth's golden age. Set 1.5 miles west of Bournemouth Pier, this award-winning subtropical enclave dates from the 1920s. Plants include those from the Canary Islands, New Zealand, Mexico and the Himalayas; their bright-red bracts, silver thistles and purple flowers frame views of a glittering sea.

In the centre of Bournemouth, the **Pleasure Gardens** stretch back for 1.5 miles from behind Bournemouth Pier in three colourful sweeps; in the east,

Boscombe Chine Gardens are also home to a water play area and minigolf course.

♥ RUSSELL-COTES ART GALLERY & MUSEUM // EXPLORE THE WORLD OF AN INVETERATE VICTORIAN COLLECTOR

This eclectic **museum** (☎ 01202-451858; www.russell-cotes.bournemouth.gov.uk; Russell-Cotes Rd; admission free; ☺ 10am-5pm Tue-Sun) is an ostentatious mix of Italianate villa and Scottish baronial pile and is framed by Japanese gardens. It was built at the end of the 1800s for Merton and Annie Russell-Cotes as somewhere to showcase the remarkable range of souvenirs gathered on their world travels. Look out for a plaster version of the Parthenon frieze by the stairs, Maori woodcarvings and Persian tiles. The house also boasts fine art, including paintings by Rossetti, Edwin Landseer and William Frith.

♥ OCEANARIUM // MEET STINGRAYS, PIRANHAS AND SHARKS

This enjoyable **aquarium** (☎ 01202-311933; www.oceanarium.co.uk; Pier Approach; adult/child £9/6.40; ☺ 10am-5pm) whisks you from the watery worlds of Key West to the Ganges via the Amazon, Africa and the Med. A highlight is the underwater tunnels that bring you eye-to-eye with mean-looking sharks, massive moray eels and giant turtles. Touch-screen games and feeding sessions deliver the educational side, while Global Meltdown explores the consequences of rising temperatures.

♥ JURASSIC CLIFFS // SAIL TO THE START OF A WORLD HERITAGE–LISTED COAST

A quirk of geological fate means Dorset's **Jurassic Coast** (p89) allows you to explore 185 million years of the earth's history in a 95-mile stretch of shore.

The wealth of rock formations, petrified forests and fossil deposits have won it Unesco World Heritage Site status. The coast ends at Exmouth in Devon, but starts some 5 miles west of Bournemouth at the white chalk **Old Harry Rocks**.

Dorset Cruises (☎ 0845 468 4640; www.dorsetcruises.co.uk; Bournemouth Pier; adult/child £12.50/5; ☺ Apr-Sep) runs a 2½-hour trip to Old Harry Rocks from Bournemouth Pier, an exhilarating journey across the mouth of Poole Harbour to cliffs where bright white columns rear up from the water. The stacks used to be massive arches before erosion brought the tops tumbling down, and huge scooped-out sections of cliff clearly show how the sea begins the process by eating away at the chalk.

GASTRONOMIC HIGHLIGHTS

♥ PRINT ROOM ££

☎ 01202-789669; Richmond Hill; mains £10-25; ☺ breakfast, lunch & dinner

This charismatic brasserie exudes Parisian chic, from the black-and-white tiled floors to the burnished wooden booths. Dishes are well travelled too; try the beet-root gnocchi, grilled calf's liver or steak with black truffle potato. Or that most excellent French tradition, the *plat du jour* – including wine – for only £10.

♥ WEST BEACH ££

☎ 01202-587785; Pier Approach; mains £11-18; ☺ breakfast, lunch & dinner

A firm favourite with Bournemouth's foodie crowd, this buzzy restaurant delivers top-notch dishes and the best views in town. The seafood is exemplary: rock oysters with shallot vinegar, monkfish medallions with Parma ham, and platters crammed with crab claws, lobster, razor clams and crevettes (from £25 per person). The white and blue decor is deliciously crisp and the decked dining terrace juts out over the sand.

TRANSPORT

TO/ FROM THE AIRPORT

AIRPORT // Bournemouth Airport (BOH; ☎ 01202-364000; www.bournemouthairport.com) links the city with Dublin, Edinburgh, Jersey and a range of European cities. An hourly **shuttle** (☎ 01202-557007; per person £4; ☺ 7am-6pm) runs between the airport, the train and bus stations and the town centre.

ACCOMMODATION

The availability of accommodation in Dorset varies wildly depending on location and season. Big resorts like Bournemouth and Weymouth are stacked with options; elsewhere there are fewer places to stay. Booking is advisable everywhere in high season (Easter, July and August).

We have in-depth reviews in our Accommodation chapter (p287), but here are some highlights:

★ **Urban Beach** (p291) Bournemouth's top hipster hotel

★ **Saltings** (p292) Poole's 1930s B&B overflows with Art Deco style

★ **Beach House** (p293) Sleek and chic with views of Lulworth Cove

★ **Beggar's Knap** (p293) An utterly opulent Dorchester guesthouse

★ **Hotel Alexandra** (p295) A Lyme Regis institution: serene, refined and full of English charm

DORSET

GETTING AROUND

BUS // Bournemouth has good intercity and local bus links; key routes include those shuttling every 10 minutes between Poole, Bournemouth and Christchurch. Bus X3 runs half-hourly to Salisbury (1¼ hours).

CAR // The nearest motorway, the M27, is 22 miles away. Bournemouth is circled by a series of roads, including the A338 and A348.

PARKING // There are numerous car parks, especially around the central Pleasure Gardens; there's also seafront parking around Boscombe Pier.

TRAIN // Trains run every half-hour from London Waterloo (£35, two hours) and go on to Poole, Dorchester South and Weymouth.

AROUND BOURNEMOUTH

· · · · · ·

Away from Bournemouth's bright 'n' breezy core the atmosphere changes. Poole provides all the bustle of an ancient port, as well as ferry trips to the homes of the super-rich – Sandbanks district boasts some of the world's most expensive properties, and a raft of tempting water sports. Mudeford Quay delivers an insight into life on the fishing boats, while local restaurants, including one run by TV chef Gary Rhodes, transform the day's catch into something fabulous on your plate. To the north and east the priory and minster at Christchurch and Wimborne resound with religious history, while at Kingston Lacy, dazzling interior design means an entire room shimmers with gold, gilded leather and semiprecious stones.

ESSENTIAL INFORMATION

TOURIST INFORMATION // Christchurch tourist office (☎ 01202-471780; www.visit christchurch.info; 49 High St, Christchurch; ۞ 9.30am-5pm Mon-Fri, 9.30am-4.30pm Sat) **Poole tourist office** (☎ 01202-253253; www.pooletourism.com;

Poole Quay, Poole; ۞ 9.15am-6pm Jul & Aug, 10am-5pm May, Jun, Sep & Oct, 10am-5pm Mon-Fri, 10am-4pm Sat Autumn half-term–Easter)

EXPLORING AROUND BOURNEMOUTH

☙ **POOLE //** DISCOVER BOURNEMOUTH'S HISTORIC, ARCHITECTURE-RICH NEIGHBOUR
Pubs, smart restaurants and shops line **Poole Harbour**; pleasure boats and impossibly pricey motor cruisers tie up alongside.

Poole's most striking sight is the 2300-year-old **Iron Age logboat**, dredged up from Poole Harbour and now on show in the town's excellent **Waterfront Museum** (☎ 01202-262600; 4 High St; admission free; ۞ 10am-4pm Tue-Sat, noon-4pm Sun Apr-Oct). This beautifully displayed, 10m-long, 14 tonne vessel is the largest to be found in southern Britain. It's thought to have carried 18 people and was hand-chiselled from a single tree; centuries later, you can still see the blade marks in the wood. Replicas of the tools used in its construction line up alongside.

Poole's past is also visible in its buildings. Beside the Waterfront Museum (itself a former 15th-century warehouse), Sarum St leads down to Thames St. It then heads left past the Tudor **King Charles pub**. A few paces away is the cream **Old Harbour Office**. Built in the 1820s, it is evidence of Poole's prosperous transatlantic trade; look out for the painted stone carving of local mayor Benjamin Skutt in an alcove.

The impressive, red-brick **Custom House** (1813) sits opposite, and boasts a Union Jack and gilded coat of arms. The wooden post and beam at the front was used to weigh goods for duty. 'Traders' often disagreed with excise men; in 1747 a consignment of illegally imported tea

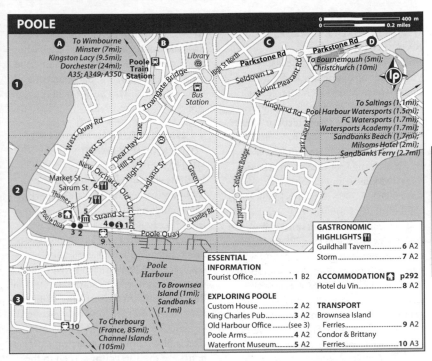

POOLE

To Wimbourne Minster (7mi); Kingston Lacy (9.5mi); Dorchester (24mi); A35; A349; A350

To Bournemouth (5mi); Christchurch (10mi)

To Saltings (1.1mi); Pool Harbour Watersports (1.5mi); FC Watersports (1.7mi); Watersports Academy (1.7mi); Sandbanks Beach (1.7mi); Milsoms Hotel (2mi); Sandbanks Ferry (2.7mi)

Poole Harbour

To Brownsea Island (1mi); Sandbanks (1.1mi)

To Cherbourg (France, 85mi); Channel Islands (105mi)

GASTRONOMIC HIGHLIGHTS
Guildhall Tavern 6 A2
Storm 7 A2

ESSENTIAL INFORMATION
Tourist Office 1 B2

EXPLORING POOLE
Custom House 2 A2
King Charles Pub 3 A2
Old Harbour Office ....(see 3)
Poole Arms 4 A2
Waterfront Museum 5 A2

ACCOMMODATION p292
Hotel du Vin 8 A2

TRANSPORT
Brownsea Island Ferries 9 A2
Condor & Brittany Ferries ...10 A3

DORSET

was seized, prompting 60 armed smugglers to break down the door of the site's previous building and make off with the contraband.

Poole Quay is lined by an attractive array of mismatched historic buildings; the atmospheric **Poole Arms** (☎ 01202-673450; ☻ lunch & dinner) makes for a good pit stop. This pub is the oldest on the quay and is faced with bright green tiles, a legacy of the town's historic pottery industry.

Poole's tourist office (p94) sells the *Poole Cockle Trail* leaflet (30p), a guide to the old town.

☙ SANDBANKS // STROLL THE BEACH BESIDE BRITAIN'S MILLIONAIRES' ROW

Curling round the entrance to Poole Harbour, Sandbanks is a 2-mile, wafer-thin **peninsula** with a bobble of land at

the end. It's backed by a stunning stretch of sand with magnificent views out to sea and the Jurassic Coast, and is lined with **exclusive homes**; property here regularly ranks as amongst the most expensive in the world, keeping pace with New York's Fifth Ave, Tokyo's Shibuya district and London's Belgravia. Homeowners include pop- and sports stars (look out for retired cricketers and footballers) and celebrity spotting is a popular local game.

The **2-mile beach** (ⓟ) itself consistently notches up seaside awards and offers a plethora of water sports. There are car parks along the peninsula and at each end. Or arrive in style courtesy of **Brownsea Island Ferries** (☎ 01929-462383; www.brownseaislandferries.com; Poole Quay; adult/child return £8/5; ☻ 10am-5pm Apr-Oct); boats shuttle between Poole Quay and Sandbanks every half-hour.

DORSET

❦ WATER SPORTS // SKIM THE WAVES IN EUROPE'S LARGEST NATURAL HARBOUR

Poole Harbour's sheltering coasts provide tempting opportunities for getting on the water. Many operators cluster near the start of the Sandbanks peninsula. They include **Pool Harbour Watersports** (☎ 01202-700503; www.pooleharbour.co.uk; 284 Sandbanks Rd, Lilliput), which offers lessons in windsurfing (per three-hour session £45) and kitesurfing (one/two/three days £99/175/240), as well as kayak tours (half-/full day £40/80).

The nearby **FC Watersports** (☎ 01202-708283; www.fcwatersports.co.uk; 19 Banks Rd) provides similarly priced kite- and windsurfing lessons, as does the **Watersports Academy** (☎ 01202-708283; www.thewatersportsacademy.com; Banks Rd), which also runs sailing courses (per two hours/two days £55/165) and wakeboarding and waterskiing (per 15 minutes from £20).

❦ BROWNSEA ISLAND // SALUTE YOUR INNER BOY SCOUT

This 200-hectare **island** (NT; ☎ 01202-707744; adult/child £5.50/2.70; ☺ 10am-5pm late Mar-Nov) in the middle of Poole Harbour played a key role in a global movement famous for three-fingered salutes, shorts and toggles. Lord Baden-Powell staged the first ever scout camp here in 1907 and **camping**, **archery** and **canoeing** all still go on.

Trails weave through heath and woods, past peacocks, red squirrels, red deer and a wealth of birdlife. Themed **guided walks** (at 11am and 2pm in July and August) include ones on the wartime island, smugglers and pirates. Brownsea is also often named as the inspiration for Enid Blyton's Whispering Island in the Famous Five story *Five Have a Mystery to Solve*. Blyton holidayed in the area repeatedly with her family in the decades from 1931.

Several ferries run to the island. Try **Brownsea Island Ferries** (☎ 01929-462383; www.brownseaislandferries.com; Poole Quay), whose boats run from Poole Quay (adult/child return £8.50/5.50) and Sandbanks (adult/child return £5/4). The last boat is about 4.30pm.

❦ CHRISTCHURCH // TOUR ONE TOWN'S RICH RELIGIOUS AND MILITARY HISTORY

With its elegant 11th-century priory, Norman castle ruins and grassy parks, Christchurch is dramatically different from breezy Bournemouth to the west.

Christchurch Priory (☎ 01202-485804; www.christchurchpriory.org; Quay Rd; suggested donation £3; ☺ 9.30am-5pm Mon-Sat, 2.15-5.30pm Sun, subject to services) was started in 1094 by Ranulf Flambard, one of King William II's right-hand men, and only escaped destruction during the Reformation after a plea from the townspeople. Highlights are the 1360 **altar screen** in the Great Quire, which depicts a peopled version of Christ's family tree, and the exquisite **Norman arches** in the nave. In the **West Tower** (adult/child £2.50/1) 176 steps lead to first-class views over the town and sea.

The evocative ruins of **Christchurch Castle** cling to a tiny rise just north of the priory. Steep stone steps lead up to its crumbling Great Tower, all that's left of a fortification that was built around 1300 on the site of an earlier motte-and-bailey affair. The castle saw action during the Civil War, when the Parliamentarians held it in the face of an attack by 1000 Royalists. Today the massive, honeycombed walls frame views onto the red-brick town and the serene priory beyond.

Below the castle, a quaint bowling green sits beside the **Norman Hall** ruins; head inside to see one of the best examples of a Norman chimney in the country. The footbridge beside the Norman Hall leads to a riverside path; follow it past the tranquil **Convent Meadow** at the rear of the Priory, to the well-weathered **Place Mill**. Mentioned in the Domesday Book (1086), it's now a composite of medieval, Tudor and 18th-century brick and stone. From there it's a few steps to **Christchurch Quay**, a calm blend of bandstands, tearooms and yachts with pinging rigging.

☙ MUDEFORD BY FERRY // CATCH A BOAT ACROSS THE SEA
Mudeford Sandbank
This slender spit of grass-backed beach curls across the mouth of **Christchurch Harbour**. It's a precarious mile-long slither of land, sandwiched between a surging sea and calmer inland waters. The sandbank is fringed by brightly painted beach huts and tufted dunes; the **Hengistbury Head Nature Reserve (P)** sits at the far south end.

The most atmospheric way to arrive is by the 1930s ferries run by **Bournemouth Boating Services** (☎ 01201-429119; return £5.30; 5 sailings daily Apr-Oct). These highly varnished vessels chug to the sandbank from **Christchurch Quay**, a 30-minute voyage that glides past rows of yachts, hundreds of wading birds and swathes of wet meadows.

Mudeford Quay
A narrow strip of turbulent water separates Mudeford Sandbank from Mudeford Quay – it's called the **Race** and watching yachts navigate it makes for compelling viewing. Get a taste of that voyage by taking a second, much shorter boat trip, the **Mudeford Ferry** (☎ 07968-334441; Mudeford Quay; adult/child return £2.40/1.20;

DORSET

⊙ Apr-Oct), which shuttles between the sandbank and quay.

Mudeford Quay is the hub of the local fishing industry. Its no-nonsense jumble of boats and lobster pots is an ideal spot to watch the catch being landed. Then sample it at the **cafe** and wet fish stall, where pots of cockles, mussels and whelks are ready to eat for £2.

The **Haven House Inn** (☎ 01425-272609; Mudeford Quay; mains from £6; ⊙ lunch & dinner) is an unreconstructed seafarers pub featuring stone floors, wooden settles and fishermen in sea boots. It's rightly famous for flavoursome crab sandwiches.

By car, Mudeford Quay is 2 miles from Christchurch; there's a car park alongside.

☙ WIMBORNE MINSTER // DRINK IN CENTURIES OF ECCLESIASTICAL HERITAGE
Wimborne Minster is the name of both a town and its religious building. The **church** (☎ 01202-884753; donation suggested; ⊙ 9.30am-5.30pm Mon-Sat, 2.30-5.30pm Sun) is a patchwork of honey-grey and worn red

stone. It was started by the Normans in 1120 and built on the site of a nunnery founded in around 700 by Cuthburga, sister to Ine, King of the West Saxons.

The highlight is the church's rare **chained library** (10.30am-12.30pm & 2-4pm Mon-Fri, 10.30am-12.30pm Sat Easter-Oct), which is set in a tiny room at the top of a winding staircase. Established in 1686, it's filled with some of the country's oldest medieval books. The handwritten *Regimen Animarum* dates from 1343, while the printed works of St Anselm date from 1495. There are also 12th-century manuscripts written on lambskin, and ancient recipes for making ink from oak apples.

The church's aisles are lined with heraldic crests, vivid stained glass and ornate tombs of knights. Near the altar are the twin marble figures of John Beaufort, Duke of Somerset, and his wife, Margaret – grandparents to **Henry VII**. Look out too for the 12th-century **Moses Corbel**, a beautiful carving, alongside. A brightly painted 14th-century **astronomical clock** sits in the west belltower. Note in this medieval depiction of the solar system the sun and moon orbit the earth.

Outside, the minster's 15th-century west tower features the **Quarter Jack**, a red-coated infantryman, complete with knee-boots and tricorne hat, who strikes the hours and quarters. He was originally a Benedictine monk, but was recarved as a soldier during the Napoleonic Wars.

❧ KINGSTON LACY // REVEL IN LAVISH INTERIORS AND WORLD-CLASS ART

This is Dorset's must-see **stately home** (NT; 01202-883402; adult/child £10.50/5.25; 11am-5pm Wed-Sun mid-Mar–Oct,). Looking every inch the setting for a period

drama, it overflows with rich decor, most famously in the **Spanish Room** which is smothered with gold and gilt. The gleaming ceiling and gilded leather wall hangings are said to come from Venetian palaces; they're topped off by panels of semiprecious stones from Florence.

Other highlights include the hieroglyphics in the **Egyptian Room**, and the elegant marble staircase and loggia. The house became the home of the aristocratic Bankes family when they were evicted from **Corfe Castle** (p101) by the Roundheads. In the loggia, look out for the bronze statue of Dame Mary Bankes; she's shown still holding the keys to her much-loved castle in her hand.

Works of art include the overwhelming ceiling fresco *The Separation of Night and Day* by Guido Reni in the Library, and paintings by Rubens, Titian and Van Dyck. Outside, wide sweeps of lawns lead to extensive **landscaped grounds** (grounds-only adult/child £6/3); hunt out the restored **Japanese tea garden**, and the Iron Age hillfort of **Badbury Rings**.

Kingston Lacy is 2.5 miles west of Wimborne off the B3082.

GASTRONOMIC HIGHLIGHTS

❧ GUILDHALL TAVERN // POOLE ££
 01202-671717; 15 Market St; mains £15-20, 2-/3-course lunch £15/19; lunch & dinner Tue-Sat
More Provence than Poole, the food at this French-run brasserie is Gallic gourmet charm at its best. Expect double-baked cheese soufflé, chargrilled sea bass flambéed with Pernod, or Charolais beef with peppercorns. Exquisite aromas fill the dining room, along with the quiet murmur of people enjoying very good food.

☙ RHODES SOUTH // CHRISTCHURCH £££

☎ 01202-484434; 95 Mudeford; mains £17-25, 2-course lunch £16; 🕑 lunch & dinner Tue-Sat

At this Gary Rhodes eatery the setting almost steals the show: tables overlook the vast sweep of Christchurch Harbour, and on summer evenings glass walls roll back turning the whole restaurant into a covered terrace. The food is supremely assured: expect prime cuts of meat, super-fresh fish and unusual vegetables to be transformed into fine dining fare.

☙ SPLINTERS // CHRISTCHURCH ££

☎ 01202-483454; 12 Church St; 2-/3-course dinner from £19/25; 🕑 lunch & dinner Tue-Sat

The awards line the walls of this intimate restaurant – and with good reason. Just a few steps from the priory, it delivers robust, deeply satisfying dishes; highlights are a rich wild-mushroom risotto laced with truffle oil, and a gooey confit of duck with red cabbage. The raspberry crème brûlée makes a fitting finale and the set lunch is a snip (two/three courses £12/15).

☙ STORM // POOLE ££

☎ 01202-674970; 16 High St; mains £17; 🕑 lunch & dinner Mon-Sat

The tables here are huge and rough-hewn; the menu is similarly robust. It also changes daily according to what the owner (a keen fisherman) catches. Great flavour combos include pan-fried scallops with green mango salad, and grey mullet with a fennel-and-samphire dressing. Or try a whole succulent, cracked crab with zesty lemon mayonnaise.

TRANSPORT

BICYCLE // Watersports Academy
(☎ 01202-708283; www.thewatersportsacademy.com;

DORSET

Banks Rd, Sandbanks, Poole) rents bicycles (per half-/full day £13/20).

BUS // Buses 1A/B/C shuttle between Poole, Bournemouth and Christchurch every 10 minutes. Bus 52 runs from Poole to Sandbanks (hourly Monday to Saturday, plus Sunday in July and August). Bus 3 links Poole and Wimborne Minster at least hourly, while bus X12 runs between Christchurch and Mudeford Quay (half-hourly Monday to Saturday, every two hours on Sunday).

CAR // It's sometimes better to avoid the ring roads when driving between Poole, Bournemouth and Christchurch. The smaller A35 is often a more direct route.

FERRY // Sandbanks Ferry (☎ 01929-450203; www.sandbanksferry.co.uk; one way per pedestrian/car £1/3.20; 🕑 7am-11pm) takes cars from Sandbanks to Studland every 20 minutes. It's a short cut from Poole to Swanage, Wareham and the Isle of Purbeck, but the summer queues can be horrendous. **Brittany Ferries** (☎ 0871 244 0744; www.brittany-ferries.com) sails from Poole to Cherbourg (France); **Condor Ferries** (☎ 01202-207216; www.condorferries.co.uk) runs between Poole and the Channel Islands.

TRAIN // Poole, Bournemouth and Christchurch are on the well-served London Waterloo–Weymouth main line, with at least hourly services.

THE ISLE OF PURBECK

· · · · ·

The Isle of Purbeck boasts arguably the most beautiful stretch of shore in Dorset. Curling underneath Poole, this is the start of the Jurassic Coast; the rocks here have been carved by the sea into glittering bays and towering cliff formations – making swimming irresistible and hiking memorable. Lulworth Cove, Durdle Door and the Fossil Forest are just a few highlights. The 'Isle' is really a peninsula; inland the immense, fairytale ruins of Corfe Castle sit amid verdant hills, while the area around the town of Wareham sheds light on the mysterious figure of Lawrence of Arabia.

ESSENTIAL INFORMATION

TOURIST INFORMATION // Lulworth Cove Heritage Centre (☎ 01929-400587; www. lulworth.com; Lulworth Cove; ⊗ 10am-5pm Apr-Oct, till 4pm Nov-Mar) Purbeck tourist office (☎ 01929-552740; www.purbeck.gov.uk; Holy Trinity Church, South St, Wareham; ⊗ 9.30am-4pm Mon-Sat, plus 10am-4pm Sun Jul & Aug)

EXPLORING THE ISLE OF PURBECK

❦ TRACKING LAWRENCE OF ARABIA // FOLLOW IN THE FOOTSTEPS OF THIS ENIGMATIC CHARACTER
Clouds Hill
TE Lawrence's simple **cottage** (NT; ☎ 01929-405616; near Bovington; adult/child £4.50/2; ⊗ noon-5pm Thu-Sun mid-Mar–Oct; ℗) provides a compelling insight into a complex man. Its four rooms are filled with collections and innovations that reflect his travels and experiences.

In the downstairs **Book Room**, walls are lined with copies of photos Lawrence took during his desert campaign; drawings of French crusader castles he sketched for his degree; and brass rubbings he made as a child. Next door is a surprisingly comfortable cork-lined bathroom, while the aluminium foil–lined **Bunk Room** upstairs acted as a pantry.

The heavily beamed 1st-floor **Music Room** features the desk where he abridged *Seven Pillars of Wisdom*, and a huge gramophone; Mozart and Beethoven were favourites. This was where Lawrence entertained guests, including EM Forster and Thomas Hardy. Refreshments were limited to tinned fruit, cheese, tea and water. There's minimal electric light in the cottage and it becomes all the more atmospheric when you're handed a wind-up torch to help with explorations. Clouds Hill is 7 miles northwest of Wareham.

Other Sites
In the nearby red-brick market town of **Wareham**, the delightful 11th-century church of **St Martin's on the Walls** (North St; ⊗ 10am-4pm Mon-Sat Easter-Oct) has a marble effigy of Lawrence in full Arab dress. If it's locked within shop hours, get the key from Joy's Outfitters in North St. The two-room **Wareham Museum** (☎ 01929-553448; East St; admission free; ⊗ 10am-4pm Mon-Sat Easter-Oct) displays a good potted history of Lawrence's life and the speculation surrounding his death.

The Purbeck tourist office in Wareham stocks free *Lawrence Walking Route* leaflets. This 7-mile walk goes from his **Bovington** army base, now a **tank museum** (☎ 01929-405096; www.tankmuseum. org; Bovington; adult/child £11/7.50; ⊗ 10am-5pm), via Clouds Hill to **St Nicolas Church** (☎ 01305-854046; ⊗ 10am-4pm) in **Moreton**,

TE LAWRENCE IN DORSET

British scholar, military strategist and writer, **Thomas Edward Lawrence** (1888–1935) is legendary for his role in helping unite Arab tribes against Turkish forces in WWI. His hit-and-run guerrilla raids on railway lines proved a telling drain on the enemy. Having risen to the rank of colonel, by the end of the war Lawrence had become fiercely disillusioned by what he saw as a British betrayal of Arab independence. He rejected his rank and re-enlisted under a batch of assumed names. But he failed to achieve the anonymity he craved and was exposed in a series of press articles. His actions ensured he was a source of fascination for many during his lifetime; David Lean's 1962 biopic *Lawrence of Arabia* assured his mythical status for decades to come.

While stationed at Bovington, 6 miles from Wareham, Lawrence worked on his epic account of the desert campaign, *Seven Pillars of Wisdom*, and eventually retired to Clouds Hill (p100), a nearby labourer's cottage that he'd transformed into a retreat. In 1935 he had a motorcycle accident on the Dorset roads. He died six days later at the age of 46. Conspiracy theories have abounded about his death ever since. The **TE Lawrence Society** (www.telsociety.org.uk) was founded in Dorset in 1985 to advance an understanding of his life and works.

DORSET

where his funeral took place. Lawrence's gravestone is at the far end of the churchyard, on the right.

❧ MONKEY WORLD // PREPARE TO SAY: 'DON'T THEY LOOK QUITE HUMAN?'

This **sanctuary** (☎ 0800 456600; www.monkey world.co.uk; Longthorns; adult/child £10.75/7.50; ☺ 10am-5pm, till 6pm Jul & Aug; ℗) overflows with the 'aah' factor. Its 65 acres are home to bounding, noisy colonies of chimpanzees, orang-utans, gibbons, marmosets and some ridiculously cute ringtailed lemurs. Most have been rescued from circuses, laboratories, working on Spanish beaches, or being mistreated as pets. The centre is near **Wool**, 5 miles west of Wareham.

❧ CORFE CASTLE // CLIMB THE KIND OF RUINS CINEMATOGRAPHERS DREAM OF

The massive, shattered ruins of this vast fortification loom so dramatically from the landscape it's like blundering onto a film set. The defensive fragments tower over an equally photogenic and eponymous **village**, creating a compelling, ever-present backdrop.

The **castle** (NT; ☎ 01929-481294; Corfe Castle; adult/child £5.60/2.80; ☺ 10am-6pm Apr-Sep, 10am-5pm Mar & Oct, 10am-4pm Nov-Feb; ℗) was begun in 1068 by William the Conqueror, then extended by Kings John, Henry III and Edward I. By the time of the English Civil War it was home to Sir John Bankes, Charles I's right-hand man. It was besieged by Cromwell's forces for six weeks, its robust defence being directed by the formidable Lady Bankes. Ultimately the castle fell after being betrayed from within. The Roundheads then blew it up with gunpowder.

The legacy of that violence is still startling today: turrets and soaring walls sheer off at precarious angles; the gatehouse in particular splays out as if it's just been blasted apart. You can roam over most of the site, peeping through slit windows and prowling the fractured battlements. Among the child-friendly gory bits, try hunting out the 'murder holes' or prescribing medieval medicine in the main **NT visitor centre**.

Some of the best views of the castle are from the west, from the junction of a cluster of trails leading off the circular **Castle Walk**.

♥ LULWORTH COVE // SWIM BESIDE THE AWE-INSPIRING EFFECTS OF EROSION

The Shore

Lulworth Cove is a perfect circle of white cliffs broken only by a distant segment of sea. It sits in a shoreline that's been carved by erosion into intricate bays, caves, stacks and weirdly wonderful rock formations. Lulworth Cove was formed when a river breached the outer Portland Limestone layer, and over millennia waves gouged out the softer Wealden rocks behind. The **Lulworth Cove Heritage Centre** (☎ 01929-400587; admission free; ☽ 10am-5pm Apr-Oct, till 4pm Nov-Mar; Ⓟ) does a superb job of explaining the process in engaging style.

Just 230m behind the heritage centre, **Stair Hole** is a tiny oblong cove with alarming sections of landslips and cliffs that have been eroded into caves, arches and worn-down stacks; in rough weather waves surge into the cavities sending water shooting into the air. Stair Hole is also home to the delightfully named **Lulworth Crumple**, a wedge of cliff that's been folded into a wavy 'S' shape by the same massive earth movements that created the Alps.

The Village

Lulworth Cove shares its name with this happy-go-lucky **village** – a string of thatched and tiled cottages, pubs and shops leading down to the fishing boats that back onto the beach. In the height of summer visitor numbers can make Lulworth a victim of its own success, but otherwise it's a charismatic place to stay.

♥ EAT JUST-COOKED CRAB // SAMPLE SHELLFISH FRESH FROM THE BEACH

Tucking into locally landed crab is a sure way to connect with a place and its past. More than a dozen fishing boats used to work out of **Lulworth Cove**; now there are only two. One is run by husband-and-wife team Joe and Christine. Their **fish shack** (☎ 01929-400807; ☽ Fri-Wed Easter-Oct, Sat & Sun Nov-Easter), beside the path to the cove, is piled with plaice, sole and brill. Settle at the tiny table outside, ask Christine to crack a freshly cooked **crab**, then devour a shellfish feast that's travelled food yards, not miles.

♥ DURDLE DOOR // SWIM BESIDE A 150-MILLION-YEAR-OLD ROCK FORMATION

Extraordinary even by this coast's standards, this towering **stone arch** plunges into the sea near Lulworth Cove. It was formed when massive earth movements tilted the rocks up; softer layers were exposed and a cave was formed. Over the millennia, constant pounding by the sea expanded the hole to form today's majestic arch. The next stage will be an eventual collapse of the top, to leave just a standing stack.

Either side of the 15m arch, hundreds of steps lead down to perfect bays – bring a swimsuit and take a dip beside a 150-million-year-old limestone arch.

There's a car park in a campsite at the top of the cliffs, but it's more fun to **hike** the mile along the coast path from Lulworth Cove's car park. The path heads west, steeply uphill and passes the exquisite, merged coves at **Man O'War Bay**.

DORSET

❦ FOSSIL FOREST // DISCOVER AN ANCIENT FOREST, DROWNED BY GLOBAL WARMING

A half-mile **hike** east along the coast path from Lulworth Cove leads to the remains of a **Jurassic jungle**. Here huge, raised donuts of rock (called 'tufa') sprout from the cliff, all that's left of the tree trunks of a 144-million-year-old forest. In the early Purbeck period a wetter climate and flooding killed the trees, and algae gathered round the stumps, preserving them in calcareous sediment.

The forest is at the foot of **Bindon Hill**, just inside an army live-firing range. The path tends to be open most weekends and school summer holidays, but it does vary. Check by calling the army's recorded info line: ☎ 01929-404819.

❦ KAYAKING // PADDLE THROUGH THE SEA ARCHES OF THE JURASSIC COAST

This three-hour kayaking trip offers a jaw-dropping view of the Isle of Purbeck's heavily eroded coast. The tours, led by **Secondwind Watersports** (☎ 01305-834951; www.jurassic-kayaking.com; Lulworth Cove; per person £50; ☺ up to 2 tours daily; ℗), glide from Lulworth Cove, through **Stair Hole's** intricate caves and stacks, across **Man O'War Bay** and under the massive stone arch at **Durdle Door**, with plenty of picnic and swimming stops along the way. From water level, the soaring cliffs are even more awe-inspiring – an unforgettable trip.

❦ TYNEHAM // TOUR A LOST VILLAGE WITH A SOBERING PAST

The ruined shells of buildings in this **evacuated village** tell a compelling story. In 1943 residents in 106 local properties were given a month to leave so the area could be used for D-Day preparations. Despite expectations, postwar they were never allowed to return home and the village remains inside an army firing range.

Tyneham's ruined cottages have panels featuring archive photos, which introduce who lived where: the Driscolls at the Post Office; the Whitelocks at Labourer's Cottage; and Miss Woodman at the School House. The school has rows of benches, dusty books and children's names above their coat pegs, while the door of **St Mary's Church** re-creates a sign pinned there by locals, asking servicemen to treat their village kindly until they returned.

SELF-CATERING & CAMPSITES

We detail Dorset's hotels and B&Bs in our Accommodation chapter (p287). But here are some great DIY options:

★ **Harbourside** (Map p112; ☎ 01305-776757; www.mallamsrestaurant.co.uk; 5 Trinity Rd; per week from £500; ℗ �ⓦ) Gorgeous two-bedroom apartment with Weymouth Harbour views

★ **Up Down** (www.updowncottage.co.uk; Gold Hill; per week from £500; ℗ �ⓦ) A whitewashed, four-bedroom cottage on Shaftesbury's irresistible Gold Hill (p109)

★ **Elworth Farmhouse** (☎ 01305-871693; www.elworth-farmhouse.co.uk; Abbotsbury; per week £300-600; ℗ ☎) A thatched cottage in a sleepy south Dorset hamlet

★ **Gypsy Caravan & Shepherd's Hut** (☎ www.canopyandstars.co.uk; per night from £85; ℗) Quirky, kooky and comfy – roughing it's never been so smooth

★ **Durdle Door Holiday Park** (☎ 01929-400200; www.lulworth.com; tent sites from £15; ☺ Mar-Oct; ℗) Camp on the cliffs above the famous rock arch

Inside, a timeline charts the history of the village, the evacuation and the families' failed campaign to be allowed back home.

Tyneham is 6 miles east of Lulworth Cove. It's only open when there is no live firing; normally most weekends and school summer holidays. Check by calling the army's recorded info line: ☎ 01929-404819.

♥ LULWORTH CASTLE // DELIGHT IN A JACOBEAN ARCHITECTURAL GEM

A creamy, dreamy white, this **castle** (☎ 01929-400352; www.lulworth.com; East Lulworth; adult/child £8.50/4; ⏱ 10.30am-6pm Sun-Fri Apr-Sep, till 4pm Oct-Mar; P) looks more like a French chateau than a traditional English fortification. Built in 1608 as a hunting lodge, it has survived extravagant owners, extensive remodelling and a disastrous fire in 1929. It's now been sumptuously restored. Check out the massive four-poster bed, and the suits of armour in the basement.

TRANSPORT

BUS // Bus 40 shuttles between Poole, Wareham, Corfe Castle and Swanage (every one to two hours). Bus 103 (daily, Monday to Saturday) links Lulworth Cove with Wool, on the X53 Weymouth–Wareham–Poole route.
TRAIN // Wareham is on the main line between London Waterloo, Wareham, Wool, Dorchester and Weymouth. The **Swanage Steam Railway** (☎ 01929-425800; www.swanagerailway.co.uk; adult/child return £9/7; ⏱ hourly Apr-Oct, limited services Nov-Mar) chuffs between Swanage and Norden, stopping at Corfe Castle.

DORCHESTER & INLAND DORSET

· · · · · ·

The country around Dorchester is Thomas Hardy country; his writing is steeped in the landscape. Here you can see the lush, gentle hills that inspired him and the towns and buildings that hide in his novels. Interestingly, Hardy himself is now an attraction: Dorchester boasts a museum with a world-class collection of his manuscripts, as well as two of his former homes. Literature aside, the area also contains the most impressive Iron Age hillfort in England; the sauciest chalk figure in the country; the architectural ornament that is Blandford Forum; and a string of bewitching, ancient towns – Sherborne to the north is a particular delight.

ESSENTIAL INFORMATION

TOURIST INFORMATION // Dorchester **tourist office** (☎ 01305-267992; www.westdorset. com; Antelope Walk, Dorchester; ⏱ 9am-5pm Mon-Sat Apr-Oct, 10am-4pm Mon-Sat Nov-Mar) **Sherborne tourist office** (☎ 01935-815341; www.westdorset. com; Digby Rd, Sherborne; ⏱ 9am-5pm Mon-Sat Apr-Oct, 10am-3pm Nov-Mar)

EXPLORING DORCHESTER & INLAND DORSET

♥ A THOMAS HARDY TRAIL // TRACK DOWN THOMAS HARDY'S LITERARY LOCATIONS

Official Sites

The Hardy collection at the **Dorset County Museum** (p106) is the biggest in the world. It offers an extraordinary insight into his creative process; manuscripts full of his cramped handwriting reveal where he's crossed out one word and substituted another. There's also a letter from Siegfried Sassoon, a handwritten outline of a dramatisation of *Jude the Obscure,* and an atmospheric reconstruction of his book-lined study at Max Gate, complete with pens, inkwell, blotters and a rickety old table on which he wrote his earlier works.

A trained architect, Hardy designed **Max Gate** (NT; ☎ 01297-262538; Alington Ave; adult/child £3/1.50; ⊗ 2-5pm Mon, Wed & Sun Apr-Sep; ℗), where he lived from 1885 until his death in 1928. *Tess of the D'Urbervilles* and *Jude the Obscure* were both written here, and the house contains several pieces of original furniture. Max Gate is a mile east of Dorchester on the A352.

The small cob-and-thatch **Hardy's Cottage** (NT; ☎ 01297-489481; admission £4; ⊗ 11am-5pm Sun-Thu Apr-Oct; ℗), where the author was born, has been little changed since he left. It's in Higher Bockhampton, 3 miles northeast of Dorchester.

DIY Investigations

Because Dorchester doubled as Casterbridge, **literary locations** crop up repeatedly amid the town's white Georgian terraces and red-brick buildings. The *Country of the Mayor of Casterbridge* pamphlet (50p) is sold at the tourist office. It highlights the **Maumbury Rings**, the location of Henchard's secret meetings; **Lucetta's House**, a grand Georgian affair with ornate doorposts near the tourist office; and in parallel South St, a red-brick mid-18th-century building (now a bank) that matches the description of the **Mayor of Casterbridge's house**.

Inside **St Peter's Church** in High West St, there's a copy of a signed plan of the church drawn by Hardy when he was an apprentice architect. Tucked away on a pillar near the altar and dated 4 August 1856, it even details how many people each pew could hold.

THOMAS HARDY

Poet, prolific novelist and Dorset's best PR man, **Thomas Hardy** (1840–1928) drew heavily on the county's landscape to produce deeply lyrical writings that blend rural idyll and romance with reality and tragedy.

Hardy was born at Higher Bockhampton, just north of Dorchester. The son of a stonemason, he became an apprentice architect before turning to writing. The novels flowed: *Far from the Madding Crowd*, *The Return of the Native*, *The Mayor of Casterbridge*, *Tess of the D'Urbervilles* and *Jude the Obscure*. When *Jude* received some scathing reviews (largely because it challenged conventional morality), a disillusioned Hardy switched to poetry; *Poems of the Past and the Present* and *Wessex Poems* are amongst the most famous.

Hardy married twice; first Emma Gifford and then, after her death, his secretary Florence Dugdale, who was 40 years his junior. Hardy died in his late 80s and his ashes were placed in Poet's Corner at Westminster Abbey. His heart though is buried in the same grave as his first wife in Stinsford, just northeast of Dorchester.

Hardy revived the then-defunct name Wessex and used it as a location for his stories. He also borrowed specific features, such as forts and Roman ruins, as well as whole towns to create his 'partly real, partly dream country'. So in Hardy's books Dorchester becomes Casterbridge, Cerne Abbas is dubbed Abbot's Cernel, Sherborne gets the new name Sherton Abbas and Higher Bockhampton is rechristened Upper Mellstock. The result is a literary scavenger hunt for Hardy enthusiasts. The **Thomas Hardy Society** (☎ 01305-251501; www.hardysociety.org) publishes a series of 'tour guides' (50p) to his novels, available at the Dorchester tourist office.

DORSET

❦ DINOSAUR DORSET // DISCOVER THE COUNTY'S FOSSIL-FILLED HERITAGE

A huge ichthyosaur skeleton in the Jurassic Coast gallery of **Dorset County Museum** (☎ 01305-262735; www.dorsetcounty museum.org; High West St; admission £6; ⏰ 10am-5pm Jul-Sep, 10am-5pm Mon-Sat Oct-Jun) sets the scene for an engaging exploration of Dorset's dinosaur era. Exhibits include locally found fossilised wood, worm casts, mammoth teeth and a crocodile skull, as well as a huge six-foot fore paddle of a plesiosaur. Imaginative

displays feature drawers full of fossils to pull out and discover, cartoons on fossil-fraudsters and a series of minia-ture, motorised dinosaur worlds to peer in on.

The museum also charts the history of fossil hunting, including a profile of Lyme Regis' formidable Mary Anning (p117).

❦ MAIDEN CASTLE // CLIMB THE RAMPARTS OF A 2500-YEAR-OLD FORT

Occupying a massive slab of horizon on the fringes of Dorchester, this is the larg-

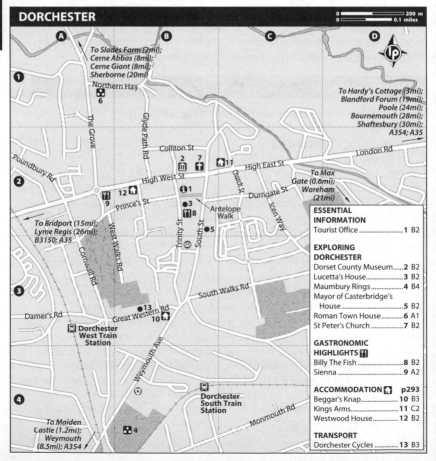

DORCHESTER

0 ___ 200 m
0 ___ 0.1 miles

To Slades Farm (2mi);
Cerne Abbas (8mi);
Cerne Giant (8mi);
Sherborne (20mi)

Northern Hay

To Hardy's Cottage (3mi);
Blandford Forum (19mi);
Poole (24mi);
Bournemouth (28mi);
Shaftesbury (30mi);
A354; A35

To Max
Gate (0.6mi);
Wareham
(21mi)

To Bridport (15mi);
Lyme Regis (26mi);
B3150; A35

Dorchester
West Train
Station

Damer's Rd

Dorchester
South Train
Station

To Maiden
Castle (1.2mi);
Weymouth
(8.5mi); A354

ESSENTIAL INFORMATION	
Tourist Office	1 B2

EXPLORING DORCHESTER	
Dorset County Museum	2 B2
Lucetta's House	3 B2
Maumbury Rings	4 B4
Mayor of Casterbridge's House	5 B2
Roman Town House	6 A1
St Peter's Church	7 B2

GASTRONOMIC HIGHLIGHTS	
Billy The Fish	8 B2
Sienna	9 A2

ACCOMMODATION	p293
Beggar's Knap	10 B3
Kings Arms	11 C2
Westwood House	12 B2

TRANSPORT	
Dorchester Cycles	13 B3

est and most complex **Iron Age hillfort** in Britain. The huge, steep-sided chalk defences flow along the contour lines of a hill and surround 48 hectares – the equivalent of 50 football pitches. The first hillfort was built on the site around 500 BC and in its heyday was densely populated, with clusters of roundhouses and a network of roads. The sheer scale of the surviving ramparts is awe-inspiring, especially from the ditches immediately below, while the winding complexity of the west entrance reveals just how hard it would have been to storm.

Those defences were put to the test in AD 43 when a Roman army, skilled at using *ballistas* (crossbows), massacred a local Durotriges tribe armed with slings and stones. The **Dorset County Museum** (p106) has an 'ammunition dump' of 20,000 slingstones, as well as Durotrige skeletons excavated from Maiden Castle's mass graves – one skeleton still has a Roman *ballista* bolt lodged in the spine.

Maiden Castle is 1.5 miles southwest of Dorchester.

❦ ROMAN DORCHESTER // STROLL AROUND ENGLAND'S BEST-PRESERVED ROMAN HOME

After the Romans defeated the local Durotriges tribe at Maiden Castle in AD 43, they created the new Roman town of Durnovaria: modern Dorchester. One remnant is the 4th-century **Roman Town House** (☎ 01305-262735; www.roman townhouse.org; High West St; admission free; ☿ open access).

Its knee-high flint walls outline the building's floor plan, while a glass-sided structure perched just above echoes its style and shape. Taking a peek into the Summer Dining Room, wide entrance hall or owner's study, reveals well-preserved **mosaics**. Some of these cream,

orange, yellow and black designs have 8200 *tesserae* (tiles) per sq metre. There are also exposed sections of the *hypocaust* (underfloor heating system), where charcoal-warmed air circulated around stone pillars, easily achieving a toasty 18°C.

There are more local mosaics at **Dorchester County Museum** (p106), along with a hoard of 70 gold coins found at Maiden Castle, a nail cleaner and even a Roman ear pick.

❦ THE CERNE GIANT // GIGGLE AT ENGLAND'S RUDEST CHALK FIGURE

Some 8 miles north of Dorchester is **Cerne Abbas**, a quintessential Dorset village with a real nudge-nudge, wink-wink tourist attraction on its fringes. The Cerne Giant is a **huge chalk figure**. He's nude, full frontal, notoriously well endowed and in a state of some excitement.

Around 60m high and 51m wide, the figure's age remains a mystery. Some argue he's a depiction of the Roman god Hercules, but the first known reference to him is in 1694, when three shillings were set aside for his repair. The Victorians found it all deeply embarrassing and allowed grass to grow over his most outstanding feature. Today the hill is grazed by sheep and cattle; only the sheep though are allowed to do their nibbling over the giant – the cows would do too much damage to his lines.

The village itself is a jumble of architectural styles. Half-timbered houses frame the honey-coloured, 12th-century **St Mary's Church**. Following the roadside stream alongside leads past a Georgian red-brick terrace, thatched cottage, propped-up barn and delightful duck pond to the picturesque remains of **Cerne Abbey** (adult/child £1/20p; ☿ 10am-4pm

Easter-Oct). Founded by the Benedictines in 987, it was dissolved by Henry VIII in 1539. The mid-15th-century flint-and-stone guesthouse has fine window arches, while the Abbot's Porch is an exquisite red-gold structure complete with lattices, shields and oriel windows.

☙ BLANDFORD FORUM // TOUR ONE TOWN'S WEALTH OF GEORGIAN ARCHITECTURE

Although today a feast for the eye, **Blandford Forum's** buildings were borne of disaster. The whole town was consumed by a massive fire in 1731 and the subsequent rebuilding programme resulted in a rarity: a town centre that dates from just one period.

Blandford's fire began in a tallow chandler's (candlemaker's) – 13 people lost their lives and 480 families were made homeless. Local builders the Bastard brothers (coyly pronounced 'B'stard' locally) were commissioned to do the rebuilding work and, over the next 30 years, they created a satisfying collection of graceful streets and elegant buildings.

In the central Market Place, the stately **Parish Church of St Peter and St Paul** was among the first buildings to go up in 1739. It has an arched white cupola on the tower instead of a spire. The colonnaded former **town pump** is just outside. Turned into a monument to the Bastard brothers, it remembers 'God's dreadful visitation by fire', noting 'Divine Mercy has raised this town like a phoenix from the ashes'.

The imposing **Town Hall** is to the left; further left again Salisbury St heads uphill – look out for the bow window and mathematical tiling at **number 6**, and fine bow and oriel windows at **number 20**. The fire started nearby, where the

Kings Arms now stands. Opposite, a narrow street called the **Plocks** leads sharply off to the right. It features a cluster of weathered red-brick buildings that include the old **County Court** and the **Blandford Fashion Museum**, with its beautiful ornate porch. The grand 1750 **Conpar House** is opposite.

A robust flint wall bears right to Blandford's first **police station** (1836–39) and the old **Rectory**, with its facing of oval tiles above the door. From there **Church Walk** cuts behind the church, past the creamy canopy of the **Old Bank House** and back to the town pump.

The **tourist office** (☎ 01258-454770; West St; ☼ 10am-5pm Mon-Sat Apr-Sep, till 3pm Oct-Mar) sells an excellent town trail leaflet (£1). Blandford Forum is 19 miles northeast of Dorchester, on the A354.

☙ SHAFTESBURY // NOSEY AROUND A QUAINT SAXON TOWN

Crowning a ridge and gathering around its historic abbey ruins, **Shaftesbury** is somehow both typically English and reminiscent of an ancient French hill town. At the central Park Walk, lawns fringe a terrace at the edge of a steep escarpment, providing sweeping views over the field-filled **Blackmore Vale**.

Alongside, **Shaftesbury Abbey** (☎ 01747-852910; www.shaftesburyabbey.org.uk; Park Walk; adult/child £2.50/1; ☼ 10am-5pm Apr-Oct) was founded by Alfred the Great in 888. Alfred's daughter, Aethelgifu, was its first abbess and it went on to house the largest community of nuns in England. King Knut died at the abbey in 1035, and it's thought his heart is buried here.

The abbey **museum** features intricate Saxon stonework, painted 15th-century statuary and illustrations from illuminated manuscripts. The abbey was dismantled during Henry VIII's dissolution of the monasteries. Most of it is now in ruins, but its buildings emphasise just how big the community was, with its dove house, laundry, brewhouse, granary and stables – and what a seismic change Henry's clerical landgrab was.

Tiny Park Lane peels off from Park Walk, leading to the impossibly pretty **Gold Hill**, a steep cobbled slope lined with chocolate-box cottages topped by thatch and tile roofs. This picture-perfect scene feels like a film set – bakers Hovis fittingly shot their famous 'Boy on a Bike' commercial here, where a lad struggles up the street to the strains of a brass band, before bobbling down again having got his loaf.

The nearby **Mitre Inn** (☎ 01747-852549; 23 High St; mains £6-10; ✆ lunch & dinner Mon-Sat, lunch Sun) is an atmospheric town-centre pub with drink-them-in views from its decked terrace.

Shaftesbury is 30 miles northeast of Dorchester.

☙ **SHERBORNE // EXPLORE AN ANCIENT ABBEY AND TWO GLORIOUS CASTLES**
Sherborne Abbey & Town
Sherborne is one of Dorset's prettiest towns. It gleams with a mellow, orangey-yellow stone that's been used to build the 15th-century shops and houses that cluster around the impressive **Abbey Church of St Mary the Virgin** (☎ 01935-812452; suggested donation £3.50; ✆ 8am-6pm mid-Mar–Oct, till 4pm Nov–mid-Mar). At the height of its influence, this was the central cathedral of the 26 Saxon bishops of Wessex. It was established early in the 8th century, became a Benedictine abbey in 998 and functioned as a cathedral until 1075. The church has mesmerising fan vaulting that's the old-est in the country; a central tower supported by Saxon-Norman piers; and an 1180 Norman porch. Its **tombs** include the elaborate marble effigy belonging to John Lord Digby, Earl of Bristol, and those of the elder brothers of Alfred the Great, Ethelred and Ethelbert.

The beautiful, 15th-century **St Johns' Almshouses** (admission £2; ✆ 2-4pm Tue & Thu-Sat May-Sep) are beside the abbey. Look out too for the six-sided conduit now at the foot of Cheap St. This arched structure used to be the **monks' lavatorium**, or washhouse, but was moved to provide the townsfolk with water when the abbey was disbanded.

Sherborne Old Castle
These days the epitome of a picturesque ruin, **Sherborne Old Castle** (EH; ☎ 01935-812730; adult/child £3/1.50; ✆ 10am-6pm Jul & Aug, till 5pm Apr-Jun & Sep, till 4pm Oct; Ⓟ) was built by Roger, Bishop of Salisbury, in around 1120. Queen Elizabeth gave it to her one-time favourite Sir Walter Raleigh in the late 16th century. He spent large sums of money modernising it before opting to build Sherborne New Castle.

His old home became a Royalist stronghold during the English Civil War, but Cromwell all but destroyed the 'malicious and mischievous castle' after a 16-day siege in 1645, leaving the crumbling southwest gatehouse, great tower and north range.

Sherborne New Castle
Having had enough of his (by then) 400-year-old Sherborne Old Castle, Sir Walter Raleigh began building **Sherborne New Castle** (☎ 01935-813182; www.sherbornecastle.com; adult/child £9.50/free; ✆ 11am-4.30pm Tue-Thu, Sat & Sun Apr-Oct; Ⓟ) in 1594. Really a splendid manorhouse, Sir Walter only got as far as the central

DORSET

block before falling out of favour with James I and ending up back in prison. In 1617 James sold the castle to Sir John Digby, the Earl of Bristol, who added four wings – look out for the heraldic beasts on the central hexagonal turrets. The interior is sumptuous; all intricate plaster ceilings, plush carpets, fine china and vast, gilt-framed oils.

In 1753, the **grounds** (grounds-only admission £5) received a mega-makeover at the hands of landscape gardener extraordinaire, Capability Brown. He added a massive lake and a remarkable 12 hectares of lush waterside gardens.

GASTRONOMIC HIGHLIGHTS

☙ BILLY THE FISH // DORCHESTER £
☎ 01305-757428; Trinity St; mains from £8; ☙ lunch Mon-Sat, dinner Thu-Sat
Former fisherman Billy doesn't catch his own anymore; he's too busy cooking up a storm at this kooky bistro. The walls are hung with fabric, lobster pots and buoys; the tables are lined by locals enjoying skilfully cooked seafood. Try the superfresh turbot, brill and scallops, or the intensely flavoured fish soup.

☙ FLEUR DE LYS // SHAFTESBURY £££
☎ 01747-853717; Bleke St; mains £23, 2-/3-course dinner £25/30; ☙ prebooked lunch Wed-Sun, dinner Mon-Sat
Time to put the diet on hold – this classy eatery delivers flavours you wouldn't want to miss: lobster ravioli, venison in Armagnac, and lemon sole with a dash of vermouth. Then add extra calories with honey, halva and fig crème brûlée.

☙ GREEN // SHERBORNE ££
☎ 01935-813821; 3 The Green; mains £9-17; ☙ lunch & dinner Tue-Sat

As mellow as the honey-coloured building it's set in, this intimate restaurant's menu is packed full of local ingredients; try the mushroom and thyme risotto with roasted butternut squash, or the guinea fowl with apples and redcurrants.

☙ NEW INN // CERNE ABBAS ££
☎ 01300-341274; 14 Long St; bar meals £9, mains £11-22; ☙ lunch daily, dinner Fri & Sat
With delicious, unconscious English irony, the New Inn was 'new' in the 13th century. Sophisticated bar meals include local venison casserole, while robust restaurant dishes include gurnard and spiced belly pork. The well-travelled wine list roams from the Veneto to Champagne, via Marlborough, Rioja and Bordeaux.

☙ SIENNA // DORCHESTER £££
☎ 01305-250022; 36 High West St; 2-course set lunch/dinner £22/33; ☙ lunch & dinner Tue-Sat, booking required
Dorchester's finest restaurant is notching up the accolades, including a Michelin star. The modern British menu is laced with seasonal produce; in spring look out for wild garlic and pungent white truffles, or partridge that might be teamed with spiced pear. The cheeseboard bears the best of the west, served with fig chutney and Bath Oliver biscuits.

TRANSPORT

BICYCLE // Dorchester Cycles (☎ 01305-268787; 31 Great Western Rd; adult/child per day £12/8).
BUS // Bus 31 goes hourly from Weymouth via Dorchester to Lyme Regis. Bus D12 (two to three daily, Monday to Friday) runs from Dorchester to Sherborne, via Cerne Abbas. Buses 57 and 58 provide an hourly service between Yeovil and Sherborne. From Shaftesbury, buses 309 and 310 run to Blandford Forum (two to six Monday to Saturday); bus 183 links Blandford Forum with Dorchester and Weymouth (two to five daily).

TRAIN // Trains run twice-hourly between Weymouth and London Waterloo via Dorchester South. Dorchester West has connections with Bath and Bristol (every two hours). Sherborne is on the Exeter–London Waterloo main line, an hourly service.

WEYMOUTH & THE WEST COAST

· · · · · ·

The shoreline stretching west from Weymouth to Devon is where the Jurassic Coast really comes into its own. Weymouth's breezy seaside charms give way to the hard, high cliffs of the Isle of Portland; they in turn flow down to Chesil Beach, a remarkable, 17-mile, lagoon-backed pebble ridge. Sheltering behind are Abbotsbury's captivating subtropical gardens and an absolutely unique attraction: a swannery of 600 nesting birds. Then in the far west comes Lyme Regis. With literary links to John Fowles and Jane Austen, it's also got an irresistible whiff of fossil fever – a bit of coastal rummaging here could unearth a seaside souvenir that's 190 million years old.

WEYMOUTH TO ABBOTSBURY

At just over 200 years old, Weymouth is a grand dame of an English resort: think ice cream, cockles and chippies and prepare for a sandy stroll down seaside memory lane. The old girl also pulls some surprises from her faded sleeve: a revitalised historic harbour and, at the neighbouring Isle of Portland, state-of-the-art sailing facilities for the 2012 Olympics. Meanwhile Portland also offers an engrossing insight into a historic quarrying industry and jaw-dropping views onto the vast ridge of Chesil Beach. Its pebbles shelter the Fleet, Britain's

biggest tidal lagoon and home to a profusion of birds.

ESSENTIAL INFORMATION

TOURIST INFORMATION // Weymouth tourist office (☎ 01305-785747; www.visitweymouth.co.uk; The Esplanade; ⊗ 9.30am-5pm Apr-Oct, 9.30am-4pm Nov-Mar)

EXPLORING WEYMOUTH TO ABBOTSBURY

❦ SEASIDE KITSCH // INDULGE IN A HOLIDAY NOSTALGIA-FEST
King George III put **Weymouth** on the seaside map when he took an impromptu dip here in 1789 to cure his 'nervous disorder'. That single swim launched the resort's Georgian heyday. Its legacy is a line of tall, sometimes worn, seafront buildings with a huge brightly painted statue of the king, from a decidedly grateful town, in the middle.

These days Weymouth's 3-mile **beach** (℗) is the place to surrender to your inner kitsch. Rent a deck chair, sun lounger or hire a **pedalo** (per hr £6) or, just south of George III's statue, watch battling puppets at the candy-striped **Punch and Judy tent**. Nearby **donkey rides** set off across the golden sands – the animals' care has been given welfare awards by the Sidmouth Donkey Sanctuary (p137).

Just south is Weymouth's **sand sculpture** area. Famous since Victorian times, designs today include intricately carved dragons, maidens and fantasy castles. Signs even provide tips on creating your own masterpieces: Weymouth's sand is particularly fine and is best mixed with water, hand packed then carved.

Bunting-draped **St Alban Street** caters for seaside kitsch shopping. Stock up on windbreaks, pop-up tents, Frisbees, cricket sets and, of course, buckets and spades.

DORSET

DORSET

✹ WEYMOUTH'S HISTORIC HARBOUR // EXPERIENCE AN AUTHENTIC SLICE OF NAUTICAL LIFE

Weymouth's harbour is full of the smells and bustle of a working port. At Custom House Quay fishing boats unload the catch, dive vessels prepare to go out and people wearing waterproofs and sea boots wander around. Pubs line the quay and their scattered chairs – and the harbour wall itself – are popular spots to sip a drink and survey the scene; at local favourite the **Royal Oak**, a worn wooden shelf-bench juts out from the wall.

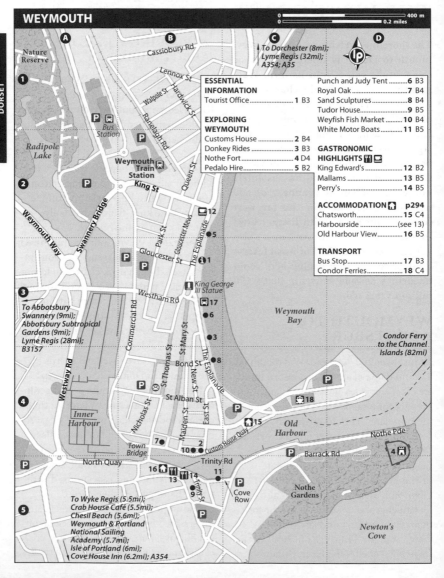

WEYMOUTH

0 — 400 m
0 — 0.2 miles

ESSENTIAL INFORMATION
Tourist Office **1** B3

EXPLORING WEYMOUTH
Customs House **2** B4
Donkey Rides **3** B3
Nothe Fort **4** D4
Pedalo Hire **5** B2

Punch and Judy Tent **6** B3
Royal Oak **7** B4
Sand Sculptures **8** B4
Tudor House **9** B5
Weyfish Fish Market **10** B4
White Motor Boats **11** B5

GASTRONOMIC HIGHLIGHTS 🍴 🍷
King Edward's **12** B2
Mallams **13** B5
Perry's **14** B5

ACCOMMODATION 🏠 p294
Chatsworth **15** C4
Harbourside .... (see **13**)
Old Harbour View **16** B5

TRANSPORT
Bus Stop **17** B3
Condor Ferries **18** C4

Nature Reserve

Cassiobury Rd

Lennox St

Walpole St

Hardwick St

Ranelagh Rd

To Dorchester (8mi);
Lyme Regis (32mi);
A354; A35

P 🚌 Bus Station

Radipole Lake

P

Weymouth Train Station 🚉

Swannery Bridge

King St

Queen St

Weymouth Way

P

🖥 12

Park St

Gloucester Mews

● 5

The Esplanade

Gloucester St

🛈 ● 11

P

King George III Statue

To Abbotsbury Swannery (9mi);
Abbotsbury Subtropical Gardens (9mi);
Lyme Regis (28mi);
B3157

Westham Rd

Commercial Rd

🚏 17

● 6

● 3

Weymouth Bay

St Mary St

St Thomas St

Bond St

● 8

The Esplanade

New St

St Alban St

Condor Ferry to the Channel Islands (82mi)

Westway Rd

Inner Harbour

Nicholas St

Maiden St

East St

P

P

🏠 15

P

P 🚗 18

Old Harbour

Nothe Pde

Town Bridge

7 ●

North Quay

Custom House Quay

2

10 ● ●

Trinity Rd

16 🏠 🍴 14

13 🍴 11

P

Barrack Rd

P

4 🏰

Nothe Pde

9 ●

Trinity St

Cove Row

Nothe Gardens

Newton's Cove

To Wyke Regis (5.5mi);
Crab House Café (5.5mi);
Chesil Beach (5.6mi);
Weymouth & Portland National Sailing Academy (5.7mi);
Isle of Portland (6mi);
Cove House Inn (6.2mi); A354

Fine 18th- and 19th-century buildings line the harbour. Part-way along Customs House Quay, the grand red-brick Georgian **Customs House** has white bay windows and a gilded crest. Flat-fronted, 19th-century warehouses lead to the pronounced overhanging eaves of the **Weyfish Fish Market** (☎ 01305-761277; Custom House Quay; ☺ 9am-4.30pm Mon-Sat). Built in 1855, it still sells wet fish and pots of cockles, mussels and whelks.

The entire **Town Bridge**, complete with road, pavements and railings, splits in two and rises (like London's Tower Bridge) every two hours, on the hour from 8am, letting masted boats through and stopping pedestrians and cars in their tracks.

On the harbour's south side, Trinity Rd winds past an appealing collection of pastel-painted houses, shops and eateries; look out for the furnished, late-16th-century **Tudor House** (☎ 01305-812341; Trinity St; adult/child £3.50/1; ☺ 1pm-3.45pm Tue-Fri May-Oct). At the end of Nothe Pde, the 19th-century **Nothe Fort** (☎ 01305-766626; adult/child £6/1; ☺ 10.30am-5.30pm May-Oct; ℗) details the Roman invasion of Dorset, a Victorian soldier's drill and Weymouth in WWII.

❦ **WATER SPORTS** // TAKE TO THE WAVES IN WORLD-CLASS WATERS
Sailing & Windsurfing
Just south of Weymouth, the 890-hectare **Portland Harbour** is the sailing venue for the 2012 Olympics. The brand-new **Weymouth & Portland National Sailing Academy** (☎ 0845 337 3214; www.wpnsa. org.uk; Portland Harbour; ℗) runs sailing tuition (per two/four days £170/325) and hires lasers (per two hours/day £40/85). **Windtek** (☎ 01305-787900; www.windtek.co.uk; 109 Portland Rd, Wyke Regis) runs lessons in windsurfing (per half-/full day £90/150) and kitesurfing (per day £95).

Diving
Local waters have a huge variety of depths, seascapes and wrecks, from paddle steamers and East Indiamen to WWII vessels. Rigid inflatable boats (RIBs) normally run to shallower sites from Portland Harbour; deeper dives accessible by hard boat leave from Weymouth. Operators include **Underwater Explorers** (☎ 01305-824555; www.underwater explorers.co.uk; 15 Castletown, Portland) and **Fathom & Blues** (☎ 01305-766220; www. fathomandblues.co.uk; 262 Portland Rd, Wyke Regis). Lessons start at around £95 a day; some operators shuttle qualified divers to a site (per person around £20) and rent equipment (per person from £50).

❦ **FERRY RIDE** // SURGE ACROSS AN OLYMPIC SAILING VENUE
Portland Harbour's vast breakwaters were begun by convict labour in the mid-1800s. **White Motor Boats** (☎ 01305-785000; Cove Row, Weymouth Harbour; adult/child return £7.50/6; ☺ Apr-Oct) runs three to four trips daily from Weymouth to **Portland Castle** on the Isle of Portland – a cracking 3-mile voyage that cuts right across Portland Harbour; that it takes 40 minutes emphasises its sheer scale.

❦ **ISLE OF PORTLAND** // EXPLORE QUARRYING HERITAGE AND TAKE IN REMARKABLE VIEWS
The Isle of Portland is a hard, high comma of rock fused to the mainland by the ridge of Chesil Beach. In places it feels half finished; its central plateau is pockmarked by limestone quarries, while huge slabs of quarried rock lie around. Then crenellated minicastles of moneyed quarry owners suddenly pop up, like surreal scenes in a David Lynch film.

Portland's industrial past is best explored at **Tout Quarry** (admission free;

DORSET

TOP FIVE

FERRY RIDES & BOAT TRIPS

* ★ **Jurassic Coast Kayaking** (p103) Take in a seal's-eye view of exquisite coves
* ★ **Mudeford Ferry** (p97) Sail to a sea-dashed sand spit
* ★ **Old Harry Rocks** (p92) Cruise to the chalk-white cliffs that herald the start of the Jurassic Coast
* ★ **Portland Harbour** (p113) Surge across an Olympic sailing venue
* ★ **Sandbanks** (p95) Take a ferry to a beach beloved by the super-rich

open access; P), a disused working where more than 90 artists have created 53 sculptures in situ. The result is a fascinating combination of the raw material, the detritus of the quarrying process and the beauty of chiselled pieces of work. Labyrinthine paths snake through hacked-out gullies and around jumbled piles of rock, revealing the half-formed bears, bison and lizards that emerge out of stone cliffs. Highlights include *Still Falling* by Antony Gormley, *Woman on Rock* by Dhruva Mistry, the well-hidden *Green Man* and the optimistic *Ascent*. Weymouth's tourist office sells a leaflet guide (40p). The views from the quarry down onto Chesil Beach are breathtaking.

In the far south, the rugged **Portland Bill** headland emphasises the isle's remote nature. It features a 13m-high, candy-striped **lighthouse** (☎ 01305-820495; adult/child £2.50/1.50; 11am-5pm Sun-Fri Apr-Sep; P); climbing to the top reveals the Race, a surging vortex of conflicting tides. The coast here is particularly rich in **bird life**: migrants in spring; guillemots, kittiwakes and occasional puffins in summer.

Portland Castle (EH; ☎ 01305-820539; Castletown; adult/child £4.20/2.10; 10am-6pm Jul & Aug, till 5pm Apr-Jun & Sep, till 4pm Oct; P) is one of the finest examples of the fortifications constructed during Henry VIII's castle-building spree. Inside you can try on period armour and enjoy wide views over Portland Harbour.

Around **Chiswell**, ancient terraces of fishermen's cottages stretch down to the sea. Portland's east coast has the ruined **Rufus Castle** and good swimming at **Church Ope Cove** (via 150-odd steps).

CHESIL BEACH // SCRAMBLE UP EVIDENCE OF ANCIENT GLOBAL WARMING

Chesil Beach is one of the most breathtaking shorelines in Britain. This mind-boggling, 100-million-tonne **pebble ridge** is a shade over 17 miles long, 15m high and is moving inland at the rate of 5m a century. Tucked in behind is **the Fleet**; at 8 miles long, Britain's largest saline lagoon.

The beach is the baby of the Jurassic Coast, a mere 6000 to 10,000 years old, and was probably formed when falling sea levels deposited chert and flint in what is now Lyme Bay. That was then swept inland when the waters rose at the end of the last ice age.

The pebble ridge is highest at the Portland end; 15m compared with 7m at Abbotsbury. For good views head to the **Chesil Beach Centre** (☎ 01305-760579; Ferrybridge; admission free; 10am-5pm Apr-Sep, 11am-4pm Oct-Mar; P) on the A354 to Portland. From here an energy-sapping hike up sliding pebbles leads to the constant surge and rattle of sea on stones and dazzling views of the sea, the thin pebble line and the expanse of the Fleet behind. The centre details the area's geology, bird and plant life, which includes ringed plover, redshank and oyster catchers, and drifts of thrift and sea campion.

Chesil is also the setting for Ian McEwan's acclaimed novel about sexual awakening, *On Chesil Beach*.

🏵 **ABBOTSBURY SWANNERY // GET CLOSER TO SWANS THAN YOU'D NORMALLY DARE**
A visit to this **swannery** (☎ 01305-871858; New Barn Rd, Abbotsbury; adult/child £9.50/6.50, combined ticket with Abbotsbury Subtropical Gardens £15/10; ☼ 10am-5pm or 6pm late Mar-Oct; Ⓟ) puts you right in the middle of 600 nesting birds. The swans are free flying and are drawn to Abbotsbury by food and fresh water. There's been a colony here for more than 600 years, and it's the only place in the world where you can walk into the heart of a nesting mute swan colony.

Trails meander between waterways, revealing the extraordinary number of birds that choose to nest beside and directly on the paths. Between mid-May and late June hundreds of fluffy cygnets emerge from their eggs, but at any time it's an awe-inspiring experience; with occasional territorial displays (think snuffling-cough and stand-up flapping), even the liveliest children are stilled.

The swannery is at the picturesque village of **Abbotsbury**, 10 miles from Weymouth off the B3157.

🏵 **ABBOTSBURY SUBTROPICAL GARDENS // GET HORTICULTURAL INSPIRATION FROM EXOTIC TREES AND SHRUBS**
These **gardens** (☎ 01305-871387; Bullers Way, Abbotsbury; adult/child £9.50/6.50, combined ticket with Abbotsbury Swannery £15/10; ☼ 10am-5pm or 6pm mid-Mar–Oct, till dusk Nov–mid-Mar; Ⓟ) are an 8-hectare indulgence, overflowing with the spikes and vivid petals of plants from around the world.

They started life in the 1760s as a kitchen garden for the Countess of Ilchester.

DORSET

THE JURASSIC COAST

The Jurassic Coast is England's first natural **World Heritage Site**, putting it on a par with Australia's Great Barrier Reef and the USA's Grand Canyon. This exquisite shoreline stretches from Exmouth in East Devon to Swanage in Dorset, encompassing 185 million years of the earth's history in just 95 miles.

It began when layers of rocks formed, their varying compositions determined by different climates as desert-like conditions gave way to higher and then lower sea levels. Massive movements in the earth's crust then tilted the rock layers to the east. Next, erosion exposed the different strata, leaving most of the oldest formations in the west and the youngest in the east.

The differences are very tangible. Devon's rusty-red Triassic rocks are 200 to 250 million years old. **Lyme Regis** (p117) has fossil-rich, dark clay and 190-million-year-old cliffs. Pockets of much younger, creamy coloured Cretaceous rocks (a mere 65 to 140 million years old) also pop up, notably around **Lulworth Cove** (p102), where erosion has sculpted a stunning display of bays, stacks and rock arches.

The website www.jurassiccoast.com is a great information source, with a free downloadable miniguide; also look out for the highly readable *Official Guide to the Jurassic Coast* (£4.95), available at local tourist offices and bookshops. For tips on responsible fossil collecting, see p119.

Today the lush valley is full of eucalyptus trees, silver birch and towering palms; their bark peeling, smooth and fibrous in turn. Clumps of bright-green bamboo pop up beside vivid magnolias and camellias; paths trace trails under stone arches, past ponds and over bridges. Meanwhile extensive labelling allows you to identify what is what. Highlights include the glimpses of the 14th-century **St Catherine's chapel**, viewed through a 'window' cut out of the trees, and the Jurassic-era swamp, complete with murky water and swathes of tree ferns.

GASTRONOMIC HIGHLIGHTS

☙ COVE HOUSE INN // ISLE OF PORTLAND £

☎ 01305-820895; Chiswell; mains £9; ☺ lunch & dinner

For a fabulously friendly old fishermen's pub, head to the east end of Chesil Beach. Oars, lead weights and sepia shipwreck photos hang from its rough stone walls, while the local fish is delicious. Tuck into just-caught hand-dived scallops, Portland crab spaghetti or seafood chowder on a blustery sea-view terrace overlooking the 17-mile pebble ridge.

☙ CRAB HOUSE CAFÉ // WYKE REGIS ££

☎ 01305-788867; Ferrymans Way, Portland Rd; mains £16; ☺ lunch & dinner Wed-Sat, lunch Sun

At this funky cabin right beside the Fleet lagoon the menu changes twice a day, depending on what fish has just been landed. Oyster beds are right alongside, meaning the molluscs are in your mouth minutes after leaving the water (per half-dozen £8.50). Gutsy dishes include skate with chorizo and paprika, or get cracking on crab still in its shell (per half/whole £11/19). The cafe is near the start of the road onto Portland.

☙ KING EDWARD'S // WEYMOUTH £

☎ 01305-786924; 100 The Esplanade; mains £6; ☺ lunch & dinner

It's got to be done in Weymouth: tuck into Britain's national dish, fish and chips. This classic Victorian chippy is lined with burgundy tiles and wrought iron. Lime and ginger crab cakes feature on the menu, alongside firm favourites: battered fish, chipped potatoes, mushy peas and pickled eggs.

☙ MALLAMS // WEYMOUTH ££

☎ 01305-776757; 5 Trinity Rd; 2/3 courses £24/30; ☺ dinner Mon-Sat

With its subdued lighting and old stone walls, this romantic harbourside eatery has been a feature of Weymouth's restaurant scene for 20 years. Find out why they've lasted by eating chargrilled local venison with lemon and gin sauce, or a fragrant fish and shellfish pie with a dash of vermouth.

☙ PERRY'S // WEYMOUTH ££

☎ 01305-785799; 4 Trinity Rd; mains £12-20; ☺ lunch Tue-Fri & Sun, dinner Tue-Sat

This Georgian town house is a study of effortless elegance. Snowy white tablecloths combine with flashes of pink – for a fabulous harbour view ask for the 1st-floor bay-window table. The local seafood is irresistible: sea bass with crushed saffron potatoes, and spiced tian of Portland crab. The set lunch menu (per two/three courses £12/16) is a real bargain.

TRANSPORT

BUS // Weymouth has bus connections to Dorchester (three per hour), Lyme Regis (hourly) and Axminster. Bus X53 (two to six daily) goes to Poole, Abbotsbury and Lyme Regis. Bus 1 runs from Weymouth to Fortuneswell on the Isle of Portland every half-hour; between June and September it also goes on to Portland Bill.

FERRY // **Condor Ferries** (☎ 01202-207216; www.condorferries.co.uk) shuttle daily between Weymouth and the Channel Islands (two to three hours).

TRAIN // Trains run twice-hourly between Weymouth and London Waterloo (£50, three hours) via Dorchester South (£3.40, 11 minutes) and Bournemouth (£10.90, one hour), and hourly to Bath (£15.60, two hours) and Bristol (£20.60, 2½ hours).

LYME REGIS & AROUND

pop 3504

Lyme Regis is fantastically fossiliferous. Rock-hard relics of the past pop out at regular intervals from the cliffs, exposed by the landslides of a retreating coast. Lyme (the Regis is dropped locally) is now a pivot point of the Jurassic Coast World Heritage Site (p115) and fossil fever is definitely in the air. Everyone, from proper palaeontologists to those out for a bit of fun, can engage in a spot of coastal rummaging. Add delightful pastel-painted cottages, sandy beaches and some great places to stay and eat, and you get a charming base for explorations.

ESSENTIAL INFORMATION

TOURIST INFORMATION // **Lyme Regis tourist office** (☎ 01297-442138; www.westdorset. com; Church St; 🕒 10am-5pm Mon-Sat & 10am-4pm Sun Apr-Oct, 10am-3pm Mon-Sat Nov-Mar)

EXPLORING LYME REGIS & AROUND

🌱 FOSSIL HUNTING // UNEARTH YOUR VERY OWN AMMONITE

Fossil fever is catching, even for those with no previous palaeontologic tendencies. The beaches around Lyme are prime sites because mudflows bring fossil-filled deposits onto the shores. The sea then washes the silt away, leaving prehistoric treasures waiting to be found.

Regular two-hour **fossil walks** (adult/child £9/5) are run by the Lyme Regis Museum (p118) and local expert **Brandon Lennon** (☎ 07944 664757; www.lymeregis fossilwalks.com; adult/child £7/5; 🕒 Sat-Tue). At Charmouth, 3 miles east of Lyme, the **Charmouth Heritage Coast Centre** (☎ 01297-560772; www.charmouth.org; admission free; 🕒 10.30am-4.30pm Easter-Oct, 10.30am-4.30pm Wed-Sun Nov-Mar; 🅿) holds two to four walks weekly (adult/child £7/5). Booking is advised for all.

You can also search for fossils yourself at low tide. The mudflow at **Black Ven**, just west of Charmouth, is a key site but is only accessible from Charmouth and within 1½ hours of low tide (the tourist office has tide times); be aware it's easy to get cut off. For more safety tips, see Responsible Fossil Collecting (p119).

At Lyme, a mile's walk west along **Monmouth Beach** (🅿) leads to the extraordinary **Ammonite Pavement**, where hundreds of fossilised, swirling sea creatures are embedded in layers of rock – the best displays are at low water. Landslips in the headland at the far end of the beach have also exposed some collectable fossils.

🌱 FOSSIL MUSEUMS // MEET A PIONEERING COLLECTOR – AND A PLESIOSAUR

Lyme's fame as a fossil hot spot began in 1811 when Mary Anning found the first full ichthyosaur skeleton on a beach. She discovered the first complete plesiosaur in 1824; the first British flying reptile followed a few years later. The bonneted, self-taught Miss Anning was an incredibly famous fossilist in her day and pioneered the science of modern-day palaeontology.

DORSET

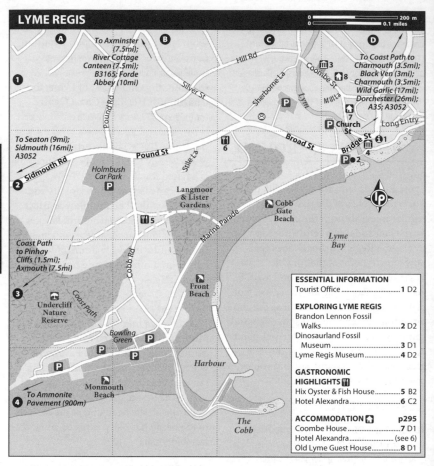

LYME REGIS

0 ——————— 200 m
0 ——————— 0.1 miles

To Axminster (7.5mi);
River Cottage Canteen (7.5mi);
B3165; Forde Abbey (10mi)

To Coast Path to Charmouth (3.5mi);
Black Ven (3mi); Charmouth (3.5mi);
Wild Garlic (17mi); Dorchester (26mi);
A35; A3052

Hill Rd
Coombe St
Silver St
Sherborne La
Lym
Mill La
Church St
Long Entry
Broad St
Bridge St

To Seaton (9mi);
Sidmouth (16mi);
A3052

Pound Rd
Sidmouth Rd
Pound St
Stile La
Holmbush Car Park

Langmoor & Lister Gardens
Cobb Gate Beach
Lyme Bay

Marine Parade
Cobb Rd

Coast Path to Pinhay Cliffs (1.5mi);
Axmouth (7.5mi)

Undercliff Nature Reserve
Coast Path
Front Beach
Bowling Green
Harbour

To Ammonite Pavement (900m)
Monmouth Beach
The Cobb

ESSENTIAL INFORMATION
Tourist Office **1** D2

EXPLORING LYME REGIS
Brandon Lennon Fossil
  Walks..**2** D2
Dinosaurland Fossil
  Museum **3** D1
Lyme Regis Museum **4** D2

GASTRONOMIC HIGHLIGHTS 🍴
Hix Oyster & Fish House..............**5** B2
Hotel Alexandra..............................**6** C2

ACCOMMODATION 🏠   p295
Coombe House **7** D1
Hotel Alexandra.........................(see **6**)
Old Lyme Guest House................**8** D1

DORSET

The site of Mary's former home is now the **Lyme Regis Museum** (☎ 01297-443370; Bridge St; adult/child £3.50/free; ⏰ 10am-5pm Mon-Sat, 11am-5pm Sun Apr-Oct, 11am-4pm Wed-Sun Nov-Mar). The museum traces her story and features her fossil-extracting hammer and other evocative prehistoric finds.

The **Dinosaurland Fossil Museum** (☎ 01297-443541; www.dinosaurland.co.uk; Coombe St; adult/child £5/4; ⏰ 10am-5pm mid-Feb–Nov) is a mini, indoor Jurassic Park, packed with the remains of belemnites, thrissops and the graceful plesiosaur. Its

timeline emphasises what an insignificant blip humans are, and lifelike dinosaur models will thrill youngsters, while the fossilised tyrannosaurus eggs and 73kg dinosaur dung will have them in raptures.

❦ **THE COBB // GAZE OUT TO SEA LIKE MERYL STREEP**
The half-dozen deeply worn steps leading onto this curling **harbour wall–cum–sea defence** make for an atmospheric climb. The Cobb's surface is uneven and sloping, and at the end a feisty

RESPONSIBLE FOSSIL COLLECTING

Responsible fossil hunting is positively encouraged by the authorities; otherwise these nuggets of prehistory would be lost to the sea. The coast though is highly unstable in places. Official advice is to observe warning signs, keep away from the cliffs, stay on public paths, check tide times, always collect on a falling tide, only pick up from the beach (never dig out from cliffs) and always leave some behind for others. Oh, and tell the experts if you find a stunner.

sea slaps up against stonework; across the harbour Lyme's brightly painted houses line the shore.

First referred to in 1294, the Cobb may be even older. It's always been susceptible to storms and has been repeatedly remodelled, most notably in 1817 resulting in the core of today's structure.

The Cobb's main movie moment is in *The French Lieutenant's Woman*, by John Fowles, when a cloaked Meryl Streep gazes out to sea from its tip. Fowles was the curator of the Lyme Regis Museum for 10 years and wrote a series of heritage walks. One details the Cobb; allowing you to tour the sea wall Fowles immortalised, with the author himself as your guide. Pick up Fowles' *Lyme Regis, Three Town Walks* (£2.50) from the tourist office.

❦ THE UNDERCLIFFE // HIKE THROUGH AN OTHER-WORLDLY LANDSCAPE OF LANDSLIPS

This wildly undulating, 304-hectare **nature reserve** just west of Lyme has been formed by massive landslides. The most famous, in 1839, saw an immense section of cliffs weighing 8 million tonnes slide partway towards the sea, creating a deep chasm. Today the reserve's slipped cliffs, fissures and ridges are smothered in dense vegetation, exposed tree roots and tangles of brambles, with the tree canopy

parting occasionally to reveal glimpses of sea.

The 8-mile path between Lyme Regis and **Axmouth** leads through the Undercliffe – an arduous, four-hour hike (note the route-side safety information). Or try walking the first mile of the reserve from the Lyme Regis end; the chalk-white bulk of **Pinhay Cliffs** makes a handy point to double back.

The Undercliff starts a mile's walk west of central Lyme Regis; follow footpath signs from **Holmbush Car Park**. Or, from beside the bowling green near the neck of the Cobb, pick up signs for the **Coast Path** (west) leading through the chalets, then follow signs for Seaton.

❦ FORDE ABBEY // INHALE THE SCENT OF WISTERIA AMID HISTORIC PLANTING

A former Cistercian monastery 10 miles north of Lyme Regis, this **manor house** (☎ 01460-221290; www.fordeabbey.co.uk; house & gardens adult/child £10.50/free; ⊗ noon-4pm Tue-Fri & Sun Apr-Oct; ℗) was built in the 12th century, updated in the 17th and has been a private home since 1649. The building boasts magnificent plasterwork, ceilings and fine tapestries, but it's the outstanding **gardens** (adult/child £8.50/free; ⊗ 10am-4.30pm) that are the main attraction: 12 hectares of lawns, ponds, shrubberies and flowerbeds; a glorious blend of

DORSET

18th-century landscaping and 19th-century trees.

GASTRONOMIC HIGHLIGHTS

❦ HIX OYSTER & FISH HOUSE // LYME REGIS ££

☎ 01297-446910; Cobb Rd; mains £8-20; ☾ lunch & dinner Wed-Sun

This super-stylish open-plan cabin is full of happy diners and views of Lyme Bay and the Cobb. The highly imaginative food dazzles too: cuttlefish and ink stew, ray with hazelnuts, and steak with baked bone marrow. There's also less grand but still great fare: fish pie, potted Morecambe Bay shrimps on toast and, of course, oysters: choose from Brownsea Island or Falmouth at £2 to £3 a pop.

❦ HOTEL ALEXANDRA // LYME REGIS £

☎ 01297-442010; Pound St; cream tea £5.20; ☾ 2.30-5.30pm

For an utterly English indulgence head to Lyme's Hotel Alexandra (p295) for afternoon tea. The kind of effortlessly classy establishment where you'd expect to find the butler Jeeves, it also has beautiful views down onto the Cobb from wide lawns. Just the place to sample trays full of sarnies (try the crab and cucumber), toasted teacakes, strawberries and cream, and thoroughly satisfying pots of tea, complete with scones, jam and Devonshire cream.

❦ WILD GARLIC // BEAMINSTER ££

☎ 01308-861446; 4 The Square; mains £12-18; ☾ lunch & dinner Wed-Sat, lunch Mon & Tue

Having wowed the judges in British TV's *MasterChef* contest, the 2009 winner Mat Follas is now impressing diners at his rustic-chic eatery. Zesty flavours include butternut squash and goat's cheese salad, pan-fried pigeon breast with beetroot, and a zingy lemon tart with rhubarb sorbet.

TRANSPORT

BUS // Bus 31 runs to Dorchester and Weymouth hourly (every two hours on Sunday). Bus X53 goes west to Exeter and east to Weymouth (six to nine daily, three on Sunday).

DRIVING TOUR: THE JURASSIC COAST

map p121
Distance: 30 miles
Duration: one day

After touring Weymouth's **historic harbour** (1; p112) pick up the A354, which sweeps onto the Isle of Portland. A winding road climbs sharply to **Tout Quarry** (2; p113); it features industrial heritage, innovative art and breathtaking views down onto 17-mile Chesil Beach – revealing the route of your day's drive. At the **Chesil Beach Centre** (3; p114) hike the ridge's sliding pebbles before an early lunch at nearby **Crab House Café** (4; p116). The B3157 leads to the thatched

LITERARY LYME

The cultural credentials of Lyme are top notch. Jane Austen visited in 1804 and the town subsequently featured in her novel *Persuasion*. Centuries later John Fowles set *The French Lieutenant's Woman* here; the film version immortalised the iconic Cobb harbour defences in movie history. Now Tracy Chevalier (author of *Girl with a Pearl Earring*) has penned *Remarkable Creatures*, the story of pioneering local fossilist Mary Anning, securing Lyme's ongoing literary legacy – a film option has already been signed.

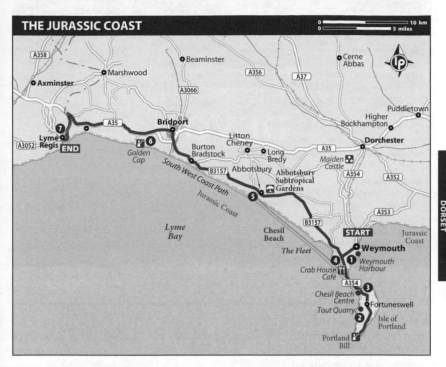

THE JURASSIC COAST

village of **Abbotsbury** (5), home to a swannery (p115) and subtropical gardens (p115). After Bridport, the coast road climbs steeply, revealing extraordinary views; drink them in at the car park at **Golden Cap** (6), the highest point on England's south coast. Look east to see your earlier viewpoint on the Isle of Portland, 25 miles away. Continue onto **Lyme Regis** (7; p117), perhaps in time for fossil hunting (p117), afternoon tea (p120) or an innovative meal at Hix (p120).

DEVON

3 PERFECT DAYS

❧ DAY 1 // A GOURMET MYSTERY TOUR

From bewitching Dartmouth, where fishing boats are landing your lunch, catch a ferry to Greenway (p152), Agatha Christie's captivating riverside home. Explorations over, cruise back to Dartmouth for a fish lunch at Seahorse (p158), or the Michelin-starred New Angel (p158) alongside. Next, meander to Sharpham Vineyard (p150) for tours, tutored tastings and snacks on a vine-view terrace. Sneak in a Totnes architectural trail (p149), then dine at Riverford Field Kitchen (p151); a pioneering eco-restaurant.

❧ DAY 2 // DARTMOOR: WILDERNESS ESCAPE & LOCAL LIFE

Hunt out shabby-chic gems in Tavistock's antiques-packed market (p170), then motor through honey-tinged moors to Princetown, for an atmospheric Hound of the Baskervilles hike (p172). Next, trace narrow lanes to appealing Widecombe-in-the-Moor for lunch in a rustic pub (p173). Then journey past wild ponies and wilderness to Jazz Age Castle Drogo (p175). For dinner, top tips are ubergourmet Gidleigh Park (p176) and 22 Mill Street (p176). Or pick up a pasty and join an unforgettable Megaliths by Moonlight guided walk (p172).

❧ DAY 3 // LANDSCAPES, GARDENS & ART

Drink in the beauty of the Royal Horticultural Society's inspirational gardens at Rosemoor (p181). Next, head to Broomhill (p180) for cutting-edge sculpture and an exquisite slow-food lunch. Take in the breathtaking expansive of 3-mile Saunton Sands, then motor round the headland to Croyde (p179) for surfing, or Mortehoe for an exhilarating hike. Finish with supper at Damien Hirst's Ilfracombe restaurant (p183), surrounded by parts of his *Pharmacy* installation and fish in formaldehyde.

EXETER

· · · · · ·

pop 111,078

Well-heeled and comfortable, Exeter is steeped in evidence of its centuries-old role as the spiritual and administrative heart of Devon. Relics include its exquisite, ancient cathedral and winding chunks of Roman wall. But the city also has a youthful vibe visible in bursts of ultramodern construction and a thriving arts scene. Down by the River Exe, the atmospheric quayside is a launch pad for explorations by bike or kayak. Add a unique movie museum, the chance to go on subterranean tours and some super-stylish places to stay and eat, and you have a relaxed but lively touring base.

ESSENTIAL INFORMATION

TOURIST INFORMATION // Exeter
Central Tourist Office (☎ 01392-665700;
www.exeterandessentialdevon.com; Paris St; ☉ 9am-
5pm Mon-Sat, 10am-4pm Sun Jul & Aug) **Quay
House Visitor Centre** (☎ 01392-271611; The
Quay; ☉ 10am-5pm Easter-Oct, 11am-4pm Sat & Sun
only Nov-Easter)

EXPLORING EXETER

❧ **EXETER CATHEDRAL //** TAKE
TIME OUT AMID EXQUISITE
ARCHITECTURE

The site of Exeter's magnificent **cathedral** (☎ 01392-255573; www.exeter-cathedral.org.
uk; The Close; adult/child £5/free; ☉ 9.30am-4.45pm
Mon-Sat) has been a religious one since
at least the 5th century. The Normans
started the current building in 1114 and
the towers visible today date from that
period. In 1270 Bishop Bronescombe
remodelled the whole building, a 90-year
process that introduced Early English
and Decorated Gothic styles.

You enter via the gorgeous **Great
West Front**. Above the door, scores
of weather-worn figures line an image
screen that was originally brightly painted. Now it forms the largest collection
of 14th-century sculpture in England.
Inside, the ceiling is mesmerising. The
longest unbroken **Gothic vaulting** in
the world, it sweeps up to meet ornate,
vividly-coloured ceiling bosses.

In the north transept, the 15th-century
Exeter Clock, in keeping with medieval
astronomy, shows the earth as a golden
ball at the centre of the universe, with
the sun, a fleur-de-lys, travelling round.
Still ticking and whirring, it chimes
on the hour. Further down, the tiny **St
James Chapel** was built to replace one
destroyed in the Blitz in 1942. Its unusual carvings include a cat, a mouse
and, oddly, a rugby player.

In the atmospheric **Refectory** (☎ 01392-
285988; ☉ 10am-4.45pm Mon-Sat) vaulted ceilings sit over trestle tables and stained-
glass windows – a place to tuck into
excellent cakes and quiches surrounded
by carved stone busts of the great, the
good and the dead.

Informative 45-minute, free **guided
cathedral tours** run at 11am and 2.30pm
Monday to Friday, 11am on Saturday.
Intensely atmospheric evensong services
are at 5.30pm Monday to Friday and
3pm on Saturday and Sunday.

❧ **TOUR HISTORIC EXETER //** DO
SOME DIY HERITAGE DETECTIVE
WORK

Exeter's past is evident in its architecture.
The Romans marched in around AD 55
and put up a 17-hectare fortress, complete
with a 2-mile russet-red **city wall**. A surprising 70% is still standing and springs
up beside shops, car parks and parks, often

(Continued on page 128)

DEVON

DEVON

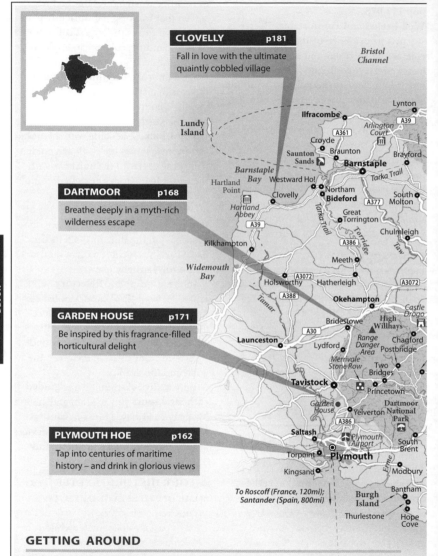

CLOVELLY   p181
Fall in love with the ultimate quaintly cobbled village

DARTMOOR   p168
Breathe deeply in a myth-rich wilderness escape

GARDEN HOUSE   p171
Be inspired by this fragrance-filled horticultural delight

PLYMOUTH HOE   p162
Tap into centuries of maritime history – and drink in glorious views

To Roscoff (France, 120mi); Santander (Spain, 800mi)

GETTING AROUND

Devon is beautiful, but big: the 3½-hour north–south drive is the same mileage as London to Bristol. Summer brings jams to key routes, such as the M5 and A361 around Braunton. You can easily tour cities, towns and main resorts without wheels. Car-free explorations off the beaten track are much harder–in reality most people drive; expect steep Dartmoor roads and winding country lanes. And to avoid ever-narrowing farm tracks, don't follow the satnav too blindly.

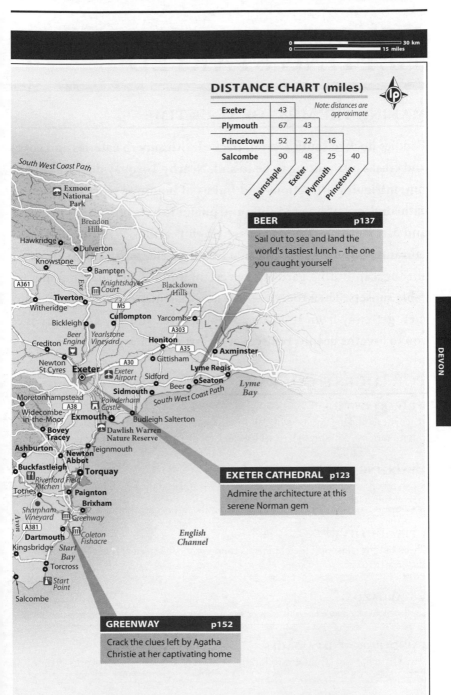

0 ⊢――――――――――――――⊣ 30 km
0 ⊢――――――――――――――⊣ 15 miles

DISTANCE CHART (miles)

Exeter	43	Note: distances are approximate		
Plymouth	67	43		
Princetown	52	22	16	
Salcombe	90	48	25	40
	Barnstaple	Exeter	Plymouth	Princetown

South West Coast Path

Exmoor National Park

Brendon Hills

Hawkridge

Dulverton

Knowstone

Bampton

A361

Knightshayes Court

Tiverton

Witheridge

Exe

Blackdown Hills

M5

Bickleigh

Cullompton

Yarcombe

Beer Engine

Crediton

Yearlstone Vineyard

Honiton

A303

A35

Axminster

Newton St Cyres

A30

Gittisham

Lyme Regis

Exeter

Exeter Airport

Sidford

Seaton

Lyme Bay

Moretonhampstead

Sidmouth

Beer

South West Coast Path

A38

Powderham Castle

Widecombe-in-the-Moor

Exmouth

Budleigh Salterton

Bovey Tracey

Dawlish Warren Nature Reserve

Ashburton

Newton Abbot

Teignmouth

Buckfastleigh

Riverford Field Kitchen

Torquay

Totnes

Paignton

Sharpham Vineyard

Greenway

Brixham

Avon

A381

Coleton Fishacre

English Channel

Dartmouth

Kingsbridge

Start Bay

Torcross

Start Point

Salcombe

BEER   p137

Sail out to sea and land the world's tastiest lunch – the one you caught yourself

EXETER CATHEDRAL   p123

Admire the architecture at this serene Norman gem

GREENWAY   p152

Crack the clues left by Agatha Christie at her captivating home

DEVON

DEVON GETTING STARTED

MAKING THE MOST OF YOUR TIME

Foodies flock to south Devon, packed with superb eateries and coves and creeks just waiting to be found. Nearby Torquay delivers seaside fun, intriguing attractions and bursts of boutique-chic. For a serene cathedral, crumbling red cliffs and quaint fishing ports head to Exeter and east Devon – they also boast Hugh Fearnley-Whittingstall's restaurants and an inky sky full of stars. In quieter north Devon discover surfing, captivating gardens, sweeps of untouched sands and memorable sunsets. Then there's wilderness Dartmoor: the ultimate gourmet, get-away-from-it-all escape. Wherever you go, Devon nudges you to breathe deeply, rediscover, reinvent, recharge and revive.

TOP TOURS & COURSES

✿ RIVER COTTAGE
Learn bread making, meat curing, allotment gardening and fish skills on the courses at Hugh Fearnley-Whittingstall's east Devon headquarters (p139).

✿ PAINTING
Brush up on watercolour techniques (per day £28) amid the bewitching blooms and bracts at the Garden House (p171).

✿ PLYMOUTH GIN
Check out the stills, sniff the botanicals then sample the spirit at this 18th-century distillery (p165).

✿ STARGAZING
See the night sky on a telescopic tour of the heavens in an east Devon observatory (p137).

✿ UNDERGROUND PASSAGES
Don a hard hat and scramble around the tunnels of a medieval waterworks (p129).

GETTING AWAY FROM IT ALL

* **Dartmoor** In this 368-sq-mile wilderness, there's always room to dodge the summertime crowds – especially in the remote higher moor around Okehampton (p174).

* **Saunton Sands** This 3-mile beach is backed by 2000 acres of dunes, the biggest network in the UK. Expect vivid wildflower displays and very few people (p179).

* **Exeter Cathedral** Step away from the shoppers, into a cool, hushed interior and gaze up at a ceiling with the longest unbroken Gothic vaulting in the world (p123).

* **The River Dart** Explore this enchanting waterway by boat or on foot – and discover your very own special, secret spot beside the creek (p155).

ADVANCE PLANNING

* **Greenway** (p152) Agatha Christie's riverside house and garden is proving hugely popular. By far the best way to arrive is by boat, but if you do have to drive, book one of the few car-parking spaces well in advance.

* **Restaurants** At peak times Devon's most popular eateries fill up fast. Booking is advised at weekends year round and any time in July and August.

* **Activities** From surfing and canoeing to painting and cooking – Devon has plenty of tempting things to do. But in the height of summer demand can outstrip supply – book to be sure.

TOP EATING EXPERIENCES

RIVERFORD FIELD KITCHEN
Fabulous food, plucked from the furrows in front of you (p151).

RIVER COTTAGE
Fine dining or canteen-style fare from Hugh Fearnley-Whittingstall (p139).

SHARPHAM VINEYARD
Tour the vines; sample the wines (p150).

BRIMPTS FARM
Quintessential Devon cream tea (p174).

ROOM IN THE ELEPHANT
Torquay's innovative Michelin-starred eatery (p147).

DEVON

RESOURCES

* **Dartmoor** (www.dartmoor.co.uk) In-depth info on the national park

* **English Riviera** (www.englishriviera.co.uk) The lowdown on Torquay, Paignton and Brixham

* **Essential Exeter** (www.exeterandessentialdevon.com) Information for Exeter and east Devon

* **Stay North Devon** (www.staynorthdevon.co.uk) North Devon database

* **Visit Devon** (www.visitdevon.co.uk) Devon's official visitor website

* **Visit South Devon** (www.visitsouthdevon.co.uk) Info for the south of the county

(Continued from page 123)

accompanied by information panels. Pick up a free **City Wall Trail** leaflet at the tourist office. Alternatively, track down sections yourself. **Rougemont** and **Northernhay Gardens** are good places to hunt for sub-

stantial remnants; there's also clear evidence of where later defences, particularly Civil War ones, have been built on top.

At the end of nearby **Castle St**, look out for the tree-fringed ruins of the city's 11th-century **castle**. It was built by the Normans after an 18-day siege in 1068,

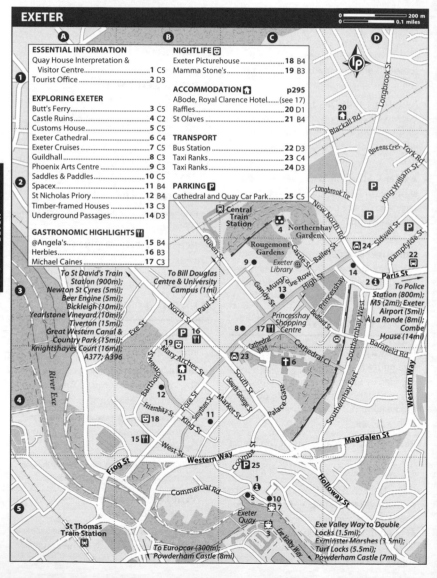

EXETER

0 ────── 200 m
0 ────── 0.1 miles

ESSENTIAL INFORMATION
Quay House Interpretation &
  Visitor Centre.................................**1** C5
Tourist Office **2** D3

EXPLORING EXETER
Butt's Ferry.......................................**3** C5
Castle Ruins......................................**4** C2
Customs House................................**5** C5
Exeter Cathedral.............................**6** C4
Exeter Cruises..................................**7** C5
Guildhall..**8** C3
Phoenix Arts Centre.......................**9** C3
Saddles & Paddles........................**10** C5
Spacex..**11** B4
St Nicholas Priory..........................**12** B4
Timber-framed Houses.................**13** C3
Underground Passages..................**14** D3

GASTRONOMIC HIGHLIGHTS
@Angela's..**15** B4
Herbies..**16** B3
Michael Caines...............................**17** C3

NIGHTLIFE
Exeter Picturehouse.......................**18** B4
Mamma Stone's...............................**19** B3

ACCOMMODATION   p295
ABode, Royal Clarence Hotel.....(see 17)
Raffles...**20** D1
St Olaves..**21** B4

TRANSPORT
Bus Station......................................**22** D3
Taxi Ranks..**23** C4
Taxi Ranks..**24** D3

PARKING
Cathedral and Quay Car Park.......**25** C5

when the city refused to surrender to William the Conqueror. The gatehouse has a plaque commemorating three Devon women who were tried here for **witchcraft** in 1685, becoming the last in the country to be hanged for the crime.

Near the junction with Cathedral Close, Exeter's High St has some fine timber-framed houses, dating from its Tudor woollen boom. Nearby the medieval **Guildhall** (☎ 01392-665500; High St; admission free) dates in part from the 1330s and features an intricately carved oak door, ornate barrel roof and crests of dignitaries. The oldest municipal building still in use in the country, the mayor still sits in the huge thronelike chair at the end. Opening hours depend on civic functions.

Around 300m southeast, just off **Fore St**, the 900-year-old **St Nicholas Priory** (☎ 01392-665858; Mint Lane; adult/child £2/free; ☺ 10am-5pm Mon-Sat school holidays) is built out of beautiful russet stone and vividly evokes life inside a late-Elizabethan town house, with brightly coloured furnishings and ornate plaster ceilings.

During Exeter's Blitz of 1942, in just one night 156 people died and more than 12 hectares of the city were flattened; even the cathedral took a direct hit. The postwar years saw an ambitious rebuild in red brick and cream stone; look out for its clean lines above the shopfronts in the **High St** between Cathedral Close and **Bedford St**. Nearby, the attention-grabbing £220 million **Princesshay Shopping Centre** was built in 2007. Much of it is shimmering glass and steel; some sections also echo the neighbouring 1940s to 1950s designs.

❧ UNDERGROUND PASSAGES // CLAMBER ROUND SOME INTRIGUING ANCIENT WATERWORKS

Prepare to crouch down, don a hard hat and even get spooked in what is the only system of its kind open to the public in the country. These medieval, vaulted **tunnels** (☎ 01392-665887; Paris St; adult/child £5/3.50; ☺ 9.30am-5.30pm Mon-Sat Jun-Sep, 11.30am-4pm Tue-Sun Oct-May) were built to house pipes bringing fresh drinking water from local springs into the city. The pipes often sprang leaks and, unlike modern utility companies, the authorities opted to have permanent access for repairs, rather than dig up the streets each time – genius.

Entertaining guides lead groups through part of this vast, dank network of passages, telling tales of ghosts, the Civil War, escape routes, the Blitz and cholera outbreaks. The hard hat comes in handy when navigating the rock arches and narrow bends; one section involves a real bent-knees scramble; those who are too big (or too unwilling) can take an easier detour.

The last tour is an hour before closing. The passages get very busy; it's best to turn up, book a tour, then come back at the appointed time.

❧ BILL DOUGLAS CENTRE // CHART FILM HISTORY, FROM MAGIC LANTERNS TO MARILYN

A delightful homage to film and fun, this **movie museum** (☎ 01392-264321; www.bill douglas.org; Old Library, Prince of Wales Rd; admission free; ☺ 10am-5pm Mon-Fri) is a lively celebration of all things celluloid. Collections include 18th-century magic lanterns, zograscopes, shadow theatres and a hand-held panorama reel of George IV's coronation. You even get to glue an eye to a saucy 'what the butler saw' machine.

Movie **memorabilia** includes programs, posters, sheet music, games and toys – highlights include Charlie Chaplin bottle stoppers, Ginger Rogers playing cards and *Star Wars* merchandise. Alongside, thought-provoking displays cover a wealth of subjects ranging from Disneymania to Cinema as Institution and the Cult of Celebrity.

The Bill Douglas Centre is a 15-minute walk northwest from the city centre, on the University of Exeter campus.

❧ GHOST & MURDER TOURS // GET SPOOKED ON A NIGHT-TIME TRAIL
Exeter claims to be one of the most haunted cities in England and these 1½-hour, free **guided walks** whisk you around locations laced with tales of murder, treachery and ghouls. The city's history emerges in engaging style, including everything from the Romans, religion and riots to plague and trade, and crime and punishment.

The walks, by the **Red Coat Guides** (☎ 01392-265203), leave from outside the Royal Clarence Hotel on **Cathedral Yard** at 7pm. Ghost Tours run on Tuesday and Thursday (Tuesday only between November and March); Murder & Mayhem Tours run on Wednesday (April to October only). A range of day-time tours is also available.

❧ EXETER QUAY // CHILL-OUT IN A HISTORIC WATERSIDE SETTING
On fine sunny days the people of Exeter head to the **quay** where converted warehouses line the River Exe and cobbled paths leads between **antiques markets**, **quirky shops**, **restaurants** and **pubs**; making an ideal place for a few alfresco drinks and a spot of people-watching.

The quay is rich in evidence of Exeter's woollen processing and export business which, by the 18th century, had made the city the third most important trade centre in the country. Look out for the stately 17th-century, red-brick **Customs House** (complete with cannons) and the gabled 18th-century **Wharfinger's House**; home to the man who collected the wharfing fees.

The nearby **Quay House** was built in 1680 as a wool store and today houses the **Quay House Visitor Centre** (☎ 01392-271611; The Quay; 10am-5pm Easter-Oct, 11am-4pm Sat & Sun only Nov-Easter). Inside are wool trade artefacts, including 'tillet blocks'; carved wooden tiles used by merchants to stamp their crests onto fabric – one shows a weaver sitting at a loom. The centre also stocks leaflets detailing other stops on **Exeter's Woollen Trail**.

There are more shops and cafes on south side of the River Exe. The bathtub-like **Butt's Ferry** (The Quay; adult/child 20/10p; 11am-5pm Easter-Oct) is propelled across by a ferryman pulling on a wire. Technically it's a floating bridge, one of only a handful in the country.

Exeter Quay has a bustling **Potter's Market** in early July and **Dragon Boat Races** several times a summer. You can also hire bikes and kayaks (see p130).

❧ EXPLORE EXETER'S WATERWAYS // TRACE TRAILS FROM THE CITY TO THE SEA
The foot and cycle paths that head southeast from Exeter Quay join the **Exe Valley Way**, shadowing both Exeter Canal and an ever-broadening river towards the sea, around 10 miles away. They make for good **biking**, **hiking** and **kayak** trips, passing several good **pubs**, a **nature reserve** and a **stately home**. The first three miles are a blend of heritage city, countryside and light industrial landscape; the later sections are more rural.

The **Quay Visitor Centre** (☎ 01392-271611; The Quay; 10am-5pm Easter-Oct, 11am-4pm Sat & Sun only Nov-Easter) stocks Exe Valley Way leaflets. About 1½ miles south from Exeter Quay, the laid-back **Double Locks** (☎ 01392-256947; Canal Banks; mains £9; lunch & dinner) pub features scarred floorboards, excellent ale and battered board games;

as well as a waterside terrace and better-than-average bar food.

The Royal Society for the Protection of Birds' (RSPB) **Exminster Marshes nature reserve** starts about two miles further on, around two miles inside the reserve, the waterside **Turf Locks Hotel** (☎01392-833128; mains £9; ⊗ lunch & dinner Mon-Sat, lunch Sun Easter-Oct) clings to a slither of land; an idyllic setting to enjoy good grub and summer barbecues. From there a rougher trail connects with a path to appealing **Powderham Castle** (p135). You can also navigate much of the above route by **kayak**, an enjoyable, nontidal paddle past pubs.

The boats of **Exeter Cruises** (☎07984 368442; The Quay; adult/child return £5/3; ⊗ 11.30-4.30pm, daily Jun-Aug, weekends only Easter-May & Sep-Oct) shuttle down the waterway from Exeter Quay to the Double Locks pub. Check to see if its connecting boat, the White Heather, is still ferrying passengers the extra four miles to the Turf Locks Hotel.

Saddles & Paddles (☎01392-424241; www.sadpad.com; 4 Kings Wharf, The Quay; ⊗ 9.30am-5.30pm), on Exeter Quay, rents out bikes (adult per hour/day £6/15, child per hour/day £5/12) and kayaks and canoes (kayaks per hour/day £7/25, open canoe per hour/day £15/35).

❧ **GALLERIES // CATCH SOME CUTTING-EDGE CONTEMPORARY ART**
Exeter's buoyant visual arts scene includes **Spacex** (☎01392-431786; www.spacex.org.uk; 45 Preston St; admission free; ⊗ 10am-5pm Tue-Sat), which has a reputation for consistently strong, accessible, contemporary art exhibitions; it also stages regular free artists' talks. **Exeter Phoenix** (☎01392-667080; www.exeterphoenix.org.uk; Bradninch Pl, Gandy St; admission free; ⊗ 10am-5pm Mon-Sat 11.30-5pm) is a buzzing arts centre with a cinema, performance space, four galleries and a cool cafe-bar.

GASTRONOMIC HIGHLIGHTS

❧ **@ANGELA'S ££**
☎01392-499038; 38 New Bridge St; 3-course lunch £18, dinner mains £17; ⊗ dinner plus prebooked lunch Wed-Sat
Dedication to sourcing local ingredients sometimes sees the chef at this smart bistro rising before dawn to bag the best fish at Brixham Market; his Sea Bass with caramelised ginger is worth the trip alone. The lamb and beef has grazed Devon fields, while local venison is made memorable by a rich redcurrant and chocolate sauce.

❧ **HERBIES £**
☎01392-258473; 15 North St; mains £5-9; ⊗ lunch Mon-Sat, dinner Tue-Sat
Cosy and gently groovy, Herbies has been cheerfully feeding Exeter's vegetarians for more than 20 years. Tuck into delicious butterbean and vegetable pie, Moroccan tagine, cashew nut loaf or broad bean, thyme and squash risotto. The grilled vegetable salads are a work of art and they take good culinary care of vegans too.

❧ **MICHAEL CAINES £££**
☎01392-223638; Cathedral Yard; mains £25; ⊗ breakfast, lunch & dinner
This restaurant's eponymous chef has two Michelin stars at his other Devon eatery (Gidleigh Park; p176), and that style filters through here too; expect a complex fusion of Westcountry ingredients and full-bodied French flavours. Try the cauliflower and truffle soup with roasted scallops, or the slow-roast beef with celeriac purée and Madeira sauce. The set lunches are a bargain (per two/three courses £15/20), while the seven-course tasting menu (£65) really is one to linger over.

NIGHTLIFE

♥ MAMA STONE'S

www.mamastones.com; 1 Mary Arches St; ⏰ 8pm-midnight, 9pm-2am when bands play

Ubercool venue showcasing everything from acoustic sets to pop, folk and jam nights. Mama Stone's daughter, Joss (yes, *the* Joss Stone) plays sometimes too.

♥ EXETER PICTUREHOUSE

www.picture houses.co.uk; 51 Bartholomew St

An intimate, independent cinema, screening mainstream and art-house movies.

TRANSPORT

TO/FROM THE AIRPORT

Exeter International Airport (EXT; ☎ 01392-367433; www.exeter-airport.co.uk) is 5 miles east of the city. Regular UK and European flights include those to Belfast, Glasgow, Leeds-Bradford, Manchester, Newcastle and the Isles of Scilly. A key operator is **FlyBe** (☎ 0871 5226100; www.flybe.com). Buses 56 and 379 run from the bus station and Exeter St David's train station to Exeter airport (20 to 30 minutes, hourly until 6pm).

GETTING AROUND

BIKE // For bike hire, see p130.

BUS // Key routes from Exeter include: bus X9 to Bude (five Monday to Saturday) via Okehampton; bus 359 to Moretonhampstead (two hourly Monday to Friday); bus 82, the Transmoor Link (two on Sunday only, late May to September), to Plymouth via Moretonhampstead, Postbridge, Princetown and Yelverton; bus X53 (the Jurassic Coastlinx) to Weymouth or Poole (four to eight daily) via Beer and Lyme Regis and bus 52 to Sidmouth (one to three hourly).

CAR // Exeter is at the southern end of the M5 motorway; junctions 29 and 30 provide useful, if congested routes into the city. Most major car-hire firms have branches in the city or at the airport. Much of the centre of Exeter is off-limits to cars, but not buses.

PARKING // The Cathedral and Quay car park often has places when others are full. Park-and-ride buses (adult/child £2/1.30) run from Sowton (near M5, junction 30), Matford and Honiton Rd (near M5, junction 29) every 10 minutes, Monday to Saturday.

TAXI // Taxi ranks are at St David's train station and on the high street. Other options include **Capital Taxis** (☎ 01392-758472), **Club Cars** (☎ 01392-341615) and **Gemini** (☎ 01392-342152).

TRAIN // Connections to Exeter's St David's train station include hourly services to London Paddington (£45, 2½ hours) and Penzance (£17, three hours), half-hourly services to Bristol (£18, 1¼ hours) and regular trains to Torquay (£6, 45 minutes), via Teignmouth and Dawlish. The picturesque Tarka Line connects Exeter Central with Barnstaple (£8, 1¼ hours, hourly Monday to Saturday, four to six on Sunday), trains also run south to Exmouth (£4, hourly, 40 minutes).

ACCOMMODATION

Location and season dictate accommodation availability in Devon. Resorts and cities such as Torquay, Plymouth and Exeter feature a host of options; elsewhere there are fewer places to stay. Booking is advisable everywhere in high season (Easter, July and August).

We have in-depth reviews in our Accommodation chapter (p287), but here are some highlights:

★ **ABode** (p295) Gorgeously Georgian hotel with Exeter Cathedral views

★ **Seabreeze** (p298) Fall asleep to the sound of the south Devon waves

★ **Burgh Island** (p299) Indulge in film-star luxury in an Art Deco bolt-hole

★ **22 Mill Street** (p300) A boutique oasis in a quaint Dartmoor town

★ **Westwood** (p300) A kooky, colourful, ultracool north Devon B&B

DEVON

AROUND EXETER

· · · · · ·

North of Exeter, the red hills of Devon's rural heartland take over. This is one of the least touristy parts of the county where agriculture still holds sway; the main town, Tiverton, is traditional and the pubs are unreconstructed. As a result it provides a genuine insight into life in Devon's farming communities. Thatched villages such as Bickleigh snuggle in a hilly, pastoral landscape where vivid green and yellow fields are interspersed with flashes of bright red soil. The superb stately homes at Powderham Castle and Knightshayes Court are also within easy reach, as are a microbrewery, a vineyard, and horse-drawn canal trips.

ESSENTIAL INFORMATION

TOURIST INFORMATION // Tiverton Tourist Office (☎ 01884-255827; Phoenix Lane; ⏰ 9.15am-4.30pm Mon-Fri, 9.15am-3.30pm Sat)

EXPLORING AROUND EXETER

❦ **BEER ENGINE //** TAKE THE TRAIN TO AN ATMOSPHERIC MICROBREWERY
A dream-come-true for ale aficionados: this **pub** (☎ 01392-851282; www.thebeerengine. co.uk; Newton St Cyres; mains £10; ⏰ lunch & dinner) brews its own beer. What's more it's right next to a train station that's a 15-minute train trip from Exeter, so you can go car-free. The decor is varnished floorboards, leather settles and exposed red brick, but the best bit is downstairs: the gleaming stainless-steel tubs and tubes of the fermenting process. The building's past as a railway hotel inspires the brews' names: the fruity Rail Ale (3.8% abv), sharp and sweet Piston Bitter (4.3% abv) and the well-rounded Sleeper Heavy (5.4% abv). Flavoursome food includes Devon ham matured in Dragon's Tears cider, a range of ploughman's made with local Quickes cheddar and steak and Sleeper Ale pie.

Newton St Cyres is on the A377, 5 miles north of Exeter. Double-check train times, but services often chug into the village in time for supper; the one that tends to leave for Exeter just after 11pm is very handy indeed.

❦ **YEARLSTONE VINEYARD //** SAVOUR THE FLAVOURS AT DEVON'S OLDEST WINERY
The owners proudly point out this **vineyard** (☎ 01884 855700; Bickleigh; admission £3; ⏰ 11am-4pm Wed-Sun Easter-Dec; Ⓟ) is on the same latitude as the Moselle Valley. It's certainly as picturesque, set amid an amphitheatre of deeply wooded, sharply sloping hills above a rushing River Exe. It produces a range of white, red, rosé and sparkling wines that regularly scoop awards. Highlights include the pale gold Vintage Brut (£17), the light and fruity red Yearlstone No 4 (£8) and the tangy, dry white Yearlstone No 1 (£7). Tours range from guide-yourself affairs (£3.50), to detailed explorations of the winemaking process (£45). All involve a tutored tasting.

The **cafe** (⏰ 11am-4pm Wed-Sun Easter-Dec) rustles up seasonal, simple, tasty food best enjoyed on the terrace with views down the Exe Valley. Try the antipasti (£6), smoked mackerel pâté (£6) or a selection of Westcountry cheese, complete with oatcakes and an apple (£4).

Yearlstone is on the outskirts of the village of **Bickleigh**, 10 miles north of Exeter on the A396; for buses see p135.

DEVON

❦ BICKLEIGH // DISCOVER A PICTURE-PERFECT THATCHED VILLAGE

For a dollop of chocolate-box-pretty **thatched cottages**, it's hard to top Bickleigh. The buildings cluster beside a sweeping 16th-century bridge, with another clump of picturesque buildings tucked away just east of the main road.

The village bridge is famous (well, locally famous) as being Paul Simon's inspiration for *Bridge Over Troubled Water* – he visited the area in the 1960s. Comments from writing partner Art Garfunkel cast doubt on the tale, but it's still a popular claim-to-fame; ask a villager and see what answer you get.

Alongside the bridge, the **Fisherman's Cot** (☎ 01884-855237; Bickleigh; ☙ lunch & dinner) is an immense thatched pub with ornate gables, a gazebo and a large riverside beer garden; a firm favourite with locals for a pint or cream tea.

The cafe-cum-craft centre at **Bickleigh Mill** (☎ 01884-855419; www.bickleighmill.com; admission free; ☙ 10am-5.30pm Mon-Wed & Sun, to 9.30pm Thu-Sat), alongside, houses a working 18th-century water wheel, while train buffs will enjoy chugging around the 2- and 7¼-gauge tracks of the neighbouring **Devon Railway Centre** (☎ 01884-855671; www.devonrailwaycentre.co.uk; adult/child £6.40/5.10; ☙ 10.30am-5pm mid-May–early Sep).

Bickleigh is on the A396, 10 miles north of Exeter. For buses see p135.

❦ GREAT WESTERN CANAL // GLIDE ALONG ON THE WESTCOUNTRY'S LAST HORSE-DRAWN BARGE

High on a hill above Tiverton, this **canal** (☎ 01884-254072; Canal Hill, Tiverton; ☙ open access; ℗) provides an intriguing insight into life on man-made inland waterways. Built in 1814, it was originally intended to link up with a canal network stretching from Bristol to the English Channel.

Reality fell short of that ambition, but tub boats carrying limestone from local quarries worked this waterway for 130 years before the network declined. This 11-mile stretch is all that's left.

Canalside displays chart its history; there's also a **floating cafe-bar** and the chance to hire a **row boat** (one/four hours £10/25) or **Canadian canoe** (one/four hours £15/30). Or settle back and travel along on a brightly painted **horse-drawn barge** (☎ 01884-253345; www.horseboat. co.uk; adult/child from £8.50/6). These trips proceed under bridges and past fields and woods at a serene pace – the only sounds are the gurgling of the water and the clip-clop of the shire horses' hooves. The canal sits in a **nature reserve**; look out for moorhens, kingfishers, little grebes and roe deer. There are normally one to two sailings daily between May and September; booking is required.

The **Great Western Canal and Country Park** is on the outskirts of **Tiverton**. Tiverton is 15 miles north of Exeter on the A396; for public transport, see p135.

❦ KNIGHTSHAYES COURT // TAKE IN A DIZZYING ARRAY OF ARCHITECTURAL STYLES

This Victorian **country house** (NT; ☎ 01884-254665; Bolham; adult/child £7.80/3.90; ☙ 11am-5pm Sat-Thu mid-Mar–Oct) was designed by the eccentric architect William Burges for the Tiverton MP John Heathcoat Mallory in 1869. Burges' obsession with the Middle Ages resulted in a plethora of stone curlicues, ornate mantles and carved figurines. There's lavish Victorian decoration too; the smoking and billiard rooms in particular have the cosy feel of a gentlemen's club.

The **gardens** feature rare trees and shrubs, a waterlily pool, imposing topiary and terraces with extensive views. The fully restored **kitchen garden** provides inspiration for vegetable growers everywhere, and the organic ingredients for the property's **cafe**.

Knightshayes is around a mile east of Tiverton at **Bolham**; bus 398 runs to Bolham from Tiverton (10 minutes, six to eight daily Monday to Saturday).

🍃 POWDERHAM CASTLE // NOSE AROUND AN APPEALING ARISTOCRATIC HOME

Somehow this crenellated **manor house** (☎ 01626-890243; www.powderham.co.uk; adult/child £9.50/7.50; ⏰ 11am-4.30pm Sun-Fri Apr-Oct) manages to be both stately and homely. The historic seat of the Earl of Devon, it was built in 1391, damaged in the Civil War and remodelled in the Victorian era, and today has some of the best preserved Stuart and Regency furniture around.

There's a fine wood-panelled **great hall**, a glimpse of life 'below stairs' in the **Victorian kitchen**, and parkland with 650 **deer**. There are also pot-bellied pigs, sheep, goats and chickens in the old **walled garden**. The Earl and Countess of Devon are still resident and, despite the grandeur of Powderham, for delightful fleeting moments it feels like you're actually wandering through someone's sitting room.

Powderham is on the River Exe near Kenton, 8 miles south of Exeter. Bus 2 runs from Exeter (30 minutes, every 20 minutes Monday to Friday), or walk or cycle along the canal and river paths (see p130).

TRANSPORT

BUS // Buses 55/55A/55B run from Exeter to Bickleigh (25 minutes, hourly Monday to Saturday, eight on Sundays) and on to Tiverton (12 minutes). Bus 50 shuttles hourly from Exeter to Newton St Cyres (10 minutes).

TRAIN // Tiverton Parkway station is on the mainline London Paddington–Penzance route, and has hourly connections to Exeter (15 minutes). The station is 10 miles from Tiverton; hourly buses (20 minutes) connect the two.

EAST DEVON
· · · · · ·

East of Exeter, Devon's red-soil fields and even redder cliffs undulate off towards Dorset. To the south, the faded resort of Exmouth sits on the edge of the Exe estuary, a springboard for Jurassic Coast cruises and adrenaline sports. Further east Regency Sidmouth delivers old-world seaside charm, stargazing and an irresistible equine sanctuary. Next up, the captivating village of Beer offers an insight into the fishing industry, the chance to land your own lunch and an ancient network of caves to explore. Meanwhile inland are the River Cottage eateries of TV chef Hugh Fearnley-Whittingstall – waiting to cook you a meal to remember.

ESSENTIAL INFORMATION

TOURIST INFORMATION // Exmouth Tourist Office (☎ 01395-222299; www.exmouth-guide.co.uk; Alexandria Tce, Manor Gardens; ⏰ 10am-5pm Mon-Sat Easter-Sep, 10am-2pm Mon-

TOP FIVE

GARDENS & HISTORIC HOMES

★ **Greenway** (p152) Agatha Christie's holiday home, fringed by beguiling gardens

★ **Coleton Fishacre** (p153) Subtropical planting and an Art Deco house

★ **Garden House** (p171) Devon's best-kept gardening secret

★ **RHS Rosemoor** (p181) Sixty-five acres of inspiration from the Royal Horticultural Society

★ **Hartland Abbey** (p183) A 12th-century gem of a historic home

Sat Oct-Easter) **Sidmouth Tourist Office**
(☎ 01395-516441; www.visitsidmouth.co.uk; Ham
Lane; ⊗ 10am-4pm or 5pm Mon-Sat, 10am-1pm Sun
Mar-Oct, 10am-1.30pm Mon-Sat Nov-Feb)

EXPLORING EAST DEVON

❦ À LA RONDE // DISCOVER THE ECLECTIC COLLECTIONS OF TWO GEORGIAN SPINSTERS
This delightfully quirky 16-sided **cottage** (NT; ☎ 01395-265514; Summer Lane, Exmouth; adult/child £6.70/3.40; ⊗ 11am-5pm Fri-Wed Jul & Aug, 11am-5pm Sat-Wed mid-Mar–Jun & Sep-Oct) is a DIY job with a difference. It was built in 1796 for two spinster cousins to house a mass of curiosities acquired on a 10-year European grand tour. Its glass alcoves, low lintels and tiny doorways mean it's like clambering through a doll's house. Hunt out the cousins' own work: intricate paper cuts, a delicate feather frieze in the drawing room and the gallery plastered with a thousand seashells on the top floor – in a fabulous collision of old and new, this can only be seen via remote-control CCTV from the butler's pantry. The house is two miles north of Exmouth on the A376; bus 57 (every 30 minutes) runs close by.

❦ KITE & WINDSURF // HARNESS THE WIND; RIDE THE WAVES
The well-worn Georgian terraces at **Exmouth** line the wide mouth of the River Exe, an exposed position that draws fleets of windsurfers and kitesurfers who whip across the water on gusty days. A series of sandbanks ensures a wealth of shallow, flat-water areas that are ideal to learn in. **Edge** (☎ 01395-222551; www.edgewatersports.com; 3 Royal Ave) runs lessons in kitesurfing (per half/one/two days £85/130/230) and windsurfing (per one/two days £60/125) from its base near the train station.

❦ CRUISE THE JURASSIC COAST // SAIL 250 MILLION YEARS BACK IN TIME
Exmouth is the beginning, or the end, of the **Jurassic Coast** (see p115), a 95-mile shoreline awarded Unesco World Heritage site status because of its geological importance. The rusty **red cliffs** that stretch east from Exmouth were formed in the desert conditions of the Triassic period, 250 million years ago, making them the oldest on the coast. Erosion has sculpted this dramatic shoreline into a multitude of coves, headlands and rock columns, best seen from the **Stuart Line** (☎ 01395-222144; www.stuartlinecruises.co.uk; adult/child 2-3hr cruise £8/6; ⊗ 1 or 2 per week late May-Oct) cruises that leave from **Exmouth Marina**. Highlights include the impressive string of rust-red sea stacks that emerge from cliffs at Ladram Bay; the chance of dolphin sightings adds to the appeal.

❦ SIDMOUTH'S ESPLANADE // PROMENADE ALONG AN ARCHITECTURE-RICH, REGENCY SEAFRONT
The select resort of **Sidmouth** is the English seaside at its most stately, serene and salubrious. Here it's not so much kiss-me-quick as have a nap before a stroll. Hundreds of **listed buildings** line up elegantly behind its Esplanade; freshly painted pillars support bright-white balconies; well-tended flowers tumble from window boxes.

The town's tourist office (see p135) sells *Historic Sidmouth* (£2), a guide to the resort's 30 **blue plaques**. Or just investigate ones that catch your eye; the **Esplanade** is a good hunting ground. At the far west end **Clifton Place** is a strip of pretty, largely Georgian cottages set right beside the sea; look out for the Swiss-chalet style **Beacon Cottage** (1840) with its pointed black-framed windows, long verandas and crowning of thatch.

Heading east, a crenellated red-stone gateway signals the **Belmont Hotel**; further down the all-cream **Riviera Hotel** (1820) has a grand bowed entrance, while the vast lemon-yellow **Kingswood Hotel** (c 1890s) was formerly the location of the hot and cold brine baths. The white and black **Beach House** was built in 1790 and revamped in Gothic style in 1826; it was a fashionable meeting spot for the gentry.

Towards the Esplanade's east end is the **Royal York and Faulkner** (1810), with its blue and white pillars and long veranda. Sidmouth's first purpose-built hotel; notable guests have included Edward VII when he was Prince of Wales.

☙ STARGAZING // SEE THE NIGHT SKY AS NEVER BEFORE

Because of relatively low light pollution, high cliffs and an expanse of sea, east Devon is prime stargazing territory. Any of the more remote coastal spots will reveal good displays, but for truly mesmerising views spend an evening at the **Norman Lockyer Observatory** (☎ 01395-512096; www.normanlockyer.org; Salcombe Hill Rd, Sidmouth; adult/child £5/2.50; ⊙ hr vary), where the high-powered telescopes reveal astonishing clusters of constellations. Evening openings are timed to coincide with celestial events, perhaps Saturn at opposition, Mercury and Venus or the Perseid meteor shower. Book your place then hope for clear skies. The observatory is a few minutes' drive from the centre of Sidmouth.

☙ DONKEY SANCTUARY // MEET HUNDREDS OF ADORABLE RESCUED DONKEYS

This is an attraction chock-full of feel-good factor. The **sanctuary** (☎ 01395-578222; www.thedonkeysanctury.org.uk; Sidmouth; admission free; ⊙ 9am-dusk) is home to around 400 donkeys, some rescued from mistreatment or neglect, others retired from working the beaches.

Walkways pass fields full of the creatures happily grazing, trotting round and rolling in the grass. In the main yard you can mingle freely with animals specially chosen for their fondness of people. Signs alongside explain donkey body language (head down is resting; ears up is interested; a swishing tail means don't come any closer), while collars bearing names and ages allow you to know who you've just met. Because donkeys bond with each other, if they come into the sanctuary together they're kept together for life: when one goes into the veterinary hospital, their friends go in to keep them company too.

The sanctuary is a few miles northeast of Sidmouth, on the A3052.

☙ BEER // SAVOUR THE ATMOSPHERE OF AN ANCIENT FISHING VILLAGE

Tucked into a deep fissure of rock, **Beer** manages to be both thoroughly picturesque and a proper, working fishing village (not an imitation of one) at the same time. Multicoloured, snub-nosed boats line its steeply sloping pebble **beach**; piles of crab and lobster pots lie scattered around.

Boats are hauled from the sea by winches and the cables criss-cross the shore. The process involves a boat being nosed into the beach, a cable is attached, then greased timbers are placed in its path as it's inched beyond the high-water mark. A **fishmonger's shack** (☎ 01297-20297; www.beerfish.co.uk; ⊙ 8.30am-1.30pm Mon-Sat, 10am-1pm Sun) beside the slipway sells the catch, allowing you to enjoy hand-picked **Beer crab** (per 8oz pot £5) sitting on the beach where it was landed. There are also mackerel fishing trips (see p138).

Beer sits in a bay of **130m-high cliffs**. Sheer and creamy white, they're

DEVON

TOP FIVE

BEACHES

★ **Salcombe** (p159) Golden bays fringing a chic sailing haven

★ **Slapton Sands** (p156) A 3-mile pebble ridge framing a nature reserve

★ **Croyde** (p179) Chilled-out surfing hot spot

★ **Saunton Sands** (p179) A 3-mile beach backed by immense dunes

★ **Exmouth** (p136) A windsurfer's and kitesurfer's dream

dramatically different from the orangey-red sand and mudstone lining the rest of the east Devon shore. That dates from the Triassic period (250–200 million years ago), while the chalk cliffs at Beer are from the Cretaceous period – a mere 70 million years ago. This younger rock pops up at Beer because geological movements forced this layer downwards, making it level with the older rocks and so stopping it from being eroded as it has on either side. Beer's beachside **heritage centre** (☺hr vary) details the process.

Beer's **Fore St** slopes up from the coast; it's lined with water-filled leats and chalk and flint-faced houses, shops and pubs. From the clifftop beer garden of the **Anchor Inn** (☎ 01297-20386; Fore St) you can look down onto the sea, the beach and the fishing activity far below.

Beer is 8 miles east of Sidmouth; for public transport see p140.

☙ BEER QUARRY CAVES // ROAM AROUND A SUBTERRANEAN ROMAN QUARRY

The geological forces that pushed chalk to the fore of Beer's **cliffs** also ensured an accessible seam of high-quality masonry material called **Beer Stone**. It's been used in a wealth of famous buildings, including 24 cathedrals, the Tower of London and Windsor Castle. The Romans began the network of evocative quarry **tunnels** (☎ 01297-680282; www.beerquarrycaves.fsnet.co.uk; adult/child £6/4.25; ☺ 10am-5pm Easter-Sep, 11am-4pm Oct) you can explore today. On the **underground tour** you don a hard hat then head off to see 2000-year-old tool marks on the walls and a maze of arches and vaults dating from Saxon and Norman times to the early 20th century.

There are also tales of smuggling, including 18th-century excise-dodger Jack Rattenbury, who snuck barrels of French brandy ashore and secreted them in the caves. Despite being arrested repeatedly, Jack ensured local hero status by surviving to die in his own bed at the age of 66. Beer's caves also evoke harsh working conditions – the incessant ringing of hammer and chisel gives rise to the phrase 'stone deaf'.

☙ CATCH YOUR OWN LUNCH // HEAD OUT TO SEA WITH BEER'S FISHERMEN

For the ultimate DIY eating experience, sign up for a **mackerel fishing trip** (per hour adult/child £7/4) from **Beer beach**. A wheeled jetty is rolled part way into the sea, allowing you to hop aboard. The skipper then putters about hunting out the best fishing spots, perhaps just around the chalky-white cliffs at Branscombe. Next it's a case of bobbing about, marvelling at the views, waiting for a nibble.

If the fish bite ask the skipper to gut your catch, head back to the beach, fire up the disposable barbecue (bring your own or try the **village stores** at the top of Fore St) and get grilling. Pick up bread rolls from the **bakery** (Fore St; ☺ 9am-1pm, closed Wed & Sun) and oil and lemon from

Woozies Deli (☎01297-20707; Fore St; ⊙10am-4pm, closed Tue). That fish dish has never been fresher.

Mackerel fishing operators advertise on boards at the beachside heritage centre. They include **Paul** (☎0777 9040491), **Simon** (☎0777 3923120) and **Kim** (☎0798 9631321).

GASTRONOMIC HIGHLIGHTS

♣ RIVER COTTAGE CANTEEN // AXMINSTER £

☎01297-631715; Trinity Sq; mains £8; ⊙breakfast & lunch daily, dinner Thu-Sat

As befits a TV chef who campaigns on sustainable food, at Hugh Fearnley-Whittingstall's bistro the emphasis is firmly on local, seasonal and organic ingredients. Hearty flavours include pike and parsley soup, Portland crab with fennel, and garlic mushrooms on toast with sorrel and goat's cheese shavings – a kind of deeply satisfying English crostino. Drinks include Stinger Beer; brewed from (carefully) handpicked Dorset nettles, it's spicy with just a hint of tingle.

♣ RIVER COTTAGE HQ // NEAR AXMINSTER £££

☎01297-630313; www.rivercottage.net; Park Farm; 4-course dinner £60; ⊙dates vary

You've seen it on TV, but eating here really gives you a taste of Hugh F-W's 21st-century take on *The Good Life*. Normally held on Friday and Saturday nights, these four-course affairs are packed with flair and the flavours of the surrounding hills and shores. Dining in the River Cottage garden on a fine summer's night replicates the communal scene you've seen on the small screen: the warm fuzzy glow people get when they come together to enjoy fantastic food.

♣ SALTY MONK // SIDFORD ££

☎01395-513174; Church St; dinner 2/3 courses £37/40, lunch mains £17; ⊙dinner nightly, lunch Thu-Sat

This chic eatery is set in a 16th-century Benedictine monastery salt-house, and the food is as imaginative as its name: try the Chanel squid with wild garlic pasta or the richly flavoured rabbit with toasted brioche. Pudding is five perfectly ripe British cheeses. Dinner is by reservation only.

SELF-CATERING & CAMPSITES

The pick of Devon's hotels and B&Bs are outlined in our Accommodation chapter (p287). But here are some DIY highlights.

★ **Start Point Lighthouse** (☎01386-701177; www.ruralretreats.co.uk; 2 nights for 5 people from £420) The ultimate seaside sleeping experience (p157).

★ **Greenway Apartment & Lodge** (NT; ☎0844 8002070; www.nationaltrustcottages.co.uk; per week £380-2700) Doze off where Agatha Christie dreamt up her plots (p152).

★ **Holne Chase** (☎01747-828170; www.holne-chase.co.uk; per week from £470) Luxury cottages on a Dartmoor country estate. Learn to fly-fish too.

★ **Dartmoor Camping** (☎01822-890414; www.dartmoor-npa.gov.uk) Pitch your tent on the open moor – or sleep in a barn. Ask the Dartmoor National Park Authority (DNPA) where and how.

★ **Higher Rew** (☎01548-842681; www.higherrew.co.uk; sites £11-16) A tranquil campsite a mile from Salcombe's sands.

DEVON

♥ STEAMERS // BEER ££

☎ 01297-22922; New Cut; mains £10-25; ☺ lunch & dinner Tue-Sat

The place to go for a stylish supper in Beer village; the decor here is exposed stone, purple velvet and arty chandeliers. Tuck into slow braised lamb shank, grilled lobster, melting roast chicken in garlic and lots and lots of local fish.

TRANSPORT

BUS // A key route is the X53 Jurassic Coastlinx. Services run between Exeter and Weymouth or Poole (four to eight daily), stopping at Beer and Lyme Regis. Bus 157 connects Exmouth with Sidmouth (one hour, hourly Monday to Saturday) and bus 52 links Sidmouth with Exeter (45 minutes, one to three hourly).

TRAIN // Branch-line trains run to Exmouth from Exeter Central (25 minutes, every half hour Monday to Saturday, hourly Sunday); Axminster is on the well-served Exeter–Waterloo intercity route.

TORQUAY & AROUND
· · · · · ·

It may face the English Channel, rather than the Med, but the coast around Torquay has long been dubbed the English Riviera; known for palm trees, piers and russet-red cliffs. At first glance, Torquay itself is the quintessential faded English seaside resort, beloved by both the coach-tour crowd and stag- and hen-party animals. But a mild microclimate and an azure circle of bay have also drawn a smarter set and Torquay now competes with foodie-hub Dartmouth for fine eateries. The area also boasts unique attractions that range from an immense aviary to prehistoric caves – add an Agatha Christie connection, fishing ports and steam trains, and it all adds up to some grand days out beside the sea.

ORIENTATION

Torquay leads into Paignton a few miles south along the shores of Tor Bay. The fishing port of Brixham is 5 miles further south again. The resort of Teignmouth is 8 miles north of Torquay, while the nature reserve at Dawlish Warren is 5 miles north from there.

The unusual 1920s National Trust property of Coleton Fishacre (p153) lies 5 miles south of Brixham, on the way to Dartmouth.

ESSENTIAL INFORMATION

TOURIST INFORMATION // Brixham **Tourist Office** (☎ 01803-211211; www.theenglishriviera.co.uk; The Quay; ☺ 9.30am-4.30pm Mon-Sat, plus 10am-4pm Sun Jun-Sep) **Torquay Tourist Office** (☎ 01803-211211; www.theenglishriviera.co.uk; Vaughan Pde; ☺ 9.30am-5pm Mon-Sat, plus Sun Jun-Sep) **Teignmouth Tourist Office** (☎ 01626-215666; www.southdevon.org.uk; The Den; ☺ 10am-4pm Mon-Sat, plus Sun Jul-Sep)

EXPLORING TORQUAY & AROUND

♥ THE AGATHA CHRISTIE TRAIL // CRACK THE CLUES TO THE WRITER'S LOCAL LINKS

Start deductions at Torquay's tourist office (see p140) in Vaughn Pde, it stocks the informative *Agatha Christie Mile* leaflet (free). Just to the south is the **Pavilion**, where Agatha met her first husband, Archie; to the east of the old harbour is **Beacon Cove**, where she had to be rescued from drowning as a girl. It's overlooked by the **Imperial Hotel**, which doubles as the Majestic Hotel in *Peril at End House*. Towards the west of town, near the train station is the **Grand Hotel**, where Agatha honeymooned with Archie.

Torquay Museum (☎ 01803-293975; 529 Babbacombe Rd; adult/child £4/2.50; ☻ 10am-5pm Mon-Sat & 1.30-5pm Sun Jul-Sep) displays an unusual selection of Christie memorabilia, including a huge collection of photos, handwritten notes and display cases devoted to her famous detectives. It also does a superb job of evoking the genteel turn-of-the-20th-century watering hole Torquay was when Christie was a child.

But the highlight is a visit to Christie's bewitching holiday home **Greenway**, near Dartmouth, see p152. The **Greenway Ferry** (☎ 01803-844010; www.greenwayferry. co.uk) sails there from Princess Pier in Torquay (adult/child return £19/12) and from Dartmouth (adult/child return £7.50/5.50) and Totnes (adult/child return £11/7.50). Boats sail only when the property is open (Wednesday to Sunday); times vary and it's best to book.

❧ **BEACH LIFE // CONNECT WITH CENTURIES OF SEASIDE FUN**
Torquay boasts no fewer than 20 **beaches** and a surprising 22 miles of coast. It's been a holiday hot spot since the French wars of the 18th century fired its development as a watering place; touring Europe was suddenly not such a good idea. In the Victorian era, rows of seaview **villas** popped up (look out for them still stacked up like dominoes on the steeply sloping hills) and the Prince

TORQUAY'S AGATHA CHRISTIE CONNECTION

DEVON

Torquay is the birthplace of a one-woman publishing phenomenon: **Dame Agatha Mary Clarissa Christie** (1890–1976). In terms of book sales the detective writer is beaten only by the Bible and William Shakespeare, and her characters are world famous: Hercule Poirot, the moustachioed, immodest Belgian detective; and Miss Marple, the surprisingly perceptive busybody spinster.

Born Agatha Miller in Torquay's Barton Rd, the young writer had her first piece published by the age of 11. By WWI she'd married Lietenant Archie Christie and was working as a nurse in the Red Cross Hospital in Torquay Town Hall, acquiring the knowledge of poisons that laces countless plotlines, including that of her first novel *The Mysterious Affair at Styles* (1920). Christie made her name with the cunning plot device she used in *The Murder of Roger Ackroyd* six years later. In the same year her mother died, Archie asked for a divorce and the writer mysteriously disappeared for 10 days; her abandoned car prompted a massive search. She was eventually discovered in a hotel in Harrogate, where she'd checked in under the name of the woman her husband wanted to marry. Christie always maintained she'd suffered amnesia, some critics saw it as a publicity stunt.

Christie later married again, this time the archaeologist Sir Max Mallowan, and their trips to the Middle East provided masses of material for her work. By the time she died in 1976, Christie had written 75 novels and 33 plays.

Christie connections crop up all over south Devon; in **Torquay** (see p140) and near **Dartmouth**, where you can visit her holiday home, **Greenway**, see p152. Dartmouth's **Royal Castle Hotel** (p298) is the Royal George in *Ordeal by Innocence*, while **Burgh Island Hotel** (p299) features in fictional form in *And Then There Were None* and *Evil Under the Sun*. For further investigations, try the comprehensive *Exploring Agatha Christie Country* (£4), by David Gerrard.

TORQUAY

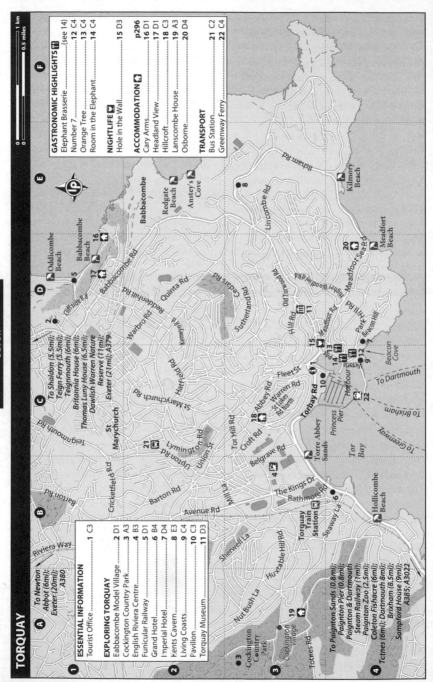

ESSENTIAL INFORMATION
Tourist Office 1 C3

EXPLORING TORQUAY
Babbacombe Model Village 2 D1
Cockington Country Park 3 A3
English Riviera Centre 4 B3
Funicular Railway 5 D1
Grand Hotel 6 B4
Imperial Hotel 7 D4
Kents Cavern 8 E3
Living Coasts 9 C4
Pavilion 10 C3
Torquay Museum 11 D3

GASTRONOMIC HIGHLIGHTS
Elephant Brasserie ....(see 14)
Number 7 ....12 C4
Orange Tree 13 C4
Room in the Elephant 14 C4

NIGHTLIFE
Hole in the Wall 15 D3

ACCOMMODATION p296
Cary Arms 16 D1
Headland View 17 D1
Hillcroft 18 C3
Lanscombe House 19 A3
Osborne 20 D4

TRANSPORT
Bus Station 21 C2
Greenway Ferry 22 C4

DEVON

of Wales bagged a few sailing victories in the **regattas**. Their modern incarnation, during **Torbay Week** in late August, still sees hundreds of vessels competing in races.

Holidaymakers flock to the central **Torre Abbey Sands** (Ⓟ), which is covered by water at very high tides; the locals opt for the sand-and-shingle beaches beside the 240ft red-clay cliffs at **Babbacombe** (Ⓟ). These can be accessed by a glorious 1920s **funicular railway** (☎ 01803-328750; adult/child return £1.75/1.20; ☽ 9.30am-5.25pm Easter-Sep), a memorable trip in a tiny wooden carriage that shuttles up and down rails set into the cliff.

Meadfoot Beach (Ⓟ) is a long strip of pebbles and sand; **Hollicombe Beach** is compact and relatively quiet; while further west Paignton seafront boasts **Paignton Sands** (Ⓟ) – a wide russet-tinged stretch. It also has **Paignton Pier** (☎ 01803-522139; ☽ open access). Built in 1879, this grand old structure offers the chance to indulge in pure holiday nostalgia: parade along the long wooden deck, jump in a dodgem; bounce around on a trampoline and have a game of crazy golf.

When the weather's foul, the wave machine and giant flumes of the pool at the **English Riviera Centre** (☎ 01803-299992; Chestnut Ave; adult/child £3.90/3.10; ☽ 9am-4pm, longer at peak times) draw the crowds.

❦ TOR BAY BY FERRY // CRUISE FROM TOURIST RESORT TO FISHING PORT
Torquay and neighbouring Paignton and Brixham all sit on the shores of **Tor Bay**, not to be confused with Torbay, the local council area. This wide sweep of water is vast and technically encompasses 16 sq miles of open sea. The sheer scale becomes apparent from the pleasure boats that make the half-hour Torquay–Brixham

trip. The voyage chugs from Torquay's old harbour, past marinas, packed beaches and Paignton Pier, beside crumbling cliffs and grand Victorian hotels to the bustling fishing port of Brixham (p145).

Several operators ply the route; their stands line the waterfront. They include the **Greenway Ferry** (☎ 01803-844010; www. greenwayferry.co.uk; adult/child return £7/4; ☽ Apr-Oct) firm, which sails from Torquay's Princess Pier 10 times a day.

❦ LIVING COASTS // STROLL AROUND WITH FREE-RANGE PENGUINS
Clinging to the cliffs beside Torquay Harbour, this open-plan **aviary** (☎ 01803-202470; www.livingcoasts.org.uk; Beacon Quay; adult/child £9.5/7.25; ☽ 10am-5pm) brings you closer to exotic birds than ever before. The immense enclosure features a series of underwater viewing tunnels and mocked-up microhabitats that include Penguin Beach, Auk Cliff and Fur Seal Cove. The result is a chance to get up close to free-roaming penguins, punk-rocker-style tufted puffins and disarmingly cute bank cormorants. The Local Coasts feature reveals the starfish, bizarre-looking cuttlefish and hugely appealing seahorses

DEVON

FAWLTY TOWERS

Torquay's most famous fictional resident is **Basil Fawlty**, the deranged hotelier memorably played by John Cleese in the classic British TV comedy *Fawlty Towers*. Written by Cleese and his then wife Connie Booth, the series was famously inspired when they visited a Torquay hotel with the Monty Python team. The owner, described by Cleese as 'marvellously rude', prompted them to set the series in Torquay – forever linking the resort to Basil, Sybil, Manuel and that rat.

that inhabit the water just offshore. For optimum squawking and waddling, time your visit to coincide with penguin breakfast (10.30am) or lunch (2.30pm).

❦ PAIGNTON ZOO // ENCOUNTER AN ARK-LOAD OF ANIMALS

The conservation charity behind Living Coasts (p143) also runs this innovative **zoo** (☎ 01803-697500; www.paigntonzoo.org.uk; Totnes Rd; adult/child £11.90/8.40; ☼ 10am-5pm). The 80-acre site is dotted with spacious enclosures recreating habitats as varied as savannah, wetlands, tropical forest and desert. Highlights are the **orang-utan island**, vast glass-walled **lion enclosure**, and a **lemur wood**, where you walk over a plank suspension bridge as the primates leap around in the surrounding trees.

Look out too for the endearing **giraffes** and the award-winning **monkey enclosures** where animals are kept stimulated by having to forage for their food rather than have it delivered on a plate. But the real must-see site is the **crocodile swamp**; a steamy enclave overflowing with tropical vegetation, where raised pathways wind over and beside Nile, Cuban and saltwater crocs, some up to 6m

---

⊳ TOP FIVE

FERRY RIDES & BOAT TRIPS

★ **Dartmouth** (p155) Hike and ferry-hop around a bewitching estuary

★ **Salcombe** (p159) Take a boat to beautiful sandy beaches

★ **Plymouth** (p167) Cross a massive harbour to a Cornish smuggling port

★ **Beer** (p138) Head out with the fishermen to catch your own lunch

★ **Jurassic Coast** (p136) Cruise past 250-million-year-old cliffs

---

long. There's also a glass-free zone where a 10m **reticulated python** sits, hopefully, just out of reach.

❦ KENTS CAVERN // TOUCH BASE WITH YOUR INNER NEANDERTHAL

Expect a stalactite to drip water on your head and temperatures to dip to 14°C in this atmospheric network of **caves** (☎ 01803-215135; www.kents-cavern.co.uk; 89 Ilsham Rd; adult/child £8.50/7; ☼ 10am-4.30pm Jul & Aug, 10am-4pm Mar-Jun & Sep-Oct, 11am-3.30pm Nov-Feb). Hour-long guided tours wind through a maze of rusty-red, uneven tunnels that link rock galleries, arcades and chambers, some of which soar to impressive heights.

The caves reveal evidence of Torbay's prehistoric animal population, in the form of the bones and teeth of **cave lions, giant mammoths** and **sabre-tooth cats**. Tours also pass **hyenas' lairs** and **cave bears' dens**; look out for the skull of one of these *ursus deningeri* embedded in the rock in the Water Gallery.

Kents Cavern is also the oldest recognisable human dwelling in Britain. Finds unearthed here include flint **hand axes** that have been dated to 450,000 years old. Another discovery, a **jawbone**, is thought to be the oldest directly dated human bone in Britain. Radio carbon tests have put it at 35,000 years old, suggesting anatomically modern humans (or Cro-Magnons) reached Britain much earlier than previously thought.

❦ BABBACOMBE MODEL VILLAGE // FIND OUT JUST HOW HUGE GULLIVER FELT

Overflowing with English eccentricity, this absorbing **model village** (☎ 01803-315315; www.model-village.co.uk; Hampton Ave; adult/child £8.50/6.25; ☼ 10am-dusk, to 6pm Jun—mid-Jul, to 10pm late Jul & Aug) is packed with thousands of tiny buildings and even tinier people. The imagination and attention to

DEVON

detail is remarkable and the Lilliputian tableaux are in turns witty, bizarre and a little unnerving.

As well as a small-scale Stonehenge, football stadium and beach there's an animated circus, a castle (under attack from a fire-breathing dragon) and a thatched village where firefighters are tackling a blaze in progress. Visit in the evening for unforgettable **illuminations** that include Piccadilly Circus, complete with flashing banner ads.

🌿 COCKINGTON COUNTRY PARK // EXPERIENCE A SLICE OF OLD-FASHIONED VILLAGE LIFE

This 182-hectare chunk of **countryside** (☎ 01803-606035; admission free; ☉ open access) provides a welcome oasis of calm, green space, just a mile from Torquay's seafront bustle. **Walking trails** wind through fields, woods and parkland surrounding a 17th-century manor house, walled garden and craft studios.

There's also a heavily **thatched village**, complete with forge, mill, gamekeeper's cottage, 14th-century church and an architectural rarity: a thatched pub designed by Sir Edwin Lutyens. The **Drum Inn** (☎ 01803-690264; Cockington; mains £7; ☉ lunch & dinner) was one of the last buildings to go up in the village in 1936; today it offers cask ales, log fires and a leafy beer garden. Check to see if there's a match taking place on Cockington's dinky **cricket pitch** (weekends provide the best chance); set amid a gently sloping natural amphitheatre, it's one of the prettiest in Devon.

🌿 PAIGNTON & DARTMOUTH STEAM RAILWAY // CHUFF YOUR WAY ALONG THE SOUTH DEVON COAST

Chugging from seaside **Paignton** to the beautiful banks of the **River Dart**, this **train trip** (☎ 01803-555872; www.paignton -steamrailway.co.uk; adult/child return £10/7.50; ☉ 4-9 trains daily May-Sep) effortlessly rolls back the years to the age of steam. The 7-mile, 30-minute journey starts with a long coastal stretch beside Goodrington Sands – look out for dolphins – then cuts inland across fields and through steeply-sloping woods. The final section sees trains steaming beside the River Dart to the village of Kingswear, where regular ferries shuttle across to picturesque Dartmouth (see p152).

The engines powering the smartly liveried, vintage coaches date from the 1920s and 1950s; some are former heavy coal trains from the Welsh valleys, others propelled Great Western Railway passenger services.

A wide range of other trips is possible; one involves cruising to Dartmouth by boat, then taking the steam train back to Paignton (adult/child £20/12).

🌿 BRIXHAM // EXPLORE DEVON'S NAUTICAL PAST AND PRESENT

Just eight miles south of Torquay, this **fishing port** offers an authentic glimpse of life along Devon's coast. It's a place of gritty charm: pastel-painted rows of fishermen's cottages lead down to a horseshoe harbour full of brightly painted boats. Fudge shops, kiosks and arcades line up alongside.

With 70 boats landing daily, Brixham is the top-earning fishing port in England and its new multimillion-pound **Fish Market** is being seen by many as a vital boost for an industry that's suffered hard times for decades. The auction isn't open to the public, but you can buy some of the day's catch from **David Walker & Son** (☎ 01803-882097; Unit B; ☉ 9am-4pm Mon-Fri, to 1pm Sat), in the market complex. The counters are piled high with fish that's just hours old, plus picnic goodies such

DEVON

as huge, cooked, shell-on prawns (per 500g £7) and dressed crab (£4.50 each).

The **quay** is at its busiest from around 6am when the auction is taking place. It's a good time to stop by one of the cafes, breakfast with those who work in the industry and watch the vessels head out. The larger beam trawlers go to sea for up to 10 days, catching sole, turbot, monkfish and plaice, much of which is exported. The smaller day boats specialise in red mullet, squid, sea bass, mackerel, cod and lemon sole. Their catch is landed daily. Look for it in the bay's top restaurants – and fish-and-chip shops.

Devon sailor and explorer Sir Francis Drake (p163) carried out a treasure-seeking circumnavigation of the globe in the late 1500s. A full-sized replica of the vessel he travelled in, the **Golden Hind** (☎ 01803-856223; adult/child £4/3; ☾ 10am-4pm Mar-Sep) is tied up in Brixham Harbour. Though remarkably small, the original ship had a crew of 60. Today, you get to cross the ship's gangplank, peer inside the tiny captain's cabin, prowl around the poop deck and listen to tales of life in the officer's quarters delivered in suitably 'arrr, me-hearties' tones. If you have youngsters, or just fancy dressing up like Johnny Depp, look out for the **Pirate Days** each Thursday.

Brixham is at the end of the A3022, but by far the most atmospheric way to arrive is by ferry from Torquay (p143).

⚘ THE TEIGN FERRY // RIDE A HISTORIC FERRY TO A SMUGGLERS' BEACH

Some 8 miles north of Torquay at the well-worn resort of **Teignmouth**, white Georgian terraces frame a red-gold sandy beach and a stately Victorian pier.

Teignmouth is also where the **River Teign** flows into the sea after a 30-mile meander from Dartmoor.

The open-sided **Teign Ferry** (☎ 07880-713420; adult/child £1.30/70p; ☾ from 8am) shuttles from Teignmouth to the appealing village of **Shaldon** on the south bank. The ferry began life around the 10th century, while the distinctive black-and-white colour scheme of the current boat is Elizabethan. It's an evocative crossing – you embark by walking up a gangplank; the voyage itself brings a crumbling, red headland ever closer. Once in Shaldon hunt out **Ness Beach**, accessed via a **smugglers' tunnel** that's been hacked out of the rock.

The ferry sails from Teignmouth's **River Beach** (℗), just behind the Point (seafront) car park. The schedule varies; times are posted on boards on the beach.

⚘ A SEA WALL WALK // HIKE TO A WAVE-DASHED NATURE RESERVE

The 5-mile stretch of coast between Teignmouth and **Dawlish Warren Nature Reserve** is edged by red sandstone cliffs that have been eroded into a series of bizarre stacks, coves and undulating headlands. Here the coast path is sandwiched between the sea and a train line that is squeezed in between rocks. It makes for an atmospheric hike – taking the coast path north out of Teignmouth actually involves walking on the breakwater. About a mile along, the trail cuts sharply inland, skirting the striking **Parson and Clerk** rock formation, before descending steeply to the seafront at the resort of **Dawlish**, a mile further on. Look out for the weirdly shaped **Horse, Old Maid** and **Cowhole rocks** on the way.

From Dawlish, a 2-mile stroll leads past deeply eroded russet cliffs and a wide beach to the Dawlish Warren Nature Reserve, which clings to the shore at the mouth of the River Exe. This slender **sand spit** arches right out into the waterway, providing exhilarating views across to Exmouth, up the Exe and out to sea. Its habitats include dunes, grasslands, salt marshes and mudflats, and is a key roost for wildfowl and wading birds.

If the walk back seems too far, you could ride the route instead: there are train stations at Dawlish Warren, Dawlish and Teignmouth. Services are regular, but vary, so check.

GASTRONOMIC HIGHLIGHTS

☙ NUMBER 7 // TORQUAY ££
☎ 01803-295055; Beacon Tce; mains £15; ☺ lunch Wed-Sat, dinner daily

Fabulous smells fill the air at this buzzing harbourside fish bistro that is packed with superfresh fruits of the sea. It specialises in local crab, lobster, skate and monkfish, often with an unexpected twist. Try the king scallops with vermouth or fish and prawn tempura. The seafood broth is packed with flavour.

☙ ORANGE TREE // TORQUAY ££
☎ 01803-213936; 14 Park Hill Rd; mains £17, ☺ dinner Mon-Sat

This award-winning brasserie brings a touch of Continental flair to dishes majoring on local fish, meat and game. Prepare to enjoy the Brixham crab lasagne with crab bisque, sea bass steamed with coriander or the south Devon steak with a rich blue-cheese sauce. Then try to resist the chocolate temptation: a brownie-mousse-parfait combo with dollops of raspberries and mango salsa.

☙ ROOM IN THE ELEPHANT // TORQUAY £££
☎ 01803-200044; 3 Beacon Tce; 6 courses £45; ☺ dinner Tue-Sat

A restaurant to remember. Torbay's Michelin-starred eatery is defined by seriously good food and imaginative flavour fusions: squid and cauliflower risotto; chicken with a liver-and-fig salad; a chocolate-fondant doughnut with hazelnut ice cream. The sumptuous cheeseboard is weighted with the very best Westcountry offerings, while the window frames bright marina views.

☙ ELEPHANT BRASSERIE // TORQUAY ££
☎ 01803-200044; 3 Beacon Tce; 2/3 courses £23/27; ☺ lunch & dinner Tue-Sat

The setting may be less formal, but the bistro below Torquay's Michelin-starred eatery (Room in the Elephant) is still superstylish. Treatments include lemon sole with shellfish ragout and Noilly Prat cream, and Devon duckling with spiced honey jus. There are real treats for dessert fans too: try the rice pudding with prune and Armagnac or the espresso-and-white-chocolate *petit pot* with pistachio madeleines.

NIGHTLIFE

Torquay has one of the busiest nightlife scenes in Devon – the area around the harbour gets particularly hectic, especially at weekends.

☙ HOLE IN THE WALL
☎ 01803-200755; 6 Park Lane, Torquay; ☺ noon-midnight

Dating from around 1540, this heavily beamed, tardislike boozer claims to be the oldest pub in Torquay – the part-cobbled floor is actually listed. At the front there's a tiny alley-cum-terrace on which to enjoy an alfresco pint.

DEVON

♥ MARITIME
☎ 01803-853535; 79 King St, Brixham;
🕒 11am-11pm

Quirky doesn't even begin to describe
this dose of full-blooded English eccentricity. This welcoming old pub is smothered in thousands of key rings, stone jugs
and chamber pots, while a vast whiskey
selection stacks up behind the counter.
The best feature though is Mr Tibbs, a
parrot who wanders around the bar say-
ing 'hello' to customers (literally).

♥ SHIP INN
☎ 01626-772674; 2 Queen St, Teignmouth; mains
£6.50; 🕒 11am-11pm, to midnight Fri & Sat

One of the most atmospheric pubs in
Teignmouth, the Ship has a mellow feel:
all rustic tables, beams and wooden
floors. Its waterside terrace is perfect for
enjoying tasty pub grub (lunch and dinner daily, except Tuesday and Sunday
evening), a glass of local Otter Ale and
memorable sunset views.

TRANSPORT

BUS // Key routes include: bus 12, from Torquay to
Paignton (20 minutes, every 15 minutes) and on to Brixham (40 minutes); bus 111, from Torquay to Totnes (one
hour, hourly Monday to Saturday, four on Sunday) and
on to Dartmouth; bus 32 from Torquay to Teignmouth
(45 minutes, every 30 minutes).

CAR // Torquay and Paignton are circled by the A380 ring
road; it heads onto Brixham as the more minor A3022. A
slower, seafront road also winds between all three.

FERRY // Regular ferries shuttle between Torquay and
Brixham, see p143.

PARKING // A seven-day permit allowing parking in all
council car parks in Torquay, Paignton and Brixham costs
£27. It's available from the tourist-office website, see p140.

TRAIN // Newton Abbot, Teignmouth, Dawlish and
Dawlish Warren are on the London Paddington–Penzance mainline. Branch-line trains run at least hourly
from Newton Abbot to Torquay (20 minutes) and on to
Paignton (10 minutes).

SOUTH DEVON
· · · · · ·

South of Torquay, Devon is transformed. Candy floss, promenades and
arcades give way to green fields and
soaring cliffs. Here historic Totnes is
home to Tudor architecture, a superb
vineyard and a counterculture vibe.
Picture-postcard-pretty Dartmouth
delivers Agatha Christie's house and
nautical history, while to the south,
captivating Salcombe boasts boat trips,
sandy beaches and a smart sailing set.
Alongside, a rural landscape offers sim-
plicity, peace and space: undeveloped
beaches, sparkling bays and a rolling
network of fields dotted with mellow villages and tranquil market towns. What's
more, it's all topped off with a rich collection of excellent eateries.

ESSENTIAL INFORMATION

TOURIST INFORMATION // Visit South
Devon (www.visitsouthdevon.co.uk) A good information source. **South Devon AONB** (☎ 01803-
861384; www.southdevonaonb.org.uk) Runs inspiring
events.

TOTNES & AROUND

pop 7443

After Torbay's kiss-me-quick delights,
Totnes is decidedly different. It's got
such a reputation for being alternative
that locals scrawled 'twinned with Nar-
nia' under the town sign. But as well as
shops stacked with tie-dye and incense,
this New Age haven is packed with history and architecture that ranges from
the Norman to the 1920s. Add the artistic Dartington Estate, a riverside walk to
an enticing vineyard and a pioneering
ecorestaurant, and you have an attractive
base for explorations.

ESSENTIAL INFORMATION

TOURIST INFORMATION // Tourist office
(☎ 01803-863168; www.totnesinformation.co.uk;
Coronation Rd; ☾ 9.30am-5pm Mon-Fri, 10am-4pm Sat
Apr-Oct, 10am-4pm Mon-Fri, 10am-1pm Sat Nov-Mar)

EXPLORING TOTNES & AROUND

❦ **HISTORIC TOTNES //** HUNT
OUT HIDDEN HISTORIC AND
ARCHITECTURAL TREASURES
Tucked away off the top of the **High St**,
the picturesque battlements of **Totnes
Castle** (EH; ☎ 01803-864406; Castle St; adult/child
£3.20/1.60; ☾ 10am-6pm Jul & Aug, 10am-5pm late
Mar-Jun & Sep, 10am-4pm Oct) crown a steeply
sloping man-made mound, providing
buzzard's-eye views over the town and
surrounding fields.

Where **Castle St** re-joins the High St,
look out for **Poultry Walk**: a wonky row
of Tudor jettied buildings propped up
by an array of columns. This was where
the town's poultry market was held;
downhill on the left, the 16th-century
Butterwalk used to shelter the town's
dairy markets. Many of the houses have
elaborate Tudor plasterwork ceilings,
two of the best preserved are at **Bogan
House**, in the **Devonshire Collection of
Period Costume** (☎ 01803-863168; 43 High St;
adult/child £2/80p; ☾ 11am-5pm Tue-Fri May-Sep).
Look out for the intricate patterns above

its excellent displays – ask to see the one
in the downstairs room too.

Church Close cuts sharply left off the
High St, leading beside the red Devon
sandstone of the 15th-century **St Mary's
Church**. Hidden in behind is the **Guildhall** (☎ 01803-862147; adult/child £1.25/50p;
☾ 10.30am-4pm Mon-Fri Apr-Oct), parts of which
were the kitchens of the Norman priory;
inside look out for cells, ceremonial
robes and an elaborate council chamber. **Ramparts Walk** curves around the
church, tracing the line of the original
Saxon town boundary.

The path re-emerges onto the High St
at the junction of Fore St, right underneath the cream, crenellated **East Gate**.
Further down, the **Totnes Elizabethan
Museum** (☎ 01803-863821; 70 Fore St; adult/
child £2/1.50; ☾ 10.30am-5pm Mon-Fri Apr-Oct), set
in a Tudor Merchants' house, recreates
interiors of the period. At the side, an
easy-to-miss gate opens onto a narrow,
cobbled path that leads to a pocket-sized
Elizabethan Garden. Signs explain
which herb cured which ailment: soap-
wort for syphilis, woad to staunch bleed-
ing, bay for bee stings.

At the bottom of Fore St, Bank Lane
features an ornate, lemon-yellow 18th-
century house built in a style known as
Strawberry Hill Gothic. Further down
the **town bridge** leads onto the leafy **Vire
Island** on the right; an appealing place to

DEVON

TRANSITION TOWN TOTNES

In 2005 in Totnes, the seeds of an almighty ecoproject were sown. The first experiment of
its kind in the UK, **Transition Town Totnes** (http://totnes.transitionnetwork.org) looked ahead to
a world with less oil and then examined the impact on every aspect of our lives; from food
and car use to health care and schools. Since then more than 180 Transition Towns have
sprung up across the UK.

In Totnes, look out for nut trees planted in public places, a plethora of solar panels
and the **tuk-tuk taxis** powered by leftover cooking oil from local restaurants. Then
there's the **Totnes Pound**, a parallel currency that aims to keep spending local.

study the renovated warehouses that line a bubbling River Dart.

🌱 DARTINGTON ESTATE // DISCOVER A TRANQUIL, HISTORIC, ARTISTIC ENCLAVE

When Dorothy and Leonard Elmhurst bought this 1000-acre **estate** in the 1920s, they set up an experiment in rural regeneration and a progressive school. The Dartington College of Arts followed in the 1960s, and the estate is still packed with art and architecture.

Dartington Hall & Grounds

Dartington's 14th-century **manor house** was in ruins when it was bought by the Elmhursts. Now beautifully restored, its weathered buildings frame a grassy, mellow space reminiscent of an Oxbridge quadrangle.

In the landscaped **gardens** impressive terraced banks frame a tiltyard, while flower-filled borders lead down to glades, meadows and thatched cottages. Amid the tiny paths and secret benches hunt out the carved stone *Memorial Figure* by Henry Moore, the swirling bobbles of

Jacobs Pillow by Peter Randall Page and the **bronze donkey** by Willi Soukop. The **Japanese Garden**, complete with raked gravel and cedar wood shelter, is beside the ruined **church**, while the estate's former kitchens now house the atmospheric **White Hart Inn**; see p151.

On the road into the estate, look out for the **Modernist Movement** building, High Cross House, sheltering behind a hedge. Now used as offices, this vivid white and bright blue structure was built in 1932.

Arts & Festivals

Dartington's exquisite **Great Hall** and neighbouring **barn** stage diverse events including music (from classical to world), dance, drama and arthouse films. See **Dartington Arts** (☎ 01803-847070; www.dartington.org) for details. Highlights include the International Summer School concerts from late July to late August, and the magical open-air Shakespeare in the gardens in June or July. The **Ways With Words** (☎ 01803-867373; www.wayswithwords.co.uk) literature festival draws key authors to Dartington in mid-July.

The Dartington Estate is 1.5 miles west of Totnes.

🌱 SHARPHAM VINEYARD & CAFE // WANDER AMID VINES; SAMPLE THE WINES

Set on the banks of the River Dart, this **vineyard** (☎ 01803-732203; www.sharpham.com; Ashprington; ☷ 10am-5pm Mon-Sat Mar-Dec, plus Sun Jun-Sep; ℗) evokes the hills of Chablis in the heart of south Devon. Row upon row of vines line up on steeply sloping hills as they hug a curving watercourse.

The most expensive **tour** (£50) involves a full trail round the vineyard, an explanation of vinification techniques, a

---

TOP FIVE

HISTORIC TOWNS & CITIES

★ **Dartmouth** (p152) Rich in painted 17th-century homes

★ **Salcombe** (p159) An ancient sailing and boat-building port

★ **Plymouth** (p164) A city's whose maritime past has helped shape the modern world

★ **Clovelly** (p181) The ultimate time-warp cobbled fishing village

★ **Exeter** (p123) A city packed with reminders of its 2000-year-old past

tutored tasting, light lunch and a bottle of Dart Valley Reserve. A full guided tour and tutored tasting costs £12, while a **self-guided walk** and instructed **tasting** costs £5. Sharpham also makes cheese, so you can nibble that while you sample the vintages too.

The decked terrace of Sharpham's **Vineyard Café** (☎ 01803-732178; mains from £8; ⏲ 10am-5pm Apr-Sep) has views over the neatly staked vines and the Dart valley. Treats range from chargrilled vegetable bruschetta and a Sharpham cheese platter to Dartmouth lobster salad. Seating is mostly alfresco; in bad weather call to check the cafe is open

Sharpham Vineyard is about 3 miles south of Totnes near **Ashprington**. Walking the tranquil **Dart Valley Trail** from Totnes is an atmospheric way to arrive; alternatively it's signposted off the A381.

GASTRONOMIC HIGHLIGHTS

☙ **WHITE HART // TOTNES ££**
☎ 01803-847111; Dartington Estate; mains £13; ⏲ lunch & dinner
Set in the former kitchen of the 14th-century Dartington Hall, this is the kind of classy pub-cum-restaurant you wish was your own local. A quality menu features local meats, fish and veggie options, such as Devon blue cheese, walnut and watercress filo pie. Winter brings a blazing fire; on fine evenings the lawnside tables are hard to beat.

☙ **WILLOW // TOTNES £**
☎ 01803-862605; 87 High St; mains £7; ⏲ lunch Mon-Sat, dinner Wed, Fri & Sat
This rustic vegetarian cafe sums up the spirit of New Age Totnes. Wobbly tables dot its bright dining room, and the menu is an array of couscous, quiches, hotpots,

homemade cakes and Fairtrade drinks. It's strong on vegan dishes too.

☙ **RUMOUR TOTNES // TOTNES ££**
☎ 01803-864682; 30 High St; mains £9-15; ⏲ lunch & dinner
A local institution, this narrow, cosy pub-restaurant features low lighting, funky local art and free newspapers. Famous for its crispy pizzas (£6), it also rustles up stylish dishes such as duck with plum and ginger jam, or mackerel with capers, olives and rosemary.

☙ **RIVERFORD FIELD KITCHEN //**
NEAR BUCKFASTLEIGH ££
☎ 01803-762074; www.riverford.co.uk; Wash Barn; 2/3 courses £18/23; ⏲ lunch daily, dinner Tue-Sat
Run by one of Britain's leading veg-box suppliers, this ecofriendly bistro is in the middle of a farm, ensuring minimal food miles: the vegetables are picked to order from the fields in front of you; the meats are organic and locally sourced. Eating is a convivial affair – big trestle tables fill a futuristic hangerlike canteen, and platters laden with food are passed around between diners. The dishes are rightly acclaimed. Rich flavours and imaginative treatments might include marinated, grilled Moroccan lamb and British veg transformed by cumin or saffron. These are truly memorable meals; a real 'don't miss'. You have to book and take a self-led or guided tour of the fields. The Field Kitchen is 3 miles west of Totnes.

TRANSPORT

BUS // Useful routes include bus 111 between Torquay, Totnes and Dartmouth (hourly Monday to Saturday, four on Sunday).
TRAIN // Totnes is on the London Paddington–Penzance mainline, services shuttle at least hourly to Exeter (45 minutes) and Plymouth (30 minutes).

DEVON

DARTMOUTH & START BAY

pop 7500

A bewitching blend of primary-coloured boats and delicately shaded houses, Dartmouth is hard to resist. Buildings cascade down steep, wooded slopes towards the River Dart, and 17th-century shops with splendidly carved and gilded fronts line narrow lanes. Its charms have drawn a yachting crowd and a string of top-notch eateries, but fleets of fishing vessels, ferries and pleasure boats ensure it's still a busy working port with an authentic tang of the sea. Hiking trails lead up the river or onto the cliffs, while a captivating Art Deco house and Agatha Christie's Greenway estate wait in the wings.

Start Bay curves out in an elongated crescent just south of Dartmouth. This is one of Devon's most spectacular sections of coast; the road climbs steeply in a series of hairpin bends, fields roll up to precipitous cliffs and villages cluster beside the sea. It's a landscape most people bypass, but it offers enchanting places to stay and unusual sights to explore, from a ruined village and a lighthouse to a massive freshwater lake.

ESSENTIAL INFORMATION

TOURIST INFORMATION // Dartmouth Tourist Office (☎ 01803-834224; www.discov erdartmouth.com; Mayor's Ave; 🕒 9.30am-5.30pm Mon-Sat, 10am-2pm Sun Apr-Oct, 9.30am-4.30pm Mon-Sat Nov-Mar)

ORIENTATION

Dartmouth is on the west side of the River Dart, near the estuary mouth; the village of Kingswear is on the opposite side. A series of car and passenger ferries shuttle between the two (see p158),

providing a key road link to Brixham, Paignton and Torquay.

The A379 runs alongside Start Bay from the village of Strete in the north, via Slapton Sands to Torcross, where it cuts inland. The villages of Beesands and Hallsands and the Start Point lighthouse are accessible via a series of lanes, or the coast path.

EXPLORING DARTMOUTH & START BAY

🌷 **GREENWAY // HUNT FOR CLUES IN AGATHA CHRISTIE'S HOLIDAY HOME**
Nestling on a bend of the River Dart, this **house and garden** (NT; ☎ 01803-842382; Greenway Rd, Galmpton; adult/child £8/4; 🕒 10.30am-5pm Wed-Sun Mar-Oct, plus Tue mid-Jul–Aug; Ⓟ) is high on Devon's must-see list. Agatha Christie owned the property between 1938 and 1959, when she gave it to her daughter, and the house has only been open to visitors since 2009. It's a unique experience: part-guided **tours** allow you to wander between rooms where the furnishings and knick-knacks are much as she left them. So you can check out the piles of hats in the **lobby**, the books in her **library** and the clothes in her wardrobe, and listen to her speak (via a replica radio) in the **drawing room**.

The **gardens** too are a delight: glorious woods hug the water, speckled with splashes of magnolias, daffodils and hydrangeas. The planting creates intimate, secret spaces; highlights are the **peach house** and the **walled gardens**; the winding **middle path** and the lush **camellia gardens**.

The **boathouse**, complete with sofas and balcony, has enchanting views of boats chugging up the river, and a chilling Georgian sea-bathing pool in the basement. In Christie's book *Dead Man's Folly*, Greenway doubles as Nasse House, with the boathouse making an appearance in a murder scene.

The property is hugely popular, entrance to the house is by timed ticket, and there are only a very limited number of parking places, which have to be booked well in advance. The best way to arrive is by boat or on foot. The **Greenway Ferry** (☎ 0845 489418; www.greenwayferry.co.uk) runs regularly from Dartmouth (adult/child return £7.50/5.50), Totnes (adult/child return £11/7.50) and Torquay (adult/child return £19/12). Times vary and it's best to book.

Alternatively, hike along the **Dart Valley Trail** from **Kingswear** (4 miles), or walk the west bank of the River Dart from Dartmouth to **Dittisham**, then cross by ferry (see p155).

❦ COLETON FISHACRE // INDULGE IN A DOLLOP OF ART DECO GLAMOUR

There's more than a touch of showbiz magic about this captivating **Arts and Crafts style house** (NT; ☎ 01803-752466; Brownstone Rd, Kingswear; adult/child £7.40/3.70; ⏰ 10.30am-5pm Sat-Wed Mar-Oct; Ⓟ). It was built in 1926 for the D'Oyly Cartes, a family of theatre impresarios and owners of London's Savoy Hotel and Claridge's. Its interiors are replete with Art Deco embellishments: original Lalique tulip uplighters, comic bathroom tiles and a saloon that's reminiscent of a stage set, complete with tinkling piano – if you know how to play, ask a room steward and they'll probably let you tap out a tune. It's a house you could really imagine living in: sitting on the monochrome furnishings in Lady Dorothy's bedroom, working at the desk in the well-stocked **library** or tucking into an alfresco lunch in the seaview **loggia**.

The **grounds** are like a three-act play, from the grassy **croquet terrace** where games were played to the scratch of a gramophone, to the deeply sloping **subtropical gardens** and the suddenly revealed vista of the sea at the **gazebo**. Expect to come across bamboo, New Zealand tree ferns and succulents from the Canary Islands; in the spring azaleas, magnolias and camellias provide bursts of colour, in the summer swaths of blue hydrangeas come to the fore.

Coleton Fishacre is 3 miles from Dartmouth on the Torquay side of the estuary. You can hike to the property along a dramatic stretch of cliff path from Kingswear (4 miles) or drive.

❦ HISTORIC DARTMOUTH // EXPLORE A HERITAGE-RICH TOWN

Dartmouth has a glorious array of **half-timbered houses** framing the South Embankment, Fairfax Place, Duke St and the streets framing the **boat float**. Many

TOP FIVE

PUBS

★ **Dolphin** Un-messed-about-with Plymouth boozer, beloved by locals, artists and fishermen (p165)

★ **Warren House Inn** Crackling fire, hearty food and great ale in the middle of wilderness Dartmoor (p176)

★ **Wreckers Retreat** Sunsets and astounding cliffs at this remote north Devon gem (p182)

★ **Double Locks** Canal views, board games and battered books at an Exeter institution (p130)

★ **Maritime** Eccentric Brixham pub where you're welcomed by the resident parrot (p148)

date from the 17th century and have brightly painted crests and gilded motifs. Look out for the 14th-century **Cherub Inn**, up steps off Fairfax Place, and the towering building opposite the entrance to **Church Close**, whose carvings include vivid bunches of grapes, a popular design for Dartmouth wine traders. A serious fire in May 2010 affected some buildings in Fairfax Place, but there are plans for a £10 million rebuild, preserving the historic facades.

Beside the boat float, the **Butterwalk** is a row of incredibly slanting 17th-century shops. It's home to the **Dartmouth Museum** (☎ 01803-832923; Duke St; admission £1.50; ☷ 10am-4pm Mon-Sat Apr-Oct, noon-3pm Mon-Sat Nov-Mar), which beautifully evokes the town's nautical past via model ships, boats in bottles and sepia photos.

The quaintly cobbled **Bayard's Cove**, just south of the lower ferry, is where the Pilgrim Fathers stopped off en route from Southampton to America in 1620. The pilgrims only put in to Plymouth to later depart from the much more famous Mayflower Steps (see p164), because one of the boats sprang a leak.

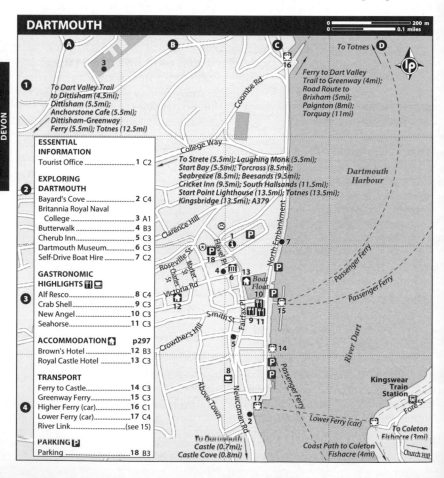

DARTMOUTH

ESSENTIAL INFORMATION
Tourist Office 1 C2

EXPLORING DARTMOUTH
Bayard's Cove 2 C4
Britannia Royal Naval
  College 3 A1
Butterwalk 4 B3
Cherub Inn.................................... 5 C3
Dartmouth Museum.................... 6 C3
Self-Drive Boat Hire 7 C2

GASTRONOMIC HIGHLIGHTS 🍴🍷
Alf Resco...................................... 8 C4
Crab Shell 9 C3
New Angel...................................10 C3
Seahorse.......................................11 C3

ACCOMMODATION 🏠   p297
Brown's Hotel 12 B3
Royal Castle Hotel 13 C3

TRANSPORT
Ferry to Castle.............................14 C3
Greenway Ferry............................15 C3
Higher Ferry (car)......................16 C1
Lower Ferry (car).......................17 C4
River Link....................................(see 15)

PARKING 🅿
Parking 18 B3

To Dart Valley Trail to Dittisham (4.5mi); Dittisham (5.5mi); Anchorstone Cafe (5.5mi); Dittisham-Greenway Ferry (5.5mi); Totnes (12.5mi)

To Strete (5.5mi); Laughing Monk (5.5mi); Start Bay (5.5mi); Torcross (8.5mi); Seabreeze (8.5mi); Beesands (9.5mi); Cricket Inn (9.5mi); South Hallsands (11.5mi); Start Point Lighthouse (13.5mi); Totnes (13.5mi); Kingsbridge (13.5mi); A379

To Totnes

Ferry to Dart Valley Trail to Greenway (4mi); Road Route to Brixham (5mi); Paignton (8mi); Torquay (11mi)

Dartmouth Harbour

Passenger Ferry

Passenger Ferry

River Dart

Kingswear Train Station

To Coleton Fishacre (3mi)

Coast Path to Coleton Fishacre (4mi)

Church Hill

Lower Ferry (car)

Passenger Ferry

To Dartmouth Castle (0.7mi); Castle Cove (0.8mi)

Boat Float

Coombe Rd

College Way

Clarence Hill

Roseville St

Market St

Charles St

Victoria Rd

Smith St

Fairfax Pl

Flavel Pl

North Embankment

Crowther's Hill

Above Town

Newcomen Rd

Ford St

0   200 m
0   0.1 miles

It's worth exploring the steps and lanes winding off Dartmouth's main routes; the tourist office also sells good town-trail leaflets (£2).

❦ BRITANNIA ROYAL NAVAL COLLEGE // GET A REVEALING INSIGHT INTO THE SENIOR SERVICE

The imposing building perched on the hills above Dartmouth is the **college** (☎ 01803-677787; College Way; ☽ tours 2pm Wed & Sun Apr-Oct) where the Royal Navy trains its officers. This vast mansion was built in 1905, replacing two training hulks that were anchored in the Dart. Guides lead you around its enormous rooms and grounds, recounting the buildings history and tales of its students. All Royal Navy officers have learnt their trade here, including Princes Charles and Andrew, and it's easy to spot today's cadets wandering the town. Visits are by pre-booked guided tour; contact the tourist office.

❦ DARTMOUTH CASTLE // A FERRY RIDE, A CASTLE AND A SWIM

The atmospheric boat trip to this fortification at the mouth of the River Dart is part of its huge appeal. The tiny, open-top **Castle Ferry** (☎ 01803-835034; return £1.40; ☽ 10am-4.45pm Easter-Oct) putters the mile downriver from Dartmouth's **South Embankment**, providing superb views of the houses and woods lining the steep banks.

The picturesque **castle** (EH; ☎ 01803-833588; adult/child £4.50/2.30; ☽ 10am-6pm Jul & Aug, 10am-5pm Apr-Jun & Sep, 10am-4pm Oct, 10am-4pm Sat & Sun Nov-Mar; ℗) started life in the 14th century to protect the harbour from seaborne raids. It was commissioned by Dartmouth's privateering mayor, John Hawley – said to be the inspiration for the 'Shipman' in Chaucer's *Canterbury Tales*. The fortification saw additions in the 15th century, the Victorian era and WWII; today its maze of passages, guardrooms and battlements provides an evocative insight into life inside. Look out too for the audiovisual recreation of a Victorian **gun drill**.

Just south of the castle, steep steps lead down to the pint-sized **Castle Cove**, a popular if bracing local spot for swimming beside battlements.

❦ EXPLORING THE RIVER DART // FIND YOUR OWN FAVOURITE STRETCH OF CREEK

Beautiful from the banks, Dartmouth is even more beguiling from the water. **River Link** (☎ 01803-834488; www.riverlink.co.uk; adult/child return £12/8; ☽ 2-4 daily Apr-Oct) runs leisurely 1¼-hour cruises to Totnes from the pontoon at South Embankment.

The dinky **Dartmouth to Dittisham Ferry** (☎ 0781 8001108; adult/child return £7.50/5 ☽ 1-2 hourly Mar-Oct) chugs to the village of **Dittisham** 4 miles north; an appealing place with a great creekside **pub** and the delightful **Anchorstone Café** (p157). From here you can catch the **Dittisham to Greenway Ferry** (☎ 0845 489418; adult/child return £3.20/2.20; ☽ 9am-6pm Mar-Oct, to 4pm Nov-Feb) to the east bank and Agatha Christie's holiday home. If the ferry isn't in sight when you arrive, summon it by ringing the ships' bell beside the pontoon.

For leisurely explorations, hire your own **motorboat** (☎ 01803-834600; North Embankment; per 1 hr/day £25/100), or charter the 12-seater **Falcon II** (☎ 07970 759172; per hr from £50), complete with skipper Tony.

A series of **car and passenger ferries** (see p158) regularly shuttle between Dartmouth and **Kingswear** on the opposite bank.

For a short circular **walk**, catch the Higher Ferry from Dartmouth to the east bank, stroll a mile downriver to

DEVON

Kingswear then catch the Lower Ferry back. Or hike the charming **Dart Valley Trail** to Dittisham and cross the river to Greenway on the **Dittisham to Greenway Ferry**, then walk down to Kingswear before crossing back to Dartmouth by ferry.

❦ START BAY WALK // STROLL BETWEEN SEA, NATURE RESERVE AND HISTORIC VILLAGE

Slapton Sands occupies a 3-mile sweep of northern **Start Bay**. The 'sands' are actually an immense pebble ridge and are backed by the largest freshwater lake in the southwest: **Slapton Ley**. There's only just enough room for a narrow strip of road between the two bodies of water, making for a memorable **drive** and some superb walking.

From the **Slapton memorial car park** halfway along Slapton Sands, walk across the road following signs for the village of Slapton. The entrance to the **Slapton Ley National Nature Reserve** (www.slnnr.org.uk) is immediately after the bridge, on the left. Fringed by reed beds and woods, the ley is alive with wildlife; look out for yellow iris, tufted ducks, great crested grebes, pochards and, if you're lucky, otters.

A series of colour-coded **trails** weaves beside the lake; the 1¾-mile one skirts the ley, crosses reed beds via a series of boardwalks, and heads up to **Slapton** itself – a quintessential Devon village where houses huddle around mazelike lanes. It has a time-warp **village shop**, robust **church** and 14th-century **ruined tower**. The **Tower Inn** (☎ 01548-580216; Church Rd; ☺ lunch & dinner daily, closed Mon Oct-Mar), next door, offers innovative food and a very decent pint. From the village, a path beside the road takes you back to the coast and your car.

❦ SHERMAN TANK MEMORIAL // DISCOVER START BAY'S TRAGIC WARTIME PAST

Wave-dashed as they are today, Slapton Sands have an even more dramatic past. During WWII, thousands of American servicemen carried out practice landings here in preparation for D-Day. Live ammunition was used to make the exercises more authentic. On one rehearsal in 1944, Exercise Tiger, a German torpedo boat sank several landing craft; more than 700 American servicemen died.

One of the **tanks** that sank during the exercise has been winched from 65ft of water just offshore. Painted black, it now sits beside the car park at **Torcross**, at the south end of **Slapton Ley**. Signs outline the remarkable role this area played in WWII; from 1943 the residents of seven local villages, including Slapton, were evacuated from their homes for a year while the D-Day rehearsals took place.

❦ SOUTH HALLSANDS // VISIT THE VILLAGE THAT FELL INTO THE SEA

The shells of the handful of houses that cling to the cliff here are all that remain of a thriving **fishing village**. In 1917 one severe storm literally washed this community out to sea. More than 20 cottages, a pub and a post office were lost overnight; remarkably, none of the 128 residents were killed. Locally, the disaster is blamed on the long-term dredging of Start Bay for building materials, which caused the village's protective strip of beach to disappear.

You can't wander amid the ruins themselves, but you can see them clearly from a cliff-side **viewing platform** where signs feature evocative sepia images of the village and its indomitable inhabitants. South Hallsands is a mile north of

Start Point Lighthouse; there is a small car park alongside.

☙ START POINT LIGHTHOUSE // CLIMB A 28M CIRCULAR TOWER FOR CRACKING VIEWS

This **lighthouse** (☎ 01803-771802; www. trinityhouse.co.uk; Start Point; adult/child £3/1.60; ◷ 11am-5pm Sun-Fri Jul & Aug, noon-5pm Wed & Sun Apr & May, noon-5pm Wed, Thu & Sun Jun & Sep; Ⓟ) sits on one of the most exposed pen insulas on the English coast. The beam from its 200,000 candela light can be seen for 25 nautical miles. Built in 1836, the lighthouse went electric in 1959 and was manned right up until 1993; it's now controlled automatically from Trinity House's HQ in Essex.

Tours last 45 minutes and wind up hundreds of steps, through tiny circular rooms. The highlight is the final climb, by ladder, to the top platform where you stand alongside the massive optics and look out over 360-degree views and down onto a boiling sea.

GASTRONOMIC HIGHLIGHTS

☙ ALF RESCO // DARTMOUTH £
☎ 01803-835880; Lower St; brunch from £4; ◷ 7am-2pm

Tucked under a huge canvas awning, this cool cafe brings a dash of chilled-out cosmopolitan charm to town. Rickety wooden chairs and old street signs are scattered around a front terrace, making it a great place for brunch alongside the riverboat crews.

☙ ANCHORSTONE CAFÉ
DITTISHAM £
☎ 01803-722365; Manor St; mains from £7; ◷ 9.30am-5pm Jun-Sep, closed Mon & Tue Easter-May & Oct

It's hard to know what is best: the view or the food. Tucked away in the charm-ing village of Dittisham, this bistro's dining terrace is right beside the creek. Watch the ferry shuttling across to Greenway and tuck into succulent Dart-mouth crab and lobster, washed down with a glass of local Sharpham wine (p150). You can cruise to this waterside idyll by boat (p155) and it's open some weekend summer evenings too.

☙ BRITANNIA SHELLFISH // BEESANDS £
☎ 01548-581186; Seafront; ◷ 10am-4.30pm

Directly opposite the fishing boats lining Beesands beach, this tiny shop allows you to revel in zero food miles. Plump for handpicked Start Bay crab; line-caught bass, pollack and mackerel; or or-der a whole cooked lobster – it even sells travel packs and ice. The shop sometimes closes early; call to check.

☙ CRAB SHELL // DARTMOUTH £
☎ 01803-839036; 1 Raleigh St; sandwiches £4; ◷ lunch, closed Jan-Mar

The shellfish in the sarnies made here have been landed on the quay a few steps away, and much of the fish has been smoked locally. Opt to fill your bread with mackerel and horseradish mayo, kiln roast salmon with dill or classic, delicious Dartmouth crab.

☙ CRICKET INN // BEESANDS ££
☎ 01548-580215; Seafront; mains £10-18; ◷ lunch & dinner

They've been serving to fishermen here since 1867 and some seafarers still prop up the bar; one of the regulars in the corner probably caught your lunch. The beautifully cooked lobsters, brill and hand-dived scallops all come from Start Bay. Options include crab soup with brandy and cream, and red mullet with carrot and coriander.

DEVON

♥ LAUGHING MONK // STRETE ££

☎ 01803-770639; Totnes Rd; mains £14; ☺ dinner Mon-Sat

This snug restaurant, set in a former school, is an object lesson in working imaginatively with local and Mediterranean flavours. Excellent combos include the carpaccio of beef with capers and parmesan, and seafood grill with crab couscous. The oozing local and Continental cheeses round things off nicely.

♥ SEAHORSE // DARTMOUTH ££

☎ 01803-835147; 5 South Embankment; mains £17-23; 2-/3-course lunch £15/20; ☺ lunch Wed-Sat, dinner Tue-Sat

The seafood served here is so fresh, the menu changes twice a day. So depending on what's been landed at Brixham (7 miles away) or Dartmouth (a few yards) you might get cuttlefish in Chianti, sea bream with roasted garlic, or fried local squid with garlic mayonnaise. The river views are charming, the atmosphere relaxed; one not to miss.

♥ NEW ANGEL // DARTMOUTH £££

☎ 01803-839425; 2 South Embankment; mains £19-27, 2 courses £19-28, 5 courses £65; ☺ breakfast, lunch & dinner Tue-Sat

The fanciest joint in town, this Michelin-starred restaurant is run by TV chef John Burton Race (of *French Leave* fame). Gallic charm suffuses the menu; expect local fish, meat and game to be transformed by complex treatments: steamed sea bass with champagne-and-oyster broth, Devon beef with snails and bone marrow, or ravioli of Dartmouth crab with bisque. Kick the evening off with a riverview cocktail in the superstylish lounge.

TRANSPORT

BUS // Bus 111 goes from Dartmouth to Torquay, via Totnes (hourly Monday to Saturday, four on Sunday). Bus 93 runs from Plymouth to Dartmouth via Kingsbridge, Torcross, Slapton and Strete (three to four daily).

FERRY // Dartmouth's Higher and Lower Ferries both take cars and foot passengers; they shuttle across the river to Kingswear (car/pedestrian £3.50/1) every six minutes between 6.30am and 10.45pm.

TRAIN // The Paignton & Dartmouth Steam Railway runs from Paignton to Kingswear Station. For details, see p145.

SALCOMBE TO BURGH ISLAND

pop 7100

Oh-so-chic Salcombe sits charmingly at the mouth of the Kingsbridge Estuary, its network of ancient, winding streets bordered by sparkling waters and sandy coves. Its beauty has drawn waves of wealthy people and at times it's more South Kensington than south Devon and a massive 43% of properties here are second homes. But despite the strings of shops selling sailing tops the port's undoubted appeal remains, offering tempting opportunities to catch a ferry to a beach and soak up some nautical history.

West of Salcombe the South Hams coast features undeveloped cliffs, golden beaches and the tucked-away villages of Hope Cove, Bantham and Bigbury-on-Sea. This is a captivating stretch, a place to catch crabs on harbour walls, learn to surf or stay in Burgh Island's sumptuous Art Deco hotel. To the east, Kingsbridge provides an insight into life in a Devon market town.

ESSENTIAL INFORMATION

TOURIST INFORMATION // Kingsbridge Tourist Office (☎ 01548-853195; www.kingsbridgeinfo.co.uk; The Quay; ☺ 9am-5.30pm Mon-Sat May-Oct, 9am-5pm Nov-Apr, plus Sun 10am-4pm May-Sep) Salcombe Tourist Office (☎ 01548-843927; www.salcombeinformation.co.uk; Market St;

⊗ 9am-6pm Mon-Sat, 10am-6pm Sun Jul & Aug, 10am-
5pm Apr-Jun & Sep-Oct, 10am-3pm Mon-Sat Nov-Mar)

ORIENTATION

Salcombe centres round its harbour on
the west bank of the Kingsbridge Estuary
(technically a drowned valley, or ria).
Whitestrand Quay lies in the heart of
town; North and South Sands are 1½ and
2 miles south respectively. On the east
side of the estuary, a string of sandy bays
sit below the village of East Portlemouth.
These coves and South Sands are linked
to the centre of Salcombe by a fleet of
ferries.

EXPLORING SALCOMBE TO BURGH ISLAND

**❦ HISTORIC SALCOMBE //
DISCOVER SUNKEN TREASURE AND A
NAUTICAL PAST**
Today it's Chelsea-on-Sea, but in the
17th century Salcombe's fishermen
worked the Newfoundland Banks; by
the 1800s scores of shipyards built fast
fruit schooners bound for the Azores. In
those days the area immediately around
Whitestrand Quay contained four boat
yards and streets full of sail lofts, landing
quays and warehouses. All competed for
a precious section of shore, resulting in
long, thin buildings, set side-on to the
harbour. Many of these remain, framed
by incredibly **narrow lanes**. Hunt them
out at the north end of Union St, and
off Fore St near Clifton Place, Robinson
Row and around the **Ferry Inn** (☎ 01548-
844000; ⊗ lunch & dinner), whose waterside
terrace provides grandstand views.

Salcombe's **Maritime Museum** (Market
St; admission £2.50; ⊗ 10am-12.30pm & 2.30-4.30pm
Apr-Oct) exhibits the now-unfamiliar
tools of the shipbuilder's trade: stretching hooks, caulking irons and drawing

knives; models of the boats they built sit
alongside.

Salcombe's role as an international
port is revealed by the treasure recovered
from local **shipwrecks**. Look out for the
museum's glittering coin haul from the
Salcombe Canon site: 500 Moroccan
gold dinars dating from the 13th to the
17th centuries. The museum also sells an
1842 map (£1) of the town, allowing for
some past-meets-present detective work.

**❦ ON THE WATER // EXPLORE THE
ESTUARY BY DINGHY, CANOE OR
FERRY**
Whitestrand (☎ 01548-843818; Whitestrand
Quay; per hr/day from £25/85) rents motorboats
and sailing dinghies and **Singing Paddles** (☎ 07754-426633; www.singingpaddles.
co.uk; per 2hr/day £10/40) does trips in both
Canadian canoes and kayaks. **South
Sands Sailing** (☎ 01548-843451; www.
southsandssailing.co.uk; per 2hr £25-45; P) runs
sailing, kayaking and surfing sessions
from South Sands beach. It also rents out
kayaks (per two hours/half-day £25/35).
Salcombe-based **South West Yacht
Charters** (☎ 07980-699936) does everything
from skippered day sails (£365) to sail-
yourself-hire (per week £1195).

The cheery **South Sands Ferry** (☎ 01548-
561035; adult/child £2.90/1.90; ⊗ 9.45am-5.15pm
Apr-Oct; P) chugs from Whitestrand Quay
to the beach at South Sands, where an ingenious motor-powered landing platform
trundles through the water to help you
ashore. The ferry runs every 30 minutes,
the trip takes 20 minutes. The half-hourly
East Portlemouth Ferry (☎ 01548-842061;
return adult/child £2.60/1.40; ⊗ 8am-5.30pm, to 7pm
August) putters to the sandy beaches on the
eastern side of the estuary. Between Easter
and October it goes from Ferry Pier (off
Fore St); from November to Easter from
Whitestrand Quay.

DEVON

❦ OVERBECK'S // ENCOUNTER SHIPWRECKS, SUBTROPICAL GARDENS AND A CURIOUS CURE
An Aladdin's cave of curios, this **Edwardian country house** (NT; ☎ 01548-842893; Sharpitor; adult/child £6.70/3.40; ☽ 11am-5pm Sat-Thu mid-Mar–Oct, plus Fri late Jul & Aug; ℗) crowns the cliffs at the estuary mouth. It's set in 3 hectares of lush, subtropical gardens, where exotic plants frame wide views. It's named after former owner Otto Overbeck, an inventor who pioneered a machine called the Rejuvenator, which claimed to cure disease using electric currents – one of these Heath Robinson-esque devices is on display.

Rooms are packed with Otto's quirky collections of stuffed animals, snuff boxes and bits of nauticalia. There are also displays about the *Herzogin Cecilie*, a beautiful four-masted barque that sank in 1936 at Starehole Bay, just a mile south of the property; a dramatic coast path leads past the spot.

You can drive to Overbeck's or walk the steep 2¼ miles from Salcombe; keep heading south on Cliff Rd until it's signposted.

❦ KINGSBRIDGE // SHOP AMID A WEALTH OF INDEPENDENT STORES
Despite being on the same estuary as chichi Salcombe to the south, Kingsbridge has avoided gentrification and kept a healthy range of local shops. **Fore St** leads steeply up from the quayside **car park**, the **Harbour Bookshop** (☎ 01548-857233; ☽ closed Sun) is on the left, just down Mill St. At traditional confectioners **Choc Amour** (☎ 01548-854471; 21 Fore St), ranks of sweet jars line the counter and your purchase is still measured out in scales. Nonchain **toy-shops**, **greengrocers**, a local **creamery** and family **butchers** range up nearby.

Further up at **Catch of the Day** (☎ 01548-852006; 54 Fore St; ☽ 9am-4pm Mon-Wed, 9am-1pm Thu & Sat, 9am-5pm Fri), they still smoke the famous Salcombe Smokies (mackerel); try the flavoursome smoked salmon and prawns too. The deli Mangetout (see p161) is right at the top of the hill. Add the kind of men's and ladies' outfitters that have simply disappeared from many high streets, and it provides a glimpse of life before chain-store retail uniformity.

❦ HOPE COVE // ENCOUNTER WRECKS AND THATCHES IN THIS SMUGGLERS' VILLAGE
A couple of pint-sized sandy coves, a tiny harbour and a gathering of thatched cottages – there's not much to this **village** situated 5 miles west of Salcombe, but what there is, is delightful. From the tiny **Mouthwell Beach** (℗), in front of the thatched **cafe**, the cliff path leads steeply north, revealing superb views of Burgh Island (p161), and a sign detailing two local wrecks: the *San Pedro*, a Spanish Armada vessel, and HMS *Ramillies*, which sank in 1760 with the loss of 700 lives.

In the village centre (technically **Outer Hope**), a terrace of pastel-painted cottages lines the **Shippen**, the steeply-sloping rock that separates Mouthwell from a sandy harbour scattered with boats. The harbour wall is ideal for a spot of **crabbing**. From here a footpath hugs the shore to **Inner Hope**, with its cluster of thatches and old lifeboat house. Next, the coast path leads a mile south to **Bolt Tail** and the 4.5m-high grassy ramparts of an **Iron Age fort**. Back in the village, the beer terrace of the **Hope and Anchor** (☎ 01548-561294; ☽ lunch & dinner) is where everyone congregates for a pint.

♣ A DAY AT THE BEACH // BEACHCOMB OR SURF ALONGSIDE VAST STRETCHES OF SAND

The pocket-sized village of **Bantham** has the best surfing **beach** (P) in south Devon and hardly anything else. Its scattering of buildings, including a pub and a shop, stretches back from a car park (£3.50) that sits between rolling dunes and (at low tide) a magnificent expanse of sand. Southwesterly swells draw rafts of surfers here; cross-shore winds see fleets of kitesurfers take to the waves. **Fir Tree Garage** (☎ 01548-550063; ☷ 9am-5pm Mon-Fri, 10am-4pm Sat & Sun, closed Sun Nov-Easter), 5 miles northwest of the beach on the A379, rents out wetsuits (per 24 hours £7), bodyboards (£7) and longboards (£12.50). Be aware: the currents at Bantham are potentially dangerous, note the signs and lifeguard's advice.

A 20-minute drive away on the other side of the estuary at **Bigbury-on-Sea**, the **Discovery Surf School** (☎ 07813-639622; www.discoverysurf.com; per 1/4 lessons £38/125) will teach you how to ride the waves.

♣ BURGH ISLAND // ROAM AROUND A PINT-SIZED ROCKY OUTCROP

A slanting chunk of grass-topped rock, this 10-hectare **tidal island** is connected to Bigbury-on-Sea by a stretch of sand at low tide. At high water the journey is made by a sea-tractor (single £2), an eccentric device where the passenger platform is perched on stilts 6ft above the tractor's wheels and the waves.

Once ashore, it takes around 30 minutes to walk around the island. At the clifftop, track down the remains of a **huers' hut**, where lookouts used to spot lucrative pilchard shoals then raise the alarm (hence 'hue and cry').

You'll also pass the gorgeous Art Deco Burgh Island Hotel (p299) where Agatha Christie stayed while writing *And Then*

There Were None. Back at the sea-tractor slipway, the 14th-century **Pilchard Inn** (☎ 01548-810514; ☷ 11am-11pm), provides snacks and a seaside beer terrace with wraparound views.

GASTRONOMIC HIGHLIGHTS

♣ DIY SALCOMBE £

For gourmet picnic supplies **Salcombe Fishmongers** (☎ 01548-844475; 11 Clifton Pl; ☷ 9am-5.30pm Mon-Sat) at the foot of Market St does tempting seafood platters and classy crab sandwiches. Next door, the Chelsea-style deli **Casse-Croute** (☎ 01548-843003; 10 Clifton Pl; ☷ 8.30am-5.30pm, 8.30am-4.30pm winter, closed mid-Jan–mid-Feb) is packed with charcuterie and organic artisanal breads; the sarnie options run to chicken with sweet lime chilli. Opposite, the **Salcombe Yawl** (☎ 01548-842143; 10a Clifton Pl) is stacked with homity pies, Scotch eggs and huge Cornish pasties.

♣ MANGETOUT // KINGSBRIDGE £

☎ 01548-856620; 84 Fore St; ☷ closed Sun

Right at the top of town, this diet-defying deli offers a smorgasbord of goodies. Choose from Devon hams, chorizo, zesty salads, olives, fresh breads, cakes and croissants. The local cheese selection is a *Who's Who* of local producers: Devon Oke, Ticklemore, Sharpham brie, Quickes Cheddar and the pungent Devon, Beenleigh and Exmoor blues.

♣ OLD BAKERY // KINGSBRIDGE ££

☎ 01548-855777; The Quay; tapas £3-8, mains £12-17; ☷ breakfast, lunch & dinner Tue-Sat

This restaurant-cum-cafe brings a slice of the sunny Mediterranean to rural south Devon. Huge pieces of modern art combine with battered leather sofas; huge bowls of olives sit alongside piles of home-baked bread. Tapas include air-dried tuna with peppers, mounds of charcuterie and garlic-laced seafood.

DEVON

On summer Friday and Saturday nights there's fine dining; think seared monkfish or lobster with garlic.

🌱 OYSTER SHACK // STAKES HILL ££
☎ 01548-810876; Milburn Orchard Farm; mains £11;
🕒 breakfast, lunch & dinner Mon-Sat plus lunch Sun Easter-Oct, closed Mon & Tue Nov-Easter
The laid-back terrace of this idyllic bistro is *the* place to indulge in local oysters, mussels, monkfish and crab; treatments range from grilled and traditional to spicy and Spanish. The shack lies just off the tidal road that hugs the estuary between Bigbury-on-Sea and Aveton Gifford to the northeast.

🌱 WINKING PRAWN // SALCOMBE ££
☎ 01548-842326; North Sands; mains £8-22;
🕒 breakfast, lunch & dinner Easter-Oct, lunch daily plus dinner Fri & Sat Nov-Easter
Overflowing with distressed driftwood-chic, this North Sands beachside brasserie features huge rowing oars, red ensigns and a seaview deck. It's a perfect spot to sample monkfish wrapped in bacon, sea bass with sweet pepper, and goat's cheese–themed veggie options. That or work through a pitcher of Pimm's. Summer sees them barbecuing mackerel, steaks, haloumi and prawns.

TRANSPORT

BUS // From Kingsbridge, bus 93 (five daily) runs east to Dartmouth, via Torcross, Slapton Sands and Strete. It also shuttles west to Plymouth (five daily). Bus 64 (two to five daily) goes between Exeter and Kingsbridge, via Totnes. Bus 606 (11 daily, Monday to Saturday) connects Salcombe with Kingsbridge; bus 162 (three daily, Monday to Saturday) runs between Kingsbridge and Hope Cove.
FERRY // The pedestrian-only **River Avon Ferry** (☎ 01548-561196; 🕒 10-11am & 3-4pm Mon-Sat Apr–mid-Sep) shuttles across the water between Bantham and Bigbury-on-Sea. Passenger ferries also ply the waters at Salcombe (see p159).

PLYMOUTH

pop 256,000
If parts of Devon are nature programs or costume dramas, Plymouth is a healthy dose of reality TV. Gritty, and certainly not always pretty, its centre has been subjected to bursts of building even the architect's mother might question. But despite being dismissed for its partying, poverty and urban problems, this is a city of huge spirit and great assets. Its location, on the edge of a stunning natural harbour and just behind Dartmoor, brings endless possibilities for boat trips, sailing or hiking. Add a rich maritime history, one of the country's best aquariums and a playful 1930s lido, and you have a place to reconnect with the real before another foray into Devon's chocolate-box-pretty moors and shores.

ESSENTIAL INFORMATION

TOURIST INFORMATION // Tourist office (☎ 01752-306330; www.visitplymouth.co.uk; 3-5 The Barbican; 🕒 9am-5pm Mon-Sat & 10am-4pm Sun Apr-Oct, 9am-5pm Mon-Fri & 10am-4pm Sat Nov-Mar)

EXPLORING PLYMOUTH

🌱 STROLLING ON PLYMOUTH HOE // TAP INTO THE CITY'S HEART AND SOUL
To get under Plymouth's skin, head for the Hoe. This **grassy headland** provides 180-degree views of rolling hills and a glittering **Plymouth Sound**; the huge natural harbour. It's where Plymothians come to stroll, fly kites, kick a football, roller skate or watch the boats in the bay.

For centuries the Hoe's been the focus of the city's community spirit. During the Blitz of WWII Plymouth suffered horrendously; more than 1000 civilians died and the centre was reduced to rubble. But, undeterred, locals famously staged morale-boosting open-air dances on the Hoe; thousands still fill it at New Year and on Bonfire Night.

The Hoe is also, supposedly, where Sir Francis Drake insisted on finishing his game of bowls before setting off to defeat the advancing Spanish Armada. The fabled green on which he lingered was probably where his **statue** now stands. A few steps away, today's enthusiasts play on a modern **bowling green**.

The Hoe is full of links to Plymouth's martial past and present. The city became a Royal Dockyard in 1690, its modern counterpart is the largest in Europe, and supports, together with the commercial yard, an estimated 24,000 jobs. Scores of **Royal Naval vessels** are Plymouth based – you can spot them in Plymouth Sound; the local paper, the *Evening Herald*, details daily shipping movements; for the best views bring binoculars. Hundreds of troops are still

Plymouth based – the **Royal Citadel**, the huge 17th-century fort at the east end of the Hoe, is home to some of them.

The biggest of the Hoe's many war memorials is the immense **Plymouth Naval Memorial**. It commemorates commonwealth WWI and WWII sailors who have no grave but the sea. It lists a total of 23,186 men. Bunches of flowers are still often propped up beside individual names.

☙ SMEATON'S TOWER // CLAMBER UP AN OLD LIGHTHOUSE

Set right in the centre of the Hoe, this former **lighthouse** (☎ 01752- 304774; The Hoe; adult/child £2/1; ☯ 10am-noon & 1-4pm Tue-Sat Apr-Oct, 10am-noon & 1-3pm Tue-Sat Nov-Mar) acts as a 70ft high, red and white candy-striped landmark. The whole structure used to stand on the Eddystone Reef 14 miles offshore and was transferred here, brick by brick, in the 1880s. For an illuminating insight into the lives of past lighthouse keepers, head up the winding stone stairs

DEVON

SIR FRANCIS DRAKE

Sir Francis Drake (1540–96) was a man with a dashing image that belies a complex reality. To Tudor England he was a hero, explorer and adventurer. To his Spanish counterparts he was 'Drake the master thief'. He was also involved, albeit briefly, in slavery when he sailed with his relative, John Hawkins; the first English captain to ply the triangular 'slave trade'.

In 1580 Drake sailed into Plymouth aboard the *Golden Hind*, having become the first man to circumnavigate the globe. His vessel was full of treasure looted from Spanish colonies, securing the favour of Queen Elizabeth I and the money to buy **Buckland Abbey** (p171) on the outskirts of Plymouth.

Eleven years later, Drake (legend has it) calmly insisted on finishing his game of bowls on Plymouth Hoe, despite the advancing Spanish Armada. The first engagement happened just off Plymouth, the second at Portland Bill – eventually the Spanish fleet was chased to Calais and attacked with fire ships. Many escaped but were wrecked off the Scottish coast.

Drake died of fever in 1596 while fighting Spanish possessions in the West Indies and was buried at sea off modern Panama. His **statue**, looking more dignified than piratical, stands on Plymouth Hoe.

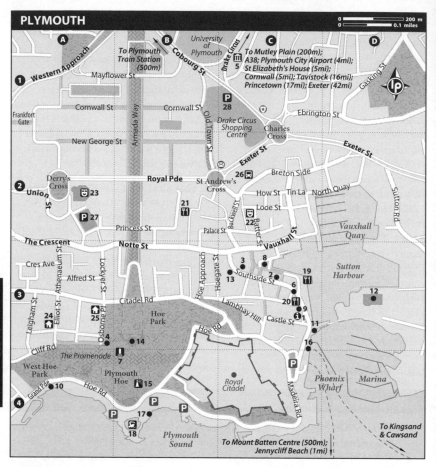

PLYMOUTH

and through a series of circular rooms. Some 93 steps later you emerge onto an open-air platform with stunning views of the city, Dartmoor and the sea.

♥ PLYMOUTH'S HISTORIC QUARTER // SEE WHERE THE PILGRIM FATHERS SET SAIL

In Plymouth's **Barbican** district, part-cobbled streets are lined with Tudor and Jacobean buildings, many of which are now galleries, restaurants and funky bars.

The **Mayflower Steps** mark the final UK departure point of the Pilgrim Fathers, a band of Puritans who sailed to the New World in 1620 in search of greater religious freedom. Having left Southampton, they were forced into Dartmouth by an unseaworthy ship and eventually left Plymouth (England) on board the *Mayflower* – going on to found New England's first permanent colony at Plymouth (Massachusetts). The Pilgrims' approximate departure point is marked by a heavily weathered honey-coloured **Doric arch** and flapping American and British flags.

Plaques alongside also mark the departures of the first emigrant ships to

New Zealand, Captain Cook's voyages of discovery, the arrival of the first-ever transatlantic flight in 1916 and, five decades later, the first solo circumnavigation of the globe by boat.

Just behind, the inventive exhibits of **Plymouth Mayflower** (☎ 01752-306330; 3-5 The Barbican; adult/child £2/1; ☺ 10am-4pm daily May-Oct, 10am-4pm Mon-Sat Nov-Apr) evoke the Barbican over the centuries, while 100yd up the Barbican, the **passenger list** of the *Mayflower* is displayed on the side of **Island House**. Look out for the descriptions of passengers as either 'Saints' (Puritan pilgrims) or 'Strangers' (those hired to support the expedition).

✿ PLYMOUTH GIN DISTILLERY // DISCOVER HOW THEY MAKE THE 'G' OF 'G&T'

This heavily-beamed **distillery** (☎ 01752-665292; www.plymouthgin.com; 60 Southside St; tours £6; ☺ tours at 11.30am, 12.30pm, 2.30pm & 3.30pm daily, plus 10.30am & 4.30pm Easter-Oct) is the oldest producer of gin in the world; they've been making it here since 1793. The Royal Navy was responsible for taking it round the world in countless officers' messes, while in the 1930s Plymouth Gin featured in the first recorded recipe for a dry martini. Distillery **tours** thread past stills and huge copper vats, while guides get you sniffing the sometimes surprising raw ingredients (called botanicals) before providing a tutored tasting. The price includes a gin and tonic in the restored medieval bar upstairs.

✿ BARBICAN ART TOUR // TAKE IN BROODING REALISM AND COMIC-BOOK CHARM

The **Barbican** has provided inspiration for artists for decades, and a healthy scattering of galleries line the streets. The district also offers the chance to track down the work of two very different Plymouth artists.

The representational painter **Robert Lenkiewicz** (1941–2002; www.lenkiewiczfoundation.org) has been described by some as a modern-day Rembrandt. The son of Jewish refugees from Germany and Poland, this brooding, eccentric philosopher was a fixture of the Barbican for decades and developed a special bond with alcoholics, drug addicts and homeless people, often offering them a meal and a bed for the night. Exploring themes of death and obsession, he also achieved notoriety in the mid-1980s when he embalmed the body of a local tramp.

His murals still dot the Barbican. Check out the *Elizabethan Mural*, the biggest and also the most peeling, in the corner of the **Parade**, alongside his former studio – there are plans to turn

DEVON ·

it into a gallery showcasing his work. Another of his huge paintings, the *Last Judgement*, is outside the **Barbican Pannier Market**. In **Prete's Café** (☎ 01752-668707; 15 Southside St) you can sip a coffee while looking up at his *Last Supper*.

In an utterly different artistic vein, Plymouth-based **Beryl Cook** (1926-2008; www.berylcook.org) was renowned for her cheerful depictions of brash, large ladies sporting unfeasibly small clothes. Her exuberant, almost comic-book artwork features a dizzying variety of Barbican scenes and one of the most popular local games is to try and spot (in the flesh) the type of characters that people her paintings.

Look out for her work in **Barbican Gallery Three** (☎ 01752-673003; 28 Southside St), then head to the gloriously unreconstructed **Dolphin Inn** (☎ 01752-660876; 14 The Barbican) for a pint. Cook immortalised this Barbican institution in several paintings, often sitting on one of the well-worn settles gathering material for her work. Two of Cook's vivid paintings (*Beach at Looe* and the impish *Lockyer Street Tavern*) also feature in a tribute to her at the **City Museum and Art Gallery** (☎ 01752-304774; Drake Circus; admission free; ⏱ 10am-5.30pm Tue-Fri, to 5pm Sat).

❦ NATIONAL MARINE AQUARIUM // COME EYEBALL TO EYEBALL WITH SAND TIGER SHARKS

The futuristic glass lines of this innovative **aquarium** (☎ 01752-220084; www.national-aquarium.co.uk; Rope Walk; adult/child £11/6.50; ⏱ 10am-6pm Apr-Oct, 10am-5pm Nov-Mar; Ⓟ) are wittily sited next to the city's pungent Fish Market; an interesting dead-fish-live-fish juxtaposition. Here sharks swim in coral seas that teem with moray eels and vividly coloured fish – there's even a loggerhead turtle called Snorkel who was rescued from a Cornish beach. Walk-through glass arches ensure huge rays glide over your head, while the immense Atlantic Reef tank reveals just what's lurking a few miles offshore. The aquarium focuses on conservation – look out for the tanks containing home-reared cardinal fish, corals and incredibly cute seahorses.

❦ CAFE CULTURE // SIP A CAPPUCCINO AND WATCH THE BOATS

On a sunny summer's day the people of Plymouth head for a waterside cafe to watch the world drift by. The **Terrace** (☎ 01752-603533; Hoe Rd; snacks £3-6; ⏱ breakfast & lunch), is a firm local favourite. Tucked away beside Tinside Lido, it boasts panoramic views across Plymouth Sound and a chilled soundtrack. To the west, the tables and chairs of the **Kiosk** (⏱ 7am-5pm daily) are scattered alongside the waterside promenade; classical music floats from the speakers.

From both, watch out for strings of yachts, dinghy races, lone canoeists, dive boats, ferries, gig boats and fishing trawlers. On a fine day it helps explain why Plymothians, although the first to admit their city is far from perfect, do tend to think of it with a sneaking sense of pride.

❦ TINSIDE POOL // TAKE A BRACING DIP IN A 1930S LIDO

The Art Deco, open-air **Tinside Pool** (☎ 01752-261915; Hoe Rd; adult/child £3.65/2.40; ⏱ noon-6pm Mon-Fri, 10am-6pm Sat & Sun late May-late Jul, 10am-6pm daily late Jul-early Sep) is an unforgettable swim-spot, with cream curves sweeping gracefully out from the foot of the **Hoe**. Built in 1935, for decades it suffered from neglect, but now it's been delicately restored in light and dark blue tiles. Plunge into its unheated salt water then recline on a sun lounger

DEVON

on the circular rim, looking straight out over Plymouth Sound.

☙ **EXPLORE THE SHORE // HOP ON A FERRY FOR WIDER VIEWS**
Seeing Plymouth from the water really conjures up its nautical past. Try the **Kingsand-Cawsand Ferry** (☎ 07971-208381; www.cawsandferry.com; adult/child return £8/4; ☼ 4-5 daily mid-Apr–mid-Sep), which does the 30-minute run from the Barbican Pontoon, across Plymouth Sound to the Cornish smuggling villages of Kingsand and Cawsand. There you can wander narrow streets, drink in some salty pubs and browse the handful of shops.

Sound Cruising (☎ 01752-671166; www.soundcruising.com; Barbican Pontoon; 1½hr trips £6) runs a Dockyard and Warship trip that shuttles along the front of the Hoe, past Drake's Island to Devonport Dockyard and some up-close views of the huge vessels of the Royal Navy.

GASTRONOMIC HIGHLIGHTS

☙ **BARBICAN KITCHEN ££**
☎ 01752-604448; 60 Southside St; mains £11; ☼ lunch & dinner, closed Sun evening
The bistro-style baby sister of Tanners Restaurant (p167) has a wood and stone interior with bursts of shocking pink and lime. The food is attention grabbing too – try the calves' livers with horseradish mash or maybe the honey, goat's cheese and apple crostini. The Devon beefburger, with a slab of stilton, is divine. It's all set in the atmospheric Plymouth Gin Distillery (p165).

☙ **CAP'N JASPERS £**
☎ 01752-262444; Whitehouse Pier, Quay Rd; snacks £3-5; ☼ 7.45am-11.45pm
Unique, quirky and slightly insane, this Barbican institution has been delight-

ing tourists and locals alike for decades. Motorised gadgets whirr around the counter and the teaspoons are attached to the counter by chains. The menu is of the burger and bacon butty school, and trying to eat the 'half a yard of hot dog' is a Plymouth rite of passage. Also on offer are fresh crab rolls – the filling could have been caught by the bloke sitting next to you; his boat's probably tied up alongside.

☙ **FISH AND CHIPS £**
Sampling just-caught fish from Plymouth's trawlers is a treat. **Platters** (☎ 01752-227262; 12 The Barbican; mains £16; ☼ lunch & dinner) is a snug restaurant with a strong local following – try the skate in butter or the locally caught sea bass. A few steps away at the classic 'chippy', the **Barbican Fish Bar** (☎ 01752-261432; 36 Southside St; ☼ 11am-9pm), the fish and chips are superb. Either take away (but watch out for diving seagulls) or settle down at a Formica-topped table; delights include pickled eggs and mushy peas.

☙ **TANNERS RESTAURANT £££**
☎ 01752-252001; www.tannersrestaurant.com; Finewell St; 2-/3-course dinner £32/39; ☼ lunch & dinner Tue-Sat
Plymouth's top fine-dining restaurant is run by the locally famous Tanner brothers and is set in a medieval building graced by soft lighting and warm stone walls. Reinvented British and French classics are the mainstay; expect lamb with gnocchi, chargrilled asparagus with soft poached egg, and roasted quail with pancetta. Their six-course tasting menu (£48, booking required) is a truly memorable meal.

NIGHTLIFE

A proper Navy city, Plymouth has a (sometimes too) lively nightlife. Union St is clubland, Mutley Plain and North Hill

DEVON

have a studenty vibe, while on the Barbican there are more restaurants amid the packed-out bars. All three areas get rowdy, especially at weekends.

❦ PLYMOUTH ARTS CENTRE

☎ 01752-206114; www.plymouthac.org.uk; 38 Looe St; ◷ 10am-8.30pm Tue-Sat, 4pm-8.30pm Sun

The city's independent cinema screens a wide range art-house flicks; it is also home to three gallery spaces, which stage innovative exhibitions, installations and talks. There's a licensed, mainly vegetarian **cafe** (◷ 11am-8.30pm Tue-Sat) too.

❦ THEATRE ROYAL

☎ 01752-267222; www.theatreroyal.com; Royal Pde; ℗

Plymouth's main theatre stages large-scale touring and home-grown productions, including West End musicals, ballet and opera. Its award-winning studio **Drum Theatre** is renowned for experimental shows and developing new writing.

TRANSPORT

TO/FROM THE AIRPORT

Plymouth City Airport (☎ 01752-242620; www.plymouthairport.com; Derriford) has four to six flights daily to London's City and Gatwick airports; other connections include those to Bristol, Dublin, Glasgow, Leeds Bradford, Manchester and Newcastle. The nearest bus stop is Derriford Roundabout, a 10-minute walk away. Regular buses (including bus 50, 30 minutes, every 20 minutes) shuttle from there to Royal Pde.

GETTING AROUND

BUS // National Express has regular coach connections between Plymouth and the rest of the country. Sample trips include Birmingham (£48, 5½ hours, four daily) and London (£32, five to six hours, eight daily). Bus X38 travels to Exeter (return £6, 1½ hours, hourly). Bus 82 (two on Sunday only, late May to September), the Transmoor Link, runs between Plymouth and Exeter via Yelverton, Princetown, Two Bridges, Postbridge, Warren House

Inn and Moretonhampstead. Bus X80 runs to Torquay (1¾ hours, hourly Monday to Saturday, two-hourly on Sunday) via Totnes (1¼ hours).

CAR // Plymouth sits just south of the A38 dual carriageway, which connects it to Cornwall to the west and Exeter and the motorway network, 43 miles to the east. Much of the city centre is pedestrianised.

PARKING // Multistorey car parks include Drake Circus shopping centre (per two/four hours £2.40/4.80), and the Theatre Royal (per two/four hours £2.20/4.40). There's also metered parking on the Hoe, and on city streets (per two/four hours £2/4).

TRAIN // Plymouth is on the intercity London Paddington–Penzance line; regular services include those to London (£40, 3½ to four hours, every 30 minutes), Bristol (£20, two hours, two or three per hour) and Exeter (£6.50, one hour, two or three per hour).

DARTMOOR NATIONAL PARK
······

Dartmoor is an ancient, compelling landscape. It's so different from the rest of Devon a visit can feel like falling into the third book of *The Lord of the Rings*. Exposed granite hills (tors) crest on the horizon – an array of crazy peaks linked by swaths of honey-tinged moors. On the fringes, streams tumble over moss-smothered boulders in woods of twisted trees. The centre is the higher moor, a vast, treeless expanse, moody and utterly empty. You'll probably find its desolate beauty exhilarating or chilling, or possibly a bit of both.

Dartmoor's villages range from brooding Princetown and picturesque Widecombe-in-the-Moor to genteel Chagford. Everywhere lies evidence of 4000 years of human history including scores of stone rows, Sir Francis Drake's former home and the last castle to be built in England. The moor offers countless explorations by car or bike, on horseback or on foot, of history, literature and myth. Mercurial weather patterns also mean it's never the same; its moods can change day by day, hour by hour.

ESSENTIAL INFORMATION

TOURIST INFORMATION // Dartmoor National Park Authority (DNPA; www.dartmoor-npa.gov.uk) runs the **High Moorland Visitor Centre** (☎ 01822-890414; ☯ 10am-5pm Apr-Oct, 10am-4pm Nov-Mar) in Princetown. Other DNPA centres include those at **Haytor Vale** (☎ 01364-661520; ☯ 10am-5pm Easter-Oct, 10am-4pm Sat & Sun Nov & Dec) and **Postbridge** (☎ 01822-880272;

☯ 10am-5pm Easter-Oct, 10am-4pm Sat & Sun Nov & Dec). Dartmoor's **official visitor website** is www.dartmoor.co.uk. **Okehampton Tourist Office** (☎ 01837-53020; www.okehamptondevon.co.uk; Museum Courtyard, 3 West St; ☯ 10am-5pm Mon-Sat Easter-Oct, 10am-4.30pm Mon, Tue, Fri & Sat Nov-Easter). **Tavistock Tourist Office** (☎ 01822-612938; Court Gate, Bedford Sq; ☯ 9.30am-5pm Mon-Sat Easter-Oct, 10am-4.30pm Mon-Tue & Fri & Sat Nov-Easter).

ORIENTATION

Dartmoor occupies a 368-sq-mile chunk of central Devon, its fringes only 7 miles

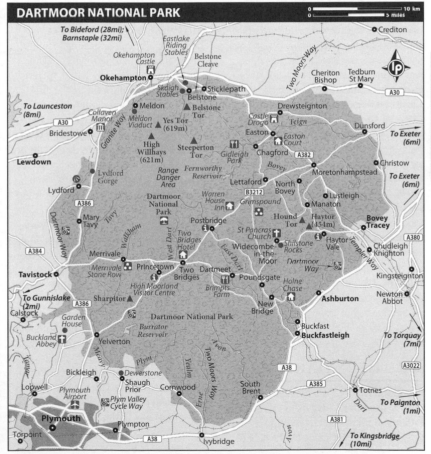

from Plymouth and 6 miles from Exeter. The northwest moor is the highest and most remote, peaking at 621m at High Willhays. The lower, southwest moor (400m to 500m) is particularly rich in prehistoric sites.

TRANSPORT

BUS // Key bus routes include: bus 83/84/86 from Plymouth to Tavistock, via Yelverton (hourly); bus 98 from Tavistock to Princetown (four daily); bus 98 from Princetown to Postbridge (one per day Monday to Friday); bus 118 from Tavistock to Barnstaple, via Lydford and Okehampton (two daily); bus X9 from Okehampton to Exeter (hourly, Monday to Saturday); bus 359 from Exeter to Moretonhampstead (two hourly Monday to Saturday); bus 179 from Okehampton to Moretonhampstead via Chagford (two daily Monday to Saturday). Bus 82 (two on Sunday only, late May to September), the Transmoor Link, runs between Plymouth and Exeter via Yelverton, Princetown, Two Bridges, Postbridge, Warren House Inn and Moretonhampstead.

CAR // The A38 dual carriageway borders Dartmoor's southeast edge, the A30 skirts it to the north, heading from Exeter via Okehampton to Cornwall. The single-lane B3212 carves a path across the centre, linking Moretonhampstead, Postbridge and Princetown. From there the B3357 leads into Tavistock. Countless single-track lanes lead away from these central routes, some becoming very steep and narrow; signs often warn when that is the case. Much of the moor is unfenced grazing and has a 40mph speed limit; be warned: you're likely to come across sheep, ponies and even cows in the road.

PARKING // Many moorland towns and villages have pay-and-display car parks. On the moor itself, there are numerous, free car parks; sometimes they're little more than lay-bys for half a dozen cars. The surface is rough to very rough.

SOUTHERN DARTMOOR

The southern moor is a tempting diversion. A 20-minute drive from Plymouth, Exeter and the A38 takes you into a world where ponies graze by the side of roads backed by endless bracken-covered hills. The Tavistock area offers a medieval manor house, a beguiling garden, prehistoric remains and markets to trawl. At Princetown a notorious prison and myths and tales of Sherlock Holmes take over; while further south Widecombe-in-the-Moor delivers pure picture-postcard charm. Add a gourmet bolt-hole, rustic pub and classic cream-tea stop, and the southern moor may be prove hard to resist.

EXPLORING SOUTHERN DARTMOOR

❦ **SCOUR THE MARKETS //** GO SHOPPING, DARTMOOR STYLE
Tavistock offers an appealing insight into moorland market town life. The centre is graced by crenellated, turreted constructions built in the 1800s during the town's copper-mining boom. Its Victorian **Pannier Market** (☎ 01822-611003; Bedford Sq; ☺ 9am-4pm Tue-Sat) is a vast covered hall where hundreds of stalls are stacked with an eclectic range of shabby-chic goodies; there's everything from silver cutlery and secondhand books, to moleskin trousers and tweed caps. Tuesday is particularly good for antiques.

Hunt out **Country Cheeses** (☎ 01822-615035; Market Rd; ☺ 9.30-5pm Mon-Sat), nearby. In this award-winning shop the aroma is all-embracing and the counters are stacked with oozing, crumbling golden delights. Many are made locally; look out for Slow Tavy (washed in Plymouth Gin), Trehill (with garlic) and Little Stinky (says it all).

On the 2nd and 4th Saturday of each month the produce-laden stalls of **Tavistock Farmers Market** (☎ 01822-820360; ☺ 9am-1pm), one of the region's best, fill Bedford Sq.

🌿 BUCKLAND ABBEY // TOUR THE HOME OF SIR FRANCIS DRAKE

Built out of honey-coloured stone, this **manor house** (NT; ☎ 01822-853607; near Yelverton; adult/child £7.80/3.90; �
10.30am-5.30pm daily mid-Mar–Oct, 11am-4.30pm Fri-Sun Nov-Dec & Feb–mid-Mar; Ⓟ) dates back to the 14th century when it was a Cistercian monastery and an abbey church. After the Dissolution, it was turned into a family residence by Sir Richard Grenville before being bought by his cousin and nautical rival Sir Francis Drake (p163) in 1581. A sumptuous interior includes Tudor plasterwork ceilings in the **Great Hall** and **Drake's Chamber**, where Drake's Drum is said to beat by itself when Britain is in danger of being invaded. There's also a monastic barn, a fine Elizabethan garden and a great program of events – look out for the night-time moth hunts or the storytelling days.

Buckland Abbey is 7 miles south of Tavistock.

🌿 GARDEN HOUSE // DISCOVER A HIDDEN, HORTICULTURAL GEM

This 8-acre **garden** (☎ 01822-854769; Buckland Monachorum, near Yelverton; adult/child £6/2.50; �
10.30am-5pm Mar-Oct; Ⓟ) is quite simply one of the best in Devon. Its enchanting blend of landscapes ranges from wildflower meadow and South African planting, to an Acer glade and walled cottage garden. Terraces cluster around the picturesque ruins of a medieval vicarage and a highlight is to clamber up its 16th-century tower for views of sweeps of blue flax, poppies and buttercups. Everywhere tucked-away benches hide in flower-filled nooks; soothing spots to drink in the fragrance and watch the bees buzz by. The **cafe** serves goat's cheese sandwiches with onion relish, and salads scattered with pomegranate seeds.

The Garden House is 5 miles south of Tavistock.

🌿 MYTHICAL DARTMOOR // GET SPOOKED BY THE MOOR'S GHOSTLY TALES

Dartmoor is laced with myth, and tales of evil forces form a big part of its heritage. Often inspired by the moor's shifting mists and stark, other-worldly nature, many revolve around the Dewer (the Devil). According to legend, he led his pack of phantom Wisht Hounds across the moor at night, rounding up sinners before driving them off a 100m granite outcrop called the **Dewerstone**. You can stroll to the Dewerstone from **Shaugh Prior**; an idyllic, but also at times chilling, half-mile riverside walk through woods of moss-smothered trees. Shaugh Prior is 12 miles southeast of Tavistock.

Many think tales of the Wisht Hounds inspired *The Hound of the Baskervilles* by Sir Arthur Conan Doyle (p172). More devilish tales crop up at Widecombe-in-the-Moor (p173) and Lydford Gorge (p174).

🌿 SIT IN A STONE CIRCLE // DISCOVER DARTMOOR'S PREHISTORIC HERITAGE

Dartmoor is ripe for **archaeological explorations**. There are an estimated 11,000 monuments on the moor and it has the largest concentration of Bronze Age (c 2300–700 BC) remains in the country; features include around 75 stone rows (half the national total), 18 stone circles and 5000 huts. The **Merrivale Stone Rows** lie near the hamlet of Merrivale on the B3357 (Tavistock to Princetown road). Heading south from the car park, a five-minute walk leads to two **parallel stone rows** (180m and

DEVON

260m long); both have large stone slabs ('terminal stones') at the eastern end. In the centre are the circular remains of a tiny stone **burial chamber** (or 'cist'). Directly south of the west end of the stone rows (around 100m) is a **stone circle** of 11 small stones; 40m southwest is a slanting, 3m **standing stone** (or 'menhir').

Another key site is the immense, enclosed prehistoric settlement at **Grimspound**, 6 miles southwest of Moretonhampstead. The DNPA runs a series of archaeology-themed walks (£3 to £8) all over the moor, and sells miniguides to some sites (£4).

❦ MEGALITHS BY MOONLIGHT // STROLL ALONG STONE ROWS AS THE SUN SETS

One of the most atmospheric ways to immerse yourself in the moor's eerie appeal is to join a **moonlit guided walk**. Knowledgeable DNPA guides lead you out into the wilds, where the sun sets over a stone row and (cloud-cover depending) a glowing, full moon rises from the tor tops. The trip back to the car is made in the gathering gloom – bring a torch. In fine weather it's an unforgettable experience; in bad weather it underlines just what a wilderness Dartmoor is.

❦ DARTMOOR PRISON // GLIMPSE LIFE BEHIND BARS

Set 427m above sea level in the heart of the remote, higher moor, the village of **Princetown** is dominated by the grey, foreboding bulk of Dartmoor Prison. The **jail** was built in 1809 to hold first French, then American, prisoners of war and became a convict prison in 1850.

Just up from its looming gates, the **Dartmoor Prison Heritage Centre** (☎ 01822-892130; www.dartmoor-prison.co.uk; Princetown; adult/child £2.50/1.50; ⏰ 9.30am-12.30pm & 1.30-4.30pm, to 4pm Fri & Sun; Ⓟ) provides a chilling insight into life inside – look out for the disturbing makeshift knives made by modern prisoners, as well as mock-up cells, straight jackets and manacles. Escapes feature too in the form of sheets tied into ropes and chair legs hammered into grappling hooks. Then there's the tale of Frankie 'the mad axeman' Mitchell, who was supposedly sprung by the '60s gangster twins, the Krays. The centre also sells the bizarrely cheerful garden ornaments made by the prisoners; don't miss the (presumably ironic) neighbourhood-watch figurines.

❦ TRACK DOWN SHERLOCK HOLMES // DISCOVER THE HOUND OF THE BASKERVILLE'S MYSTERY LOCATIONS

Sir Arthur Conan Doyle (1859–1930) once stayed at the Duchy Hotel in Princetown, now the **High Moorland Visitor Centre** (p177). Local lore recounts Dartmoor man Henry Baskerville took

WARNING

The military has three training ranges on Dartmoor where live ammunition is used. DNPA staff can explain their precise locations; they're also marked on Ordnance Survey maps. When walking you're advised to check if the route you're planning falls within a range; if it does, check if firing is taking place via the **Firing Information Service**(☎ 0800 458 4868;www.dartmoor-ranges.co.uk). In the day, red flags fly at the edges of in-use ranges; red flares burn at night. Even when there's no firing, beware of unidentified metal objects lying in the grass – don't touch anything you find; note its position and report it to the police or the **Commandant** (☎ 01837-650010).

Conan Doyle on a carriage tour, and the brooding landscape he encountered, coupled with legends of a huge phantom dog, inspired *The Hound of the Baskervilles*.

The moor around Princetown still evokes the book's locations. From the village centre, the lonely track heading southeast from beside the Plume of Feathers pub leads to **Foxtor Mires** (the book's Grimpen Mire) 2½ miles away. Many see the nearby **Nun's Cross Farm** as Merripit House (where the Stapletons lived); and the **hut circles** half a mile southwest of Princetown (beside the B3212) as the ruins Holmes camped out in.

The High Moorland Visitor Centre has displays about Holmes and sells numerous books, including a facsimile edition of *The Hound of the Baskervilles*; perfect for some atmospheric reading in the snug Plume of Feathers as the mists swirl in.

❦ WIDECOMBE-IN-THE-MOOR //
EXPLORE A QUINTESSENTIAL MOORLAND VILLAGE

The **village** of Widecombe (the 'in-the-Moor' is dropped locally) is archetypal Dartmoor, down to the ponies grazing on the village green. Honey-grey buildings cluster around the 14th-century **St Pancras Church** whose immense 37m tower has seen it dubbed the Cathedral of the Moor. Inside, search out the brightly painted **ceiling bosses**; one near the altar has the three rabbits emblem adopted by Dartmoor's tin miners. Look out too for the antique **wooden boards** telling the fire-and-brimstone tale of the violent storm of 1638 – it knocked a pinnacle from the roof, killing several parishioners. As ever on Dartmoor the Devil was blamed; said to be in search of souls.

Outside, the nearby **Church House** (now a National Trust shop) used to be almshouses, while Glebe House opposite, started life in 1527 as a farm. Complete the tour with a trip to the rustic Rugglestone Inn (p173), for a proper pint.

GASTRONOMIC HIGHLIGHTS

❦ BROWNS // TAVISTOCK ££
☎ 01822-618686; 80 West St; dinner 2/3 courses £34/40, lunch 2/3 courses £14/25; ☽ lunch & dinner

Browns' restaurant delivers moorland flavours with an imaginative twist; treatments include belly pork with goat's cheese and black pudding jus. The bistro rustles up brasserie dishes (mains £8); expect combos like seared lambs liver with roasted garlic mash. Either way, wash it all down with a glass of water from the real Roman well.

❦ HORN OF PLENTY // GULWORTHY £££
☎ 01822-832528; www.thehornofplenty.co.uk; 3-course lunch/dinner £27/47; ☽ lunch & dinner; Ⓟ

Effortlessly stylish and beautifully relaxed, this country house hotel is chockfull of class. Classic food includes Devon lamb with Madeira sauce or brill with sautéed squid – best enjoyed on the vine-shaded terrace looking out over rolling Tamar Valley views. Take a tip from the locals and visit on Monday, when dinner prices plunge to £28 for three courses. It's 3 miles from Tavistock.

❦ RUGGLESTONE INN // WIDECOMBE-IN-THE-MOOR £
☎ 01364-621327; mains £4-9; ☽ lunch & dinner

For a taste of traditional Dartmoor, head to the Rugglestone Inn. Two of the three tiny rooms are warmed by real fires; sanded wooden tables and ancient chairs are scattered around. The flavoursome food is homemade; expect hearty ploughman's and beef and ale or steak and Stilton pies. Many of the ingredients are provided by local farmers, you'll often find them eating here too.

☙ **BRIMPTS FARM // DARTMEET £**
☎ 01364-631450; cream teas £3; ⊗ 11.30am-5.30pm weekends & school holidays, 2-5.30pm weekdays

This is cream tea goes gourmet. They've been serving them here since 1913, and it's still one of the best places to tuck in on the moor. Expect freshly baked scones, homemade blackcurrant jam, a choice of teas and utterly, utterly gooey clotted cream. It's signed off the B3357, Two Bridges to Dartmoor road.

THE NORTHERN MOOR

North of Princetown and Widecombe the wilds of Dartmoor take on an even wilder feel. In the far north, sturdy Okehampton has a staging-post atmosphere and acts as a springboard for memorable hikes, and bike and horse rides. At Lydford in the west, a 30m waterfall thunders down sheer cliffs, while in the east genteel Chagford offers superb dining and an architectural oddity: the last castle to be built in England. In the middle is the mind-expanding sweep of the higher moor. Its bracken-covered slopes have no roads and no farms, just mile after mile of gorse and granite tors.

EXPLORING THE NORTHERN MOOR

☙ **POSTBRIDGE // DANGLE YOUR FEET IN THE ICY RIVER DART**
The hamlet of Postbridge owes its popularity, and its name, to its medieval stone slab or **clapper bridge**. A path leads from beside the main B3212 to the 13th-century structure, with its four, 10ft-long slabs propped up on four sturdy columns of stacked stones. Walking across the top takes you over the rushing **East Dart** river; paths alongside provide picturesque spots to sit, whip off your boots and plunge your feet into water that has quite possibly never felt so cold.

☙ **LYDFORD GORGE //HIKE TO A THUNDERING WATERFALL**
At the appealing village of **Lydford**, 3 miles of trails zigzag down what is the deepest river **gorge** (NT; ☎ 01822-820320; adult/child £5.50/2.80; ⊗ 10am-4pm or 5pm mid-Mar–Oct; ℗) in the southwest. Oak woods close in on all sides and the temperature drops. The riverside route leads to the 30m-high **White Lady Waterfall**, an impressive cascade that thunders down from sheer rocks. Rugged trails also weave past a series of bubbling **whirlpools**; you can actually walk out over the fearsome **Devil's Cauldron**, which seems to have been scooped out of the surrounding mossy rocks. Lydford is 9 miles southwest of Okehampton.

☙ **CLAMBER UP A TOR // STRETCH YOUR LEGS ON THE HIGH HILLS**
Studying Dartmoor's scenery from the road is impressive, but walking off the beaten track underlines its size and wilderness appeal. Half the entire moor (47,000 hectares) is open access and there are 450 miles of public rights of way. The area around **Okehampton** features many trails; staff at the tourist office (p177) can offer advice. One highlight is the **10-mile circular hike** from the nearby village of **Belstone**, past **Belstone Tor**, round isolated **Steeperton Tor** and back through **Belstone Cleave**. The route fringes a military live firing range; check to see if firing is scheduled before setting out (see p172).

DEVON

Pathfinder's *Dartmoor, Short Walks* (£5.99) is a great source of shorter routes. The DNPA (p177) runs a range of informative **guided walks** (per two/six hours £3/8). The Ordnance Survey (OS) Explorer 1:25,000 map No 28 *Dartmoor* (£7.99) covers the whole of the moor in good detail. Be prepared for upland weather conditions: warm, waterproof clothing, water, hats and sunscreen are essential, as is a map and compass. The military uses some sections of moor for live firing (see p172).

🌱 OKEHAMPTON CASTLE // SCRAMBLE AROUND AMID ROMANTIC RUINS

For a picturesque slice of history, it's hard to beat this ancient **castle** (EH; ☎ 01837-52844; Okehampton; adult/child £3.50/1.80; 🕑 10am-5pm Apr-Jun & Sep, 10am-6pm Jul & Aug). Its towering, crumbling walls teeter on the top of a wooded spur just above the cascading River Okement. This Norman motte-and-bailey affair has 14th-century additions and at one time was the largest castle in Devon. Paths and flights of steps trace between its apparently haunted walls, revealing views of bracken-covered moors in the distance.

🌱 PONY TREKKING // CLIP-CLIP OVER THE MOOR AT A NATURAL PACE

There's a frontier feel to the moor, making it an ideal landscape for saddling up and trotting out. At **Skaigh Stables** (☎ 01837-840917; www.skaighstables.co.uk; 🕑 Apr-Oct; Ⓟ) in Belstone, the two-hour rides (£36) head out of the picturesque village directly onto the moor. Experienced riders can set off for a gallop and jump over stone walls; novices can simply enjoy ambling along. The stables even run **day-long pub rides** (£60), which stop at a local hostelry for lunch.

Other recommended stables are **Eastlake** (☎ 01837-52515; Ⓟ) near Okehampton, **Babeny Farm** (☎ 01364-631296; Ⓟ) at Poundsgate and **Shilstone Rocks** (☎ 01364-621281; Ⓟ) at Widecombe-in-the-Moor.

🌱 GET PEDDALLING // CYCLE ALONG AN OLD RAILWAY LINE

Although today it's a wilderness, Dartmoor used to have a valuable quarrying industry and a network of rail- and tram-ways sprang up to ferry rock off the moor.

The 11-mile **Granite Way** runs along one of these old railway lines, between Okehampton and Lydford, allowing you to tap into that past. The 6-mile stretch between Okehampton and Lake Viaduct is entirely traffic-free; **Devon Cycle Hire** (☎ 01837-861141; www.devoncyclehire.co.uk; Sourton Down, near Okehampton; per half/full day £10/14; 🕑 9am-5pm Apr-Sep; Ⓟ) sits in the middle of that section. Hopping on a bike here opens up spectacular views of Exmoor, Bodmin Moor, **Okehampton Castle**, **High Wilhays** (the highest point on the moor) and the 165m **Meldon Viaduct**. The DNPA sells an off-road cycle map and can advise about countless other routes.

🌱 CASTLE DROGO // EXPLORE A TRUE ARCHITECTURAL ODDITY

This gorgeous **stately home** (NT; ☎ 01647-433306; Drewsteignton; adult/child £7.40/3.70; 🕑 11am-5pm Wed-Mon late Mar-Oct; Ⓟ) is the last castle to be built in England. The imposing grey edifice was designed by Sir Edwin Lutyens for self-made food-millionaire Julius Drewe, and was constructed between 1911 and 1931. The brief was to combine the medieval grandeur of a castle and the comforts of a 20th-century country house. The result is an appealing blend of crenellated battlements, cosy carpeted interiors and (how practical) a good central-heating system. The **gardens** are influenced by Gertrude Jekyll and the woodland trails have alpine-esque views over Dartmoor and the plunging **Teign Gorge**. Castle Drogo is 3 miles northeast of **Chagford**.

GASTRONOMIC HIGHLIGHTS

❦ 22 MILL STREET // CHAGFORD ££

☎ 01647-432244; 22 Mill St; lunch 2/3 courses £15/20, dinner 2/3 courses £36/42; ☽ lunch & dinner
Bursting with rural chic, this intimate little restaurant delivers dishes packed with produce from the moors and the shores that are transformed by imaginative treatments. Look out for seared Exmoor venison, Falmouth scallops with caraway caramel and rabbit with parmesan risotto. It's all best rounded off with the roasted pears and white chocolate ice cream.

❦ GIDLEIGH PARK // CHAGFORD £££

☎ 01647-432367; 2-/3-course lunch £35/45, 3-course dinner £95, 9-course tasting menu £115; ☽ lunch & dinner
Welcome to Devon's top eatery: a double Michelin–starred restaurant set in a luxury Arts and Crafts–era hotel. Classic French techniques are teamed with local ingredients; Devon quail, Brixham scallops and Dartmoor lamb are all accompanied with purée, velouté or jus – the effect is stunning and the meals truly memorable. Considering the standard of cooking, the service and the setting, the two-course lunches are a bargain.

❦ WARREN HOUSE INN NEAR POSTBRIDGE £

☎ 01822-880208; mains £7-10; ☽ food noon-9pm Mon-Sat, noon 8.30pm Sun, to 4pm Mon & Tue Nov-Mar
Plonked amid miles of open moor, this former tin miner's haunt exudes the kind of hospitality you only get in a pub in the middle of nowhere. A Dartmoor legend, its stone floors, trestle tables and hearty food are given an extra glow by a fire that's been crackling since 1845. Try its warrener's (rabbit) pie; named after the men who used to farm the creatures on the moor. It's on the B3212, two miles north of Postbridge.

DRIVING TOUR: A DARTMOOR ROAD TRIP

Map p177
Distance: 20 miles
Duration: one day
Driving on Dartmoor is like being inside a feature film: compelling 360-degree views are screened all around. One of the most scenic routes is a transmoor traverse from Tavistock to Chagford. From **Tavistock (1)** the B3357 to Princetown climbs steeply (expect ears to pop), crosses a cattle grid and crests a hill to reveal swaths of honey-coloured tors. At **Merrivale (2**; p171) a short stroll reveals atmospheric stone rows and circles. Next comes the **Dartmoor Prison Heritage Centre (3**; p172) and then the **prison (4)** itself, at rugged **Princetown (5)**. Pick up the B3212 towards Two Bridges; the **lay-by (6)** here provides the best views of Dartmoor Prison. Follow signs for Moretonhampstead, a route that sees an expansive landscape unfurl. At **Postbridge (7**; p174), park up and stroll over the 700-year-old bridge, perhaps cooling hot feet in the River Dart. A few miles further on, the **Warren House Inn (8**; p176) is a great spot for lunch. Around **Lettaford (9)** take one of the signed, smaller roads to **Chagford (10)** to experience tiny lanes, sharp bends and

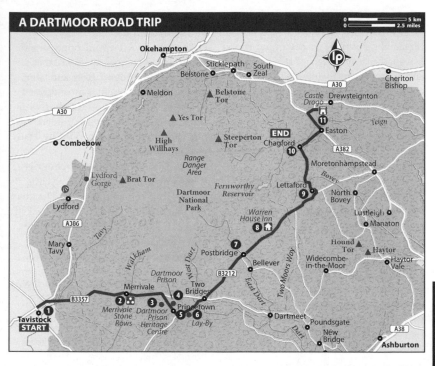

A DARTMOOR ROAD TRIP

plunging valleys, before emerging into Chagford's quaint, thatch-dotted square. Perhaps scour some of its wonderfully old-fashioned shops, or head to **Castle Drogo** (11; p175) to explore a 1920s stately home. Finish the day at **22 Mill Street** (see **10**; p176), a truly classy spot to eat.

NORTH DEVON

······

Intensely rugged and in places utterly remote, this is a coast to inspire. It's peppered with drastically concertinaed cliffs, expansive sandy beaches and ancient fishing villages. The area offers a smorgasbord of delights, from surfing lessons at cool Croyde to Damien Hirst's artistic restaurant in Ilfracombe. Swimming experiences range from snorkelling safaris to Victorian bathing. Then there's Braunton's immense sand dunes, impossibly pretty Clovelly, phenomenal rock formations at Hartland Point, and, sitting on the horizon 10 miles out to sea, Lundy Island – a truly get-away-from-it all escape.

ESSENTIAL INFORMATION

TOURIST INFORMATION // Barnstaple **Tourist Office** (☎ 01271-375000; www.staynorthdevon.co.uk; The Square; ☯ 9.30am-5pm Mon-Sat) **Braunton Tourist Office** (☎ 01271-816400; www.brauntontic.co.uk; Caen St; ☯ 10am-3pm Mon-Fri, 10am-2pm Sat) **Ilfracombe Tourist Office** (☎ 01271-863001; www.visitilfracombe.co.uk; Landmark Theatre, the Seafront; ☯ 10am-5pm daily Easter-Sep, 10am-4pm Mon-Sat Oct-Mar) **North Devon Marketing Bureau** (☎ 0845 241 2043; www.northdevon.com)

ORIENTATION

Ilfracombe sits in the far east of north Devon; the surfing beaches at Croyde and Braunton are 10 miles to the south and west. The Taw and Torridge estuaries cut deeply inland at the key towns of Barnstaple and Bideford. Next comes the village of Clovelly and the rugged Hartland Peninsula – the last piece of land before Cornwall.

Although parts of Exmoor National Park fall within north Devon, we've covered the whole of Exmoor in our Somerset chapter (p80).

EXPLORING NORTH DEVON

❦ ILFRACOMBE // PLUNGE INTO THE PAST IN VICTORIAN BATHING POOLS

Ilfracombe's heyday was in the Victorian era and echoes of faded grandeur still pepper the resort: town houses with cast-iron balconies edge its sloping streets, while formal gardens, crazy golf and ropes of twinkling lights line the promenade.

But the best insight into 19th-century watering-hole life comes at **tunnels beaches** (☎ 01271-879882; www.tunnelsbeaches. co.uk; Granville Rd; adult/child £2/1.50; ⏰ 10am-5pm or 6pm Easter-Oct, to 7pm Jul & Aug). Here passageways hacked out of the cliffs lead to a **tidal swimming pool** and a clutch of shingle **beaches**. The tunnels were hand-carved by hundreds of Welsh miners in the 1820s – they cut through 960 cu metres of rock.

The site's evocative displays convey a Victorian world of woollen bathing suits, segregated swimming and the characters of the era, including an extraordinary-looking Professor of Ornamental Swimming, Harry Parker. There are also signs detailing boating etiquette: 'gentlemen who cannot swim should never take ladies upon the water'.

The tidal pool itself still offers superb swimming, a unique experience that's at its best three hours before and after low tide when the pool is most defined. Alongside are rock pools crawling with life; look out for the regular guided rambles staged by the **Devon Wildlife Trust** (www.devonwildlifetrust.org).

Ilfracombe's tiny, sandy **harbour** is framed by dramatically crinkled cliffs and brightly coloured terraces. The **quay** is home to No 11 (p183), the art-packed eatery run by Damien Hirst, while the photogenic 14th-century **St Nicolas' Chapel** crowns nearby **Lantern Hill**.

❦ LUNDY ISLAND // GET CAST AWAY ON AN ISOLATED, SEA-FRINGED ROCK

For the ultimate great escape, head for this tranquil **island** (☎ 01271-863636; www.lundyisland.co.uk). Three miles long and half a mile wide, it's anchored 10 miles off the north Devon coast, a two-hour ferry ride away.

In May and June, **puffins** nest on the island's 400ft cliffs, the only place in Devon where they do; fittingly Lundy means 'Puffin Island' in Norse. Other **wildlife** on the island include Lundy ponies, sika deer and Soay sheep, while basking sharks float by offshore. Pack a swimsuit – the wardens here lead **snorkelling safaris**. The island also has **standing stones**, a 13th-century castle and a couple of **lighthouses** to explore. Car free, it's an extraordinarily peaceful place and, with rich star displays, takes on a magical quality at night.

Lundy has a shop and a welcoming pub, the **Marisco Tavern** (☎ 01237-431831; ⏰ lunch & dinner), as well as **camping** and 20 holiday lets, ranging from cottages and former lighthouses to the single-bed

Radio Room, which used to house Lundy's wireless transmitter.

Between late March and October, the **MS Oldenburg** shuttles to the island from Ilfracombe or Bideford (day returns adult/child £33/17, two hours, four to five sailing per week). The return fare rises to £56 (child £28) if you stay overnight. In winter a **helicopter service** (return adult/child £95/50) runs from Hartland Point. It only flies on Monday and Friday between November and mid-March and can't be done as a day trip. The **Lundy Shore Office** (☎ 01271-863636) takes all transport bookings.

✿ ARLINGTON COURT // RIDE IN A CARRIAGE ROUND A REGENCY ESTATE

Clip-clopping up the drive towards this honey-grey **manor house** (NT; ☎ 01271-850296; Arlington; adult/child £8.60/4; ◷ 11am-5pm daily Mar-Oct; P) is the epitome of arriving in style. Built in the early 1800s, Arlington exudes charm, from the model ships and shells collected by the owners, to the produce-packed walled kitchen garden.

Its stables are home to the **National Trust's carriage collection**. The burnished leather and soft fabrics of its 40 vehicles summon up an era of stately transport, as do the daily harnessing demonstrations and trips in jangling, rattling carriages. Another highlight is the tiny **Pony Phaeton**, a four-wheeled carriage belonging to Queen Victoria. Her Majesty drove it herself, but for safety reasons a servant walked alongside, ready to apply the handbrake (think Billy Connolly's Mr Brown to Judi Dench's Queen Victoria). Arlington also has a **heronry** and colony of **lesser horseshoe bats**, viewable via a 'bat-cam'.

Arlington Court is 8 miles north of Barnstaple on the A39.

✿ SURFING // HANG 10 (OR JUST HANG ON), HAWAII STYLE

Perfectly positioned to make the most of wave sets rolling in from the Atlantic, north Devon's coast offers some truly superb surfing and bodyboarding. Good beaches to try are **Croyde** (P), **Woolacombe** (P) and **Westward Ho!** (P). Beginners benefit from lessons, for safety and sheer frustration's sake. The **Nick Thorn Hunter Surf Academy** (☎ 01271-871337 www.nickthornhuntersurfacademy.com; per half-day £30; ◷ 9am-5pm Apr-Sep) operates from Woolacombe beach. At Croyde and Saunton Sands, **Surf South West** (☎ 01271-890400; www.surfsouthwest.com; per half-day £30; ◷ Mar-Nov) is approved by the British Surfing Association, as is **Surfing Croyde Bay** (☎ 01271-891200; www.surfingcroydebay.co.uk; 8 Hobbs Hill, Croyde; per half-day £35). At Westward Ho! try **North Devon Surf School** (☎ 01237-474663; www.northdevonsurfschool.co.uk; per 2hr/full day £28/50).

Racks of wetsuits, surf- and bodyboards line up in north Devon's top surf spots. In Croyde, **Le Sport** (☎ 01271-890147; Hobbs Hill; ◷ 9am-5.30pm, at peak times 9am-9pm) is among those hiring wetsuits (half/full £5/8) and boards (half-/full day £8/12). It also has a Woolacombe **branch** (☎ 01271-870044; 1 Barton Rd).

✿ BEACH LIFE // DISCOVER SAND DUNES, SALTMARSHES AND JAGGED CLIFFS

Surfing aside, north Devon's 80-mile coast still boasts some of the region's most tempting **beaches**. Some are undeveloped affairs with mile after mile of golden sand and not much else.

Five miles south of Ilfracombe, **Woolacombe** (P) is a traditional family resort with 3 miles of sand. For a leg-testing **hike**, take the coast path a few miles north past the jagged rock-ridge of

Morte Point, to the appealing village of Mortehoe.

Just to the south is Croyde (ℙ), a cheerful, chilled village where surf culture meets olde worlde: thatched roofs peep out over racks of wetsuits, crowds of cool guys in boardshorts sip beer outside 17th-century inns. The wide beach at this mini-Maui is backed by green fields and sand dunes.

From Croyde, a jaw-dropping coast road (and coast path) winds down to Saunton Sands (ℙ), a 3-mile stretch of beach that's overlooked by a sumptuous Art Deco hotel (p301). This is one of north Devon's most rural beaches and is backed by Braunton Burrows (ℙ), a 2000-acre Unesco World Biosphere Reserve and the UK's largest dune system. Paths wind past sandy hummocks, saltmarshes and rich plant life; in early July there are scatterings of purple thyme, yellow hawkweed and pyramidal orchids. Braunton Burrows was also the main training area for American troops before D-Day and mock landing craft are still hidden in the tufted dunes near the car park at its southern tip.

The family-friendly resort of Westward Ho! (ℙ) is on the south side of the wide Taw-Torridge Estuary; from Braunton Burrows it's a 17-mile detour via Barnstaple and Bideford. The 2-mile

WESTWARD HO!

Westward Ho! is the only place in England with an exclamation mark after its name. The resort owes its existence to the best-selling 1855 novel *Westward Ho!* by Charles Kingsley, which featured this stretch of then-undeveloped coast. Speculators targeted the area, built a town and gave it the same name to cash in on the book's popularity.

beach at Westward Ho! is backed by a natural pebble ridge and Northam Burrows (ℙ). This expanse of grassy plains, sand dunes and saltmarshes is grazed by sheep and horses, and is particularly rich in bird life. Look out for wheatear, linnet, pied wagtail, stonechat, curlew and little egret.

After Westward Ho! north Devon's precipitous cliffs take over, but for sheer atmosphere the tiny beach at Clovelly (p181) is a good spot for a swim.

❦ BROOMHILL SCULPTURE GARDENS // HUNT OUT HUNDREDS OF QUIRKY PIECES OF ART

This 10-acre wooded valley (☎ 01271-850262; Muddiford Rd, near Barnstaple; adult/child £4.50/1.50; ⏱ 11am-4pm; ℙ) is home to 300 sculptures, making it one of the largest permanent collections of contemporary art in the southwest. Slivers of burnished steel, painted columns and a series of mystical figures pop out from behind trees; sculptural silhouettes emerge from flood planes and 25 polished stone Zimbabwean Shona statues sit on a plateau. There's a fairy-tale, often comic feel to much of it – Greta Berlin's 23ft-tall, red-leather stiletto tends to raise a smile.

Broomhill also has a contemporary art gallery (admission free; ⏱ 11am-4pm Wed-Sun), where works are for sale, a great slow-food restaurant, Terra Madre (p183), and an art hotel (p300).

Broomhill Sculpture Gardens are 3 miles north of Barnstaple at Muddiford, on the B3230.

❦ TARKA TRAIL // CYCLE TRANQUIL PATHS IN SEARCH OF OTTERS

This 30-mile, traffic-free trail (☎ 01237-423655; www.devon.gov.uk/tarkatrail) gets its name from the Henry Williamson book *Tarka the Otter*, which was in turn inspired by the lush north Devon landscape. The trail starts at coastal **Braunton** and traces the route of disused train lines. The 6-mile stretch to **Barnstaple** makes for flat, family-friendly cycling alongside the banks of a River Taw that's rich in bird life.

From Barnstaple, a 9-mile section traces the Taw-Torridge Estuary to **Bideford**, before heading beside the River Torridge upstream for 6 miles to **Great Torrington**. This section passes the **Beam Aqueduct**, described by Williamson as Tarka's birthplace and there are still **otters** here today. The final 11-mile stretch to **Meeth** is the quietest and winds through north Devon's hilly farming heartland.

Bike-hire options include **Otter Cycle Hire** (☎ 01271-813339, The Old Pottery, Station Rd; per day adult/child £12/8; ☻ 9am-5pm Mar-Oct) in Braunton and **Tarka Trail Cycle Hire** (☎ 01271-324202; per day adult/child £11/8; ☻ 9.15am-5pm late Mar-Oct) at Barnstaple train station.

☙ RHS ROSEMOOR // BE INSPIRED BY A TRANQUIL GARDENER'S PARADISE

Run by the Royal Horticultural Society (RHS), this **garden** (☎ 01805-624067; www.rhs.org.uk; adult/child £7/2.50; ☻ 10am-6pm Apr-Sep, 10am-5pm Oct-Mar; ℗) is a must-see source of green-fingered inspiration. One of only four RHS centres open to the public nationwide, its 65 enchanting acres are a vivid, fragrant oasis, full of colour, serenity and tips on best practice.

A wealth of garden styles and features are represented, ranging from **arboreta** and croquet lawns to **shade**, **terrace** and **town gardens**. The **fruit and veg section** is an object lesson in how to grow produce, whether in traditional rows, raised beds or containers. Other highlights include the tree ferns, bananas and ginger lilies in the **exotic garden**, the sweeps of colour in the **cottage garden** and, ever popular at Rosemoor, the heady scents of the **rose garden**.

Events and talks take place through the year; themes include colour and fragrance, alpines, rhododendrons, apples, pumpkins and fungi. Rosemoor is one mile south of Great Torrington, off the A3124.

☙ TORRINGTON 1646 // SPIN THE CLOCK BACK TO THE CIVIL WAR

This irrepressible **attraction** (☎ 01805-626146; www.torrington-1646.co.uk; South St; adult/child £8/5.50; ☻ 10am-3pm Mon-Fri Apr-Sep) is a vivid audiovisual recreation of a key English Civil War battle. In the eponymous 1646 Sir Thomas Fairfax and his Parliamentarians surged into Great Torrington, confronting and defeating the Royalists under Lord Hopton – a battle that spelled the end of Royalist resistance in the Westcountry.

Tours are led by cheeky costumed guides who tease visitors remorselessly and pepper their spiel with tales of leech-breeders, urine-takers and Puritans. Discover a **physic garden**, wave a **sword**, learn about the **bum roll**, and ladies – if you sit with crossed legs, expect to be the butt of more than a few jokes.

The last tour is at 3pm. Torrington 1646 is in the centre of Great Torrington.

☙ CLOVELLY // FALL IN LOVE WITH AN IMPOSSIBLY PRETTY VILLAGE

At this traffic-free **fishing village** white cottages cascade beside steep cliffs and a crab-claw harbour curls out into a deep blue sea. Cobbles are everywhere. They smother houses, garden walls and the incredibly steep lanes, and give the whole village the air of flowing down the hill into the sea. Inevitably it's a tourist honeypot, but despite Colvelly's sometimes stage-set feel around 98% of its houses have year-round tenants – in some Westcountry villages almost half the properties are second homes.

Clovelly is privately owned and you have to pay to get in. The overwhelming **visitor centre** (☎ 01237-431781; www.clovelly. co.uk; adult/child £6/4; ☺ 8.45am-6.30pm Jun-Sep, 9am-5pm Apr & May, 10am-4pm Nov-Apr; ℗) leads to a cobbled lane that's so steep cars can't negotiate it; instead supplies are brought in by **sledge**: you'll see these big breadbaskets on runners leaning outside people's homes.

Fisherman's Cottage (High St; admission free; ☺ 8.45am-6.30pm Jun-Sep, 9am-5pm Apr & May, 10am-4pm Nov-Apr) recreates the interior of a 1930s village house, the **Kingsley Museum** (High St; admission free; ☺ 8.45am-6.30pm Jun-Sep, 9am-5pm Apr & May, 10am-4pm Nov-Apr) pays tribute to Charles Kingsley, author of *The Water Babies,* who lived in Clovelly as a child. The museum also features Kingsley's poem *The Three Fishers,* about three fishermen's wives waiting in vain for their husbands to return, a recurring theme locally.

Until the 1990s donkeys ferried goods up and down Clovelly's steep streets – some animals still make appearances for the cameras. **Temple Bar Cottage** arches right over the High St; the space underneath was a donkey shelter. Beside the **beach**, the 15th-century **Crazy Kate's Cottage** is named after a fisherman's wife driven made with grief when he failed to return. The **lifeboat station** was built in 1870 after a storm that claimed many lives. The far end of the beach has a **waterfall**, with a hidden cave.

In its herring-fishing heyday 400 donkeyloads of fish were landed at **Clovelly Quay** in one day. Today you can buy wet fish, crab and lobster from the **Fish Shop**

alongside, or charter a boat for **fishing trips** or journeys to **Lundy Island**. Try **Remo** (☎ 07977 782059), **Dave** (☎ 07817 974963) or **Clive** (☎ 07774 190359). The quayside **Red Lion** has an atmospheric bar, complete with a locally caught stuffed shark's head; it also makes a superb place to stay (p301).

Clovelly is 12 miles north from Bideford, on the A39.

❧ HARTLAND QUAY & POINT // ENCOUNTER SHIPWRECKS, CLIFFS, STARS AND SUNSETS

A rugged right-angle of land, the **Hartland Peninsula** has the kind of coast that makes you gasp. It feels like the edge of Devon, and it is; the county stretches no further west from here and Cornwall lies just a few miles south.

The towering cliffs at **Hartland Quay** (℗) are among the most spectacular in the region – the peninsula rises 350ft above sea level. Russet strata of sand and mudstone have been scrunched vertical by incredible natural force to stick out at crazy angles – not unlike a giant, deeply folded lasagne. The 16th-century quay has a rocky beach and compact **Shipwreck Museum** (☎ 01237-441218; adult/child £1/50p; ☺ 11am-5pm Easter-Oct), which uses artefacts and powerful photographs to evoke some of the hundreds of vessels that have foundered on the jagged shore. The welcoming **Wreckers Retreat Pub** in the **Hartland Quay Hotel** (☎ 01237-441218) has a beer terrace with spectacular views.

A mile north, the coast around **Hartland Point** (℗) offers superb hiking. Tucked just under the point is the short white column of a **lighthouse,** which was built in 1874. You can't go in but there's a viewing platform just to the west, where you can also see the rusting hull fragments of the coaster *Johanna*. She came to grief on New Year's Eve in 1982 (the crew was rescued by the Clovelly lifeboat); the ship's bell now sits in Hartland Quay's Shipwreck Museum.

The unspoilt, west-facing coast of the Hartland Peninsula reveals overarching sunsets, while its remoteness ensures rich star displays at night. Superb constellation **viewing points** are Hartland Quay and the Wreckers Retreat beer terrace.

❦ HARTLAND ABBEY // STROLL ROUND A LAVISH FAMILY HOME

This warm grey **manor house** (☎ 01237-441264; www.hartlandabbey.com; adult/child £9.50/2.50; ☙ gardens noon-5pm Sun-Fri Apr-Sep, house 2-4.30m Wed, Thu & Sun Apr & May, Sun-Thu Jun-Sep; ℗) is rich in history and plush furnishings. Built in the 12th century, it was a monastery until Henry VIII grabbed it in the Dissolution; he then gave it to the sergeant of his wine cellar in 1539. Today its sumptuous interiors house a sequence of vivid **murals**, an ornate **Alhambra Passage**, a **Regency library** designed in the Strawberry Hill Gothic style, and a hugely evocative collection of **Victorian photographs** – many were taken during the 1898 Sudan campaign.

The gardens were inspired by Gertrude Jekyll, a frequent guest, and are rich in camellias, hydrangeas, rhododendrons and azaleas. Other highlights are the **Baronet's Bog Garden**, the **Victorian Fernery** and the displays of woodland **bluebells**.

Hartland Abbey is a mile south of Hartland Point and 5 miles west of Clovelly.

GASTRONOMIC HIGHLIGHTS

❦ 11, THE QUAY // ILFRACOMBE ££

☎ 01271-868090; www.11thequay.com; 11 The Quay; snacks £2-9, mains £13-22; ☙ restaurant lunch & dinner Wed-Sat, dinner Sun; bistro lunch, dinner & snacks all day

Full of Chelsea-chic, this distinctive eatery is owned by the artist Damien Hirst, a man famous for exhibiting dead cows and sharks. The menu's less controversial; sample cured ham with pickled garlic or lobster risotto with chives while admiring Hirst's artwork. It includes his *Pharmacy* installation and, with delicious irony, fish in formaldehyde.

❦ LA GENDARMERIE // ILFRACOMBE ££

☎ 01271-865984; 63 Fore St; mains £14; ☙ dinner Tue-Sat, Sun bookings only

One of several smart restaurants winding up Ilfracombe's Fore St, this one is all wooden floors and exposed stone. Try the sea bass with lobster ravioli and cognac, or be bold and plump for the pigs trotters with béarnaise sauce.

❦ TERRA MADRE // MUDDIFORD £

☎ 01271-850262; Muddiford Rd; 3 courses £14; ☙ lunch Wed-Fri & Sun

The tables at Broomhill Sculpture Gardens' slow-food bistro overflow with local, organic produce, including Lundy Island crab, Red Ruby beef and free-range chicken. Dishes are infused with Mediterranean flavours – they even make their own air-dried chorizo with free-range pork from a farm just 4 miles away. The evening jazz and tapas buffets are a snip at £7.50.

❦ MASON'S ARMS // KNOWSTONE ££

☎ 01398-341231; mains £18-23; ☙ lunch & dinner Tue-Sat, lunch Sun

A surprise: a Michelin-starred eatery in a thatched, 13th-century pub deep in rural north Devon. Expect modern takes on European classics; try the scallops with pear vanilla and vermouth sauce, or lamb with toasted cumin jus. But leave

DEVON

room for the sticky rhubarb crumble tart with clotted-cream ice cream. The Mason's Arms is 20 miles southeast of Barnstaple; it's worth the drive.

TRANSPORT

BUS // Bus 3 (every 30 minutes Monday to Saturday, hourly Sunday) runs between Ilfracombe and Barnstaple, via Braunton. Bus 308 (hourly Monday to Saturday, five on Sunday) goes from Barnstaple to Braunton, Saunton Sands and Croyde. Bus 315 (seven daily Monday to Saturday, two on Sunday) goes from Exeter to RHS Rosemoor, Great Torrington, Biddeford and Barnstaple. Bus 118 (two daily) shuttles between Barnstaple and Tavistock via Okehampton. Bus 319 (four to six Monday to Saturday, two on Sunday between May and September only) goes between Barnstaple, Bideford, Clovelly and Hartland Village.

TRAIN // The Tarka train line runs between Barnstaple and Exeter (hourly Monday to Saturday, six on Sunday).

DEVON

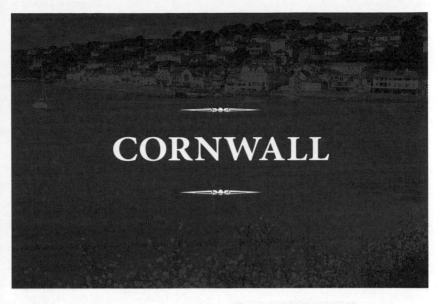

CORNWALL

3 PERFECT DAYS

❦ DAY 1 // NORTHERN EXPOSURE
Begin with a spin along the Atlantic Highway (p190) via Boscastle (p190) and Tintagel (p192), en route to Cornwall's culinary capital, Padstow (p194). Lunch at Paul Ainsworth at No 6 (p198) or Margot's Bistro (p197), then work off the calories around the Seven Bays (p196) or the Camel Trail (p194). Finish in boutique style at the Scarlet (p302) with supper at Lewinnick Lodge (p202) or Fifteen (p201).

❦ DAY 2 // ARTISTIC ST IVES
Spin on along the north coast, factoring in scenic stops at Chapel Porth (p203) and beachy Perranporth (p203). If time is short, head straight down to St Ives (p206) to explore the Tate (p206) and the Barbara Hepworth Museum (p207), stopping for lunch at the Porthminster Beach Café (p210). Catch the sunset from the cliffs at Gwithian (p209), have supper at Alba (p209) or the Loft (p210) and kip at Primrose Valley (p303) or the Boskerris (p303).

❦ DAY 3 // WAY OUT WEST
On day three, follow the breathtaking Zennor coast road (p211), leaving time for a visit to Pendour Cove (p211), the Men-an-tol (p212) or the Iron Age village of Chysauster (p213). Book in for lunch at the Gurnard's Head (p216), then plumb the depths of Geevor Mine (p211) or hike the glorious stretch of coast path between Sennen (p214) and Land's End (p215) before overnighting at the luxurious Cove (p304). Round things off with a memorable meal at Mousehole's top restaurant, Two Fore St (p221).

CORNWALL

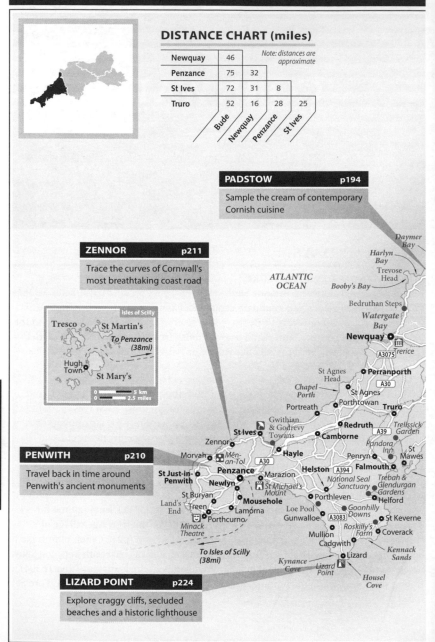

DISTANCE CHART (miles)

	Bude	Newquay	Penzance	St Ives
Newquay	46			
Penzance	75	32		
St Ives	72	31	8	
Truro	52	16	28	25

Note: distances are approximate

PADSTOW   p194

Sample the cream of contemporary Cornish cuisine

ZENNOR   p211

Trace the curves of Cornwall's most breathtaking coast road

PENWITH   p210

Travel back in time around Penwith's ancient monuments

LIZARD POINT   p224

Explore craggy cliffs, secluded beaches and a historic lighthouse

ATLANTIC OCEAN

Isles of Scilly

Tresco   St Martin's
To Penzance (38mi)
Hugh Town   St Mary's
0 ___ 5 km
0 ___ 2.5 miles

Daymer Bay
Harlyn Bay
Trevose Head
Booby's Bay
Bedruthan Steps
Watergate Bay
Newquay   Trerice
A3075
St Agnes Head   Perranporth
A30
Chapel Porth   St Agnes
Portreath   Porthtowan   Truro
Gwithian & Godrevy Towans   Redruth   Trelissick Garden
St Ives   Camborne   A39
Zennor   Hayle   Pandora Inn
Morvah   Mên-an-Tol   A30   Penryn   St Mawes
St Just-in-Penwith   Penzance   Marazion   Helston   Falmouth
Newlyn   St Michael's   A394   National Seal Sanctuary   Trebah & Glendurgan Gardens
St Buryan   Mount   Porthleven   Helford
Land's End   Treen   Lamorna   Loe Pool   Goonhilly Downs   St Keverne
Porthcurno   Gunwalloe   A3083   Roskilly's Farm   Coverack
Minack Theatre   Mullion   Kennack Sands
To Isles of Scilly (38mi)   Cadgwith   Lizard
Kynance Cove   Lizard Point   Housel Cove

CORNWALL

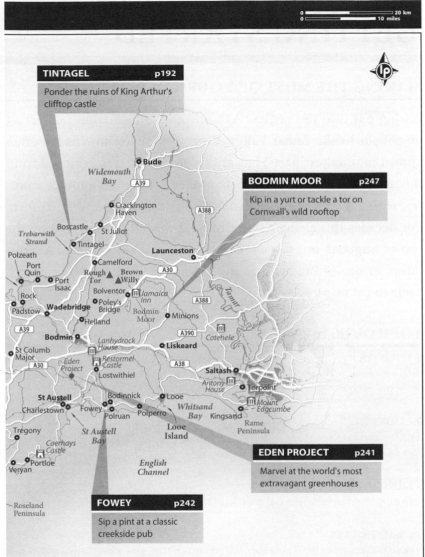

0 20 km
0 10 miles

TINTAGEL p192

Ponder the ruins of King Arthur's clifftop castle

BODMIN MOOR p247

Kip in a yurt or tackle a tor on Cornwall's wild rooftop

Widemouth Bay Bude

Crackington Haven

Boscastle St Juliot
Trebarwith Strand Tintagel

Launceston

Polzeath
Port Quin Camelford
Port Isaac Rough Tor Brown Willy
Rock Bolventor Jamaica Inn
Padstow Wadebridge Poley's Bridge Bodmin Moor Minions
Helland
Bodmin Lanhydrock House Cotehele
St Columb Major Eden Project Restormel Castle Liskeard
Lostwithiel Saltash
St Austell Bodinnick Antony House Torpoint
Charlestown Fowey Looe Mount Edgcumbe
Polruan Polperro Whitsand Bay Kingsand
Tregony Looe Island Rame Peninsula
Caerhays Castle St Austell Bay
Portloe
Veryan *English Channel*

EDEN PROJECT p241

Marvel at the world's most extravagant greenhouses

Roseland Peninsula

FOWEY p242

Sip a pint at a classic creekside pub

CORNWALL

GETTING AROUND

Cornwall is a lot easier to get around these days: the newly dualled A30 has cut down considerably on driving times, but you're still bound to snag traffic jams in peak season. The main route along the county's southern side is the A38, which crosses the Tamar Bridge into Plymouth and south Devon. Public transport is patchy outside the main towns, especially out of season and around the county's more remote corners. Bring a decent map: satnav is more a hindrance than a help.

CORNWALL
GETTING STARTED

MAKING THE MOST OF YOUR TIME

Jutting out into the restless Atlantic and cut off from its nearest neighbour by the Tamar Valley, Cornwall (or Kernow, as it's often known round these parts) has always stood one step removed from the rest of the nation – not just another county but another country, with a distinct culture, landscape and language all of its own. For decades this slender sliver of land was all but ignored by the rest of England, but more recently Cornwall has garnered a reputation as one of the nation's most desirable and creative corners. Time to get inspired.

TOP TOURS & COURSES

❦ WILD FOOD
Forage for some authentic Cornish bush tucker – wild berries, samphire, rock oysters, edible mushrooms – then cook up your very own feast (p215).

❦ COOKING
If you've always wanted to know how to cook the perfect pollack, where better to learn than Rick Stein's fantastic seafood school (p195).

❦ MINE TOURS
Take an underground tour of Geevor Tin Mine in the company of an ex-miner (p211).

❦ LIGHTHOUSES
Bask in the scenery at the Lizard Point lighthouse (p224), now a fascinating maritime heritage centre.

❦ WINE
Visit one of Cornwall's three working vineyards: Camel Valley (p247), Polgoon in Penzance (p219) and St Martin's in the Isles of Scilly (p253).

GETTING AWAY FROM IT ALL

* **South West Coast Path** The beaches might be packed, but you can nearly always find some solitude just by strapping on your boots and striking out on the coast path. And with nearly 300 miles to explore, there's more than enough to go around.

* **Bodmin Moor** Cornwall's windswept roof might not have many beaches, but for big, desolate views, there's nowhere better. You might even spot the legendary beast, so remember to pack a camera (p247).

* **Rame Peninsula** Most visitors buzz by the county's southeastern corner without a second glance, leaving its country estates serene and coast trails unspoilt (p244).

ADVANCE PLANNING

* **Crowds & Traffic** Let's face it – when the sun's shining, you're just not going to escape the crowds and the traffic jams. By far the worst times are between July and August and around bank holiday weekends. Visit in the shoulder months if you want to see Cornwall at its best.

* **Bookings** Cornwall's big-name restaurants and hotels – especially those with a celebrity name attached – get booked out way in advance. Plan accordingly.

* **Train Travel** Travelling to Cornwall by train can be seriously pricey if you leave it till the last minute. Book as early as possible for the best-value fares.

TOP RESTAURANTS

☙ PAUL AINSWORTH AT NO 6
Step aside, Mr Stein – there's a new boy in town (p198)

☙ SEAFOOD RESTAURANT
The restaurant that kickstarted Padstow's renaissance (p198)

☙ NATHAN OUTLAW SEAFOOD & GRILL
Michelin-starred, multitalented chef now in new premises in Rock (p197)

☙ THE GURNARD'S HEAD
Cornwall's finest gastropub, bar none (p216)

☙ KOTA
Fusion cuisine on the Porthleven quayside (p227)

RESOURCES

* **Visit Cornwall** (www.visitcornwall.com) Comprehensive tourist site

* **Cornwall 24** (www.cornwall24.co.uk) Lively (and often heated) discussion forum

* **Cornwall Beach Guide** (www.cornwallbeachguide.co.uk) Online guide to the county's sands

* **Cornwall Online** (www.cornwall-online.co.uk) Community-based site covering accommodation, walks and activities

* **Stranger Mag** (www.stranger-mag.com) Digital magazine with reviews, interviews and cultural news

NORTH COAST

· · · · · ·

If it's the classic Cornish combination of lofty cliffs, sweeping bays and white-horse surf you're after, then make a beeline for the north Cornwall coast. Battered by Atlantic breakers and whipped by year-round winds, the stretch of shoreline between St Ives and Bude is arguably the county's most dramatic. Unsurprisingly, this was John Betjeman's favourite corner of Cornwall, but it's far from a well-kept secret these days; the north coast has become a magnet for every one from weekend surfers to gourmet chefs and celebrity second-homers.

BUDE & THE ATLANTIC HIGHWAY

Travelling west along the Atlantic Hwy (or the A39, as it's more prosaically known to locals) carries you through some of the county's most inspiring vistas. Every twist and turn in the road unfurls a fresh panorama of postcard views. Take your time: this is a trip to be savoured.

ESSENTIAL INFORMATION

TOURIST OFFICES // Bude (☎ 01288-354240; www.visitbude.info; The Crescent; ⏱ 10am-5pm Mon-Sat, plus 10am-4pm Sun summer) **Boscastle** (☎ 01840-250010; www.visitboscastleandtintagel. com; The Harbour; ⏱ 10am-5pm Mar-Oct, 10am-4.30pm Nov-Feb) **Tintagel** (☎ 01840-779084; www. visitboscastleandtintagel.com; Bossiney Rd; 10am-5pm Mar-Oct, 10am-4.30pm Nov-Feb)

EXPLORING THE ATLANTIC HIGHWAY

❦ **BUDE** // SAND, SURF AND SEAPOOLS

First stop across the Cornish border is **Bude**, a blustery beach town which has been reeling in the day trippers and

beachgoers since the Victorian tourist boom in the late 19th century. Tucked away at the end of the River Neet, Bude briefly flourished in the mid-19th century thanks to the construction of the Bude Canal, but the town's industrial ambitions were scuppered by the arrival of the railway, and the canal's now frequented mainly by kingfishers, dragonflies and the occasional otter.

Heritage apart, it's Bude's beaches that warrant a visit. Closest of all is **Summerleaze**, a classic bucket-and-spade affair flanked by the **Bude Sea Pool** (⏱ 10am-6pm May-Sep), dating from the 1930s. Be prepared for a chilly dip: the water's fed straight from the Atlantic, so it's bracing even at the best of times.

The traditional surfers' choice is **Crooklets** (sometimes dubbed the 'Bondi of Britain'; ℗), home to Bude's Surf Life Saving Club, while to the north are the pebbly sand and rockpools of **Northcott Mouth** (℗), **Sandymouth** (a quiet beach with its own waterfall; ℗), and **Duckpool** (℗), a moody, secluded cove dominated by the craggy bulk of Steeple Point.

Three miles south of town, **Widemouth Bay** (pronounced widmuth; ℗) is Bude's best family beach, offering good swimming and plenty of facilities. Though it looks like one long continuous stretch at low tide, it's officially two beaches (North and South) divided by the spiny spur of Black Rock.

Two miles further south is rocky **Millook**, renowned for birdwatching and seal-spotting and a distinctive 'zigzag' cliff. Another 6 miles on is **Crackington Haven** (℗), backed by imposing bluffs, but the most impressive scenery is saved for **the Strangles**, 12 miles south of Bude, where the perilously sheer cliffs plunge straight into the booming surf. At

223m (731ft), the appropriately named High Cliff is the loftiest in Cornwall.

♣ BOSCASTLE // EXPLORE A BEAUTIFUL NATIONAL TRUST VALLEY

Cornwall's north shore has its share of pretty harbours, but none hold a candle to **Boscastle**. Nestled in the crook of a steep valley at the meeting point of three rivers, it's the perfect image of a Cornish harbour, but Boscastle's chocolate-box setting backfired in dramatic fashion in August 2004, when a combination of freak rainfall and the village's unique geography resulted in the worst flash floods to hit Britain in over 50 years. Six years on, things are just about back to normal; flood-prevention schemes have been installed upriver, although in a globally warming world, no one's sure if the floods were a freak event or a sign of things to come.

Other than its Elizabethan-era **harbour** (built in 1584 by Sir Richard Grenville), Boscastle's main draw is its coastal setting. The cliffs provide the perfect backdrop for a blustery picnic, especially at the tiny, tucked-away cove of **Bossiney Haven**, accessible via farmland and steps cut into the cliff. The beach is halfway between Boscastle and Tintagel, and is practically submerged at high tide.

Also worth a visit is the **Museum of Witchcraft** (☎ 01840-250111; www.museumofwitchcraft.com; The Harbour; admission £3; ☺ 10.30am-6pm Mon-Sat, 11.30am-6pm Sun Apr-Oct) founded by the occult expert and ex-MI6 spy Cecil Williamson in 1960. Renovated postflood, its exhibits include witch's poppets (a kind of voodoo doll), divination pans, enchanted skulls, pickled beasts and a horrific 'witch's bridle', designed to extract confessions from suspected hags.

♣ ST JULIOT // A CHURCH WITH THOMAS HARDY CONNECTIONS

Inland from Boscastle along the River Valency, a 3-mile walking trail leads

TOP LOCAL FOOD SHOPS

A few of our favourite places to get your grub from down on the farm.

* **Trevaskis Farm** (☎ 01209-713931; www.trevaskisfarm.co.uk; 12 Gwinear Rd, Hayle; ☺ farm shop 9am-6pm summer, 9am-5pm winter) This Gwithian farm sells choice cuts from the farm butchery, homemade chutneys in the market and 70 varieties of homegrown fruit and veg in the kitchen garden. The farm restaurant also does a popular Sunday roast.

* **Trevathan Farm** (☎ 01208-880164; www.trevathanfarm.com; ☺ 10am-5pm) Pick your own fruit near Port Isaac.

* **Lobbs Farm Shop** (☎ 01726-844411; St Ewe; ☺ 9.30am-5pm Mon-Fri) Part of the Heligan Estate, this is arguably the best farm shop in Cornwall. Stock up on smoked fish, farm-reared meats and marmalades, or pick up a prepacked hamper.

* **Gear Farm** (☎ 01326-221150; www.gearfarmcornwall.co.uk; St Martin, Helston) The Lizard's organic operation, with meat and dairy supplied from a herd of Aberdeen Angus reared on the farm.

* **Kingsley Village** (☎ 01726-861111; www.kingsleyvillage.com) Purpose-built shopping complex on the A30 near Fraddon, with a massive food hall stocked with luxury goods from Cornish suppliers, and excellent fresh-fish and meat counters.

CORNWALL

through old oak woodland to a brace of historic churches: pint-sized **Minster** (sometimes known as St Merthiana's), partly dating from the 12th century; and **St Juliot**, best known for its association with Thomas Hardy. Hardy arrived here in 1870 as a young architect contracted to oversee the church's restoration, and promptly fell head-over-heels for the rector's sister-in-law, Emma Lavinia Gifford (a tale recounted in his novel *A Pair of Blue Eyes*). Hardy buffs can even stay at the rectory where their love affair played out (p301).

Trail leaflets for this walk and several others around Boscastle can be found at the tourist office (p190).

☙ TINTAGEL // KING ARTHUR'S FABLED BIRTHPLACE

The spectre of King Arthur looms large over Tintagel and its clifftop **castle** (EH; ☎ 01840-770328; adult/child £5.20/2.60; ☯ 10am-6pm mid-Mar–Sep, 10am-5pm Oct, 10am-4pm Nov-Mar). Though the ruins mostly date from the 13th century, archaeological digs have revealed the foundations of a much earlier fortress, fuelling speculation that the legendary king may have been born at the castle as local legend claims. Fables aside, the site has been occupied since Roman times and served as a seasonal residence for Cornwall's Celtic kings, but the present castle is largely the work of Richard, Earl of Cornwall, who established the fortress to cash in on its Arthurian connections and curry favour with the local populace.

King Arthur notwithstanding, it's hard to think of a more soul-stirring spot for a stronghold: part of the crumbling castle stands on a rock tower cut off from the mainland, accessed via a wooden bridge and dizzying cliff steps. Though much of the castle has long since crumbled, it's

still possible to make out the footprint of the Great Hall and several other key rooms. A short walk inland leads to the tiny Norman **Church of St Materiana**, in a windblown spot above Glebe Cliff.

After the natural splendour of the Tintagel headland, the **village** itself is a letdown, although it's worth stopping off at the **Old Post Office** (NT; ☎ 01840-770024; Fore St; adult/child £3.20/1.60; ☯ 10.30am-5.30pm Jun-Sep, 10.30am-5pm Apr-May, 11am-4pm Oct-Mar), a 16th-century Cornish longhouse that once served as the village post office.

☙ PORT ISAAC // SAVOUR THE SEA-TANG OF A CLASSIC CORNISH PORT

A few miles southwest of Tintagel is the teeny fishing harbour of Port Isaac, a cluster of cobbled alleyways, slender opes (narrow alleys) and cob-walled cottages collected around a medieval harbour and slipway. Though still a working harbour, Port Isaac is best known as a filming location: the Brit film *Saving Grace* and the TV series *Doc Martin* have both used the village as a ready-made backdrop (a sign near the quayside directs tourists straight to **Doc Martin's cottage**).

A short walk west leads to the neighbouring harbour of **Port Gaverne**, while a couple of miles west is **Port Quin**, now owned by the National Trust. Local folklore maintains that the entire fishing fleet of Port Quin was lost during a great storm in the late 17th century. The remaining families, including some 20 widows, were all subsequently relocated to Port Isaac.

☙ THE SIX CHURCHES // MAKE A PILGRIMAGE TO BETJEMAN'S BURIAL PLACE

Three miles inland from Port Isaac is the pretty church of **St Endellion** (www.stendellion.org.uk), whose tower is still used as a daymark by local fisherman. The church now hosts the **St Endellion Festivals** (www.endellionfestivals.org.uk), a series of classical concerts held during Easter and summer.

It's also one of the Six Churches, a collection of historic chapels that includes **St Minver** and **St Peter's** in Port Isaac, **St James the Great** at St Kew and **St Michael's** at Porthilly. Most famous of all is **St Enodoc**, nestled amongst the dunes of the local golf course, which John Betjeman commemorated in one of his greatest Cornish poems, *Trebetherick*. Fittingly, it was at St Enodoc that Betjeman was buried on a memorably grey, drizzly Cornish day in May 1984. Even without its Betjeman associations, the walk up to St Enodoc is well worth the effort, affording views across the Camel Estuary and the shining sands of Daymer Bay.

GASTRONOMIC HIGHLIGHTS

❦ THE CASTLE // BUDE ££
☎ 01288-350543; www.thecastlerestaurantbude. co.uk; The Wharf; lunch £8-12, mains £14-18; ⏰ lunch & dinner

Housed inside Sir Goldsworthy Gurney's faux folly in Bude, this restaurant is a relaxed, informal place offering Mediterranean-influenced flavours. Chef Kit Davis honed his craft in the capital before setting up shop in Bude, so quality's the watchword.

THE ONCE AND FUTURE KING

For many people the southwest is inextricably bound up with **King Arthur**, the mythic warrior-king, heroic knight and fabled protector of the British Isles; but despite endless research, countless archaeological digs and dubious movies, it's still a matter of complete conjecture if Arthur even really existed.

So here are the facts. There was a Celtic soldier by the name of Arthur or Arthurus who led a counterattack against invading Saxons sometime in the 6th century. A Welsh monk called Nennius is the first to mention Arthur by name in his *Historia Brittonum,* written around AD 800, although Arthur is noticeably absent in the works of other chroniclers of the period such as Bede and Gildas.

The 12th-century historian Geoffrey of Monmouth, a notoriously unreliable scholar, was the first to establish the basics of Arthur's biography, including his birth and death (c AD 500–42), genealogy and ascension to the throne. But Geoffrey almost certainly used a large dollop of Celtic myth to embellish his facts, and it's possible he just made much of it up for the sake of a good yarn. Medieval writers including Chrétien de Troyes and Thomas Mallory's epic poem *Le Morte d'Arthur* embellished the story, inspiring Tennyson's *Idylls of the King* and TH White's *The Once & Future King*.

Many areas in the southwest have staked their claim to an Arthurian connection. **Glastonbury Abbey** (p70) is the supposed burial place of Arthur and Queen Guinevere, while **Glastonbury Tor** (p69) is rumoured to be the legendary Isle of Avalon, where Arthur was carried after being mortally wounded by his illegitimate son/nephew, Mordred.

Cornwall has by far the most King Arthur connections, including **Tintagel** (p192) and **Slaughterbridge** near Camelford, asserted to be the site of Arthur's last battle at Camlann. Meanwhile **Dozmary Pool** (p247) and **Loe Pool** (p223) both claim to be home of the Lady of the Lake, who gave Arthur his legendary sword, Excalibur.

CORNWALL

✿ LIFE'S A BEACH // BUDE ££

☎ 01288-355222; www.lifesabeach.info; Summerleaze Beach; lunch £4-6, mains £16-21.50; ✤ Mon-Sat

Dangling above Summerleaze, this beachside establishment has a split personality: by day it's a surfy cafe churning out ciabattas, coffees and ice cream, but by night it transforms into something slinkier, offering thick slabs of halibut in prosciutto, and roasted whole bream in a super seafront setting.

✿ MILL HOUSE INN // TREBARWITH ££

☎ 01840-770200; www.themillhouseinn.co.uk; mains £12-18; ✤ lunch & dinner

Tucked between Tintagel and Trebarwith Strand, this 18th-century corn mill suits all moods. Aaron Calverd trained at Jamie Oliver's parents' pub, so he knows a trick or two. The pub is a cockle-warming spot, dishing up fishcakes and snakebite-battered haddock, while the river-view restaurant is a more sophisticated concern.

✿ ST KEW INN // ST KEW ££

☎ 01208-841259; www.stkewinn.co.uk; mains £8-16; ✤ 11am-3pm & 6-11pm

Mix the hugger-mugger feel of a village local with the quality grub of a bona fide gastropub and you've got something close to the superb St Kew. Chef/landlord Paul Ripley is a Rick Stein alumnus and former Michelin-star chef, and it shows: the food is up there with the best Cornwall has to offer.

TRANSPORT

BUS // Bus 584 (six daily, four on Sunday) runs between Camelford and Wadebridge, stopping at Port Gaverne, Port Isaac, St Endellion and Port Quin. Bus 594 (every two hours Mon to Sat, four on Sunday) from Bude stops at Boscastle, Widemouth, Crackington Haven, Bossiney and Tintagel.

CAR // Whatever you do, don't try to drive down into Port Isaac; the main car park is at the top of the hill for a reason…

PADSTOW & AROUND

pop 3162

Spin the clock back a couple of decades and Padstow was just another sleepy little port on the north Cornwall coast. Fast forward to the present and the town has become the capital of Cornwall's fast-growing culinary scene, largely thanks to the efforts of one man: celebrity chef, TV star and local-food champion Rick Stein, who earned his spurs in the nation's top kitchens before moving to Cornwall in the late '80s to lay the foundations of his gastronomic empire.

Since his arrival, Padstow has been transformed into one of Cornwall's most cosmopolitan corners, with a profusion of posh boutiques and upmarket eateries rubbing shoulders with the pubs, pasty shops and lobster boats clustered around the town's old quay. It's an occasionally uneasy mix, but it's hard not to be charmed by the setting – and if you're looking to sample contemporary Cornish cuisine, this is most definitely the place.

ESSENTIAL INFORMATION

TOURIST INFORMATION // Padstow tourist office (☎ 01841-533449; www.padstowlive.com; North Quay; ✤ 10am-5pm Mon-Sat)

EXPLORING PADSTOW & AROUND

✿ THE CAMEL TRAIL // CORNWALL'S MOST FAMOUS BIKE TRAIL

In his autobiography *Summoned by Bells* John Betjeman fondly remembered the train ride to Cornwall from Waterloo, especially the coastal line that ran be-

ACCOMMODATION

As you might expect, space is at a premium in Cornwall around holiday times. The best hotels, B&Bs and campsites are booked out months in advance, especially July and August, but off-season you'll be spoilt for choice. Full listings are detailed in the Accommodation chapter (p287), but here are a few perfect picks to whet your whistle.

★ **The Scarlet** (p302) Soho style on the cliffs above Mawgan Porth.

★ **The Cove** (p304) Chic self-catering retreat perched above Lamorna Cove.

★ **Trevalsa Court** (p306) Relax in a gorgeous gentleman's residence near Mevagissey.

★ **Boskerris Hotel** (p303) Boutique sleeps within easy reach of St Ives.

★ **The Lugger** (p305) Smuggle yourself into this sexy coastal hotel.

tween Bodmin and Padstow. The original branch line closed to passenger traffic in the late 1960s, a casualty of Dr Beeching's railway cutbacks, and has since been reinvented as the Camel Trail, one of Cornwall's most popular **cycling** tracks.

The flat, easygoing trail starts in Padstow and runs east through Wadebridge (5 miles from Padstow) along the Camel Estuary before continuing on through Bodmin (10.8 miles) to Poley's Bridge (18.3 miles) on Bodmin Moor. The Padstow–Wadebridge section makes a lovely half-day excursion, but it gets crowded – an estimated 350,000 people tackle the Camel Trail every year. The Wadebridge–Bodmin section is usually quieter and, in its own rugged way, just as scenic.

Bikes can be hired from both ends. In Padstow, **Padstow Cycle Hire** (☎ 01841-533533; www.padstowcyclehire.com; South Quay; ☼ 9am-5pm, t0 9pm mid-Jul–Aug) and **Trail Bike Hire** (☎ 01841-532594; www.trailbikehire.co.uk; Unit 6, South Quay; ☼ 9am-6pm) hire bikes for similar rates (£12 to £15 per day, more for tandems, trikes and tagalongs for kids). Given Padstow's traffic problems, in summer you might find it easier to park in Wadebridge and hire bikes from **Bridge Bike Hire** (☎ 01208-813050; www.bridgebikehire.co.uk) instead.

⚘ NATIONAL LOBSTER HATCHERY // LEARN TO LOVE THE HUMBLE LOBSTER
Lobster-fishing has been a way of life on the north Cornish coast for centuries, but overfishing and pollution led to a dramatic decline in stocks during the 1970s and '80s, requiring dramatic action to ensure the industry's survival. Since 2004 the **National Lobster Hatchery** (☎ 01841-533877; www.nationallobsterhatchery.co.uk; South Quay; adult/child £3/1.50; ☼ 10am-8pm summer, 10am-4pm winter) has been overseeing a sustainability project to help stocks recover. Baby lobsters are reared in holding tanks before being released into the wild. There's plenty of background on marine conservation and the lobster life cycle: you can even adopt your own crustacean for £2.50 and track its progress back into the wild via the hatchery website.

⚘ PADSTOW SEAFOOD SCHOOL // SHARPEN YOUR KITCHEN SKILLS COURTESY OF STEIN & CO
Masterclasses in everything from French fish to perfect sushi are on offer at Rick Stein's vaunted **cookery school** (☎ 01841-532700; www.rickstein.com). Courses last between one and two days and feature hands-on demos from Stein-trained chefs (you'll be disappointed if you're

CORNWALL

expecting to pick up tips from the master himself). Courses are usually booked out months in advance; check the website for late availability.

🌼 PRIDEAUX PLACE // TOUR THE PRIDEAUX-BRUNE'S STATELY RESIDENCE

Much favoured by directors of costume dramas (particularly adaptations of Rosamunde Pilcher novels), the stately **manor** (☎ 01840-532411; www.prideauxplace. co.uk; house & grounds adult £7.50, grounds only £2; 🕑 house 1.30-4pm Sun-Thu, grounds & tearoom 12.30-5.30pm Apr-Oct) was built by the Prideaux-Brune family, purportedly descendants of William the Conqueror. Guided tours last around an hour and take in a feast of state rooms, staircases and plaster ceilings, as well as a host of Prideaux-Brune heirlooms. The house is clearly signposted from the town centre.

🌼 BOAT TRIPS // SAIL OUT TO THE DOOM BAR

Regular boat trips chug out into the Camel Estuary. The **Jubilee Queen** (☎ 07836-798457) and **Padstow Sealife Safaris** (☎ 01841-521613; www.padstowsealifesafaris. co.uk) offer trips around the bay and offshore islands, with a chance of spotting sea birds, seals and even a basking shark in summer; while 15-minute **speedboat trips** (☎ 07811-113380) zip past the treacherous sandbank of Doom Bar and the beaches of Daymer Bay, Polzeath, Hawkers Cove and Tregirls. Check **Padstow Boat Trips** (www.padstowboattrips.com) for schedules and operators.

🌼 ROCK // CORNWALL'S CELEBRITY CAPITAL

Across the estuary from Padstow is the exclusive enclave of **Rock**, now notorious as one of Cornwall's priciest postcodes thanks to an influx of cash-rich second-homers and affluent cityfolk looking to snap up their own seaside property.

The village's popularity with rich cityfolk has earned Rock a roster of nicknames (Cornwall's St-Tropez, Kensington-on-Sea), all of which are guaranteed to raise the hackles of the few remaining locals. It's all a far cry from the sleepy seaside backwater recalled so fondly by Betjeman, but Betjeman's Rock hasn't quite disappeared, at least not yet: outside the main holiday season between June and August, the white sands of **Daymer Bay** are often all but deserted.

In season, the village is best visited as a day trip from Padstow aboard the **Black Tor ferry** (☎ 01841-532239; adult/child return £3/2; 🕑 8am-7.50pm summer, 8am-4.50pm winter), which is supplemented by a nightly **water taxi** (☎ 07778-105297; www.rock-water-taxi.com; adult/ child return £6/3; 🕑 7am-midnight Easter-Oct).

🌼 THE SEVEN BAYS // SEVEN BEACHES FOR SEVEN DAYS

The coastline west of Padstow is studded with a string of beaches known locally as 'the Seven Bays'. Nearest to town are **Trevone** (1½ miles from Padstow; Ⓟ) and half-moon **Harlyn** (2 miles; Ⓟ), which both offer good, safe swimming. Nearby **Mother Ivey's Bay** (2½ miles) is reached along the cliff path; it's usually quieter than its neighbours, despite the proximity of several local caravan parks.

Further west there are stunning, surf-battered views from **Trevose Head**, a notorious shipping hazard that's been topped by a lighthouse since the mid-19th century. Near the headland are the cheek-by-jowl beaches of **Booby's Bay** (3½ miles) and **Constantine** (4 miles; Ⓟ), which lace together at low tides to form one great swash of sand. Next comes **Treyarnon** (5 miles; Ⓟ), with a natural rockpool that doubles as a swimming pool, followed by slender **Porthcothan** (6 miles; Ⓟ).

Although it's not officially one of the Seven Bays, **Hawker's Cove**, 2 miles west of Padstow, is also worth seeking out. Between 1827 and 1967 it was home to Padstow's lifeboat before it moved to Trevose Head. The town's brand-new £2.5m Tamar Class vessel, *Spirit of Padstow,* was inaugurated in 2006.

❦ POLZEATH // LEARN TO SURF AWAY FROM THE NEWQUAY HUSTLE

Around the headland from Padstow, Polzeath usually plays second fiddle to Newquay in the **surfing** stakes, but is actually a much more pleasant place to learn to ride the waves.

Surf's Up Surf School (☎ 01208-862003; www.surfsupsurfschool.com; 21 Trenant Close, Polzeath) is family run and focuses on surf coaching, while **Animal Surf Academy** (☎ 0870 242 2856; www.animalsurfacademy.co.uk; Polzeath Beach) offers female-only lessons. **Harlyn Surf School** (☎ 01841-533076; www.harlynsurf. co.uk; 23 Grenville Rd) is another quality school based at Harlyn Beach.

GASTRONOMIC HIGHLIGHTS

❦ CUSTARD // PADSTOW ££

☎ 0870 170 0740; www.custarddiner.com; 1a The Strand; mains £11-18; ☻ 11am-2.30pm daily, 6-9.30pm Wed-Sun

A promising entry to Padstow's already packed dining scene, Custard is overseen by yet another Stein graduate, Dan Gedge. Touting itself as a 'British dining room', it's really all about Cornish flavours – spiced mackerel, salted cod, sea bass – and the retro decor makes it feel more relaxed than many fine-dining temples around town.

❦ MARGOT'S BISTRO // PADSTOW ££

☎ 01840-533441; www.margotspadstow.blogspot. com; 11 Duke St; mains £12-15; ☻ lunch Wed-Sat, dinner Tue-Sat

Just one sitting and a handful of tables at this dinky bistro, so you'll need to book, but for those in the know this is one of Padstow's secret gems. The menu takes its inspiration from the daily catch and the changing seasons, and owner-chef Adrian Oliver is a real character, so you're in for an offbeat treat.

❦ NATHAN OUTLAW SEAFOOD & GRILL // ROCK £££

☎ 01208-863394; www.nathan-outlaw.com; St Enodoc Hotel, Rock; tasting menu per person from £65, seafood & grill mains £13-20; ☻ lunch & dinner

Rick Stein protégé Nathan Outlaw made his name at the Fowey Hall Hotel, but upped sticks to the St Enodoc Hotel in

CORNWALL

'OSS ANTICS

Padstow is famous for its annual street party, the **'Obby 'Oss ceremony**, a May Day festival (or 2 May if it falls on a Sunday), believed to derive from an ancient pagan fertility rite. The ritual begins just before midnight on 30 April, when revellers announce to the innkeeper at the Golden Lion that summer is 'a-come'. At 10am the Blue Ribbon (or Peace) Oss – a man garbed in a hooped sailcloth dress and snapping horse headdress – dances around the town, accompanied by a baton-wielding 'teazer' and a retinue of musicians, dancers, singers and drummers, all singing the traditional May Song.

An hour later he's followed by the Old (or Red) Oss and, after a day of revelling, singing, carousing and general high jinks, the 'osses are both 'stabled' for another year. It's all eerily reminiscent of *The Wicker Man,* but unlike Sgt Howie you'll need to book well ahead if you're planning on staying in town.

THE STEIN EFFECT

Building on the success of the Seafood Restaurant, Stein's property portfolio now seems to encompass half of Padstow. Start out munching a muffin from **Stein's Patisserie** (Lanadwell St; ⊗9am-5pm Mon-Sat, 10am-5pm Sun), then dine at **St Petroc's Bistro** (New St; mains £11-25; ⊗lunch & dinner), or tuck into battered cod from **Stein's Fish & Chips** (South Quay; takeaway £6.65-10.95; ⊗noon-2.30pm & 5-8pm).

Afterwards, pick up chutneys, choc and cheeses at **Stein's Deli** (South Quay; ⊗9am-7pm Mon-Sat, 10am-5pm Sun), browse for cookbooks at **Stein's Gift Shop** (Middle St; ⊗9am-7pm Mon-Sat, 10am-5pm Sun), and kip at **St Edmunds House** (St Edmunds Lane; r £270), cosy **St Petroc's Hotel** (New St; d £135-210) or one of several Stein cottages.

As if that wasn't enough, Rick's latest ventures include a **fish-and-chip shop cum champagne-and-oyster bar** in Falmouth (p231), plus a revamped pub in St Merryn, the **Cornish Arms** (Churchtown, St Merryn; mains £5.20-13.25; ⊗11am-11.30pm).

Bookings for the Stein empire are handled by a **central switchboard** (☎01840-532700; www.rickstein.com).

Rock in 2008 and has since earned a national reputation and a shiny Michelin star. There's a choice of two Outlaws: foodies plump for the exclusive (and expensive) Restaurant Nathan Outlaw, but we prefer his seafood and grill, where his passion for local produce is expressed at a more affordable price.

❤ PAUL AINSWORTH AT NO 6 // PADSTOW ££

☎01840-532093; www.number6inpadstow.co.uk; 6 Middle St; mains £13.50-15.50; ⊗lunch & dinner
If you're looking for the chef most likely to inherit Rick Stein's crown, our money's on Paul Ainsworth, who took over the reins at this bijou townhouse in 2008 having cut his teeth under Gary Rhodes and Gordon Ramsay. Imaginative, inventive and refreshingly unpretentious, Ainsworth's trademark is reinventing classic dishes with his own distinctive spin: the end result is modern Brit cooking at its very, very best.

❤ RELISH // WADEBRIDGE £

☎01208-814214; www.relishwadebridge.co.uk; Foundry Ct; mains £4.50-8.50; ⊗9am-5pm Mon-Sat

Wadebridge isn't blessed with exciting eateries, but this fab cafe-deli makes up for the shortfall. Owner Hugo Hercod won the UK Barista Championship in 2008, so the coffee is about the best you'll find this side of the Tamar: follow up with a Blacky ham sandwich, a savoury scone laced with Godminster cheddar or a plate of goodies from the inhouse deli, and you've got one of the best little lunch stops in Cornwall.

❤ SEAFOOD RESTAURANT // PADSTOW £££

☎01840-532700; www.rickstein.com; Riverside; 3-course lunch £35, mains £17.50-45; ⊗lunch & dinner
The brick that built the Stein empire, and still the best of the bunch. It's less starchy than you might think, with a light-filled conservatory for predinner tipples and a classy dining room draped with potted plants and local art. Unsurprisingly, seafood is the menu's cornerstone, but you'll need friends in high places to bag a table. Space is usually easier to come by at **Rick Stein's Café** (Middle St; mains £8.50-15; ⊗closed Sun), Rick's Continental brasserie a bit further into town.

CORNWALL

TRANSPORT

BUS // Most useful is the 556 (hourly in summer, reduced service in winter), which runs between Padstow and Newquay with stops including Trevone, Harlyn, St Merryn, Constantine, Porthcothan, Bedruthan Steps, Newquay Airport, Watergate Bay and Porth. Bus 555 (half-hourly Mon to Sat, six on Sunday) travels from Padstow to Bodmin via Little Petherick, St Issey and Wadebridge.

NEWQUAY & AROUND

After years of touting itself as Cornwall's party town *par excellence,* Newquay is currently suffering an identity crisis. Blessed with a breathtaking location smack bang in the middle of Cornwall's finest stretch of coastline, over the last decade the town has become more infamous for its after-dark antics: every summer the town plays host to a tsunami of stag-dos, sun-bleached surfers and barely legal drinkers looking for some high jinks by the seashore.

But the bubble seems to have burst. Rampant property development, spiralling house prices and the town's reputation for booze-fuelled bad behaviour have led many residents to question the direction in which Newquay's headed. The issue was thrown into sharp focus in 2009 following the deaths of two teenagers, who fell from the town cliffs after an evening of heavy drinking, prompting a band of placard-waving residents to march on County Hall demanding a zero-tolerance approach to underage drinking and antisocial behaviour.

While the debate about Newquay's future rumbles on, it's hard not to be seduced by its natural charms. Some of Cornwall's best beaches are just a stone's throw from the town centre, and the steady drip-drip of quality restaurants and accommodation suggest Newquay might finally be ready to leave its teenage antics behind.

ESSENTIAL INFORMATION

TOURIST INFORMATION // Newquay tourist office (☎ 01637-854020; www.newquay. co.uk; Marcus Hill; ⏱ 9.30am-5.30pm Mon-Sat, 9.30am-12.30pm Sun)

EXPLORING NEWQUAY & AROUND

❦ **NEWQUAY BEACHES //** THE COUNTY'S MOST FAMOUS SANDS
Like many north-coast towns, Newquay started life as a bustling harbour and pilchard port. Until they were fished out in the early 20th century, the Newquay shoals were some of the largest in Cornwall (one catch of 1868 netted a record 16.5 million fish). The only remnant of this once-thriving industry is the 14th-century **Huer's Hut**, a lookout once used for spotting approaching shoals, perched on the headland between Towan and Fistral.

These days, however, Newquay's all about the beaches. **Great Western**, **Tolcarne** and **Towan** are nearly always crammed thanks to their proximity to town. Things are usually quieter out east at **Lusty Glaze** and **Porth** (Ⓟ), while out west beyond Pentire Head, surfers brave the breakers of **Fistral** (Ⓟ), England's most famous surfing beach.

If the town beaches are too hectic, you'll find more elbow room further afield. Three miles southwest is **Crantock** (Ⓟ), sandwiched between the headlands of East and West Pentire backed by dunes and the fast-flowing River Gannel. Further west is tiny **Porth Joke** (known locally as Polly Joke), but it's tricky to find and has no facilities; families will be better off at **Holywell Bay** (Ⓟ), with

CORNWALL

powder-soft sand plus rockpools and caves to explore at low tide.

One-and-a-half miles east of Newquay is **Watergate Bay** (Ⓟ), home to Jamie Oliver's Fifteen restaurant and a fast-growing centre for adventure sports. Five miles from Newquay is **Mawgan Porth** (Ⓟ), home to Cornwall's super eco-chic hotel, the Scarlet (p302).

❦ BEDRUTHAN STEPS // WATCH NATURE'S HEAVY MACHINERY AT WORK

Seven miles east of Newquay loom the stately rock stacks of **Bedruthan Steps** (Carnewas), carved out by the relentless action of thousands of years of wind and waves. Accessed via a vertiginous staircase, the beach is practically swallowed up at high tide, but the surrounding cliffs are great for clifftop walks and birdspotting, and there's a National Trust **cafe**

(☽ 10am-5.30pm mid-May–Sep, 11am-4pm mid-Feb–mid-May & Oct–mid-Dec) for when the Atlantic wind really whips up.

❦ TRERICE // HEIRLOOMS APLENTY IN AN ELIZABETHAN MANORHOUSE

Built in 1751, the charming Elizabethan **manor** (NT; ☎ 01637-875404; adult/child £6.70/3.30; ☽ 11am-5pm Sat-Thu Mar-Oct) is most famous for the elaborate barrel-roofed ceiling of the Great Chamber, but has plenty of other intriguing features, including ornate fireplaces, original plasterwork and fine period furniture. Outside, the grounds contain a traditional Cornish orchard, a lawnmower museum and a bowling green where you can try traditional medieval sports: anyone for a game of slapcock?

Trerice is 3.3 miles southeast of Newquay. Bus 527 runs from Newquay to Kestle Mill, less than a mile from the house.

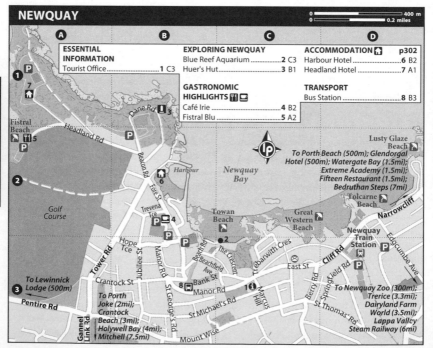

CORNWALL'S BEST BEACHES

* **For families:** Holywell Bay (p199), Perranporth (p203), Praa Sands (p220), Kennack Sands (p224), Summerleaze (p190)

* **For surfers:** Fistral (p199), Gwithian (p209), Crooklets (p190), Polzeath (p197)

* **For hikers:** Portheras Cove (p214), Porthgwarra (p215), Porthchapel (p215)

* **For views:** Bedruthan Steps (p200), Chapel Porth (p203), Kynance Cove (p225)

* **For solitude:** Housel Bay (p225), Nanjizal (p215)

* **For adventure sports:** Watergate Bay (p201), Widemouth Bay (p190), Lusty Glaze (p201)

♣ ADVENTURE CORNWALL // THRILLS AND SPILLS ON THE NEWQUAY BEACHES

Newquay is a haven for outdoor activities, from abseiling, kitesurfing and sea kayaking to the latest craze of coasteering, which combines clambering along the cliffs in a full-bodied wetsuit prior to taking a plunge into the briny blue.

There are lots of operators. On Lusty Glaze, the **Adventure Centre** (☎ 01637-872444; www.adventure-centre.org; Lusty Glaze) runs multiactivity sessions on land, sea and cliff-face (although some such as zip-lining aren't suitable for younger children).

At Watergate, the **Extreme Academy** (☎ 01637-860543; www.watergatebay.co.uk/extreme academy.htm; Watergate Bay) offers watersports including paddle-surfing and traction kiting, while over at Holywell, **EboAdventure** (☎ 0800 781 6861; www.penhaleadven ture.com; Holywell Bay) offers land-based activities including orienteering and mountain-biking.

FESTIVALS & EVENTS

Boardmasters (www.relentlessboardmasters.com) Surf and sports hit Fistral, while bands strut stages on Watergate Bay in early August.
Run to the Sun (www.runtothesun.co.uk) Thousands of VW Beetles and Campers descend on Newquay for this May mash-up.

GASTRONOMIC HIGHLIGHTS

♣ CAFÉ IRIE // NEWQUAY £

☎ 01637-859200; www.cafeirie.co.uk; 38 Fore St; lunch £3-8; 🕙 9am-5.30pm Mon-Sat

Run by surfers for surfers, this cafe's famous for its coffee and hot chocolate (just the ticket after a morning in the ocean swell), plus veggie wraps, piping-hot jacket spuds and gooey cakes. The decor's cool, too: vintage vinyl on the walls, multicoloured plates and coffee mugs, and chalkboards scrawled with daily specials.

♣ FIFTEEN CORNWALL // WATERGATE BAY £££

☎ 01637-861000; www.fifteencornwall.com; Watergate Bay; 3-course lunch menu £26, dinner menu £55; 🕙 8.30-10am, noon-2.30pm & 6.15-9.15pm

Jamie Oliver opened his Cornish Fifteen franchise on Watergate Bay in 2006, and despite inevitable grumblings about style over substance, it's proved a big hit. Staffed with student chefs from Cornwall College, Fifteen ticks plenty of boxes: fabulous beachside setting, buzzy atmosphere and a menu stuffed with Oliver's trademark Italian food. It's a red-hot ticket, though, and often gets too busy for its own good: plan weeks ahead.

TOP FIVE

FAMILY OUTINGS

Attractions in and around Newquay that'll keep the tots entertained.

* **Blue Reef Aquarium** (☎ 01637-878134; www.bluereefaquarium.co.uk; Towan Promenade; adult/child/family £9.20/7.20/30.80; ⏲ 10am-5pm Mar-Oct, 10am-4pm Nov-Feb) Touch-pools and deep-sea denizens on Towan Beach.

* **Newquay Zoo** (☎ 01637-873342; www.newquayzoo.co.uk; Trenance Gardens; adult/child/family £10.95/8.20/30.50; ⏲ 9:30am-6pm Apr-Sep, 10am-5pm Oct-Mar) Red pandas, sloths, penguins, great-horned owls and a python called Monty (ha ha).

* **St Eval Kart Circuit** (☎ 01637-860160; www.cornwallkarting.com; St Eval, Wadebridge; adult/child from £22/4; ⏲ 9.30am-6pm Mon-Sat) The southwest's biggest go-kart centre, offering four tracks and five different karts.

* **Lappa Valley Steam Railway** (☎ 01872-510317; www.lappavalley.co.uk; St Newlyn East; adult/child/family £9.95/7.95/30; ⏲ closed winter) Ride the rails aboard Lilliputian steam trains.

* **Dairyland Farm World** (☎ 01637-510246; www.dairylandfarmworld.com; admission £8.35; ⏲ 10am-5pm Mar-Oct) Ride the ponies, pet the billy goats and milk the cows. Oo-ar.

❦ FISTRAL BLU // NEWQUAY ££
☎ 01637-879444; www.fistral-blu.co.uk; Fistral Beach; mains £8-20; ⏲ noon-3pm & 6-9.30pm
If you can't bag a spot at Fifteen, this place makes a decent fall-back. Lodged inside Fistral's glass-fronted retail complex, it offers big beach views and Med cuisine, supplemented by Cornish standards such as fish pie, mussels and scallops. Fish and chips and Ben & Jerry's ice cream are available at the ground-floor cafe.

❦ LEWINNICK LODGE // NEWQUAY ££
☎ 01637-878117; www.lewinnick-lodge.info; Pentire Head; mains £10-18; ⏲ 9am-11pm
What this clifftop bistro-bar lacks in exterior charm it makes up for in setting. Nestled on Pentire Head, teetering on the cliff edge, the Lewinnick would be worth a recommendation simply for the vistas. Thankfully, the food's good too, mixing zingy Continental flavours with quality Cornish produce.

❦ PLUME OF FEATHERS // MITCHELL ££
☎ 01872-510387; www.theplume.info; Mitchell; mains £10-18.75; ⏲ 11am-11pm
Run by the team behind Lewinnick Lodge, this village boozer is worthy of investigation. The gloomy interior and eight B&B rooms have been attractively overhauled, and the menu's bursting with gastropub credentials: big hunks of pork belly and sirloin steak, Cornish bangers with herby bacon mash, roast chicken with greens and dauphinoise potatoes.

TRANSPORT

TO/FROM THE AIRPORT
AIRPORT // Newquay Airport (NQY; ☎ 01637-860600; www.newquaycornwallairport.com) is 5 miles from town. There are several daily flights to London Gatwick and London City, plus less frequent departures to Belfast, Bristol, Edinburgh, Glasgow and Newcastle. For flights to Scilly, see p249.
BUS // Bus 556 runs to Newquay Bus Station (22 minutes, £2.80, hourly in summer, reduced service in winter)

plus Padstow and nearby villages. **Summercourt Travel** (☎ 01726-861108; www.summercourttravel. com/410.pdf; adult £11.50) also runs prebooked taxibus services from Newquay.

TAXI // There is no taxi rank at Newquay airport. Official transfers are provided by ecofriendly **BioTravel** (☎ 01637-880006; www.biotravel.co.uk). Local taxi firms offering airport transfers include **A2B Newquay Travel** (☎ 01637-875555; www. newquaytravel.co.uk), **Henver Cabs** (☎ 0792-882-5668; www.newquayairporttaxis.org) and **Carbis Cabs** (☎ 01637-260360; www.newquay-airport-taxis. co.uk). Guide prices: to/from Newquay £15 to £20; Padstow £25 to £30; Truro £40 to £50.

GETTING AROUND

BUS // There are regular services to Truro: buses 585 and 586 are the fastest (50 minutes, twice-hourly Monday to Saturday), while the hourly 587 follows the coast via Crantock (14 minutes), Holywell Bay (25 minutes) and Perranporth (50 minutes).

TRAIN // Newquay is at the end of the branch line to Par (£3.80, 49 minutes) on the main London–Penzance route.

PERRANPORTH TO PORTREATH

🌱 PERRANPORTH // TEST YOUR KITE-BUGGYING SKILLS

East of Newquay, the coast road tracks through craggy scenery all the way to **Perranporth**, another breezy beach town blessed with a fabulous 3-mile stretch of sand. The town isn't much to look at – an untidy sprawl of concrete chalets, holiday villas and clifftop bungalows – but the beach itself is a stunner, sweeping in a great arc all the way to the grassy dunes of **Penhale Sands**. On the southern edge of the beach, a staircase leads to Perran's giant **sundial**, built to commemorate the millennium and show Cornish time (rather than GMT).

Reliable swells make Perranporth popular with surfers and bodyboarders, and the level sands make it ideal for wind-powered sports such as kite-buggying, powerkiting and landboarding. **Mobius Kite School** (☎ 08456 430 630; www.mobiuson line.co.uk) has its home base in Perran, and offers taster sessions in all these sports, as well as guided mountain-bike trips.

For a cold one as the sun goes down, you can't beat the **Watering Hole** (☎ 01872-572888; www.the-wateringhole.co.uk; mains £4-14; ⏱ 11am-11pm) plonked right on Perran's sands, always packed with postbeach punters when the sun's been shining.

🌱 ST AGNES & CHAPEL PORTH // WANDER AMONGST CLIFFS AND CHIMNEY STACKS

Abandoned engine houses litter the hilltops around **St Agnes**, which once resounded to the thump and clang of mine pumps and steam engines, and now echoes only to the strains of crashing surf and calling gulls. Smart slate-roofed houses hint at the town's former prosperity as one of the Cornwall's tin-mining boom towns: the local landmark of the **Stippy Stappy** consists of a terrace of miners' cottages built in a stepped pattern down the hill to **Trevaunance Cove**.

A century or two ago there were several mines around St Agnes working the area's rich mineral lodes. The best-known is **Wheal Coates**, a clifftop engine house which still boasts its original brick chimney. The mine is a steep walk up from the National Trust cove of **Chapel Porth** (Ⓟ), a mile's drive from St Agnes. The beach cafe (recently rebuilt after a fire) is renowned for its house speciality of hedgehog ice cream (vanilla ice cream, clotted cream and chopped hazelnuts).

After all those calories, the coast path around St Agnes is just crying out to be explored. Westwards, the trail meanders across the cliffs to the small coastal town of **Porthtowan**, with its sandy beach and surfy hangout, the Blue Bar (p204). Eastwards, the trail winds through windswept gorse to the plunging bluffs around **Tubby's Head** and **St Agnes Head**. Inland, **St Agnes Beacon** offers one of the best vantage points in Cornwall; see www.st-agnes.com/walks/beacon.php for several circular routes.

☙ BLUE HILLS // POLISH YOUR KNOWLEDGE AT A WORKING TIN STREAM

Two miles east of St Agnes, a turn-off from the B3285 (signed to Wheal Kitty) leads down a perilously steep single-track road into **Trevellas Coombe**, known locally as Blue Hills, a reference to the vivid blue heather that grows on the surrounding slopes. Halfway down the valley, surrounded by crumbling mine workings, is **Blue Hills Tin Streams** (☎ 01872-553341; www.bluehillstin.com; adult/child £5.50/3; ☼ 10am-4pm Mon-Sat Jul-Aug, 10am-2pm Mon-Sat late-Mar–late-Oct), where the Wills family has been working tin for the last three decades. Guided tours take in the whole process, from mining and smelting through to casting and finishing. There's also a small shop where you can pick up souvenirs including brooches, earrings, cufflinks and tableware, all made from 100%-certified Cornish tin.

☙ THE COAST TO COAST TRAIL // CYCLE THROUGH THE HEART OF CORNWALL'S MINING HERITAGE

A couple of miles west of St Agnes is **Portreath**, from where vast quantities of Cornwall's mineral ore was once shipped out to Swansea for smelting. In its heyday in the mid-19th century, around 100,000 tonnes of ore were passing out of Portreath's harbour every year; in order to streamline the process a mineral tram-way was built from Portreath to connect the harbour with the productive Gwennap copper mines around Camborne, Redruth and the Gwennap area.

The tramway itself has long since closed down, but has been resurrected as the **Coast to Coast Cycle Trail** (11 miles), which runs to the villages of **Bissoe** and **Devoran** through the rugged mining country around Scorrier, Chacewater and the Poldice Valley. It's mostly flat and easy, although there are a few uphill and off-road sections, and at several points the trail crosses a minor road.

Bikes and maps can be hired from the Portreath end at the **Bike Barn** (☎ 01209-891498; www.cornwallcycletrails.com; ☼ 10.30am-5.30pm), or at the Devoran end from **Bissoe Bike Hire** (☎ 01872-870341; www.cornwallcyclehire.com; ☼ 9.30am-6.30pm summer, to 5pm winter), which also has a good cafe. There's plenty of car parking at both ends if you want to bring your own bike.

☙ TEHIDY COUNTRY PARK // WEST CORNWALL'S LARGEST WOODLAND

This 250-acre **country park** formerly belonged to the Bassets, one of Cornwall's four richest tin-mining families, who made their fortune from extensive mineral rights across west and central Cornwall. The estate has been owned by the council since 1983 and run as public woodland, criss-crossed by trails, peaceful lakes and wildlife reserves. The park maintains an area of woodland especially reserved for barbecues (per day £15), as well as a pleasant **cafe** (mains £4-8; ☼ 9.30am-5pm).

GASTRONOMIC HIGHLIGHTS

☙ **BLUE BAR** // PORTHTOWAN £
☎ 01209-890329; www.blue-bar.co.uk; mains £6-14; ☼ 10am-11pm Mon-Fri, to midnight Sat, to 10pm Sun

Over at Porthtowan, this thriving locals hangout brings some Bondi flair to Cornwall's social scene. It is suitably surfy, featuring bold primary colours and an open-plan interior, as well as big booths and patio tables that overlook the beach. Decent après-surf grub and regular gigs, too.

🍴 **DRIFTWOOD SPARS //**
ST AGNES ££
☎ 01872-552428; www.driftwoodspars.com; Trevaunance Cove; mains £10.95-16.95; ☯ lunch & dinner

Hunkered by the pebbly sands of Trevaunance Cove, the Driftwood is an old warhorse but it's as popular as ever. The pub's bars are full of low-beamed character, while the upstairs restaurant is light, bright and pine-filled. Bookings are recommended for Monday Pie Night and the ever-popular Sunday roast.

🍴 **THE TIN FIN // PERRANPORTH ££**
☎ 01872-572117; 4 Beach Rd; mains £12-18; ☯ breakfast, lunch & dinner

A welcome addition to Perran's lean dining scene. Slate floors, multicoloured chairs and pine tables give it a fresh seaside feel, while the simple, bistro-style food is a cut above most places round town. Shame there's no beach view.

TRANSPORT

BUS // Local buses include bus 583 (12 daily Monday to Saturday) between Truro, St Agnes and Perranporth and bus 304 (10 to 12 Monday to Friday, six on Saturday) from Truro to Porthtowan. Bus 85 (hourly Monday to Saturday) is the most regular from Truro to St Agnes. Bus 403 also runs between Truro, St Agnes, Perran and Newquay.

CORNISH MINING & THE WORLD HERITAGE SITE

Since 2006, Cornwall's historic mining areas have formed part of the UK's newest Unesco World Heritage Site, the **Cornwall and West Devon Mining Landscape** (www.cornish-mining. org.uk). This site covers huge tracts of land around the county, with the largest concentration in St Just, St Agnes, Gwennap and the former mining towns of Camborne and Redruth, where the last working tin mine at South Crofty closed down in 1998 after almost four centuries of production.

Despite various attempts to restart the industry since South Crofty's closure, the huge costs of draining the now-flooded shafts, coupled with the double whammy of cheap extraction and labour costs in the developing world, have so far proved prohibitive and, for now at least, Cornwall's pumps and engines look set to remain silent.

The **Cornish Mines & Engines** (☎ 01209-315027; cornishmines@nationaltrust.org.uk) centre in Pool, near Redruth, makes an ideal place to get acquainted with this once-great industry. At the heart of the complex are two working beam engines, both once powered by steam boilers designed by local engineer Richard Trevithick (who was born in Redruth in 1771, and whose cottage at Penponds is now open to the public).

Elsewhere films, photos and artefacts trace the area's rich mining history, while you can see more mining gear in action at **King Edward Mine** (☎ 01209-614681; www. kingedwardmine.co.uk; adult/child £5/1; ☯ 10am-5pm May-Sep), which also marks the start of the 7.5-mile **Great Flat Lode Trail**, a circular trail that can be used by cyclists, walkers and horse riders alike, and which encompasses the major historic mines between Camborne and Redruth. The trail links up with several other sections of the Cornish Way (p242).

CORNWALL

WEST CORNWALL

· · · · · ·

While most visitors head for the tourist honey pots of the north coast, the wild west of Cornwall receives relatively few visitors outside St Ives and Land's End. And that's a shame, as it's one of Cornwall's starkly beautiful areas, where stone monuments rise up from the hilltops, ancient moorland butts up against gorse-topped cliffs, and forgotten mine stacks stand in sharp relief against the skyline.

ST IVES

pop 9870

Huddled in the lee of a shimmering curve carved out of the west Cornish coastline, St Ives was historically one of Cornwall's important pilchard harbours, but reinvented itself as a haven for the arts after a stream of influential painters and sculptors set up studios along the town's streets during the 1920s and '30s. Art galleries aplenty still line St Ives'

alleyways, but in recent years the town has also benefited from an explosion of enticing bistros, boutiques and cafes.

Traffic can be hellish during the peak season, so many people plump to arrive aboard the endearing old single-carriage railway, which chugs its way along the coastline from St Erth and offers grandstand views of coast, sea and countryside.

ESSENTIAL INFORMATION

TOURIST INFORMATION // St Ives tourist office (☎ 01736-796297; www.stives-cornwall.co.uk; Street-an-Pol; ☉ 9am-5.30pm Mon-Fri, 9am-5pm Sat, 10am-4pm Sun) Inside the Guildhall.

EXPLORING ST IVES

❦ **TATE ST IVES //** MODERN ART AND ARCHITECTURE ON PORTHMEOR BEACH

There's no shortage of art galleries in St Ives, but the **Tate St Ives** (☎ 01736-796226; www.tate.org.uk/stives; Porthmeor Beach; adult/ child £5.75/3.25, incl Barbara Hepworth museum £8.75/4.50; ☉ 10am-5pm Mar-Oct, 10am-4pm Tue-Sun Nov-Feb) is the undisputed centrepiece. Hovering like a white concrete

---

TOP FIVE

QUIRKY CAMPING

Bored of the old B&Bs but not quite enamoured about sleeping under canvas? Then try these offbeat camping options, handpicked for their eccentric character.

* **Lovelane Caravans** (p305) Ditch those preconceptions – the caravan goes cool at this brilliantly barmy place in Constantine.

* **Yurtworks** (☎ 01208-850670; www.yurtworks.co.uk; yurt per week £320-700; ℗) Camp Mongolian-style in these yurts on Bodmin Moor.

* **Quirky Holidays** (p307) Period railway wagons decked out in retro style near Launceston.

* **The Bodrifty Farm Roundhouse** (☎ 01736-361217; www.bodriftyfarm.co.uk; near Penzance; from £130 per night) Kip in an Iron Age hut on the moors of West Penwith.

* **Ekopod** (☎ 01179-247-877; www.canopyandstars.co.uk/our-places/ekopod; near Launceston; from £90 per night) Low-carbon camping in a geodesic dome.

curl above Porthmeor Beach, the gallery's architecture intentionally echoes its seaside setting. Themed exhibitions are matched with a permanent collection rich in works by artists connected with the St Ives School. Terry Frost, Naum Gabo, Patrick Heron, Ben Nicholson, the potter Bernard Leach and the naive Cornish painter Alfred Wallis are all represented, alongside sculptures by Barbara Hepworth. On the top floor is a cafe with a glass-walled patio overlooking Porthmeor Beach.

❦ BARBARA HEPWORTH MUSEUM & SCULPTURE GARDEN // VISIT THE STUDIO OF ST IVES' FAMOUS SCULPTOR

Barbara Hepworth was one of the leading abstract sculptors of the 20th century, and a key figure in the St Ives art scene, so it seems fitting that her former studio is now a **museum** (☎ 01736-796226; www.tate.org.uk/stives; Barnoon Hill; adult/child £4.75/2.75, incl Tate St Ives £8.75/4.50; ☟ 10am-5.30pm Mar-Oct, 10am-4.30pm Tue-Sun Nov-Feb). The studio has remained practically untouched since her death in a fire in 1975, and the adjoining garden contains some of her most famous sculptures. Among the shrubs, look out for the harplike *Garden Sculpture (Model for Meridian)* and *Four Square,* the largest work Hepworth ever created. Her art is also liberally sprinkled around town; there's a Hepworth outside the Guildhall, and her moving *Madonna and Child* inside St Ia Church commemorates her son Paul Skeaping, who was killed in an air crash in 1953.

❦ ART GALLERIES // PICK UP A ST IVES SOUVENIR

The **Sloop Craft Market** (☟ around 9am-5pm) is a treasure trove of artists' studios selling everything from handmade cards

to silkscreen art. You can watch the artists at work through the studio windows: look out for handcrafted brooches, rings and pendants at **Smith Jewellery** (☎ 01736-799876; www.smithjewellery.com); stained-glass artwork by **Debbie Martin** (☎ 01736-796051); and one-off pieces of driftwood furniture by **Beach Wood** (☎ 01736-796051).

The **St Ives Society of Artists** (☎ 01736-795582; www.stivessocietyofartists.com; Norway Sq) – one of Cornwall's oldest and most influential collectives, founded in 1929 – has its gallery in a converted church on Norway Sq, with a separate 'Mariners Gallery' in the crypt. Another well-respected name is the **New Millennium Gallery** (☎ 01736-793121; www.newmillenniumgallery.co.uk; Street-an-Pol), which houses one of the largest local collections in town.

Modern work is the focus at the **Salthouse Gallery** (☎ 01736-795003; http://salthousegallery.110mb.com; Norway Sq) and the **Wills Lane Gallery** (☎ 01736-795723; www.willslanegallery.co.uk; Wills Lane; ☟ 10.30am-5.30pm Wed-Sat, 11am-4pm Sun), run by a former director of the Contemporary Art Society, while **Art Space** (☎ 01736-799744 www.artspace-cornwall.co.uk; The Wharf; ☟ 10.30am-5.30pm summer, 11am-4.30pm winter) showcases talented local artists.

❦ LEACH POTTERY // PONDER THE WORK OF A GENIUS POTTER

While Hepworth was breaking new sculptural ground, the potter Bernard Leach was hard at work reinventing British ceramics in his studio in Higher Stennack. Drawing inspiration from Japanese and Oriental sculpture, and using a unique hand-built 'climbing' kiln based on ones he had seen in Japan, Leach's pottery created a unique fusion of Western and Eastern ideas.

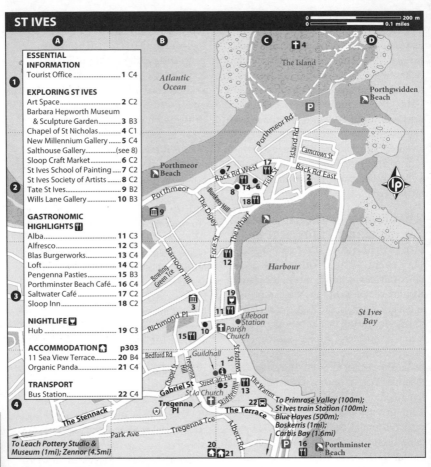

ST IVES

ESSENTIAL INFORMATION
Tourist Office 1 C4

EXPLORING ST IVES
Art Space 2 C2
Barbara Hepworth Museum
  & Sculpture Garden............. 3 B3
Chapel of St Nicholas............. 4 C1
New Millennium Gallery 5 C4
Salthouse Gallery.................(see 8)
Sloop Craft Market................. 6 C2
St Ives School of Painting 7 C2
St Ives Society of Artists 8 C2
Tate St Ives............................. 9 B2
Wills Lane Gallery 10 B3

GASTRONOMIC HIGHLIGHTS
Alba.. 11 C3
Alfresco.................................. 12 C3
Blas Burgerworks................. 13 C4
Loft.. 14 C2
Pengenna Pasties................. 15 B3
Porthminster Beach Café.. 16 C4
Saltwater Café 17 C2
Sloop Inn............................... 18 C2

NIGHTLIFE
Hub 19 C3

ACCOMMODATION   p303
11 Sea View Terrace............. 20 B4
Organic Panda...................... 21 C4

TRANSPORT
Bus Station........................... 22 C4

Atlantic Ocean

The Island

Porthgwidden Beach

Porthmeor Rd

Carncrows St

Island Rd

Back Rd East

Porthmeor Beach

Back Rd West

Fish St

Bunkers Hill

Porthmeor

The Digey

The Wharf

Fore St

The Harbour

Barnoon Hill

Bowling Green Tce

Richmond Pl

St Ives Bay

Lifeboat Station

Parish Church

Bedford Rd

Guildhall

Chapel Hill

Street-an-Pol

Gabriel St

St Ia Church

Tregenna Pl

Skidden Hill

St Andrews St

The Warren

The Terrace

To Primrose Valley (100m); St Ives train Station (100m); Blue Hayes (500m); Boskerris (1mi); Carbis Bay (1.6mi)

The Stennack

Park Ave

Tregenna Tce

Albert Rd

To Leach Pottery Studio & Museum (1mi); Zennor (4.5mi)

Porthminster Beach

0   200 m
0   0.1 miles

His former **studio** (☎01736-796398; www.leachpottery.com; adult/child £4.50/3.50; ☺10am-5pm Mon-Sat, 11am-4pm Sun) displays examples of his work, and has been enhanced by a brand-new **museum** and working pottery studio. The shop contains work by contemporary potters, as well as souvenirs from the Leach tableware range.

❧ ART COURSES // PAINT LIKE THE PROS
St Ives makes a fine place to indulge your inner artist. The **St Ives School of Painting** (☎01736-797180; www.stivesartschool.co.uk;

Back Rd West) has been tutoring budding painters from its studios near Porthmeor Beach for decades. Founded as a hangout for the town's artistic elite, the school holds regular drop-in sessions open to all on Monday, Wednesday, Friday and Saturday, as well as longer courses lasting from one to six days, covering everything from landscapes to life drawing.

❧ BEACHES // KICK BACK ON THE ST IVES SEAFRONT
St Ives boasts three excellent town beaches. Furthest west is **Porthmeor**, just

CORNWALL

below the Tate. Nearby, beside the grassy headland known as the Island, is the little cove of **Porthgwidden**. On the promontory is the pre-14th-century **Chapel of St Nicholas**, patron saint of sailors, and the oldest (and certainly smallest) church in St Ives. On the other side of town is **Porthminster**, with a horseshoe of soft golden sand that's sheltered by the cliffs. Two miles east of town is the busy resort of **Carbis Bay**, worth a visit for its sheltered (if touristy) Blue Flag beach.

❦ GWITHIAN & GODREVY TOWANS // GOLDEN SAND AND GRASSY DUNES

The dune-backed flats of **Gwithian** (Map p212; ℗) and **Godrevy** (Map p212; ℗) unfurl in a glimmering sea-fringed curve that joins together at low tide to form Hayle's much-lauded '3 miles of golden sand'. At the southwestern end is the **Hayle Estuary**, once a busy industrial harbour, while at the opposite end, the **Godrevy Lighthouse** perches on a rocky island and supposedly inspired Virginia Woolf's stream-of-consciousness classic *To the Lighthouse*.

The beaches are about 4 miles' drive from St Ives. Both have car parks, but spaces can be hard to come by on summer days (Godrevy Point is National Trust–owned, so members can park for free assuming they can find a space). Next to the Godrevy car park is the **Godrevy Café** (☎ 01736-757999; www.godrevycafe.co.uk; ☒ 10am-5pm), a split-level timber cafe with a top-deck patio overlooking the beach. Further along the dunes towards Gwithian is the **Sunset Surf Shop & Café** (☎ 01736-752575; www.sunsetsurfshop.co.uk; 10 Gwithian Towans), another good spot for postbeach coffee, cake and ice cream.

The best place for surf lessons in and around Gwithian is the **Gwithian Surf Academy** (☎ 01736-757579; www.surfacademy.co.uk), one of only four BSA Schools of Excellence.

FESTIVALS & EVENTS

St Ives September Festival (www.stivesseptemberfestival.co.uk) Annual arts fest featuring music, exhibitions and live events all over town; early to mid-September.

GASTRONOMIC HIGHLIGHTS

❦ ALBA ££

☎ 01736-797222; www.thealbarestaurant.com; Old Lifeboat House; mains £11.95-18.95; ☒ lunch & dinner
This seafood restaurant blazed the gourmet trail in St Ives, and it's still one of the top places in town. Beige pine and crisp white tablecloths create a cool and contemporary space, while the menu offers a smorgasbord of seafood, mostly sourced straight from St Ives day-boats. The best tables are in the picture window overlooking the harbour; ask when you book.

❦ ALFRESCO ££

☎ 01736-793737; info@alfrescocafebar.co.uk; The Wharf; lunch £8.95-11.95, mains £14.95-18.95; ☒ lunch & dinner
Watch the world spin by at this cosy wharfside bistro, with a handful of tiny wooden tables and sliding doors opening onto the harbour. It's especially strong on fish, but finds space for traditional country favourites too (foie gras and rabbit terrine, duck breast with kale and pancetta).

❦ BLAS BURGERWORKS £

☎ 01736-797272; www.blasburgerworks.co.uk; The Warren; burgers £4-8
The humble burger becomes a work of art at this ecoconscious burger joint, surely the first to grace the pages of the Good Food Guide. Burgers are 100% local, served with Cornish blue

CORNWALL

or Westcountry cheddar, while veggies could plump for beetburgers with horseradish and watercress, or grilled mushroom with spinach and Béarnaise. It's crammed into a teeny space along the Warren, so there's precious little space to sit. Beware of marauding seagulls if you opt for takeaway.

☙ THE LOFT ££
☎ 01736-794204; www.theloftrestaurantandterrace.co.uk; Norway Lane; mains £10.95-19.95; ☽ lunch & dinner

Lost amongst the old artists' quarter, the Loft has only been in business since mid-2009, but it's established itself as a town favourite. In a converted sail loft overlooking the St Ives rooftops, it feels like dining inside a ship's galley: tables are packed in under the A-frame roof, while sea views unfold from the patio. Simple, unfussy food and a shipshape atmosphere.

☙ PORTHMINSTER BEACH CAFÉ ££
☎ 01736-795352; www.porthminstercafe.co.uk; Porthminster Beach; mains £10.50-21.95; ☽ 9am-10pm

Fresh from scooping top prize in a recent *Times* survey to find Britain's top coastal cafe, the Porthminster boasts a sexy Riviera vibe, a suntrap patio overlooking Porthminster's sands, and a seasonal menu ranging from Provençal fish soup to pan-fried scallops. The result? Cornwall's top beach cafe, bar none.

☙ SALTWATER CAFÉ ££
☎ 01736-794928; www.saltwaterstives.co.uk; 14 Fish Street; mains £12.95-15.95; ☽ dinner Tue-Sat

Small doesn't do justice to the Saltwater: we've seen broom cupboards that are more spacious. The Franco-Italian food is simple and classic, designed to emphasise quality Cornish ingredients rather than chefy showiness. It really is tiny though: bookings are essential and tables are crammed in ridiculously tight.

☙ SLOOP INN £
☎ 01736-796584; www.sloop-inn.co.uk; The Wharf; mains £5.95-15.95; ☽ 11am-11pm Mon-Sat, 10am-10pm Sun

Old Speckled Hen, Doom Bar and Bass ales make this beam-ceilinged boozer a comfy old favourite. Settle into a booth for the night, or bag one of the coveted wharfside tables – there's no better place for a pint and a crab butty when the sun's shining.

NIGHTLIFE

☙ THE HUB
☎ 01736-799099; www.hub-stives.co.uk; 4 The Wharf; ☽ 10am-late

Coffee, cake, ciabattas or cocktails, this open-plan cafe-bar is the heart of St Ives' social scene. Funky murals by local design collective A-Side Studio create a big-city vibe quite out of keeping with the quayside location. Tables spill onto the flagstones on hot days, while DJs provide late-night entertainment.

TRANSPORT

BUS // The regular bus 17 (twice hourly Monday to Saturday, hourly on Sunday) runs from St Ives to Penzance, while bus 14 travels to Truro via Hayle, Camborne and Redruth. Bus 516 (hourly Monday to Saturday) is another option to Penzance. For travel to Zennor and Land's End, see p217.

TRAIN // The branch line from St Erth (£3, 14 minutes, half-hourly) links up with the main London–Penzance line.

THE PENWITH PENINSULA

Taking its name from two Cornish words – *penn* (headland) and *wydh* (end) – Penwith juts like a crooked finger stretching from St Ives to the most westerly point on the British mainland at Land's End. Wild and remote, spotted with minestacks, ancient farmland and windswept moor, Penwith was originally one of the Cornish Hundreds (a network of administrative districts dating back to the Domesday Book) but the first settlers arrived long before – this corner of west Cornwall boasts one of Europe's highest concentrations of prehistoric sites, many of which predate Stonehenge and Avebury. Later Penwith became a hub of mining activity and the area now provides a fantastic insight into the unimaginably tough lives of Cornwall's tinners.

A great way to tour the Penwith area is aboard the open-top double-decker bus 300 (Penwith Explorer), which runs from May to October; see p217 for details.

EXPLORING THE PENWITH PENINSULA

❦ ZENNOR & PENDEEN // DRIVE THROUGH DAZZLING SCENERY

The wild B3306 coast road between St Ives and **St Just-in-Penwith** is a jewel, winding through a panorama of patchwork fields and granite-strewn moorland. Five miles west of St Ives is the miniscule village of **Zennor**, set around the medieval **Church of St Senara**. DH Lawrence famously sojourned here between 1915 and 1917 before being drummed out of the village as a suspected communist spy (an episode recounted in his novel *Kangaroo*), but the village is best known for its associations with the local legend of the Mermaid of Zennor, who is said to have fallen in love with the singing voice of local lad Matthew Trewhella. A carved bench-end inside the church depicts the mermaid holding a mirror and comb; her favourite haunt of **Pendour Cove** can be reached along the coast path.

Downhill from the church, the **Wayside Folk Museum** (☎ 01736-796945; admission £3; ☯ 10.30am-5pm Sun-Fri May-Sep, 11am-5pm Sun-Fri Apr & Oct) houses folksy ephemera gathered by Colonel 'Freddie' Hirst in the 1930s, from blacksmiths' hammers and reclaimed watermills to an 18th-century Cornish kitchen.

The village youth hostel, the **Old Chapel Backpackers** (☎ 01736-798307; www.backpackers.co.uk/zennor) has an excellent cafe, while heartier fare can be found at the village pub, the Tinner's Arms (p217).

❦ MINING SITES // DELVE INTO THE WORLD OF THE HARD-ROCK MEN

Tin mining was once the staple industry in west Cornwall, and deserted engine houses still punctuate the crag-backed coastline. **Geevor Tin Mine** (☎ 01736-788662; www.geevor.com; adult/child £9.50/4.50; ☯ 9am-5pm Sun-Fri Mar-Oct, 9am-4pm Sun-Fri Nov-Feb) was the last mine in west Cornwall to close (in 1990), and has since been resurrected as a fascinating museum. Above ground you can wander around the old machinery where the tin ore was extracted, while below ground you can take a guided tour into the mine itself – a maze of dank shafts and tunnels where miners worked for hours at a stretch, enduring ever-present dangers of rockfalls, air pollution and underground explosions.

More mining heritage comes to life at the **Levant Mine & Beam Engine** (NT; ☎ 01736-786156; www.nationaltrust.org.uk/main/w-levantmineandbeamengine; adult/child £5.80/2.90; ☯ 11am-5pm Tue-Fri & Sun Jul-Sep, Wed-Fri & Sun Jun, Wed & Fri Apr-May & Oct), one of the world's only working Cornish beam engines. These pioneering steam-powered engines were used to pump floodwater from the deep underground shafts and bring ore back to the surface, and transformed the Cornish mining industry into a world leader; the engine design was later exported across the world.

CORNWALL

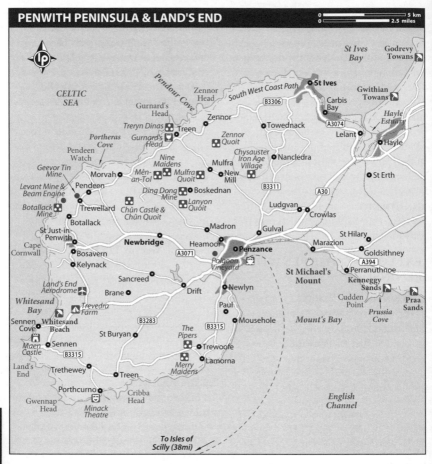

PENWITH PENINSULA & LAND'S END

Clinging to the sea-battered cliffs nearby is **Botallack Mine**, whose shafts once extended right out beneath the raging Atlantic waves (it's said that miners could hear the rumble of rocks being moved around by the ocean currents). Further west along the B3306 is **Carn Galver**, situated near the mining ruins of the Porthmeor Valley, while **Ding Dong Mine**, perched on the hilltops near the Mên-an-tol (p213), is reputed to be Cornwall's oldest mine. Official records date back to the 17th century, although legend has it the mine has been working for over 2000 years, and was once visited by Jesus and Joseph of Arimathea.

🌿 **PENWITH'S ANCIENT SITES //**
GET CLOSE TO THE ANCESTORS
Quoits and Stones
Penwith is littered with archaeological remains, built by Neolithic settlers sometime between 4000 BC and 2500 BC. Most dramatic are the **quoits**, three or more upright stones topped by a capstone, built on top of a chamber tomb. Most were probably once covered by a barrow of earth or stones, but over the

centuries the stones have been plundered or worn away to reveal the supporting structure.

Most impressive is **Lanyon Quoit**, topped by a 13.5-tonne capstone and situated right beside the road between Madron and Morvah. In the 18th century, the monument was tall enough to shelter a man on horseback, but an 1815 storm blew the quoit down and broke one of the four uprights; it was re-erected nine years later. **Chûn Quoit** (near the Chûn Castle hillfort) is also very well-preserved, although others such as **Zennor Quoit** and **Mulfra Quoit** haven't fared so well over the centuries.

Five miles southeast of Morvah is the curvy **Mên-an-tol** (Cornish for stone-of-the-hole), a weird formation consisting of two menhirs flanking a hollow stone. Squeezing through the stone was said to be a cure for infertility and rickets.

Hillforts & Settlements

The area is dotted with Iron Age hillforts, most of which date from around 1000 BC to 500 BC (although some were probably built on the site of earlier fortifications), including **Chûn Castle**, signposted from the road past Mên-an-tol. A pile of rubble and two upright stones are all that remains of the fortress, but in the 18th century the walls stood 4.5m high; much of the stone was subsequently plundered for local construction projects (including Penzance's north pier). Other ruined hillforts can be seen at Maen Castle near Sennen (p215), Logan Rock near Treryn Dinas (p216 and Kenidjack, near St Just).

Marginally more intact is the Iron Age village of **Chysauster** (adult/child £3.20/1.60; ☉ 10am-6pm Jul & Aug, to 5pm Apr-Jun & Sep, to 4pm Oct), thought to have been built between 400 BC and AD 100. Consisting of eight stone-walled houses, each with its own central courtyard, it gives you a real sense of daily life during the Iron Age – you can still see the stone hearths and platforms used to grind corn, and wander the gardens where the residents kept livestock and grew arable crops.

Stone Circles

Penwith's stone circles include the **Merry Maidens**, near Lamorna, which supposedly mark the petrified remains of a group of 19 girls turned to stone for dancing on the Sabbath. Nearby are the **Pipers**, who earned the same fate for tootling a tune on a Sunday. There's another circle east of the Mên-an-Tol, the **Nine Maidens**; the name derives from the Cornish word *maedn* (later *mên*) meaning stone. There are lots more to find: the useful pages at www.pznow.co.uk/historic1/circles.html provide a good overview.

☙ ST JUST-IN-PENWITH & CAPE CORNWALL // VISIT BRITAIN'S ONLY CAPE

Not to be confused with its namesake on the Roseland, St-Just-in-Penwith (usually known simply as St Just) might not be the hive of activity it was during the heyday of Cornish tin-mining, but it's still a hub for Penwith's artistic community. All roads lead to the Market Sq, ringed by grey granite buildings, the small parish church and the **Plen-an-gwary**, an open-air auditorium once used to stage outdoor theatre, mystery plays, Methodist sermons and Cornish wrestling.

Jutting out from the cliffs a couple of miles from St Just is **Cape Cornwall**, a rocky headland topped by an abandoned chimneystack (the last remains of the Cape Cornwall Mine, which closed in

CORNWALL

CORNWALL CAMPSITES

There's nowhere better to sleep out under the stars than Cornwall. Check out our favourite handpicked sites:

★ **South Penquite** (☎ 01208-850491; www.southpenquite.co.uk; adult/child £6/3; ☺ May-Oct) Delightful site on an organic farm on Bodmin Moor, between Blisland and St Breward, which also offers bushcraft courses, nature walks and food from the farm.

★ **Treloan Farm** (☎ 01872-580989; www.coastalfarmholidays.co.uk; Gerrans; sites £13.25-19; ☺ year-round) Rural country camping a stone's throw from Portscatho. There's plenty of space, decent facilities and the Roseland's on your doorstep. Pick your spot and you'll even have ocean views.

★ **Henry's Campsite** (☎ 01326-290596; www.henrys.co.uk; adult £6-8, child £2-4; Caerthillian Farm, the Lizard; ☺ year-round) Endearingly eccentric site in a private subtropical garden in Lizard village. Nearly all sites have views of the sea, and the Lizard's beaches, shops and cosy pubs are all within easy reach.

★ **Treen Farm** (☎ 07598-469322; www.treenfarmcampsite.co.uk; St Levan; adult/car £4/1, child £1.50-2, tent £2.50-4; ☺ Easter-Oct) If it's coastal camping you want, this is the site for you. The spacious family-friendly field offers stunning vistas stretching to Logan Rock, and you can pick up organic milk and eggs from the shop.

★ **Dennis Farm** (☎ 01841-533513; Padstow; sites around £16.50; ☺ Easter-Sep) Padstow doesn't have to break the bank at this tents-only site above town. Unsurprisingly, it gets busy in summer, but there's usually space to spare in the overspill field.

1875). Below the cape is the rocky beach of Priest's Cove, while nearby are the ruins of **St Helen's Oratory**, one of the first Christian chapels built in West Cornwall.

A century ago, the surrounding cliffs (especially Gurnard's Head) were among the most treacherous in Britain, accounting for hundreds of costly shipwrecks. To prevent further wrecks, construction of a new lighthouse at **Pendeen Watch** began in 1900. Standing barely 17m tall, the lighthouse was originally oil-powered, before being electrified in 1926 and automated in 1995.

Half a mile east is **Portheras Cove**, a lovely slash of sheltered sand reached via a 15-minute walk along the cliff path. The high cliffs around the beach take the brunt of the Atlantic winds, and the water is deep and crystal clear – although the remains of an exploded wreck in the

1960s still supposedly wash up from time to time, so take care.

❦ SENNEN // SEASIDE SPLENDOUR ON A BLUE FLAG BAY

Tucked into the arc of Whitesand Bay, **Sennen Cove** (Ⓟ) boasts Penwith's best surf and sand. With vivid blue waters and a mile of beach backed by dunes and marram grass, it's one of Cornwall's most impressive bays – but apart from the scenery, there's not much to the village itself save for the lifeboat station (in operation since 1853), a handful of shops, cafes and galleries and the venerable Old Success Inn (p216).

When you're done lazing about on the beach, Sennen makes a fine spot for coastal walks. One of the best routes is the 1.5-mile hike west around the headland of **Pedn-men-du** to Land's End. En route you'll pass the remains of the Iron Age hillfort of **Maen Castle** (thought to date from around 500 BC) and the peculiarly named promontory of **Dr Syntax's Head**. Plentiful seabird colonies make the Sennen cliffs great for wildlife-spotting, and if you're really lucky you might even spy a dolphin or seal. Bring binoculars just in case.

On a clear day you should also be able to spot the **Longships Lighthouse**, jutting out from the ferocious Atlantic atop a perilous set of reefs about a mile offshore. The first lighthouse was built by the architect Samuel Watts in the 18th century, before being replaced by the present granite version in 1875 at a cost of over £40,000.

All told it's a walk of about a mile-and-a-half, although it can feel a good deal longer on a blazing hot day.

✿ LAND'S END // LAST STOP KERNOW, NEXT STOP AMERICA

A mile from Whitesand Bay, the Penwith Peninsula comes to a screeching halt at **Land's End**, the last port of call for countless charity walkers on the 874-mile slog from John O' Groats. The scenery doesn't get much more dramatic – black granite cliffs and heather-covered headland teeter above the booming Atlantic surf, and in good weather you can glimpse the Isles of Scilly, 28 miles out to sea. Even the construction of a tacky **theme park** (☎ 0871 720 0044; www.landsend-landmark. co.uk; adult/child £10/7; ⏱ 10am-5pm Easter-Oct, 10.30am-3.30pm Nov-Mar) on the headland in the 1980s hasn't quite spoiled the scenery, although it certainly hasn't helped – wiser heads will give it a wide berth and just pay for the car park (£3) and head off along the coast path instead.

✿ WILD FOOD // FORAGE FOR PICNIC SUPPLIES

Longing for the good life? Then how about a weekend delving through the undergrowth in search of wild berries, edible roots and samphire in the company of **Fat Hen** (☎ 01736-810156; www.fathen.org; Boscawen-noon Farm, St Buryan). Head forager-ecologist Caroline Davey leads guided trips in search of wild goodies, before retiring to headquarters to see the raw materials transformed into something tasty by the Fat Hen chefs. There are day courses, or you can opt for a wild food weekend (£165), which includes three slap-up meals in the Goat Barn. Hedge-row cocktails, anyone?

✿ PORTHCURNO // CATCH A CLIFFTOP PLAY

From Land's End, the coastline zigzags past a string of remote coves, including **Nanjizal**, **Porthgwarra** and teeny **Porthchapel**, where you'll find the 'holy well' of St Levan (one of many holy wells sprinkled around Penwith) hidden amongst the gorse-cloaked cliffs.

Further east is the steep wedge of sand of **Porthcurno** and the gravity-defying **Minack Theatre** (☎ 01736-810181; www.minack .com), dreamt up in the 1920s by local eccentric Rowena Cade and built largely by hand over the next 30-odd years. With its vertiginous seating and clifftop amphitheatre overlooking the Atlantic, it's an unforgettable place to watch a play (although aficionados always bring pillows, blankets and umbrellas in case the weather takes centre stage). Above the theatre there's a cafe and **visitor centre** (adult/child under 12yr £3.50/free; ⏱ 9.30am-5.30pm Apr–mid-Sep, closed Wed & Fri afternoons May–mid-Sep) exploring the Rowena Cade story; you can wander around the auditorium on nonmatinée days.

CORNWALL

Long before the Minack, Porthcurno was a hub for Britain's burgeoning telecommunications network. During the 19th century, a network of subterranean cables owned by the Eastern Telegraph Company stretched from Porthcurno all the way to Spain, Gibraltar, northern France and India; the subterranean tunnels now house the **Porthcurno Telegraph Museum** (☎ 01736-810966; www.porthcurno.org.uk; adult/child £4.50/2.50; ⏲ 10am-5pm Mar-Nov, 10am-5pm Sun & Mon Nov-Feb).

☙ LOGAN ROCK // THE ROCK THAT DOESN'T ROCK

A couple of miles from Porthcurno, just off the B3315, is the miniature village of **Treen**, best known for the geological oddity known as the **Logan Rock**. Perched on the headland near Treryn Dinas, the site of one of Cornwall's largest **Iron Age hillforts**, this massive boulder once famously rocked back and forth on its own natural pivot with only the slightest pressure; its name supposedly derives from the Cornish verb *log*, meaning 'to rock', often used to denote the motion of a drunken man.

The Logan Rock has been a tourist attraction since at least the 18th century, but became infamous after it was knocked off its perch by a young naval lieutenant, Hugh Goldsmith (the nephew of the Restoration playwright Oliver Goldsmith), in an attempt to show the physical prowess of the British Navy. Unfortunately, the locals were so incensed by his actions, Goldsmith was forced to restore the rock to its original position under threat of his naval commission – a considerable undertaking that required the efforts of 60 men, winches borrowed from Devonport Dockyard and a total cost of £130 8s 6d (a copy of the bill can be seen in the Logan Rock Inn, p216).

Unfortunately, Goldsmith's efforts were in vain: the Logan Rock hasn't rocked since.

GASTRONOMIC HIGHLIGHTS

☙ THE BEACH // SENNEN COVE ££
☎ 01736-871191; Sennen Cove; pizzas £7.65-13.95, mains £8.75-14.95; ⏲ breakfast, lunch & dinner

There's been a beach cafe since the late '50s, but over the last few years it's been brought bang up to date and, unusually, is still owned by the same family. Simple pizzas, pastas, salads and tapas are the menu's mainstays, but you couldn't wish for a better spot: the deck looks straight out over Whitesand Bay.

☙ GURNARD'S HEAD // NEAR ZENNOR ££
☎ 01736-796928; www.gurnardshead.co.uk; lunch £5.50-12, dinner £12.50-16.50; ⏲ 12.30-2.30pm & 6.30-9.30pm

It's way out on the Zennor coast road, but you can't miss the Gurnard's – its name is written in big letters on the roof. Run by the Inkin brothers, this sublime country pub has defied its isolated location to become one of Cornwall's destination addresses (bookings are a must). Book-lined shelves, sepia prints, scruffy wood and rough stone walls create a reassuringly lived-in feel, and the menu's crammed with cockle-warming fare – haddock and mash, spring lamb and pork belly, followed by lashings of Eton Mess or sticky marmalade pudding. A modern Cornish classic.

☙ LOGAN ROCK INN // TREEN £
☎ 01736-810495; mains £6-14; ⏲ 10.30am-11pm, closed mid-afternoon in winter

This village pub's been around for four centuries, so it's crammed with old-time atmosphere – head-scraping ceilings, wooden seats, a crackling hearth and

CORNWALL

brassy trinkets, backed up by hearty grub and St Austell ales (plus a rather incongruous collection of cricketing memorabilia in one corner).

♥ OLD SUCCESS INN // SENNEN COVE £

☎ 01736-871232; Sennen Cove; mains £5-15; ⏰ 11am-11pm

Recently snapped up by St Austell Brewery, the Old Success has been slaking the thirst of Sennen punters (and the local lifeboat crew) for centuries. It's currently a bit of a work in progress: the food is still standard pub fare, but it's full of local charm and the rooms are set for an upgrade soon.

♥ TINNER'S ARMS // ZENNOR £

☎ 01736-792697; www.tinnersarms.co.uk; mains £5.95-14.95; ⏰ 11.30am-11pm, closed 3.30-6.30pm winter

Built for masons working at St Senara's Church, this is a quintessential Cornish inn, complete with slate roof, roaring fireplaces and zero commercial clutter (no TV, no jukebox, no mobile signal). The food is hearty – ploughman's for lunch, breaded fish for supper – and there's a host of Cornish ales on tap. Next door, the 'White House' provides fresh, spotless rooms (singles/doubles £55/95).

TRANSPORT

BUS // Bus 508 shuttles between Penzance and St Ives, with stops at Towednack, Zennor, Gurnard's Head and New Mill (for Chysauster). Bus 1/1A (eight daily, five on Saturday) runs from Penzance to Land's End (half the buses go via Sennen; the other half via Treen and Porthcurno). Bus 10A runs from Penzance to St Just via Botallack and Cape Cornwall. Best of all is bus 300 (May to Oct), an open-top double-decker that runs three to five times daily taking in Penzance, St Ives and all the main Penwith spots.

PENZANCE & AROUND

pop 21,168

Gulls wheel overhead, fishing trawlers ply the coast and there's a scent of brine on the breeze around the elegant old harbour town of Penzance. Stretching along the western edge of Mount's Bay, Penzance has marked the end of the line for the Great Western Railway since the 1860s, and the town still feels one step removed from the rest of Cornwall. It's faded in spots, but unlike many of its sister towns along the coast, Penzance has resisted the urge for over-gentrification and still boasts the kind of rough-edged authenticity many of Cornwall's daintier towns lost long ago.

Like Truro and Falmouth, Penzance's wealth was founded largely on the booming maritime trade of the 18th and 19th centuries, and there are some fine Georgian and Regency townhouses dotted around town, especially along Chapel St and Queen St; look out for the extraordinary Egyptian House, which looks like a cross between a Georgian townhouse and an Egyptian sarcophagus, and was originally built for a wealthy local mineralogist, John Lavin, as a geological museum.

ESSENTIAL INFORMATION

TOURIST INFORMATION // Penzance **tourist office** (☎ 01736-362207; penzancetic@cornwall.gov.uk; Station Approach; ⏰ 9am-5pm Mon-Sat, 10am-1pm Sun)

EXPLORING PENZANCE & AROUND

♥ GALLERIES // FROM OLD MASTERS TO CONTEMPORARY ART

Penzance has long been a focus for West Cornwall's art scene. West of town along the seafront, the **Newlyn Art Gallery** (☎ 01736-363715; www.newlynartgallery.co.uk;

CORNWALL

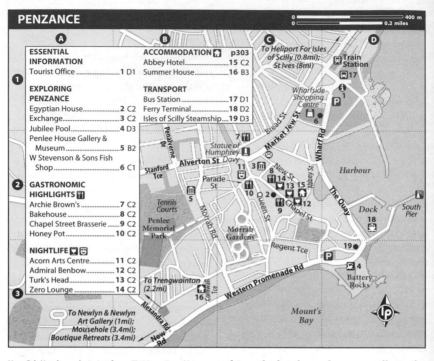

PENZANCE

ESSENTIAL
INFORMATION
Tourist Office 1 D1

EXPLORING
PENZANCE
Egyptian House..................... 2 C2
Exchange................................ 3 C2
Jubilee Pool.......................... 4 D3
Penlee House Gallery &
  Museum............................ 5 B2
W Stevenson & Sons Fish
  Shop.................................. 6 C1

GASTRONOMIC
HIGHLIGHTS
Archie Brown's 7 C2
Bakehouse............................. 8 C2
Chapel Street Brasserie 9 C2
Honey Pot 10 C2

NIGHTLIFE
Acorn Arts Centre............... 11 C2
Admiral Benbow.................. 12 C2
Turk's Head 13 C2
Zero Lounge 14 C2

ACCOMMODATION   p303
Abbey Hotel........................ 15 C2
Summer House 16 B3

TRANSPORT
Bus Station 17 D1
Ferry Terminal....................18 D2
Isles of Scilly Steamship....19 D3

To Newlyn & Newlyn
Art Gallery (1mi);
Mousehole (3.4mi);
Boutique Retreats (3.4mi)

New Rd, Newlyn; admission free; 10am-5pm Mon-Sat summer, 10am-5pm Tue-Sat winter) benefited from a £1.7m refit in 2007, which also added a sleek new sister establishment, the **Exchange** (☎ 01736-363715; www.newlyn artgallery.co.uk; Princes St, Penzance; admission free; 10am-5pm Mon-Sat summer, 10am-5pm Tue-Sat winter) in Penzance's former telecoms building, complete with its own pulsing light installation by the artist Peter Freeman. More traditional stuff is displayed at the **Penlee House Gallery & Museum** (☎ 363625; www.penleehouse.org.uk; Morrab Rd, Penzance; adult/child £3/free, Sat free; 10am-5pm Mon-Sat May-Sep, 10.30am-4.30pm Mon-Sat Oct-Apr), which owns a fine collection of paintings by artists of the Newlyn and Lamorna Schools (including Stanhope Forbes, Norman Garstin and Walter Langley). There's no permanent collection; what you see is down to a bit of pot luck. Even if the art's not your

thing, the lovely gardens are well worth a stroll.

JUBILEE POOL & BATTERY ROCKS // SWIM IN A LISTED LIDO
Penzance's 19th-century **promenade** stretches along the sea wall between the South Pier and New Rd. At the eastern end is the **Jubilee Pool** (www.jubileepool. co.uk; adult/child £4/2.90; 10.30am-6pm May-Sep), a stunning Art Deco lido built in 1935 to mark George V's silver jubilee. Since falling into disrepair in the 1980s, the triangular pool has been impeccably renovated and is now a listed monument – it even boasts its own poolside cafe. The views over Mount's Bay are utterly glorious – just don't expect the water to be warm.

The rocky shoreline around the pool known as **Battery Rocks** has recently become the focus of a heated dispute over proposals to transform it into a new terminal for ferries to Scilly. Two online lobby groups – the anti-development **Friends of Penzance Harbour** (www.friends ofpzharbour.org) and the pro-development **True Friends of Penzance Harbour** (www.truefriend.org.uk) – have been slugging it out with increasing ferocity; as we go to press, the fight has gone all the way to the top with a decision due from the Secretary of State. If there's building happening on Battery Rocks when you visit, you'll know what the outcome was.

❦ **TRENGWAINTON // A HILLSIDE GARDEN WITH MOUNT'S BAY VIEWS**
Two miles north of Penzance near Madron is the walled garden of **Trengwainton** (NT; ☎ 01736-363148; trengwainton@ nationaltrust.org.uk; Madron; adult/child £5.60/2.80; ⏰ 10am-5pm Sun-Thu mid-Feb–Nov), famous for its ferns, shrubs, magnolias and rhododendrons, as well as a stunning vista over Mount's Bay. Peculiarly, the kitchen garden was laid out to match the dimensions of Noah's Ark.

Nearby is the **Madron Holy Well**, whose cure-all waters have been sought out by ailing pilgrims for at least six centuries. The ruins of the chapel date from the early Middle Ages, but the well was also a sacred site for pre-Roman Celts.

❦ **POLGOON VINEYARD // SAMPLE CORNWALL'S MOST WESTERLY WINES**
Braving the vicissitudes of the Cornish weather, former fish merchants John & Jim Coulson set up Penzance's first-ever vineyard, **Polgoon** (☎ 01736-333946; http:// polgoonvineyard.vpweb.co.uk; Rosehill, Penzance), on a derelict farm just outside town in 2006. Despite a couple of disastrous harvests in 2007 and '08, the farm has scooped several national awards: the current crop includes a rosé and a red, as well as Peren (a sparkling pear drink) and Aval (a champagne-style cider; also available in a raspberry version).

There are guided tours of the vineyard from April to November, and you can pick up Polgoon vintages from the **wine shop** (⏰ 10am-5pm).

❦ **FRESH FISH // THE PICK OF THE DAY'S CATCH**
Two miles along the Penzance prom, the salty old harbour of **Newlyn** has weathered the storms in the wider fishing industry and clung on as Britain's busiest working port. The town has recently received a welcome boost following the announcement of a £2.3 million grant to redevelop its fish market, while the old Cornish staple, the pilchard, has recently received a rebrand as the 'Cornish sardine' in an effort to boost consumer appeal (it's not entirely sleight of hand: pilchards are in fact simply juvenile sardines).

Although the town's last pilchard cannery closed in 2005, ending a tradition stretching back over three centuries, Newlyn still has many suppliers where you can pick up fish literally straight off the boats. Newlyn's largest (and oldest) fishing family is **W Stevenson & Sons** (☎ 01736-362982), who own the Newlyn market and run two fish outlets on Harbour Rd in Newlyn and Wharf Rd in Penzance (beneath the Wharfside Shopping Centre). You can buy from the fish shops, or place an order by phone or online. Other suppliers:
JH Turner (☎ 01736-363726; The Coombe, Newlyn; www.jhturner.co.uk; ⏰ 9am-3pm Mon-Fri) Stocks whatever's in season.
Trelawney Fish (☎ 01736-361793; www.cornish fishonline.com; 78 The Strand; ⏰ 8am-5pm Mon-Fri, 8am-1pm Sat) Fish shop and deli on the Newlyn harbour.
W Harvey & Sons (☎ 01736-362983; www. crabmeat.co.uk; The Coombe, Newlyn; ⏰ 8am-4.45pm Mon-Fri, 8am-11.45pm Sat) Specialists in crab and lobster.

CORNWALL

❦ MOUSEHOLE // THE HOME OF
STARGAZY PIE
In contrast to rough-and-ready Newlyn,
the next-door harbour of **Mousehole**
(pronounced *mowzel*) is an altogether
gentler affair. Once a bustling pilchard
port, and now a hot spot for second
homes, Mousehole's muddle of slate-
roofed cottages, meandering lanes and
granite quays is undeniably attractive,
although the village is swamped by a sea
of visitors throughout summer and the
Christmas lights in December. Whatever
you do, leave the car on the outskirts – or
better still, follow the coast path on foot
from Newlyn.

Mousehole's main claim to fame is
as the home of stargazy pie, a baked
pilchard pie in which the fish heads are
left poking through the crust. It's eaten
on 23rd December, **Bawcock's Eve**, in
commemoration of Tom Bawcock, a
local lad who ended a village famine
by braving tempestuous seas to land a
bounty of fish. The traditional recipe is
still a closely-guarded secret at the **Ship**
(☎ 01736-731234; www.shipmousehole.co.uk; South
Cliff; mains £7.95-12.95).

Halfway along the Newlyn road, look
out for the old Penlee Lifeboat Station just
below the cliff. On 19 December 1981 the
Solomon Browne lifeboat went to the aid
of the stricken coaster *Union Star,* which
was being driven onto rocks near **Lamorna** by heavy seas. Both ships were lost
with all hands; since then the boathouse
has remained as a monument to the 16
men who lost their lives, and every year
Mousehole's lights are dimmed on December 19 as an act of remembrance.

❦ ST MICHAEL'S MOUNT // CROSS
THE CAUSEWAY TO AN ISLAND ABBEY
Looming from the waters of Mount's
Bay, **St Michael's Mount** (NT; ☎ 01736-
710507; www.stmichaelsmount.co.uk; castle & gardens
adult/child £8.75/4.25; ☺ house 10.30am-5.30pm
Sun-Fri late-Mar-Oct, gardens 10.30am-5.30pm Mon-
Fri May & Jun, 10.30am-5.30pm Thu & Fri Jul-Nov)
is one of Cornwall's iconic landmarks.
Connected to the mainland by a cobbled
causeway that's submerged by the rising
tide, there's been a monastery here since
at least the 5th century, but the island
was used long before as a trading stop
for Cornish tin and copper. After the
Norman Conquest, the island was gifted
to the Benedictine monks of Mont St
Michel in Normandy, who raised a new
chapel on the site in 1135. The mount
later served as a fortified stronghold and
is now the family seat of the St Aubyns,
although since 1954 it has been under
the stewardship of the National Trust.

At low tide, you can walk across to the
island from the village of **Marazion,** or
when the tide's up you can catch a ferry
(£1) from the quay. The tiny chapel with
its rose window and 15th-century ala-
baster panels is a highlight; there's also
a rococo drawing room, ornate library,
an island garrison and the grand Chevy
Chase Room (named after a medieval
hunting ditty, not the *National Lampoon*
star). Around the edge, subtropical gardens cling precariously to the cliffs, with
a cornucopia of blooms and shrubs nurtured by the temperate Gulf Stream.

Further east along the coast brings
you to the friendly-family beach of **Praa
Sands** (pronounced pray; ℗) and the
rocky cliffs of **Prussia Cove**, once an
infamous hideaway for Cornwall's most
celebrated smuggler, John Carter (aka
the King of Prussia).

FESTIVALS & EVENTS

Golowan Festival (www.golowan.com) Ten days
of music, art and Cornish culture, plus a big street parade
on Mazey Day; held in Penzance in late June.

Newlyn Fish Festival (www.newlynfishfestival.
org.uk) Newlyn celebrates its piscatorial heritage at this
festival, held over the August Bank Holiday.

GASTRONOMIC HIGHLIGHTS

❦ ARCHIE BROWN'S // PENZANCE £

☎ 01736-362828; Bread St; mains £3-10; ☯ 9.30am-
5pm Mon-Sat

Veggie salads, wedge sarnies and hearty
soups are what this much-loved wholefood cafe is all about, with filling eats in
the cheerful 1st-floor cafe, and a smorgasbord of lentils, pulses and whole-
grains in the ground-floor shop.

❦ BAKEHOUSE // PENZANCE ££

☎ 01736-331331; www.bakehouserestaurant.co.uk;
Chapel St; mains £8.95-19.50; ☯ lunch Wed-Sat,
dinner daily

Ask a local where to eat and chances
are they'll send you to the Bakehouse,
a double-floored diner down an alley
off Chapel St. Steaks take the honours:
choose your cut and match it with your
choice of sauce or spicy rub. Seafood
and veggie options are more limited, but
that doesn't seem to deter the punters –
booking is advisable.

❦ CHAPEL STREET BRASSERIE // PENZANCE ££

☎ 01736-350222; www.chapelstbrasserie.com; 13
Chapel St; lunch £10, mains £15; ☯ 10am-11pm

Old Coco's has recently been reinvented as this smart Gallic bistro-bar,
as suitable for an afternoon aperitif as
for a late-night feed. Black rattan, white
walls and big windows provide the setting; big plates of herby pan-roasted
chicken, confit of duck and classic
steak-frites provide the inexpensive
French-inspired food. The two-course
prix fixe menu is amazing value at
£12.50, and it's served at lunch and
supper.

❦ THE CORNISH RANGE // MOUSEHOLE ££

☎ 01736-731488; www.cornishrange.com; 6 Chapel
St; lunch £6.95-9.50, mains £13.50-17.50; ☯ lunch &
dinner

Another well-respected Mousehole
restaurant squeezed inside a former pilchard processing house. The food is elegant – choose from shellfish steamed in
cider, roast hake with crayfish risotto or
crispy duck with fennel and watercress –
but it is expensive and the place can feel
claustrophobic when it gets crowded.
Lunch is better value for money, or
there's a two-course £17.50 menu between 6pm and 7pm.

❦ THE HONEY POT // PENZANCE £

☎ 01736-368686; 5 Parade St; mains £4-10;
☯ 9am-5pm Mon-Sat

For afternoon tea and crumbly cakes,
there's nowhere better in Penzance than
the Honey Pot, opposite the Acorn Arts
Centre. It attracts punters across the
Penzance spectrum, from arty types
supping cappuccinos to earth-mums
tucking into fruit teas and homity pie.
Naturally, nearly everything's homemade and local.

❦ TWO FORE ST // MOUSEHOLE ££

☎ 01736-731164; www.2forestreet.co.uk; 2 Fore St;
mains £11.50-14.95; ☯ lunch & dinner

Riviera sophistication on the Mousehole seafront. It's young but has already
gained plenty of admirers, including
Harden's (www.hardens.com) and the *Good
Food Guide*. Inside, stripped wood, cool
colours and harbour views; outside, a
sweet garden shaded by palms and canvas
umbrellas. The emphasis is on simple
dishes designed to bring out the best
from the Cornish-sourced ingredients.
One to watch.

CORNWALL

NIGHTLIFE

❦ ACORN ARTS CENTRE

☎ 01736-363545; www.acorn-theatre.co.uk; Parade St, Penzance

Lively arts centre hosting film, theatre, comedy and live bands. There are currently question marks about its future: fingers crossed it'll still be there when you read this.

❦ ADMIRAL BENBOW

☎ 01736-363448; 46 Chapel St, Penzance

On historic Chapel St, the salty old Benbow looks like it's dropped from the pages of *Treasure Island*, with nautical decor mostly reclaimed from shipwrecks: anchors, lanterns, figureheads and all.

❦ TURK'S HEAD

☎ 01736-363093; Chapel St, Penzance

Purportedly the town's oldest pub; there's been a tavern on the site of the Turk's Head since the 13th century, and it was supposedly a favourite hangout for Penzance's 'free traders'; a subterranean smugglers tunnel once led straight to the harbour from the cellar (now the dining room). Skinner's and Sharp's ales on tap.

❦ ZERO LOUNGE

☎ 01736-361220; Chapel St, Penzance

In stark contrast to Chapel St's other pubs, this new boy is more urban chic than olde-worlde. There's a big open-plan bar serving quality coffees, beers and cocktails, and a sprawling patio out back that's popular with Penzance's trendy set.

TRANSPORT

BOAT // For ferries to the Isles of Scilly, see p249.
BUS // Penzance is the main local bus hub. Useful connections include bus 1/1A to Land's End, bus 6/6A to Newlyn and Mousehole, bus 17 to St Ives and bus 18/X18 to Truro, plus most places around the Penwith area. It's also served by National Express coaches.

TRAIN // Penzance is the last stop on the main line from London Paddington (six hours, eight to 10 daily) – booking early and off-peak gets the best fares. For trains to St Ives (£3.30), change at St Erth.

THE LIZARD
· · · · · ·

Cornwall's southern coastline takes a sudden wild turn around the Lizard Peninsula, where fields and heaths plunge into a melee of ink-black cliffs, churning surf and saw-tooth rocks. Cut off from the rest of Cornwall by the River Helford, and ringed by treacherous seas, the Lizard was once an ill-famed graveyard for ships, and the peninsula still has a wild, untamed edge.

ESSENTIAL INFORMATION

TOURIST INFORMATION // Helston tourist office (☎ 01326-565431; 79 Menage Street; ☯ 10am-5pm Mon-Sat)

EXPLORING THE LIZARD

❦ HELSTON // HOME OF THE FURRY DANCE

The only town of any size on the Lizard is **Helston**, which started life as a bustling river port and one of the county's four Stannary towns, where local tin was assayed and stamped before being shipped all over Britain. The town received another lease of life with the arrival of the naval airbase at Culdrose, which hosts a popular annual air-day in late July, and is still the county's main base for air-sea rescues.

The best time to visit is on **Flora Day** (www.helstonfloraday.org.uk) on 8 May. Believed to be the last remnant of a pagan celebration marking the coming of spring, this ancient festival is a mix of street dance, musical parade and floral pageant. The two main events are the Hal-An-Tow, in which St Michael and the devil do battle; and the Furry Dance, which kicks off at noon and proceeds around the town's streets (participants take part by invitation only, and the dance is always led by a local couple).

There's plenty of background on the Furry Dance at the **Helston Folk Museum** (☎ 01326-564027; Market House; ✆ 10am-1pm Mon-Sat), where the displays include replica shopfronts, a 5-tonne cider press and a display on local hero Bob Fitzsimmons, the first man to simultaneously hold the world titles for middleweight, light heavyweight and heavyweight boxing.

Outside the museum, look out for one of the **cannons** recovered from the wreck of the HMS *Anson,* which foundered on Loe Bar in 1807. This traumatic event inspired local cabinet-maker Henry Trengrouse to devote his life to inventing new life-saving tools, including the winch-powered 'Bosun's Chair' and a rocket-propelled rescue line.

🌱 PORTHLEVEN & THE LOE // AN UNSPOILT LIZARD PORT
Three miles southwest of Helston is **Porthleven**, a quiet port set around the massive walls of its stone quay, built to shelter the harbour from ferocious winter storms. It's a pleasant little town with a burgeoning foodie scene, epitomised by the bustling Wednesday-morning market and the **Porthleven Food Festival** (www.porthlevenfoodfestival.co.uk). You'll also find a good deli, a fishmonger and the excellent Kota Restaurant (p227) dotted round town. Porthleven is also renowned for its challenging surf, but it's not for novices – you'll get acquainted with the harbour wall if you don't know what you're doing.

A mile south is the treacherous sandbank of **Loe Bar** – scene of many a shipwreck down the centuries – and **Loe Pool**, Cornwall's largest freshwater lake, said by some to be the resting place of King Arthur's magical blade, Excalibur. Walking trails wind their way around the lakeshore and the surrounding Penrose Estate, but swimming is dangerous due to unpredictable rip currents.

🌱 GUNWALLOE // DIG FOR SPANISH TREASURE
Also part of the Penrose estate is **Gunwalloe Church Cove** (Ⓟ), five miles from Porthleven, with its tiny 15th-century **Church of St Winwaloe** half-buried amongst the dunes behind the beach. Out on the headland, the hulking, 200ft mass of Halzephron Cliff was an infamous shipwreck spot – in 1785, the Spanish ship *Vrijdag* was wrecked offshore along with its 2.5-tonne cargo of silver dollars, and local legend maintains that the pirate John Avery once buried a fabulous horde somewhere in the Gunwalloe dunes. Don't be surprised if you see a few metal-detectors hard at work on nearby Dollar Cove.

🌱 MULLION // THE HOME OF WIRELESS
Tucked away on the Lizard's west side is **Mullion**, handily placed for three of the peninsula's prettiest beaches. A mile south is little **Mullion Cove** (Ⓟ), with a characteristically Cornish cluster of harbour, boats and cottages; **Polurrian**, the most remote and dramatic of the three, only accessible via the coast path; and **Poldhu** (Ⓟ), favoured by families thanks to its facilities (and nearby ice-cream shop).

Poldhu's other claim to fame is as the site of the world's first radio transmission, sent from Poldhu Point across 2000 miles of the Atlantic to St John's in Newfoundland by the Italian engineer Guglielmo Marconi in 1901. The little **Marconi Centre** (☎ 01326-574441; http://marconi-centre-poldhu. org.uk; ⊗ times vary, check website) was opened in 2001 to mark the centenary. Volunteer radio enthusiasts fill you in on the Marconi story, and there are short-wave radio sets to mess about with. A plaque in a nearby field marks the site of the original transmission station.

❦ GLORIOUS GARDENS // TWO OF THE LIZARD'S GREAT ESTATES

Two of Cornwall's landmark gardens lie within easy reach of Helston. **Trelowarren** (☎ 01326-221224; www.trelowarren.com; Mawgan; admission free) has been in the hands of the Vyvyan family for six centuries and languishes over 1000 acres of land between Goonhilly and the Helford River. The estate has lots of woodland walks and country trails, including one to the **Halliggye Fougou**, an underground chamber on the site of an old Iron Age hillfort. Recent sidelines also comprise a plant nursery, craft centre, superb restaurant (see p226) and some seriously luxurious ecofriendly holiday cottages.

Nearby **Trevarno** (☎ 01326-574274; www. trevarno.co.uk; Crowntown, nr Helston; adult/child £6.85/2.40; ⊗ 10.30am-5pm) has been owned by several notable families since its 13th-century beginnings, including the aristocratic Arundels and the industrious Bickford-Smiths, but the estate owes its recent regeneration to two businessmen, Mike Sagin and Nigel Helsby, who bought the estate in 1994. Again, the sweeping grounds are the centrepiece, with woodland, formal gardens, daffodil collections and a lake with its own photogenic boathouse (look out for Trevarno's famous peacocks, which can

often be seen strutting across the lawns). Afterwards, there's a museum of garden memorabilia to browse, a conservatory for afternoon tea and an organic shop where you can buy soaps and lotions handmade on the estate.

❦ LIZARD POINT // HOW LAND'S END SHOULD BE

Five miles south from Mullion, Britain reaches its southernmost tip at **Lizard Point**, historically one of Britain's deadliest patches of coast. Hundreds of ships have come to grief around the point over the centuries, from Spanish treasure galleons and naval frigates to tiny fishing smacks. With all those wrecks it's a mecca for scuba divers, as well as coastal walkers who flock to the clifftops to bask in the scenery.

With its conglomeration of fudge-sellers and souvenir shops, **Lizard village** makes a pretty disappointing gateway, so most people just park in the village and make the mile-long stroll down to the point itself. A steep track leads down to the long-disused lifeboat station and shingly cove, while shack cafes at the top of the cliff provide a fine vantage point for drinking in the views. In May and June the Lizard is one of the best places in Cornwall to spot basking sharks, and if you're really lucky you might catch sight of a Cornish chough (see p225).

Just inland from the point is the **Lizard Lighthouse Heritage Centre** (☎ 01255-245011; www.lizardlighthouse.co.uk; adult/ child £4/2; ⊗ times vary, check website). Commissioned in 1752, the lighthouse was automated in the '90s and since 2009 has housed a museum exploring the area's maritime history, encompassing everything from weather prediction to semaphore and shipwrecks. A guided tour costs extra (adult/child £2/1), but

THE CORNISH CHOUGH

While you won't have any trouble spotting a seagull in Cornwall, you'll be extremely lucky to see the chough (pronounced *chuff*). A member of the crow family distinguished by its jet-black plumage and bright orange beak, the bird is a symbol of Cornish culture – legend has it that the chough embodies King Arthur's spirit, and the bird still features on Cornwall's coat of arms. The chough was once common but suffered a huge decline in the 20th century due to intensive farming and habitat destruction. Happily, the first pair of choughs to nest in Cornwall for over 50 years arrived in 2002, and the success of recent breeding programmes has fuelled hopes that the chough will re-establish itself along the county's cliffs.

it's worth it for the chance to climb up into the light-tower; ask nicely and you might even get to let off a blast from the station foghorn.

More craggy scenery can be found further east at **Housel Bay** and the wild promontories of Pen Olver and Bass Point. Further along the coast past **Church Cove** is **Cadgwith**, an idyllic huddle of thatched houses and fishermen's cottages at the foot of a lung-bustingly steep hill. On the cliffs above the village is the 200ft collapsed blowhole colloquially called the **Devil's Frying Pan**, which gets its name from the way it spits out water during heavy seas.

Five miles from Lizard Point near Kuggar is **Kennack Sands** (Ⓟ), a family paddling spot with plenty of sand, seaweed-stocked rockpools and beach shops.

✤ KYNANCE COVE // COASTAL SCENERY AT ITS FINEST

The Lizard has some special coves, but top of the pile is **Kynance Cove** (NT; ☎ 01326-561407; lizard@nationaltrust.org. uk; Ⓟ), an impossibly pretty pocket of coast tucked under towering cliffs and wildflower-strewn headland. Once an important source of the red-green serpentine rock favoured by the Victorians, the cove is now owned by the National Trust. A rough path leads down from

the cliff car park, allowing Kynance's panorama of rock stacks, arches, caves, islands and vivid sapphire seas to unfurl in dramatic fashion. It's dreamy stuff, no matter whether the sun's blazing or the winter storms are raging – but take care when swimming and be careful not to be cut off by the fast tide, especially if you're venturing across the sand towards Asparagus Island and Gull Rock.

There's a tearoom behind the beach, but this is a perfect place for packing your own beach picnic.

✤ ST KEVERNE // ICE CREAM, SHIPWRECKS AND SATELLITES

Centred around a market square ringed by stone cottages and two village pubs, **St Keverne** is one of the Lizard's oldest market towns. The spire of the parish church has been a vital day-mark for sailors and fishermen for more than five centuries, and the nearby coastline is dotted with attractive fishing ports, including **Porthoustock**, **Porthallow** (locally pronounced *pralla*) and the arc-shaped harbour of **Coverack**, once an infamous haunt for smuggled contraband, now a haven for the Lizard's artistic community. Out to the east are the **Manacles**, a treacherous offshore reef that's a source of terror for sailors and delight for wreck divers.

CORNWALL

Just outside St Keverne is **Roskilly's Farm** (☎ 01326-280479; www.roskillys.co.uk; ⏰ 10am-6pm), an ice-cream maker and organic farm which has scooped several awards for its ice creams, yoghurts, fudges, sorbets and fruit jams. Roskilly goodies are served at the Croust House restaurant (p226), while the Bull Pen Gallery showcases local craftwork and furniture. You can even watch the cows being milked most days; phone ahead for times.

Across the centre of the Lizard sprawl the barren **Goonhilly Downs**, home to one of the world's largest satellite stations. For some reason the Goonhilly dishes are all named after Arthurian characters; the oldest, Arthur, was built in 1961 and is now a listed monument.

❦ THE HELFORD // CORNWALL'S MOST EXCLUSIVE CREEK

Flowing along the Lizard's northern edge, lined with overhanging oaks and hidden creeks, the **River Helford** feels far removed from the rest of the peninsula. There are few corners of Cornwall which have remained as naturally unspoilt, and it's a haven for marine wildlife, as well as one of Cornwall's last remaining oyster fisheries at Porth Navas, not to mention a liberal smattering of rock-star mansions and palatial houses sprinkled along the riverbanks.

The southern bank is much less accessible than the northern shore, and is ideal for exploring on foot. **Helford River Boats** (☎ 01326-250770; www.helford-river-boats. co.uk; adult/child £4/2; ⏰ 9.30am-9.30pm Jun-Aug, 9.30am-5.30pm Apr, May, Sep & Oct) runs pedestrian ferries from Helford Passage (near Falmouth) to **Helford village**. With its jumble of creek-front cottages and shady lanes, this idyllic river village is one of the priciest in the whole of Cornwall,

but while you might not be able to afford the real estate, but you should at least be able to stretch to a pint in the village pub (p227) or a cream tea at the **Down by the Riverside Café** (☎ 01326-231893; www.downby theriverside.co.uk), in a converted chapel beside the village car park.

From here, the coast trail leads east to **Frenchman's Creek** (inspiration for Daphne du Maurier's classic tale of Cornish smuggling). If you're feeling ambitious, you could continue on to **Tremayne Quay** (part of the Trelowarren estate, p224). To the east, the coast path leads past Treath Beach to Dennis Head and the village of **St-Anthony-in-Meneage**, picturesquely plonked beside Gillan Creek. Locals can often be spotted trigging (cockle-picking) in the nearby mudflats. Further still is the isolated headland of **Nare Point**, from where the views unfurl all the way to Pendennis Point.

You can get the lowdown on the Helford's natural environment from the **Helford Marine Conservation Society** (www.helfordmarineconservation.co.uk), while **Helford River Expeditions** (☎ 01326-250258; www.helfordriverexpeditions.co.uk), based at Carwinion Gardens near Falmouth, offers guided walks, wildlife trips and kayaking expeditions around the Helford estuary.

GASTRONOMIC HIGHLIGHTS

❦ CROUST HOUSE // ST KEVERNE £
☎ 01326-280479; www.roskillys.co.uk; Tregallast Barton; ⏰ 9am-dusk

Family-friendly food (pies, soups and homemade pasties) is the order of the day at Roskilly's homely farm-restaurant, but the star of show is the homemade ice cream. Choose from 40-odd flavours, including esoteric options such as

Blackcurrant Cheesecake or Chocolate
Brownie & Marshmallow.

♥ HALZEPHRON INN //
GUNWALLOE ££

☎ 01326-240406; www.halzephron-inn.co.uk; mains
£10.95-18.50

You couldn't ask for a better place for a
pint of ale than this 500-year-old pub,
balanced on the cliffs above Gunwalloe.
Whitewashed, slate-roofed, full of nooks
and niches, it's run by ex-opera singer
turned landlady Angela Thomas. The
food's solid (especially the Sunday roast)
and the views are really grand.

♥ KOTA // PORTHLEVEN ££

☎ 01326-562407; www.kotarestaurant.co.uk; mains
£11.50-19.95; ☺ lunch Fri & Sat, dinner Mon-Sat

Malaysian meets Maori at this converted
mill on Porthleven's harbour, overseen
by head chef Jude Kereama, one of Cornwall's rising culinary stars. His pan-Asian
food has won lots of plaudits, blending
Pacific Rim flavours with Cornish ingredients (seabass with Thai-spiced bouillabaisse, Sichuan-spiced venison pie).
Exotic and exciting.

♥ LIZARD PASTY SHOP //
THE LIZARD £

☎ 01326-290889; www.annspasties.co.uk; The Lizard;
pasties £2.75; ☺ Tue-Sat

Long before Rick Stein bestowed his seal
of approval on this Lizard bakery, Ann
Muller was already famous for her pasty-
making. Made by hand to a tried-and-
tested traditional recipe, the steak's the
star, but wholemeal, veggie and cheese-
and-onion versions are also offered.

♥ NEW YARD // TRELOWARREN ££

☎ 01326-221224; www.newyardrestaurant.co.uk;
☺ lunch & dinner Tue-Sat, lunch Sun

Definitely not your average garden cafe:
in a super setting inside the old carriage
house at Trelowarren, this is a destination in its own right. Head chef Olly
Jackson is a poster boy for local sourcing: fruit, herbs and veg from the estate;
oysters, clams, mussels and scallops
from the Helford; dairy and cheese from
Menallack Farm – and his food's rapidly
gaining some heavyweight admirers.

♥ SHIPWRIGHT ARMS // HELFORD £

☎ 01326-231235; mains £4-10

Thatched on top, beamed inside, blessed with to-die-for river views, the Helford's waterfront pub makes a fine place
for a pint and a ploughman's. While
many of its compatriots along the river
have been spruced up and hollowed out,
the Shipwright has stayed true to its
roots and is the better for it. Betty Stogs,
Doom Bar and Helford Creek cider behind the bar.

♥ SOUTH CAFÉ // MANACCAN ££

☎ 01326-231311; www.south-cafe.co.uk; mains
£9.25-13.95; ☺ breakfast, lunch & dinner

Not what you'd expect in the uber-rural
Lizard – a bistro that feels more Covent
Garden than Cornwall. Take your pick
from the light dining room or sheltered
back garden, and sit back for a blend of
English, French and Italian: pan-fried
scallops with chilli, perhaps, or roast
chicken with chorizo and balsamic glaze.
Worth travelling for.

TRANSPORT

BUS // Buses on the Lizard are patchy. Bus 32 runs from
Helston to Gunwalloe, Gweek, Coverack and St Keverne,
while bus 33 stops at Poldhu, Mullion and the Lizard.
Helston also has regular services to Penzance, Truro and
Falmouth.

CAR // Perilously narrow streets lie in wait for un-
suspecting drivers – take our advice and leave the car
outside Cadgwith, Helford Village, Coverack and St
Anthony.

CORNWALL

FALMOUTH, TRURO & THE ROSELAND

. . . . . .

In contrast to the crags and breakers of the Atlantic coast, the area around Falmouth and the Roseland Peninsula presents a gentler side to the county. Sheltered from the brunt of the biting Atlantic winds, the coastline benefits from a balmy subtropical climate that allows exotic plants and trees to flourish along its valleys; many of Cornwall's finest gardens, including Trelissick, Glendurgan, Caerhays and Heligan, can be found along the southern coastline. In previous centuries it was an important maritime area, and the old ports of Falmouth, St Mawes and Mevagissey are all worthy of investigation.

FALMOUTH

pop 20,775

Strategically situated at the end of the River Fal, overlooking the entrance to the Carrick Roads estuary, the port of Falmouth has been a maritime hub for more than 500 years. Boasting the world's third-deepest natural harbour, Falmouth flourished as a trading port and naval harbour after the river at Truro silted up. The town reached its heyday during the era of the Falmouth Packet Service, which carried mail, bullion and supplies between Britain and its overseas colonies between 1689 and 1850.

The days of the tall ships, tea clippers and naval galleons may be gone, but the town remains an important centre for shipping and repairs, and since 2003 it's also been home to the Cornish outpost of the National Maritime Museum. More recently, especially since the spanking

new campus of University College Falmouth opened in nearby Penryn, it's also gained a buzzy after-dark scene, with a medley of bars and brasseries dotted along its streets.

ESSENTIAL INFORMATION

TOURIST INFORMATION // Falmouth tourist office (☎ 01326-312300; falmouthtic@yahoo.co.uk; 11 Market Strand, Prince of Wales Pier; ☺ 9.30am-5.15pm Mon-Sat)

EXPLORING FALMOUTH

❧ **NATIONAL MARITIME MUSEUM // SAIL INTO FALMOUTH'S SEAFARING PAST**

At the centre of Falmouth's heavily redeveloped Discovery Quay is the **National Maritime Museum Cornwall** (☎ 01326-313388; www.nmmc.co.uk; Discovery Quay; adult/child £9.50/6.50; ☺ 10am-5pm; ♿), whose maritime collection is second only to its sister museum in Greenwich. At the heart of the complex is the Flotilla Gallery, where boats dangle from the ceiling by slender steel wires, and suspended walkways wind their way amongst yachts, schooners, trimarans and other groundbreaking sailing craft. Other highlights include the Nav Station, a hands-on exhibit exploring nautical navigation; the Tidal Zone, where underwater windows peer into the murky depths; and the Look Out, offering a 360-degree panorama of Falmouth Bay.

❧ **PENDENNIS CASTLE // ONE OF BRITAIN'S FINEST TUDOR STRONGHOLDS**

On the promontory of Pendennis Point, **Pendennis Castle** (EH; ☎ 01326-316594; adult/child £5.40/2.70; ☺ 10am-6pm Jul & Aug, 10am-5pm Apr-Jun & Sep, 10am-4pm Oct-Mar) was constructed from 1540 to 1545 by Henry VIII as one of a chain of fortresses designed to defend the British mainland from

Spanish and French invasion. Falmouth's deepwater harbour made it a key strategic asset, and Pendennis was built with its sister fortress of St Mawes (p238) to defend the entrance to the Carrick Roads.

The heart of the castle is its circular keep and Tudor gun-deck, where the battlements still bristle with vintage cannons. During the Civil War, the castle was engaged in a six-month siege under the command of Captain John Arundel of Trerice (p200), during which the garrison resorted to eating the castle's dogs, rats and horses to survive; it was the last Royalist fortress in the southwest to fall. Elsewhere, you can visit the WWI-era guardhouse and the Half Moon Battery, designed to play a crucial role in the event of Nazi invasion during WWII. Underground are the guns' magazines and observation post.

Outdoor concerts are held in the grounds during summer. Less tuneful is the **Noonday Gun**, which rings out at noon sharp every day throughout July & August.

☙ A BEACH TOUR // RELAX ON THE FALMOUTH SEAFRONT

Falmouth's bucket-and-spade beaches aren't up to north coast standards, but they're nice enough for a spot of sunlounging. Nearest to town is **Gyllyngvase** (P), a flat sandy beach backed by a good beach cafe, about half a mile from the town centre. Fifteen minutes' walk along the coast path is **Swanpool** (P), with a small inland lagoon populated by grebes, coots, ducks and mute swans. A couple of miles further along the coast is **Maenporth** (P), the quietest of the three, with facilities including a beach cafe, kayak centre and smart restaurant, the Cove (p229). Bus 500 from Falmouth stops at all three beaches en route to Trebah Gardens (p232) and the Helford Passage.

TOP FIVE

PASTIES

Pasty shops are everywhere in Cornwall, but beware: not all pasties are the same. There are strict rules about what goes into a true Cornish pasty (see p282), so we've picked out some of our favourite suppliers:

★ **WC Rowe** (www.wcrowe.com) The county's main pasty baker: traditional and very reliable.

★ **Pengenna Pasties** (www.pengenna pasties.co.uk) Great pasties with a slightly different pastry style, with shops in Bude, Tintagel and St Ives.

★ **Chough Bakery** (☎ 01841-533361; www. thechoughbakery.co.uk) Ace pasties on the Padstow harbour.

★ **Lizard Pasty Shop** (p227) Rick Stein's favourite, near Lizard Village.

★ **Aunty May's Pasty Company** (☎ 01736-364583; The Coombe, Newlyn) This Newlyn stalwart unusually uses flaky rather than shortcrust pastry in its pasties.

FESTIVALS & EVENTS

Falmouth Oyster Festival (www.falmouthoys terfestival.co.uk) Expect dance, music and cookery classes (plus plenty of oyster eating) at this October festival.
Cornwall Film Festival (www.cornwallfilmfes tival.com) Three days of Cornish shorts, workshops and premieres, held in November.

GASTRONOMIC HIGHLIGHTS

☙ THE COVE £££

☎ 01326-251136; www.thecovemaenporth.co.uk; Maenporth; mains £14.25-22.50; ☺ lunch & dinner
Falmouth's fanciest food is on Maenporth, at this modern building with a memorable beach-view balcony. Chef

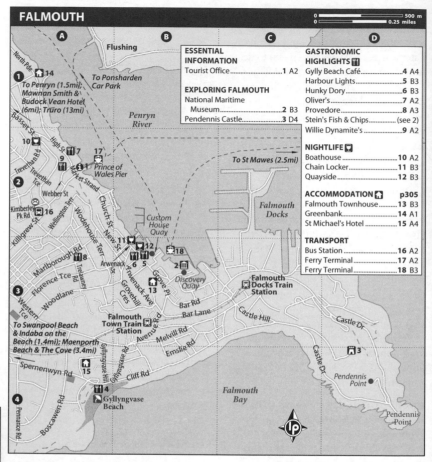

FALMOUTH

0 _____ 500 m
0 _____ 0.25 miles

ESSENTIAL INFORMATION
Tourist Office.........................1 A2

EXPLORING FALMOUTH
National Maritime
  Museum...........................2 B3
Pendennis Castle..................3 D4

GASTRONOMIC HIGHLIGHTS
Gylly Beach Café....................4 A4
Harbour Lights.......................5 B3
Hunky Dory...........................6 B3
Oliver's................................7 A2
Provedore............................8 A3
Stein's Fish & Chips............(see 2)
Willie Dynamite's...................9 A2

NIGHTLIFE
Boathouse.........................10 A2
Chain Locker.......................11 B3
Quayside............................12 B3

ACCOMMODATION   p305
Falmouth Townhouse...........13 B3
Greenbank..........................14 A1
St Michael's Hotel................15 A4

TRANSPORT
Bus Station.........................16 A2
Ferry Terminal......................17 A2
Ferry Terminal......................18 B3

Arty Williams is known for his classy Brit food, and a short but carefully considered menu that refreshes every couple of months with seasonal meat, fish and game (veggies are also well catered for). It's really rather good, but the secret's spreading fast: one to book for.

❤ HUNKY DORY £££

☎ 01326-212997; www.hunkydoryfalmouth.co.uk; 46 Arwenack St; mains £12.25-24.95; ☾ dinner
Seafood again features heavily at this split-level restaurant near the old Customs House. The menu marries Euro-

pean and Asian cuisine with Cornish-caught fish, plus a more limited choice of meat and game. The setting is nicely minimal, mixing cool blues with pale wood and whitewashed walls.

❤ GYLLY BEACH CAFÉ ££

☎ 01326-312884; www.gyllybeach.com; Gyllyngvase Beach; mains £10.95-15.95; ☾ breakfast, lunch & dinner
A great location and a decked patio over Gyllyngvase are the main draws at this lively beach restaurant. It covers all bases: fry-ups and pancakes for brekkie,

CORNWALL

platters of antipasti for lunch, quality steak, seafood and pasta after dark. It's open late for drinks but gets very busy.

🌱 INDABA ON THE BEACH ££

☎ 01326-311886; www.indabafish.co.uk; Swanpool; mains £10.50-20, 2-person seafood platter £97.50; ⏰ lunch & dinner Mon-Sat, lunch Sun

Recently acquired by the people behind Indaba Fish (p237), this airy restaurant sits on the bluff beside Swanpool. Like its sister restaurant in Truro, it's a seafood specialist, offering everything from single oysters through to copious seafood platters. Blackboards take their fishy cue from local markets.

🌱 OLIVER'S ££

☎ 01326-218138; 33 High St; mains £12.95-19.95; ⏰ lunch & dinner Tue-Sun

Things are stripped back to the essentials at this new arrival. The bare-bones decor (plain white walls, plain pine tables) is matched by simple, impeccably presented dishes: delicate noisettes of lamb with bubble-and-squeak, chunky pork and apple sausages, or sea bass with seafood risotto. Quietly impressive, refreshingly unpretentious and just about the top place to eat in Falmouth.

🌱 THE ORIGINAL WILLIE DYNAMITE'S DINER

☎ 01326-212112; 10 Webber St; mains £5-10; ⏰ 10am-4pm Mon-Sat, 10am-3pm Sun

Hey-ho, daddy-o... This American-style diner dishes up the best burgers, fries, pancakes and shakes in town. The decor's convincing – vintage signs, melamine tables, booth seats, chequerboard floor – but sadly, no waitresses on skates as yet.

🌱 PROVEDORE £

☎ 01326-314888; www.provedore.co.uk; 43 Trelawney Rd; mains £4-10; ⏰ 9am-4pm Tue & Wed, 9am-4pm & 6-10pm Thu & Fri, 9am-1.30pm Sat

It's a walk from town, but this deli-turned-cafe is worth the shoe leather. Spanish and Italian flavours feature strongly; students, locals and arty types pack in to read the papers accompanied by frothy lattes, artisan sandwiches or the legendary Saturday-morning breakfast. It's open for tapas, paella and seafood on Thursday and Friday evenings.

🌱 STEIN'S FISH & CHIPS £

☎ 01841-532700; Discovery Quay; takeaway £6.65-10.95; ⏰ 12-2.30pm & 5-9pm

Rick Stein has finally stepped out of his Padstow comfort zone and set up shop on the Falmouth seafront. Offering essentially the same menu as his Padstow fish-and-chip shop, the Falmouth version is blinged up with an upstairs **champagne and oyster bar** (mains £3.50-15.50; ⏰ 5-9pm). Whether it's worth the price premium is a matter of opinion – cheaper chips can be had at the **Harbour Lights** (☎ 01326-316934; Arwenack St; fish & chips £3-6; ⏰ 11:30am-8pm Mon-Thu & Sun, 11.30am-9pm Fri & Sat).

NIGHTLIFE

🌱 BOATHOUSE

☎ 01326-315425; Trevethan Hill

Friendly pub offering views across the river to Flushing and a good mix of Belgian and Cornish beers.

🌱 CHAIN LOCKER

☎ 01326-311685; Quay St

Shiver-me-timbers – a proper old sea-dog of a pub, with the all-important low ceilings and hugger-mugger atmosphere.

🌱 QUAYSIDE

☎ 01326-312113; Arwenack St

Along the quay from the Chain Locker, this is the place for a sunset pint, with picnic tables beside the harbour and a pub selling German lager and local beers.

CORNWALL

TRANSPORT

BOAT // **Ponsharden Park & Float**
(☎ 01326-319417; www.ponsharden.co.uk; day pass per car with 2 passengers/3-7 passengers £11/15; ☻ 10am-6pm May-Oct) allows you to catch a ferry (Monday to Friday) or bus (Saturday and Sunday) to Customs House Quay from the 500-space Ponsharden car park on the outskirts of Falmouth. The **St Mawes Ferry** (www.kingharryscornwall.co.uk; return £7.50/4.50, at least hourly in summer) shuttles across the water from Prince of Wales Pier and Customs House Quay.

BUS // Falmouth has good bus links, including bus 88 to Truro, 89 to Newquay, 2 to Penzance via Helston and 14 to St Ives via Camborne and Redruth. Bus 35 (10 daily, three on Sunday) travels to the Lizard via Helford Passage, Constantine and Gweek, while bus 500 (four daily in summer) travels from Falmouth via the town beaches en route to the Helford Passage.

TRAIN // Falmouth is at the end of the branch line from Truro (£3.20, 20 minutes, hourly), stopping at Penryn, Falmouth Town and Falmouth Docks.

AROUND FALMOUTH

Falmouth is handily placed for exploring the sleepy villages and quiet creeks around the Restronguet Estuary and the northern bank of the River Helford. Unsurprisingly, this well-to-do corner shelters some of Cornwall's priciest property (large houses around Point, Feock and Flushing regularly swap hands for a million pounds a pop) but you don't need a king's ransom to appreciate the scenery: several great estates and a handful of Cornwall's loveliest waterfront pubs are just a spin away.

EXPLORING AROUND FALMOUTH

❦ TREBAH & GLENDURGAN // THE FOX FAMILY'S HORTICULTURAL EXPLOITS

A short drive from Falmouth takes you through the hamlet of **Mawnan Smith** en route to the Helford River and two side-by-side estates, both founded by members of the Fox family, who made their fortune importing exotic plants from the New World. **Glendurgan** (NT; ☎ 01326-250906; glendurgan@nationaltrust.org.uk; adult/child £6/3; ☻ 10.30am-5.30pm Mon-Sat Jul & Aug, Tue-Sat Feb-Jun, Sep & Oct) was established by Alfred Fox in the 1820s to show off the many weird and wonderful plants being brought back from the far corners of the empire, from Himalayan rhododendrons to Canadian maples and New Zealand tree ferns. Tumbling down a stunning subtropical valley, the garden offers breathtaking views of the River Helford, as well as an ornamental maze and a secluded beach near **Durgan** village.

Just west is **Trebah** (☎ 01326-250448; www.trebahgarden.co.uk; adult/child £7.50/2.50 Mar-Oct, £3/1 Nov-Feb; ☻ 10.30am-6.30pm, last entry 4.30pm), planted in 1840 by Charles Fox, Alfred's younger brother. It's a touch less formal than Glendurgan, with gigantic rhododendrons, gunnera and jungle ferns lining the sides of a steep ravine leading down to the quay and shingle beach. Charles Fox was a notorious polymath and stickler for detail; the story goes that he made his head gardener construct a scaffold to indicate the height of each tree, barking out his orders from an attic window via a megaphone and telescope. Half-price admission is offered if you arrive on the Western Greyhound bus 500.

❦ NATIONAL SEAL SANCTUARY // FEED FISH TO AN INJURED SEAL

At the western head of the Helford near Gweek, the 'ah' factor goes into overdrive at the **National Seal Sanctuary** (☎ 0871 423 2110; www.sealsanctuary.co.uk; Gweek; adult/child £10.95/6.95; ☻ 10am-5pm May-Sep, 9am-4pm Oct-Apr), which cares for sick and orphaned seals washed up along the Cornish coastline before returning them to the wild.

TOP FIVE

SECRET GARDENS

Everyone knows about Heligan, Eden and the big National Trust gardens, but Cornwall has a wealth of private gardens where it's easier to enjoy the blooms in peace.

★ **Penjerrick** (☎ 01872-870105; www.penjerrickgarden.co.uk; Budock nr Falmouth; adult/child £2.50/1; ⌚ 1.30-4.30pm Sun, Wed & Fri Mar-Sep) Two gardens in one: exotic jungle plants in the Valley Garden; rhododendrons, magnolias and camellias in the Upper Garden.

★ **Carwinion** (☎ 01326-250258; www.carwinion.co.uk; Mawnan Smith; adult/child £4/free; ⌚ 10am-5.30pm) Famous for its bamboo collection; you can even pick up your own bamboo bikini.

★ **Chygurno** (☎ 01736-732153; Lamorna, nr Penzance; ⌚ 2-5pm Wed & Thu Apr-Sep) Perfectly formed pocket of subtropical showiness above Lamorna Cove.

★ **Bonython** (☎ 01326-240550; www.bonythonmanor.co.uk; Cury Cross Lanes, nr Helston; adult/child £6/free; ⌚ 10am-4.30pm Apr-Sep) Twenty-acre estate including allotments, herbaceous borders and a walled garden.

★ **Tregrehan** (☎ 01726-814389; www.tregrehan.org; adult/child £5/free; ⌚ 10.30am-5pm Wed-Sun mid-Mar–May, 1-4.30pm Wed Jun-Aug) Two-hundred-year-old trees in a celebrated woodland garden near St Austell.

♥ TRELISSICK // WATERFRONT WALKS ALONG THE FAL

Stretching for 200 hectares above the Carrick Roads, **Trelissick** (NT; ☎ 01872-862090; trelissick@nationaltrust.org.uk; adult/child £7.40/3.70; ⌚ 10.30am-5.30pm Feb-Oct, 11am-4pm Nov-Feb) is another of Cornwall's showpiece estates. It's particularly popular for its walking trails, which meander through a patchwork of maintained woodland, working farmland and river estuary; deep-sea tankers can often be seen moored up along the Fal, near the King Harry Ferry. If you're only here to walk, you can just pay for the car park (free to NT members; otherwise £3.50).

The estate has been owned by several families, although for the bulk of its history it belonged to the Copeland family (of Copeland china fame) before being gifted to the National Trust in 1955. Although the estate's neo-Gothic mansion is closed to the public, you can still explore the ornamental gardens, renowned for their collections of rhododendrons, camellias and hydrangeas.

♥ PENRYN, FLUSHING & MYLOR // ROUND AND ABOUT THE RIVER PENRYN

These days you'll be hard-pushed to tell where Falmouth ends and **Penryn** begins, but in bygone days this was a proud market town in its own right, as well as the site of one of Cornwall's great seats of ecclesiastical learning, Glasney College (another casualty of Henry VIII's monastery-bashing antics during the Dissolution). After decades in the doldrums, Penryn received a kick-start following the arrival of University College Falmouth just up the road, and its twisty opes and alleyways are now home to a smattering of cafes, boutiques and food shops.

Of particular note are the **Earth & Water Deli** (☎ 01326-259889; www.earthandwater.co.uk; 6 St Thomas St); **Higher Market**

Studio (☎ 01326-374191; www.highermarket studio.co.uk; 19 Higher Market St), which sells retro furniture and artworks; and the fab Miss Peapod's Kitchen Café (p234), part of the ecochic, windmill-powered development of **Jubilee Wharf** (www. jubileewharf.co.uk), which is also home to a seamstress, florist, bike shop and yoga school.

Across the river from Penryn are the well-heeled villages of **Flushing** and **Mylor**, much favoured by yachties and weekend boaters, as well as walkers trekking along the coast path between Trefusis and Penarrow Points.

GASTRONOMIC HIGHLIGHTS

❦ THE CORNISH SMOKEHOUSE // PENRYN £

☎ 01326-376244; www.cornishcuisine.co.uk; Islington Wharf; ⏱ 10am-5pm Wed-Fri

Duck, fish, cheese and game are just some of the things to find their way into the kilns of this lovable little family-run smokehouse, which employs fragrant fruitwoods to give its goodies their distinctive smoky tang.

❦ FERRYBOAT INN // HELFORD PASSAGE ££

☎ 01326-250625; Helford Passage; mains £8-18; ⏱ lunch & dinner

Having taken over the reins at the Duchy Oyster Farm along the river, the UK's premier oyster merchants, the Wright Brothers, have given this old river pub a complete revamp. Gone are the dated furnishings; in comes wood, slate and an open-plan feel, plus a proper gastropub menu. It's expensive, but for waterfront views it can't be bettered.

Follow road directions to Trebah and Glendurgan and then look out for the signs. Buses 35 and 500 both stop at Helford Passage.

❦ MISS PEAPOD'S KITCHEN CAFÉ // PENRYN £

☎ 01326-374424; www.misspeapod.co.uk; Jubilee Wharf; mains £5.25-9.25; ⏱ 10am-4pm Tue-Thu & Sun, 10am-12.30am Fri & Sat

What's not to adore about this riverfront cafe? Run with relaxed efficiency by Alice Marston and crew, and dotted with retro lamps and mix-and-match furniture, it's earned a passionate Penryn following thanks to its hearty wholefood, friendly vibe and packed programme of film, music and live events – and the waterside deck is a stunner. If there's a cooler cafe in Cornwall, we're yet to find it.

❦ PANDORA INN // RESTRONGUET CREEK ££

☎ 01326-372678; www.pandorainn.com; main £10-16; ⏱ 10.30am-11pm

Conjure up the perfect smugglers pub and chances are it'll be darn close to the Pandora. Inside, blazing hearths, snug alcoves and ships-in-cabinets; outside, thatched roof, cob walls and a pontoon snaking out onto Restronguet Creek. The location really has the wow factor, but the food's been disappointingly patchy since a recent change of ownership.

TRURO

pop 17,431

Dominated by the triumvirate spires of its 19th-century cathedral, Truro is the county's capital and its main administrative and commercial centre. The city originally grew up around a hilltop castle, and later became one of the county's four stannary towns and busiest ports, although the town's maritime ambitions were scuppered by the silting up of the river, and the town's quays (including Lemon Quay and Back Quay, both near the Hall for Cornwall) now exist

~ WORTH A TRIP ~

Three miles from Truro near Tresillian is **Tregothnan** (☎ 01872-520000; www.tregothnan. co.uk), the feudal seat of the Boscawen family, whose heirs have inherited the title of Lord Falmouth for the last 600 years.

More recently, Tregothnan has found fame as the UK's first (and only) **tea plantation**. The temperate Cornish climate allows the cultivation of several rare-leaf teas, including assam, darjeeling and earl grey. Prices command a considerable premium (tea bags from £3.50 for 10 sachets, loose tea from £7.99 for 50g). Other goodies, including manuka honey produced by the estate's bees, are sold at the **shop**.

Tregothnan House is closed to the public, although the estate's **botanic garden** can be visited on a private tour with the head gardener (£50). If you really want to educate your palate, tutored tea-tasting days (£175) are held throughout the year.

---

only in name. Traces of Truro's wealthy heritage remain in the smart Georgian townhouses and Victorian villas dotted around the city – especially along Strangways Terrace, Walsingham Place and Lemon St.

ESSENTIAL INFORMATION

TOURIST INFORMATION // Truro tourist office (☎ 01872-274555; tic@truro.gov.uk; Boscawen St; 🕑 9am-5.30pm Mon-Fri, 9am-5pm Sat)

EXPLORING TRURO

🌿 TRURO CATHEDRAL // CORNWALL'S ECCLESIASTICAL LANDMARK

Plonked like a neo-Gothic supertanker in the heart of town, **Truro Cathedral** (☎ 01872-276782; www.trurocathedral.org.uk; High Cross; suggested donation £4) dominates the city skyline from every angle. Built on the site of the 16th-century parish church of St Mary's (part of which now forms the cathedral's South Aisle), the cathedral was a massive technical undertaking for its architect John Loughborough Pearson. The foundation stones were laid in 1880 but the building wasn't completed until 1910 – the first new cathedral to be built in Britain since St Paul's. The

cathedral's copper-topped central tower reaches 76m, while the shorter western spires are 61m.

🌿 ROYAL CORNWALL MUSEUM // FROM STONE AGE TOOLS TO STANHOPE FORBES

The **Royal Cornwall Museum** (☎ 01872-272205; www.royalcornwallmuseum.org.uk; River St; admission free; 🕑 10am-5pm Mon-Sat) is Cornwall's oldest museum, and houses a varied range of exhibits covering the county's archaeological and historical past. Downstairs, the Rashleigh Gallery contains over 16,000 rare mineralogical specimens, while upstairs in the Treffry Gallery you'll find paintings by Stanhope Forbes and other Newlyn School artists alongside a small selection of old masters such as Rubens, Blake, Turner, Gainsborough and Van Dyck.

🌿 TO MARKET, TO MARKET // SHOP FOR FARM-FRESH AND FAIRTRADE

Although the city centre is largely dominated by high-street chains, it's worth having a wander around the revamped **Lemon St Market** (www.lemonstreetmarket.co.uk), where there's a deli, baker, herb seller, cafe and Fairtrade shop on the ground floor, and a smart gallery-cafe on the upper level.

CORNWALL

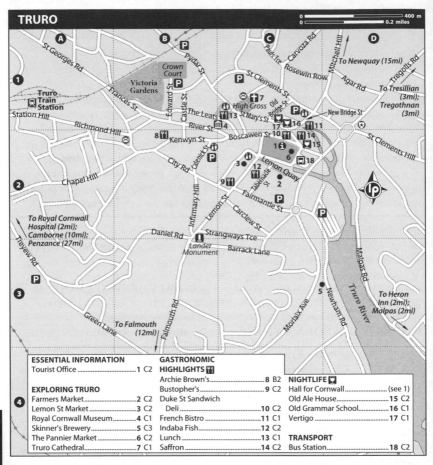

TRURO

0 ——— 400 m
0 ——— 0.2 miles

Overhead, look out for withy sculptures built for the City of Lights parade.

Local butchers, bakers, cheesemakers and veg-growers set up shop at Truro's lively **Farmers Market** (www.trurofarmers market.co.uk; 9am-4pm) on nearby Lemon Quay from Wednesday to Saturday.

♨ MALPAS // CRUISING ON THE RIVER

Two miles downriver from the city, past the green expanse of Boscawen Park, is the riverside hamlet of **Malpas**, from where ferries run by **Enterprise**

Boats (☎ 01326-374241; www.enterprise-boats. co.uk) chug out along the wooded banks of the River Fal all the way to Falmouth, sometimes stopping at Trelissick (p233) en route. Free double-deckers run from the Truro harbourmaster's office to the pontoon at Malpas, although depending on the tides you can often ride the boat all the way back to Truro.

FESTIVALS & EVENTS

City of Lights (www.trurocityoflights.co.uk) Giant withy lanterns are carried through the city centre during this December street parade.

CORNWALL

GASTRONOMIC HIGHLIGHTS

❦ BUSTOPHER'S ££

☎ 01872-279029; www.bustophersbarbistro.com; 62 Lemon St; mains £10-18; ☺ lunch & dinner

This Lemon St establishment has had a full refit, and it's now ideal for a swift, stylish bite. The interior's been lightened up with wood, chrome and an open kitchen, and the menu offers quality bistro food, including a different daily *plat du jour*. Businessy types cram in for lunchtime, and it gets busy at weekends.

❦ THE FRENCH BISTRO ££

☎ 01872-223068; www.thefrenchbistro.co.uk; 19 New Bridge St; lunch £5-8, mains £10-13; ☺ lunch & dinner Thu-Sat

A *soupçon* of Gallic flair comes to Truro courtesy of Karen Cairns, who is passionate about the flavours of classical French cooking. Old lamps, glossy chairs and velvet seats conjure a decadent feel matched by the French cuisine – shame it's only open three days a week. Wine is BYO; corkage is £3.

❦ INDABA FISH ££

☎ 01872-274700; www.indabafish.co.uk; Tabernacle St; mains £10.15-20, 2-person seafood platter £97.50; ☺ dinner

Stein-trained Rick Taylor has turned this metro-modern diner into the city's best address for seafood, from Falmouth oysters and dressed crab to Newlyn lobster picked straight from the tank. Plate glass, banquette seats and overhead pipes give things an urbane big-city feel.

❦ SAFFRON ££

☎ 01872-263771; www.saffronrestauranttruro.co.uk; 5 Quay St; mains £10-16.50; ☺ lunch Mon-Fri, dinner Tue-Sat

For ages this pint-sized restaurant was the only decent place to eat in town, and it's still a favourite. Tightly packed pine tables and sunny yellow tones make for a cosy dining space, and the seasonally inspired menu is a treat of Cornish ingredients spiced with Spanish, Italian and French flavours: mutton with turnip dauphinoise, or seared pollack with saffron mash.

ALSO RECOMMENDED

Some attractive cafes in Truro:

Archie Brown's (☎ 01872-278622; www.archiebrowns.co.uk; 105-106 Kenwyn St; dishes £2.50-8; ☺ 9am-5pm Mon-Sat) Truro outpost of Penzance's much-loved wholefood cafe.

Duke St Sandwich Deli (☎ 01872-320025; 10 Duke St; sandwiches £2.50-5; ☺ 9am-5.30pm Mon-Sat) Build your own sandwich from Cornish ingredients.

Lunch (☎ 01872-275252; The Leats; ☺ 9am-4pm Mon-Sat) Tiny, tucked-away sandwich stop.

NIGHTLIFE

❦ HALL FOR CORNWALL

☎ 01872-262466; www.hallforcornwall.co.uk; Lemon Quay

The county's main venue for touring theatre and music, housed in Truro's former town hall on Lemon Quay.

❦ THE HERON INN

☎ 01872-272773; www.heroninn.co.uk; Malpas; ☺ 11am-3pm & 6-10.30pm Mon-Thu, 11am-11pm Fri & Sat, noon-10.30pm Sun

Two miles from the city along the river estuary, this creekside pub serves good beer and grub, with outside benches where you can sup your pint.

❦ OLD ALE HOUSE

☎ 01872-271122; Quay St

One of the last pubs in Truro to retain its traditional spit-and-sawdust skin, burnished wood, beer mats and all. Guest ales are chalked on blackboards, and there are live gigs at weekends.

CORNWALL

❦ OLD GRAMMAR SCHOOL

☎ 01872-278559; www.theoldgrammarschool.com; 19 St Mary's St; ☾ 10am-late

Cool and contemporary city bar, offering open-plan drinking with big tables and soft sofas to sink into. Lunch is served from noon to 3pm; later it's cocktails, candles and imported Belgian and Japanese beers.

❦ VERTIGO

☎ 01872-276555; www.vertigo-truro.co.uk; 15 St Mary's St

Another of the buzzy bars around St Mary's St and Bridge St; the real selling point at Vertigo is the quirky decor and delightful walled patio garden.

TRANSPORT

BUS // Truro is the county's main transport hub, with connections to most destinations in Cornwall. The most useful services include bus 88 to Falmouth, 14 to St Ives, 18 to Penzance and bus 89/90 to Newquay.

TRAIN // Truro is on the London Paddington–Penzance line (sample fares £3.30 to Redruth, £5.40 to Penzance & St Ives, £41.50 to £61.50 to London), and the smaller branch line to Penryn and Falmouth (£3.20).

DRIVING TOUR: THE ROSELAND PENINSULA

Map: p239
Distance: 40km to 60km, depending on route
Duration: 1 day

South of Truro, the mudflats and tidal estuaries of the River Fal seep into the deep water of the Carrick Roads, dividing the quiet parishes of Mylor and Feock from the Roseland Peninsula. The name derives from the Cornish word *ros,* meaning promontory: it's a lovely, quiet corner of the county, carpeted with arable fields, country lanes and little-visited inlets.

Start out at **Trelissick** (**1**, p233) and catch the historic **King Harry Ferry** (**2**, ☎ 01872-862312/1916; www.kingharryscornwall. co.uk; car/pedestrian one way £5/free; ☾ every 20 min, 7.20am-9.20pm summer, 7.20am-7.20pm winter, from 9am Sun), which has been transporting passengers over to Philleigh for nigh on a century. Stop for tea at **Smuggler's Cottage** (**3**, ☾ 10.30am-8.30pm summer), recently overhauled by Tregothnan; it's a picture of tranquillity now, but in 1944 it was a major embarkation point for American troops setting sail for the D-Day landings. Continue along the B3289 to the churchyard of **St-Just-in-Roseland** (**4**), a jumble of wildflowers and overhanging yews tumbling down to a boat-filled creek.

Five miles further south brings you to the chichi harbour of **St Mawes** (**5**), where a curve of whitewashed cottages and impeccably kept gardens lead along the waterfront to clover-shaped **St Mawes Castle** (EH; ☎ 01326-270526; adult/child £4.20/2.10; ☾ 10am-6pm Jul & Aug, 10am-5pm Apr-Jun & Sep, 10am-4pm Oct & Fri-Mon Nov-Mar). Next it's time for an excellent pub lunch at the **Idle Rocks** (☎ 0800-005-3901; www.idlerocks. co.uk; St Mawes; mains £9.95-16) or the **Rising Sun** (☎ 01326-270233; www.risingsunstmawes. co.uk; St Mawes; mains £7-15).

From the St Mawes waterfront, catch the **Place Ferry** (☎ 01872-861910, 07791-283884; adult/child return £5.50/4; ☾ half-hourly 9.30am-4.30pm Easter-Oct) for a paddle on the beaches of **Little & Great Molunan**, or drive around the River Percuil to **St Anthony's Head** (**6**), crested by a candy-striped lighthouse and the remains of a WWII gun battery.

Further east is the fishing village of **Portscatho** (**7**) and the beaches of **Carne** and **Pendower** (**8**), which join together at low tide to form a huge sweep of sand. Further round the sheltered sweep of

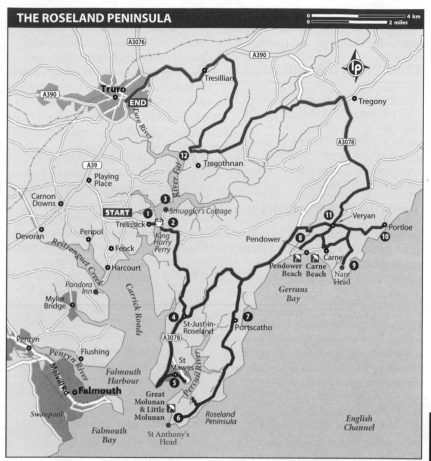

THE ROSELAND PENINSULA

0   4 km
0   2 miles

A3076

A390

Tresillian

Truro

END

Tregony

A390

A3078

A39

Playing Place

Tregothnan

Carnon Downs

START

Smuggler's Cottage

Trelissick

Veryan

Portloe

Penpol

King Harry Ferry

Pendower

Devoran

Feock

Harcourt

Pendower Beach

Carne Beach

Carne

Nare Head

Pandora Inn

Restronguet Creek

Carrick Roads

Mylor Bridge

Gerrans Bay

St-Just-in-Roseland

Portscatho

Penryn

Flushing

A3078

Falmouth Harbour

St Mawes

Pentryn

Penryn River

Mylor Rd

Falmouth

Great Molunan & Little Molunan

Roseland Peninsula

English Channel

Swanpool

Falmouth Bay

St Anthony's Head

Gerrans Bay there are some fine coastal walks around National Trust–owned **Nare Head (9)** before you reach the squeeze-guts streets of **Portloe (10)**, once a hugger-mugger haunt of pilchard boats, now frequented by designer yachts.

Inland is the village of **Veryan (11)**, set around a central green and duck pond, and famous for its twin roundhouses, whose lack of corners made them devil-proof. From here it's a 10-mile drive back to Truro, with a stop for treats at **Tregothnan (12, p239)**.

SOUTHEAST CORNWALL

· · · · · ·

East of the Roseland, Cornwall's south coast opens up through a string of beaches and ports that have long since swapped fishing gear for beach togs: Looe, Mevagissey and Polperro are among the most heavily touristed towns in Cornwall, although things are a touch more upmarket in Fowey. Further still brings you to the lovely Rame Peninsula, with some of Cornwall's least-explored countryside and a string of fabulous estates, including Antony, Mount Edgcumbe, Port Eliot and Cotehele.

ST AUSTELL & AROUND

The area's main town, St Austell, certainly isn't going to win any beauty contests, although it looks a bit more presentable thanks to the expensive redevelopment of its shopping centre. Nonetheless, it's not a place to linger, but it's a handy hub for the southeast coast.

EXPLORING ST AUSTELL & AROUND

❦ MEVAGISSEY // FISH FOR CRABS FROM A GRANITE QUAY

Flower-fronted cottages, salty pubs and a small fishing fleet shelter behind a double breakwater in **Mevagissey**, another of Cornwall's quintessential fishing ports. It won't take you long to exhaust the town's meandering alleys, but there are some intriguing beaches within easy reach, and the quay's a good spot for crab-lining. Beyond town, there's a popular holiday beach at **Pentewan**, and several tucked-away coves dotted around **Gorran Haven** and **Dodman Point**. In summer, **ferries** (adult/child return £10/5; ☉ May-Sep) run from Mevagissey Harbour to Fowey .

❦ LOST GARDENS OF HELIGAN // DISCOVER A REAL SECRET GARDEN

Before he embarked on his Eden adventure, Tim Smit's pet project was the **Lost Gardens of Heligan** (☎ 845100; www.heligan. com; Pentewan; adult/child £10/6; ☉ 10am-6pm Mar-Oct, 10am-5pm Nov-Feb). During the 19th century, Heligan was the family seat of the Tremayne family and one of Cornwall's great country gardens, but following the outbreak of WWI (where most of its staff were killed) the garden and house slid

into disrepair. Since the early 1990s, volunteers have slowly restored the garden to its former splendour, complete with a kitchen garden, fairy grotto and a 'Lost Valley' filled with palms and jungle plants.

Heligan is 1.5 miles from Mevagissey and 7 miles from St Austell. Western Greyhound's bus 526 runs regularly to Mevagissey, Gorran Haven and St Austell.

❦ CLAY COUNTRY // CYCLE THROUGH THE CORNISH ALPS

Alongside mining and fishing, Cornwall's other great industry was the extraction of 'white gold', otherwise known as china clay – a key component in everything from porcelain manufacture to medicines and paper coatings. The heartland of the industry was the St Austell claypits, where an otherworldly landscape of spoil heaps, mica dams and turquoise pools still looms dramatically on the horizon, earning them the nickname of the 'Cornish Alps'.

The best way to explore the area is along the **Clay Trails** (www.claytrails.co.uk), a network of off-road routes suitable for pedestrians, horse riders and cyclists. One route starts at the informative **China Clay Country Park** (☎ 01726-850362; www.wheal-martyn.com; adult/child £7.50/4.50; ☉ 10am-5pm) at Wheal Martyn and runs on to the Eden Project (p241); another travels north from Eden to Bugle.

❦ CHARLESTOWN // SHIPWRECK STORIES

Once a key port for shipping china clay from the St Austell quarries, Charlestown is now a favourite location for film crews: several big-budget blockbusters and costume dramas have used its quayside as a ready-made backdrop. The town's seagoing heritage is explored at the **Charlestown Shipwreck & Heritage Centre** (☎ 01726-69897; www.shipwreckcharles

town.com; adult/child £5.95/2.95; ⊙ 10am-5pm Mar-Oct), which houses a massive collection of objects and ephemera recovered from 150 global shipwrecks, ranging from telescopes, muskets, scrimshaw and coins to howitzer cannons and a few choice pieces from the *Titanic* and *Lusitania*.

❦ CAERHAYS CASTLE // A NATIONAL MAGNOLIA COLLECTION

West of Mevagissey overlooking the gentle crescent of Porthluney Beach is **Caerhays Castle** (☎ 01872-501310; www.caerhays.co.uk; gardens adult/child £7.50/3.50, incl house tour £12.50/6; ⊙ gardens 10am-5pm mid-Feb–May), a crenellated country mansion originally built for the Trevanions and later remodelled under the guidance of John Nash (who designed Buckingham Palace and Brighton Pavilion). The house is still a private residence, and is open for guided tours in spring, while the gardens are woth visiting for their wonderful displays of camellias, rhododendrons and magnolias.

❦ EDEN PROJECT // CORNWALL'S ECOLOGICAL CAUSE CÉLÈBRE

The space-age domes of the **Eden Project** (☎ 01726-811911; www.edenproject.com; Bodelva; adult/child £16/6; ⊙ 10am-6pm Apr-Oct, 10am-4.30pm Nov-Mar) scarcely need any introduction: since their opening in an abandoned clay pit in 2001, they've become one of Cornwall's most iconic sights.

The three giant greenhouses – the largest on earth – were dreamt up by former record producer Tim Smit, and recreate a stunning array of global habitats. Giant ferns, palms, banana trees, and delicate orchids fill the Humid Tropics Biome, while temperate plants such as cacti, lemon trees, vines, olive groves and aloes inhabit the Mediterranean Biome. Beyond the domes, 13 hectares of herbaceous borders, kitchen gardens and

wild flower beds radiate out from the Core, Eden's inspiring education centre (constructed according to the Fibonacci sequence, one of nature's most fundamental building blocks).

It's an amazing and hugely ambitious project that for once lives up to the hype. It's also a model of environmental sustainability – packaging is reused or recycled, power comes from sustainable sources or microgenerators, and rainwater is used to flush the loos. It's also worth visiting year-round: in summer, the biomes provide the backdrop for outdoor gigs at the **Eden Sessions** (www.edensessions.com); and in winter a full-size ice-rink springs up for the **Time of Gifts**.

Eden gets very busy; booking online allows you to dodge the queues and gets a £1 discount. It's three miles by road from St Austell. You can catch buses from St Austell, Newquay, Helston, Falmouth and Truro, but arriving on foot or by bike snags you £3 off the admission price.

❦ RESTORMEL CASTLE // CLIMB THE BATTLEMENTS OF A MEDIEVAL KEEP

High on a hilltop above Lostwithiel, the ruined castle of **Restormel** (☎ 01208-872687; adult/child £3.20/1.60; ⊙ 10am-6pm Jul & Aug, 10am-5pm Apr-Jun & Sep, 10am-4pm Oct) was built by Edward the Black Prince (the first Duke of Cornwall), although he only stayed there twice during his reign. It's one of the best-preserved circular keeps in the country, and affords brilliant views across the river and fields from its crenellated battlements.

GASTRONOMIC HIGHLIGHTS

This pocket of Cornwall isn't blessed with many stellar eateries, although the cafes at Eden and Heligan are both good for a quick lunch stop.

CORNWALL

THE CORNISH WAY

Spurred by the success of the Camel Trail, Cornwall is now covered by a series of bike trails known collectively as the **Cornish Way**. Jointly developed by Sustrans and Cornwall Council, the end-to-end route covers almost 200 miles from Bude to Land's End, but has been conveniently split up into several interlinked sections, each of which can be easily covered in a day's ride.

We've covered a few of the best sections in this book, including the **Clay Trails** (p239), the **Coast to Coast Trail** (p204), the **Camel Trail** (p194) and the **Great Flat Lode Trail** (p205), but there are lots more to discover.

For further information and useful route maps contact **Cornwall Council** (☎ 01872-222000; www.cornwall.gov.uk/default.aspx?page=13405) or **Sustrans** (☎ 0845 113 0065; www.sustrans.org.uk).

♥ FOUNTAIN INN // MEVAGISSEY £

☎ 01872-842320; St George's Sq; pub meals £5-8; ☺ lunch & dinner

Mevagissey doesn't seem to have caught Cornwall's culinary wave just yet, but who cares when you've got a pub this good? The oldest pub in town has two bars in original oak and slate, plus a smugglers' tunnel to the harbour. For sustenance, there are St Austell ales and a menu of beer-battered cod and curries.

♥ TREVALSA COURT // MEVAGISSEY ££

☎ 01726-842468; www.trevalsa-hotel.co.uk; 2-/3-course menu £26/30; ☺ dinner

Mevagissey's super hillside hotel has thrown open its doors to diners, and it's worth a peep even if you aren't staying the night. Mahogany panels contrast with puce seats and starchy tablecloths in the dining room, and the menu is especially good for fresh, unfussy fish, landed wherever possible on the Mevagissey quay.

TRANSPORT

BUS // Handy buses from St Austell are the 522 (hourly Monday to Saturday), 524 to Fowey (10 daily), 525 to Charlestown and Fowey (10 daily Monday to Saturday), 526 (hourly Monday to Saturday, four on Sunday) to Mevagissey, Heligan and Gorran Haven and 527 (hourly Monday to Saturday, six on Sunday) from Newquay to St Austell and the Eden Project.

TRAIN // St Austell is on the main London Paddington–Penzance line, with connections along the branch line to Par.

FOWEY, LOOE & THE RAME PENINSULA

Eastwards from St Austell Bay, the coastline zigzags through a pulse-quickening panorama of wooded creeks, fishing coves and secluded bays, passing through a string of harbour towns teetering right beside the water's edge. Fowey is best-known for its associations with thriller writer extraordinaire and ex-resident Daphne du Maurier, while nearby Polperro and Looe combine salty seagoing heritage with a breezy bucket-and-spade atmosphere. Beyond Looe, the coast meanders round in a lazy curve to the remote Rame Peninsula and its sprawling country estates.

EXPLORING FOWEY, LOOE & THE RAME PENINSULA

♥ FOWEY // DAPHNE DU MAURIER'S HOMETOWN

In many ways, Fowey feels rather like Padstow's south-coast sister; a workaday port turned well-heeled holiday town, with a trim tumble of pastel-coloured houses, portside pubs and tiered terraces overlooking the china-blue harbour. The town's wealth was largely founded on the export of china clay from the St Austell pits, but it's been an important port since Elizabethan times; Fowey was considered a key link in the chain of defences protecting the British mainland against Catholic invasion.

These days Fowey is a prim little place, with pricey yachts and upmarket brasseries sprinkled liberally along its barnacled quays. In the heart of town is the 15th-century **Church of St Finbarrus**, which marks the southern end of the **Saints' Way**, a 26-mile way-marked trail running all the way to Padstow. East of the church, the smart terrace of the Esplanade leads down to **Readymoney Cove** and the small Tudor fort of **St Catherine's Castle** (EH; admission free).

The town is at its busiest in mid-May, when it hosts the four-day **Daphne du Maurier Festival of Arts & Literature** (www.dumaurierfestival.co.uk) in honour of the writer, who lived for many years at nearby Menabilly Barton. There is also a small du Maurier display at the **Fowey tourist office** (☎ 01726-833616; www.fowey. co.uk; 5 South St).

From Fowey's quayside, a regular **foot ferry** (pedestrians & bikes £1) travels across to the neighbouring harbour at **Polruan**. A little further out of town the **Bodinnick Ferry** (car/pedestrian £2.20/1; ☺ last ferry 8.45pm Apr-Oct, 7pm Nov-Mar) carries cars and bikes across the estuary, cutting miles off the onward journey to Looe. If you're on foot, Bodinnick also marks the start of the lovely **Hall Walk**, a scenic 4-mile jaunt that circles round the headland back to Polruan.

❦ KAYAKING // UP THE CREEK WITH A PADDLE

It's thought that Kenneth Grahame first got the inspiration for his classic children's novel *The Wind in the Willows* while wandering around Fowey's quiet creeks, so messing about on the river is a must. **Fowey River Expeditions** (☎ 01726-833627; www.foweyexpeditions.co.uk; 17 Passage St; per person £24) runs guided kayak trips along the River Fowey to the waterside hamlets of Golant and Lerryn; if you're lucky you might spy herons, cormorants and the odd kingfisher en route. Experienced paddlers can hire their own canoes (per half-/full day £18/22).

❦ COASTAL SIGHTSEEING // SEEK OUT SOME ULTRA-SECLUDED BEACHES

There are several little-known beaches strung along the coastline towards Looe, but they can be tricky to find without a decent map. **Lansallos** is a small patch of sand and shingle reached by a half-mile trail from Lansallos village. There's more space on **Lantic Bay**, a soft-sand cove reached via a steep cliff-path.

A little further along the coast is photogenic **Polperro**, once awash with pilchards and smuggled contraband, now swamped throughout the summer by coach parties and crimson-faced daytrippers. Unless you're here in the off-season, you're probably better off giving the village a miss and heading along the coast in search of clifftop solitude around **Talland Bay**.

❦ THE GOOD LIFE // BRUSH UP YOUR GREEN CREDENTIALS

The attempts of former lieutenant colonel Dick Strawbridge to transform a 300-year-old Cornish farmhouse into an ecohaven were documented in the BBC

CORNWALL

series *It's Not Easy Being Green*. Post–TV stardom, the Strawbridges now offer courses in everything from making your own household cleaners to building your own biodiesel reactor. Courses take place chez Strawbridge at **Newhouse Farm** (www.newhousefarm.tv) in Tywardreath, near Fowey.

❦ LOOE & LOOE ISLAND // SET SAIL FOR AN ISLAND NATURE RESERVE

In contrast to Fowey, Cornwall's culinary renaissance hasn't quite reached the twin towns of East and West Looe – chip shops and chintzy B&Bs still very much rule the roost roundabouts. Looe has been a thriving holiday town ever since one of the county's first bathing machines was installed around 1800 beside **Banjo Pier** (named for its circular shape). A couple of centuries on, the town beaches of **East Looe**, **Second Beach** and **Millendreath** are still bound to be crammed on hot summer days; things are usually a quieter across the river at **Hannafore Beach**, backed by grassy banks for picnics, and plenty of rock pools to delve in at low tide.

A mile offshore from Hannafore Point is the densely wooded **Looe Island** (often known as St George's Island), a 22-acre nature reserve and a haven for marine wildlife. The island has been inhabited since the early 12th century, when Benedictine monks established a chapel; it was subsequently a favourite stash for local smugglers (the island's main house was built by Customs officials to keep a watch for smuggled contraband). In 1965 the island was occupied by Surrey sisters Babs and Evelyn Atkins, who established the nature reserve and lived there for most of their lives. Since 2000 the island has been administered by the Cornwall Wildlife Trust, which continues to pro-

tect the island's delicate habitat by monitoring visitor numbers.

Between May and September, trips are offered by the **Islander** (adult/child £6/4, island landing fee £2.50/1) from the quayside near the lifeboat station, but they're dependent on the weather and tides. Check the blackboard on the quay for the next sailing times, or call skipper Tim on ☎07814-139223.

❦ MONKEY MAGIC // PRIMATE PROTECTION

On the hills above East Looe, the **Wild Futures Monkey Sanctuary** (☎01503-262532; www.monkeysanctuary.org; St Martins; adult/child £7.50/3.50; ☷11am-4.30pm Sun-Thu Easter-Sep) is home to a colony of ridiculously cute woolly monkeys, smaller colonies of capuchin monkeys, patas monkeys and Barbary macaques (mostly rescued from captivity) and a roost of rare lesser horseshoe bats. Tickets stay valid for a year.

❦ THE RAME PENINSULA // GIVE THE DAY-TRIPPERS THE SLIP

Flung out on Cornwall's eastern edge, the Rame Peninsula receives so few visitors it's often dubbed as 'Cornwall's forgotten corner'. Despite its proximity to Plymouth, which sits just across the River Tamar, and the regular ferry traffic from the Torpoint Ferry, the Rame Peninsula remains one of Cornwall's most unspoilt pockets, and it's a fine place to head when you want to give the crowds the slip.

The bulk of the peninsula is occupied by two magnificent country estates. The Grade I–listed **Mount Edgcumbe** (☎01752-822236; www.mountedgcumbe.gov.uk; adult/child £6/4; ☷11am-4.30pm Mar-Sep) encompasses 865 acres. Originally built for the Earls of Edgcumbe, it is now owned by

Cornwall and Plymouth City Councils. Mount Edgcumbe is thought to be one of Cornwall's earliest landscaped estates, and the country park is liberally sprinkled with follies, chapels, grottoes, pavilions and formal gardens. The house was built between 1547 and 1553, but was practically destroyed by German bombing in 1941. It's since been restored in lavish 18th-century style.

Only marginally less stunning is **Antony House** (NT; ☎ 01752-812191; antony@ nationaltrust.org.uk; adult/child 7.50/4.80; ☺ house noon-5pm Tue-Thu & Sun, gardens 11am-5pm Sun-Thu), still the family home of the Carew-Poles, although it now formally belongs to the National Trust. The house's main claims to fame are its Repton-designed gardens and truly outlandish topiary, recently interspersed with modern sculptures; fittingly, Antony House was chosen as the backdrop for Tim Burton's recent reimagining of *Alice in Wonderland*.

Also worth a detour are the button-cute villages of **Kingsand** and **Cawsand**, which once sat on either side of the Devon–Cornwall border; the blowy paths around **Rame Head**; and the impressive 3-mile expanse of sand at **Whitsand Bay**.

☙ COTEHELE // TUDOR SPLENDOUR ON THE TAMAR

At the head of the Tamar Valley sits the Tudor manor of **Cotehele** (NT; ☎ 01579-351346; St Dominick; adult/child £8.70/4.35, garden & mill only £5.20/2.60; ☺ 11am-4.30pm Sat-Thu Apr-Oct), another of the Edgcumbe dynasty's modest country retreats. The cavernous great hall is the centrepiece, and the house has an unparalleled collection of Tudor tapestries, armour and furniture. Outside, the gardens sweep down past the 18th-century **Prospect Folly** to **Cotehele Quay**, where there's a discovery centre exploring the history of the Tamar Valley and a vintage sailing barge, the *Shamrock*.

A short walk inland (or a shuttle bus) leads to the restored **Cotehele Mill**, where you can watch the original waterwheel grinding corn, and watch a furniture maker and potter at work.

∼ WORTH A TRIP ∼

Stretching across the far eastern end of Cornwall is yet another huge estate, **Port Eliot** (☎ 01503-230211; www.porteliot.co.uk; house & grounds adult/child £7/free, grounds only £4/2; ☺ 2-6pm Sat-Thu Mar-Jun), the family seat of the Earl of St Germans. The 6000-acre estate has been off-limits to the public for many years, but since 2008 has opened its doors for 100 days every year. The highlight of the house is the amazing **Round Room**, whose walls are almost entirely covered by a characteristically Bacchanalian mural by the late Plymouth artist Rovert Lenkiewicz. Outside, the Grade I–listed estate was part improved by Humphrey Repton, and offers dramatic views towards the Tamar estuary.

Port Eliot has also become renowned for its annual outdoor bash, the **Port Eliot Festival** (www.porteliotfestival.com), which began life as a literary festival but has now branched out into live music, theatre and outdoor art. The festival takes place in late July.

Occasional trains from Plymouth stop at the tiny station of **St Germans**; otherwise, you'll need your own transport to get to the estate. The vehicle entrance is along the B3249, about 9 miles east of Looe.

CORNWALL

GASTRONOMIC HIGHLIGHTS

❦ COUCH'S // POLPERRO £££

☎ 01503-272554; Saxon Bridge; 3-/4-course menu £24.95/28.95; ☺ from 6.15pm Mon-Sat, from 4.30pm Sun

Richard McGeown's mentors include Gordon Ramsay, Raymond Blanc and Marco-Pierre White, so his style's all about Michelinesque *amuse-gueules*, poached truffle eggs and beef carpaccio. His restaurant is bang in the middle of Polperro, but the rustic-chic decor and slightly fusty atmosphere feel weirdly out of sync with the rest of the village.

❦ FINNYGOOK INN // CRAFTHOLE ££

☎ 01503-230338; www.finnygook.co.uk; mains £10.25-19.50 ☺ lunch & dinner

Crafthole's venerable coaching inn has been spruced up, but for once the character hasn't been stripped out. There are still plenty of log fires, heavy beams and comfy sofas, but the menu's been upgraded to gastro status with steamed Fowey mussels, Doom Bar–battered haddock and platters of cheeses, meats and seafood. Ask behind the bar if you're wondering about the name – it's a very long story.

❦ PINKY MURPHY'S CAFÉ // FOWEY £

☎ 01726-832512; www.pinkymurphys.com; 19 North St; dishes £2.75-8.95; ☺ 9am-5pm Mon-Sat, 9.30am-4pm Sun

Cafes don't come much more characterful than this oddbod establishment, where mismatching crockery is a virtue and seating ranges from tie-dyed beanbags to patched-up sofas. Ciabattas, panini and generous platters are washed down with Pinky's Cream Tease, mugs of Horlicks and fresh-brewed smoothies.

❦ SAM'S // FOWEY ££

☎ 01726-832273; www.samsfowey.co.uk; 20 Fore St; mains £5.95-13.95; ☺ lunch & dinner

Much recommended local's caff, like a cross between *Cheers* and a backstreet French bistro. Squeeze into a booth, sink a beer and tuck into mussels, calamari rings or stacked-up Samburgers. New space has recently been added upstairs, but bookings aren't taken; if it's full, there's **Sam's on the Beach** (☎ 01726-812255) on Polkerris Beach.

❦ THE VIEW // TORPOINT ££

☎ 01752-822345; www.theview-restaurant.co.uk; Treninnow Cliff Rd, Millbrook; mains £10.50-17.50; ☺ lunch & dinner

The name says it all. Matt Corner's stellar restaurant sits in a stunning position on the cliffs above Whitsand Bay, and has some heavyweight admirers in the foodie world. It's a treat, especially for classic, unfussy seafood, meat and game, stripped back to highlight the essential flavours. We really love this place. You will too.

ALSO RECOMMENDED

The little villages along the Fowey River have several fine pubs worthy of a pint stop:

Old Ferry (☎ 01726-870237; www.oldferryinn.co.uk; Bodinnick) Beside the Bodinnick slipway.
Russell Inn (☎ 01726-870292; Polruan)
Ship Inn (☎ 01208-872374; www.theshipinnlerryn.co.uk; Lerryn).

TRANSPORT

BUS // Bus 573 (hourly Monday to Saturday) runs between Liskeard, Looe and Polperro, while the 572 shuttles between East and West Looe to Plymouth via St Germans and Tideford. The 581 links Liskeard and the Torpoint Ferry, stopping at Portwrinkle, Crafthole and Antony.

TRAIN // The scenic Looe Valley Line trundles along the gorgeous stretch to Liskeard (day ranger adult/child £3.40/1.70, every two hours) on the London–Penzance line. Occasional trains from Plymouth stop at the tiny station in St Germans (£3.30) for Port Eliot.

ALL ABOARD!

For a vision of Cornwall as Betjeman might have seen it, clamber aboard the **Bodmin & Wenford Railway** (☎ 0845 125 9678; www.bodminandwenfordrailway.co.uk; rover pass adult/child £11.50/6), a vintage steam train that's been rescued by enthusiasts and runs along the old standard-gauge tracks between Bodmin Parkway, Bodmin General and Boscarne Junction.

The trains are still decked out in their 1950s livery, and the clattering carriages and chuffing engines can't fail to make you nostalgic for the days when train travel was more than a matter of simply getting from A to B. For the full-blown experience, book in for one of the regular Dining Trains or, better still, don your glad rags for a Murder Mystery or James Bond outing. See the website for forthcoming dates.

DRIVING TOUR: BODMIN MOOR

Map p248
Distance: 30 to 40 miles, depending on route
Duration: 1 day

Hugging the edge of the Devon border, the stark, barren expanse of Bodmin Moor is the county's wildest, weirdest landscape. Pockmarked by bogs and treeless heaths, Cornwall's 'roof' is often overlooked by visitors, but it's well worth taking the time to explore; lofty peaks loom on the horizon, stone circles are scattered across the hills, and ancient churches nestle at the foot of granite tors. It's also home to Cornwall's highest peaks – Rough Tor (pronounced row-tor; 400m) and Brown Willy (419m) – as well as the infamous Beast of Bodmin Moor, a black catlike creature that's been seen for many years but has still not been conclusively captured on camera.

The moor can be easily covered in a day's drive. Begin in **Bodmin (1)**, one of Cornwall's four stannary towns and, until the 1980s, the site of the county's crown court. Until the late 19th century, convicted criminals were banged up before their execution at **Bodmin Jail** (☎ 01208-76292; www.bodminjail.org; adult/child £6/3.75; ☜ 10am-dusk) and, though much of

the prison has fallen into ruin, you can still wander around several cells and the eerie hanging pit, supposedly haunted by a host of restless spooks.

Detour west to sample the vintages at the **Camel Valley Vineyard** (2, ☎ 01208-77959; www.camelvalley.com; ☜ 10am-5pm Mon-Sat), which produces world-class whites and a much lauded sparkling wine, before picking up the A30 past glassy **Colliford Lake (3)** and **Dozmary Pool (4)**, where King Arthur's sword, Excalibur, was supposedly thrown by Sir Bedivere after Arthur's death.

Near Bolventor, Daphne du Maurier conceived her classic adventure story at the **Jamaica Inn** (5, ☎ 01566-86250; www.jamaicainn.co.uk) after becoming lost during an impromptu horseriding trip; the story was apparently inspired by the spooky tales and smuggling yarns with which she was regaled by the local parson from Altarnun Church. The inn now houses a small museum of smuggling, although sadly much of its period character has been swept away since du Maurier's day.

Stop for a quick pint and a bite in **Altarnun (6)** at the **Rising Sun** (☎ 01566-86636; www.therisingsuninn.co.uk; mains £5.95-18.95; ☜ lunch & dinner) before swinging south along the B3257 and the B3254 to little **Minions (7)**. Nearby are two of the moor's major prehistoric monuments: the **Hurlers (8)**,

CORNWALL

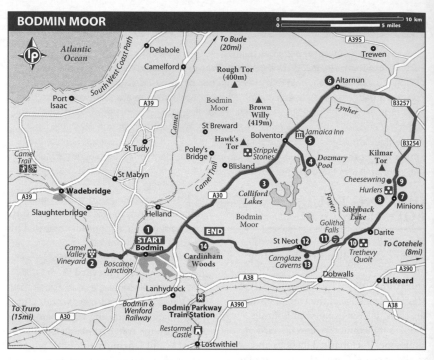

two stone circles said to be the remains of men turned to stone for hurling on a Sunday; and the **Cheesewring (9)**, a bizarre pillar of stones caused by natural erosion. Three miles south, near Darite, is **Trethevy Quoit (10)**, one of Cornwall's most striking Neolithic burial chambers, standing almost 15ft high.

Further west are the **Golitha Falls (11)**, a renowned beauty spot surrounded by the remains of the vast oak woodland which once covered much of the moor. Nearby, the parish church of **St Neot (12)** is blessed with fabulous medieval stained glass, while subterranean caves and underground pools can be seen in the old slate mine at **Carnglaze Caverns (13, ☎ 01579-320251; www.carnglaze. com; adult/child £6/4; ⏲ 10am-5pm)**

If time allows, finish up with a walk around the forested trails of **Cardinham**

Woods (14, ☎ 01208-72577; www.forestry.gov.uk/ cardinham), much favoured by mountain-bikers and horse riders.

ISLES OF SCILLY

Sprinkled across the Atlantic Ocean 28 miles southwest of Land's End, the Isles of Scilly offer a taste of what life must have been like in England a century ago. Rush-hour traffic, trilling telephones and summertime roadworks seem like a distant memory as soon as you set foot on this miniature archipelago of 140 tiny islands, only five of which are inhabited.

On Scilly the nearest thing to noise pollution is the screech of seagulls and the crash of waves breaking on the shore; it's a place where the accumulated hum of the outside world is left behind

~ WORTH A TRIP ~

Two-and-a-half miles from Bodmin, the 16th-century manor of **Lanhydrock** (NT; ☎ 01208-73320; adult/child £9.90/4.90, gardens only £5.80/3.10; ☺ house 11am-5pm Tue-Sun Mar-Oct, gardens 10am-6pm year-round) offers a fascinating insight into *Upstairs, Downstairs* life in Victorian England.

The house was originally built for the aristocratic Robartes clan, and still feels very much like a family home. Highlights include the gentlemen's smoking room (lined with old Etonian photos, moose heads and tiger-skin rugs); the children's nursery, movingly strewn with abandoned toys belonging to the Robartes children; and the original kitchens with their huge ovens and pioneering water-cooled cold store. There's also a fabulous plaster ceiling in the Long Gallery, which somehow managed to escape a huge fire in 1881 that gutted the rest of the house.

and life is dictated by the whims of the weather and the tide. Peak season on Scilly is from May to September, when you'll find most of the B&Bs and hotels are fully booked weeks ahead, while many businesses simply shut down in winter. Even the main island of St Mary's, which welcomes the vast majority of the islands' visitors, is hardly a bustling metropolis, while the smaller islands of Tresco, Bryher, St Martin's and St Agnes are home to just a few hardy castaways. Whether it's solitary walks, empty beaches or clear water you're looking for, Scilly certainly won't disappoint – just don't expect to get back on that chopper any time soon.

ESSENTIAL INFORMATION

EMERGENCIES // **Hospital** (☎ 01720-422392; ☺ 24hr) **Police station** (Garrison Lane, Hugh Town, St Mary's; ☺ 9am-10pm)

TOURIST INFORMATION // **Isles of Scilly tourist office** (☎ 01720-422536; tic@scilly.gov.uk; Hugh Town, St Mary's; ☺ 8.30am-6pm Mon-Fri, 9am-5pm Sat, 9am-2pm Sun, shorter hours in winter) is the islands' only tourist office. **Radio Scilly** (107.9FM; www.radioscilly.com) is the islands' very own FM station. **Scilly Online** (www.scillyonline.co.uk) is a locally run website with lots of info on the islands. **Simply Scilly** (www.simplyscilly.co.uk) is the official tourist site.

TRANSPORT

AIR // There are two ways to get to Scilly by air – chopper and plane – but neither's cheap. Helicopter flights are provided by **British International** (☎ 01736-363871; www.islesofscillyhelicopter.com), which flies to St Mary's and Tresco from Penzance heliport. Full return fares are adult/child £175/105. Saver fares (for travel Monday to Friday) and Daytrip fares are much cheaper. Planes are run by **Isles of Scilly Skybus** (☎ 0845 710 5555; www.ios-travel.co.uk), which offers several daily flights from Land's End (adult/child return £140/89.25) and Newquay (£165/100.25), plus at least one from Exeter, Bristol and Southampton daily in summer. Cheaper Saver fares are available for flights leaving Land's End after 2pm or St Mary's before 11am.

BIKE // Bikes are an ideal way of getting round the island of St Mary's; contact **St Mary's Bike Hire** (☎ 01720-422289; The Strand, High Town; bike hire per day around £10).

BOAT // The cheapest way to reach the islands is the **Scillonian Ferry** (☎ 0845 710 5555; www.ios-travel.co.uk; ☺ Mar-Oct), which plies the choppy waters between Penzance and St Mary's (adult/child return £95/47.50). There's at least one daily crossing in summer (except on Sunday), dropping to four a week in the shoulder months. For boats around the islands, see p251.

BUS // The only bus services are on St Mary's. The airport bus (£3) departs from Hugh Town 40 minutes before each flight, while the **Island Rover** (☎ 01720-422131; www.islandrover.co.uk; per person £7), offers a twice-daily sightseeing trip in a vintage bus in summer.

CORNWALL

TAXI // For taxis, try **Island Taxis** (☎ 01720-22126), **Scilly Cabs** (☎ 01720-422901) or **St Mary's Taxis** (☎ 01720-422555).

ST MARY'S

First stop on Scilly (unless you're in charge of your own private yacht) is St Mary's, the largest and busiest of the islands, and home to the vast majority of hotels, shops, restaurants and B&Bs. Just over 3 miles at its widest point, St Mary's is shaped like a crooked circle, with a claw-shaped peninsula at its southwestern edge – home to the island's capital,

Hugh Town, and the docking point for the *Scillonian* ferry. The main airport is a mile east near Old Town.

EXPLORING ST MARY'S

❦ **TOWNS & BEACHES //** EXPLORE THE ISLAND'S MAIN LANDMARKS
Most of the action on St Mary's centres on **Hugh Town**, which sits on a low-lying sliver of land between the main island and the old **Garrison**. By Scilly standards, it's positively hectic souvenir shops and cafes line the main thoroughfares of the Strand and Hugh St, while

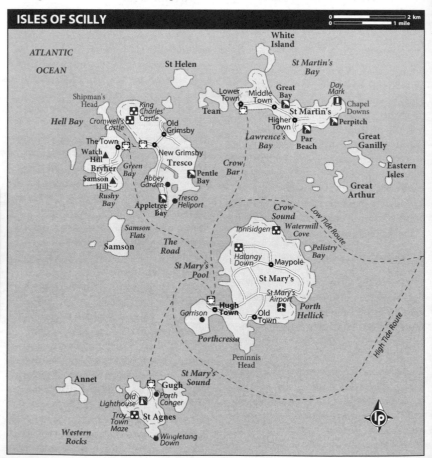

ISLES OF SCILLY

trippers dip their toes off **Town Beach** and **Porthcressa**.

A mile east of Hugh Town, reached via the coast path around **Peninnis Head**, is the island's former harbour at **Old Town**, home to a few small cafes, a village pub, a working pottery and a pleasant beach. The graveyard of the nearby church contains a memorial to Augustus Smith, founder of the Abbey Garden, as well as the grave of former prime minister Harold Wilson, who often holidayed on the Scillys.

There are lots of small inlets scattered around the island's coastline, best reached on foot or by bike, including **Porth Hellick**, **Watermill Cove** and the relatively remote **Pelistry Bay**. St Mary's also has several ancient sites, notably the small Iron Age village at **Halangy Down**, a mile north of Hugh Town.

❦ BOAT TRIPS // CATCH A LIFT WITH SCILLY'S COMMUTER SERVICE

The **St Mary's Boatmen's Association** (☎ 01720-423999; www.scillyboating.co.uk; adult/child return £7.80/3.90) runs regular day trips and ferry services to the off islands, usually leaving in the early morning and returning in late afternoon. You don't need to book, but make sure you label your luggage clearly so it can be deposited at the right harbour. It also offers fishing, sightseeing and wildlife excursions; details of forthcoming trips are chalked up on the blackboards beside the quay and at the tourist office.

Island Sea Safaris (☎ 01720-422732; www.scillyonline.co.uk/seasafaris.html) explores the islands at a racier pace, with speedboat rides (adult/child £30/20) and snorkelling trips (£35) to local seabird and seal colonies.

The traditional sport of **gig racing** is still popular on Scilly. These six-oared wooden boats were originally used to race out to rescue foundering ships, but these days gig racing is a highly competitive sport. Races are held most weekends, and every April or May St Mary's hosts the **World Pilot Gig Championships**, which attracts teams from as far away as Holland and the USA.

❦ WILD WALKS // ORNITHOLOGY AND ARCHAEOLOGY

St Mary's is a good place to get acquainted with Scilly's rich wildlife. Local boy Will Wagstaff is a mine of natural information and runs entertaining **Island Wildlife Tours** (☎ 01720-422212; www.

CAMPING & SELF-CATERING ON SCILLY

There are loads of self-catering cottages available on Scilly – contact the tourist office for full listings, or call **Island Properties** (☎ 422082; St Mary's) or **Sibley's Island Homes** (☎ 01720-422431; sibleys@scilly.fsnet.co.uk).

All the main islands, except Tresco, have at least one campsite, but you'll need to book well ahead in season. Rates quoted are for two people and a tent.

★ **Garrison Campsite** (☎ 01720-422670; www.garrisonholidays.com/camping.html; St Mary's; sites £14.50-19.50; ☺ Mar-Oct)

★ **St Martin's Campsite** (☎ 01720-422888; www.stmartinscampsite.co.uk; St Martin's; sites £16-20; ☺ mid-Mar–Oct)

★ **Troytown Farm** (☎ 01720-422360; www.troytown.co.uk; St Agnes; sites £16-25; ☺ Mar-Sep)

★ **Bryher Campsite** (☎ 01720-422886; www.bryhercampsite.co.uk; Bryher; sites from £19; ☺ Apr-Sep)

islandwildlifetours.co.uk; per person £10; ☺ Apr-Oct) in search of butterflies, birds, mammals and marine animals.

Katharine Sawyer takes a more academic slant; her three-hour **Scilly Walks** (www.scillywalks.co.uk; adult/child £5/2.50) focus mainly on Scilly's seagoing history and archaeological remains.

☙ ISLES OF SCILLY MUSEUM // A TREASURE TROVE OF SCILLY MEMORABILIA

The islands' main repository of knowledge, Hugh Town's **museum** (☎ 01720-422337; Church St; adult/child £3.50/1; ☺ 10am-4.30pm Mon-Fri, 10am-noon Sat winter) contains an eclectic muddle of stuffed birds, Bronze Age artefacts and shipwreck booty (including muskets, a cannon and a ship's bell).

GASTRONOMIC HIGHLIGHTS

☙ JULIET'S GARDEN RESTAURANT ££

☎ 01720-422228; www.julietsgardenrestaurant. co.uk; lunch £4-10, mains £12-16; ☺ 10am-5pm daily, 6pm-late Wed-Sun

Fifteen minutes' walk from Hugh Town, this old barn on Seaways Farm began life as a tiny tearoom but has blossomed into the best place to eat on St Mary's: light lunches by day, candlelit fare by night, all treated with loving care and attention. The addition of the new Balcony Room has maximised the fine harbour views.

TRESCO

A short boat hop across the channel from St Mary's brings you to Tresco, the second-largest island, once owned by the monks of Tavistock Abbey, now leased by locals from the Duchy of Cornwall. It's a proper old-fashioned island getaway – for decades there was just one pub and one hotel on the island, although the recent arrival of the Flying Boat Club has brought a dash of razzle-dazzle to this tiny corner of Scilly.

☙ ABBEY GARDEN // TRESCO'S ANSWER TO THE EDEN PROJECT

One of Scilly's great attractions is this subtropical **estate** (☎ 01720-424105; www.tresco. co.uk/see/abbey-garden; adult/child £10/5; ☺ 10am-4pm), first laid out in 1834 on the site of a 12th-century Benedictine priory by the horticultural visionary Augustus Smith. The gardens are now home to over 20,000 exotic species, from towering palms to desert cacti and crimson flame trees, all nurtured by the temperate gusts of the Gulf Stream. Admission also covers the **Valhalla collection**, made up of figureheads and nameplates salvaged from the many ships that have foundered off Tresco's shores.

☙ BEACHES & FORTS // BACKCOUNTRY TRESCO

Around the edge of the island are several well-hidden beaches, including the sand-and-shell beach of **Appletree Bay**, and the more grandiose curve of sand at **Pentle Bay**. On the northwest side of the island are the ruins of two naval forts – **King Charles' Castle** was the first to be built in the 1550s, but was later superseded by the cannon tower of **Cromwell's Castle** nearby.

GASTRONOMIC HIGHLIGHTS

☙ NEW INN ££

☎ 01720-422222; mains £9-17.50; ☺ 10am-11pm The hub of the island's social scene, where locals and trippers alike pack onto the shady terrace of the Driftwood Bar for a refreshing pint of Skinner's or Scilly Ale accompanied by a hearty plate of beer-battered pollack or bangers and mash. Be warned though – the lack of competition means prices are far from cheap.

OTHER INHABITED ISLANDS

❤ BRYHER // SCILLY'S SMALLEST AND WILDEST INHABITED ISLAND

Just over 80 people live on the remote island of **Bryher**. Blanketed with heather and bracken, and spotted with miniature hills, it's a tough place to eke out an existence; fishing and flower-growing are about the island's only industries, and even those aren't what they once were.

Bryher's **town** is little more than a huddle of a couple of dozen houses dotted along the shore overlooking the deep anchorage of New Grimsby Channel, a favourite stop for visiting yachts. From the modest summit of **Samson Hill**, you can drink in one of the finest views in all of Scilly, with a fantastic panorama taking in most of the island chain.

Bryher's eastern side is exposed to the full force of the Atlantic weather, and the appropriately named **Hell Bay** makes for a powerful sight during a winter gale. Things are usually more tranquil to the south at **Rushy Bay** and on the east side at **Green Bay**.

From the quay, **Bryher Boats** (☎ 01720-422886) trundles across to deserted **Samson Island**, where a few ruined cottages are all that's left of the last island settlers who moved out in 1855. At low tide, the remains of ancient fields swamped during the last ice age become visible at **Samson Flats**.

❤ ST MARTIN'S // PIN-DROP QUIET AND PARADISICAL

The third-largest and furthest north of the islands, **St Martin's** is one of the main centres for Scilly's flower-growing industry, and the island's fields are a riot of colourful blooms in season. It's also blessed with gin-clear waters and the kind of untouched sands you'd more usually associate with St Lucia than Cornwall.

Par Beach is right next to the main quay, while on the island's southern shore is **Lawrence's Bay**, which reveals a broad sweep of sandy flats at low tide. Along the island's northern side are **Great** and **Little Bay**, arguably the finest beaches in Scilly; from the western end, you can cross to White Island at low tide.

The main settlement is Higher Town, where you'll find a small village shop and **Scilly Diving** (☎ 01720-422848; www.scilly diving.com), which offers snorkelling and diving trips in the chilly waters around St Martin's.

Rather improbably, the island is also home to Britain's most southwesterly (and certainly the smallest) winemaker, **St Martin's Vineyard** (☎ 01720-423418; www. stmartinsvineyard.co.uk). Tours of the vineyard, which began as a holiday hobby for owners Val and Graham Thomas, are

CORNWALL

THE UNINHABITED ISLANDS

Still not left the outside world behind enough? Don't fret – **St Agnes Boating** (☎ 422704; www.st-agnes-boating.co.uk) offers day trips (around £15) to the most remote corners of Scilly, including the little-visited beaches of the **Eastern Isles**, the ruined church on **St Helen's**, the many shipwreck spots around the **Western Rocks**, and the famous **Bishops Rock Lighthouse**, a marvel of 19th-century engineering raised on a narrow sliver of rock barely 46m long by 16m wide.

offered from 11am to 4pm on weekdays throughout the summer.

For beers and ales, there's the island's Brobdingnagian boozer, the **Seven Stones** (☎ 01720-423560; www.sevenstonesinn. co.uk), named after the notorious offshore reef where the oil tanker *Torrey Canyon* came aground in 1967, causing one of Britain's worst oil spills.

🐾 ST AGNES // PEACEFUL COVES AND RUGGED REEFS

Even by Scilly standards, the rocky island of **St Agnes** is quiet; when the last day boats have departed for St Mary's, the island is all but deserted. The most southerly of the Scilly Isles, St Agnes is studded with peaceful coves, rugged reefs and a scattering of prehistoric sites, and it's a place many visitors never quite manage to reach.

The main quay is at **Porth Conger**, near the decommissioned **Old Lighthouse**, from where the road leads to two lovely inlets at Periglis Cove and St Warna's Cove, named after the patron saint of shipwrecks. The coast path between the coves passes the tiny **Troy Town Maze**, a concentric maze of stones that's thought to be around two centuries old, but might be based on a prehistoric original.

The southern side of the island is mostly taken up by the bracken-strewn sweep of **Wingletang Down**, while on the east side the little beach of **Covean** is a handsome place to settle down for an afternoon sunbathe. At low tide a sandbar connects St Martin's with the small island of **Gugh** (pronounced goo), famous for its Bronze Age remains and the slanting menhir known as the **Old Man of Gugh**. Take care not to be cut off by the rising tide, which comes in fast and is too strong for swimming.

GASTRONOMIC HIGHLIGHTS

🐾 FRAGGLE ROCK // BRYHER £
☎ 01720-422222; ⏰ 10.30am-4.30pm & 7-11pm; 📶
This relaxed cafe also doubles as the island's pub. The menu's mainly pizzas, salads and burgers, and there are a few local ales on tap and Fairtrade coffees that help support the Cornwall Wildlife Trust.

🐾 LITTLE ARTHUR FARM // ST MARTIN'S £
☎ 01720-422457; www.littlearthur.co.uk; ⏰ 10.30am-4pm daily, 6.30-8.30pm Mon-Fri
If you're looking for a taste of what life really *should* be like, look no further than this wonderful wholefood cafe and sustainable farm just off Par Beach. All the produce is home-grown, from herbs and vegetables to ham, fruit and eggs – they even make their own shoes, for heaven's sake. Soups, sarnies and scones are cooked up daily, and there's a fish-and-chips night a couple of times a week.

🐾 ST MARTIN'S BAKERY // ST MARTIN'S £
☎ 01720-423444; www.stmartinsbakery.co.uk; ⏰ 9am-6pm Mon-Sat, 9am-2pm Sun
Toby Tobin-Dougan's minuscule bakery cooks up a tempting selection of rolls, pizzas, quiches and pastries, as well as Scilly's finest homemade pasties. He also runs baking courses in the off-season between January and April. See www.cookingholidays.co.uk for details.

🐾 TEAN RESTAURANT // ST MARTIN'S £££
☎ 01720-422090; www.stmartinshotel.co.uk; St Martin's on the Isle; 3 courses £39.50; ⏰ lunch & dinner

The island's pamper-pad hotel, St Martin's on the Isle, also has one of the islands' top fine-diners, the glossy Tean Restaurant, where venison, foie gras, squab pigeon and seabass all find their way onto the upmarket *carte*. The formal dress code feels surreal on laidback St Martin's.

❧ **TURK'S HEAD // ST AGNES £**
☎ 01720-422434; mains £7-12; ☽ lunch & dinner

Quite possibly our favourite pub in the entire country, Britain's most southerly alehouse is an absolute beaut. Model ships and seafaring photos line the walls, great pub food (swordfish, crab cakes, veggie chillis) is served up in the panelled bar, and you can carry your pint of homebrewed Turk's Head down to the slipway as the sun goes down. You might even be treated to a sea shanty if the lads are in the mood.

BACKGROUND

❧ HISTORY
From ancient stones to modern architecture, the southwest packs an astonishing amount of history into a tiny space. (p257)

❧ CORNWALL & THE ARTS
West Cornwall has been a hotbed of artistic creativity since the early 19th century. (p266)

❧ OUTDOORS
This vast adventure playground offers the ultimate great escape. It could spell the start of a new passion or the rediscovery of an old. (p271)

❧ GARDENS
Step back in time and explore the stories of some of the southwest's glorious land-scaped gardens. (p277)

❧ FOOD & DRINK
Famously a gourmet hot spot and celebrity-chef-packed zone, the southwest also leads the way in green, sustainable cuisine. (p281)

HISTORY

ANCIENT STONES

It's thought that humans have inhabited southwest England for more than 100,000 years, but the first evidence of human settlement is a jawbone dating from around 35,000 BC, unearthed in Kents Cavern (p144), near Torquay, during an excavation in 1927. (Academic opinion is still divided as to whether the bone belongs to a Neanderthal or prehistoric ancestors of *Homo sapiens*.) The earliest settlers were tribes of hunter-gatherers, living seasonally from the land and travelling in pursuit of game. The oldest complete skeleton ever discovered in Britain was found in Cheddar Gorge (p65) and dates from around 7150 BC.

The first signs of organised farming and animal domestication emerged around 4000 BC. Around this time prehistoric builders developed their taste for eye-catching architecture, and built many stone rings, menhirs, quoits and barrows across Devon, Dartmoor, Bodmin Moor, Penwith and the Isles of Scilly.

'Celtic society flourished in southwest Britain and developed its own culture, architecture and language'

By 1800 BC there was already a thriving trade in gold, tin, bronze and copper between southwest mines and many parts of Europe and the Mediterranean. This trade continued following the arrival of the Celts, who established themselves in southwest Britain from around 1000 BC.

The Celts quickly conquered much of the area, establishing themselves in hilltop forts and coastal strongholds such as Maiden Castle (p106), just outside Dorchester, and Ham Hill (p79) in Somerset. Over the next few centuries, Celtic society flourished in southwest Britain and developed its own culture, architecture and language, but by the 1st century BC, a new wave of invaders had landed and brushed all but the hardiest Celtic defenders aside. *Veni, vidi, vici* – the Romans had arrived.

ROMAN RULE & THE COMING OF THE KINGS

The first Roman landings in Britain were led by Julius Caesar in 55 BC. In AD 43 Aulus Plautius invaded Britain with around 20,000 troops, who were backed by

» TO 4000 BC	» 4000–1500 BC	» 1000–500 BC
The southwest is populated by tribes of nomadic hunter-gatherers.	First evidence of organised farming. Neolithic builders construct many dolmens, quoits, stone circles and menhirs.	Arrival of the first Celts on British shores. Celtic warriors establish hillforts and fortified settlements across the region, and gradually begin to integrate with native Britons.

BACKGROUND

reinforcements from the stuttering Emperor Claudius. Over the next five years, under the orders of their commander Vespasian, the legions rampaged through southern England.

Having wrested control of the area from the ruling Celtic tribes (the Durotriges in Dorset and Somerset, and the Dumnonii in Devon and Cornwall), the Romans set about building a network of roads, settlements, ports, temples and forts. A key garrison was stationed at Exeter (Isca Dumnoniorum to the Romans) that marked the western end of the Roman road to Lincoln known as the Fosse Way. Further north, the Romans founded the spa town of Aquae Sulis (present-day Bath) to take advantage of the area's natural hot springs.

The Romans' grip on power lasted until the 4th century, when rebellions from Pictish warriors in the north, combined with Saxon invasions from the east, placed increasing pressure on Rome's dwindling resources. By 410 the last legions had been withdrawn, and the 'Dark Ages' had begun.

Over the next 500 years, southwest Britain was invaded by waves of Anglo-Saxon settlers, mainly tribes of Angles, Saxons, Jutes and Frisians from modern-day Germany, who first came as mercenaries in the Roman army. The native Celts were pushed back into their core strongholds in Wales, Dartmoor and Cornwall, creating pockets of Celtic culture, while the rest of the region was largely colonised by the Anglo-Saxons. Around this time a fearsome war leader – supposedly named Arthur or Arthurus – is said to have emerged to lead a counter-attack against the invading Saxons, checking their progress over 12 great battles, and launching the enduring legend of King Arthur (p192).

The first Christian saints arrived in the southwest around this time, probably from Ireland, although their vessels were a little unconventional – St Ia is supposed to have sailed to the north Cornish coast on a giant leaf, while St Piran, patron saint of Cornwall, allegedly arrived aboard a granite millstone.

In the early 9th century, King Egbert and the armies of Wessex swept west and brought the whole of the southwest under Anglo-Saxon control. His grandson, King Alfred, led a series of campaigns against Viking incursions (and famously burnt some cakes while hiding on the island of Athelney). After a series of power struggles between various Anglo-Saxon kingdoms over the next century, King Edward (the Peacemaker) was crowned the first king of a unified England at Bath Abbey in 973.

» 55 BC	» AD 410–600	» 838
Roman legions under Julius Caesar land in Britain and defeat native tribes, although some areas of west Cornwall and Devon remain effectively independent kingdoms.	Christianity is brought to the southwest by Irish missionaries (many of whom are subsequently made saints, including St Piran, the patron saint of Cornwall).	Armies of Wessex under King Egbert defeat final alliance of Cornish and Viking warriors at Hingston Down.

THE MIDDLE AGES

In 1066 England was invaded again by Norman armies from northern France under the command of William I (the Conqueror), who defeated the English king Harold I at the Battle of Hastings – an event that effectively marked the end of Anglo-Saxon rule in England. Following the Norman conquest, the region came under the sway of feudal lords, who developed the area's potential for trade, agriculture and industry. Wool, tin and minerals became important exports, and a series of ports sprang up around the southwest coastline, notably at Fowey, Bristol, Looe, Saltash and Plymouth.

In 1305 Edward I recognised the importance of tin mining to the area by granting official charters to the Stannaries (tin-mining districts) and establishing four stannary towns in Cornwall (Truro, Lostwithiel, Launceston and Helston) and three more in Devon (Chagford, Ashburton and Tavistock). Among other functions, these towns had the right to assay tin to determine its quality before export. Cornwall also had its own Stannary Parliament, governed by its own system of taxes and laws; tin-miners were effectively exempt from civil jurisdiction, and had the right to be tried according to Stannary law. Half a century later in 1337, Edward III established the Duchy of Cornwall for his son Edward, the Black Prince, a title still traditionally inherited by the heir to the throne.

'The first Christian saints arrived in the southwest from Ireland'

The long-held rights of the Stannaries were a major factor in the 1497 'An Gof' rebellion, a popular uprising against taxes levied by Henry VII to fund a war against the Scots, which many believed eroded the Stannaries' right to govern their own affairs. Under leaders Thomas Flamank, a Bodmin lawyer, and Michael Joseph, a blacksmith (*an gof* in Cornish) from St Keverne, an army of 15,000 Cornishmen marched on London, but despite a series of spirited battles, it was outclassed by the king's forces, and Flamank and Joseph were hanged, drawn and quartered before having their heads gibbeted on pikes outside London Bridge.

A similarly brutal end awaited the region's ecclesiastical institutions during Henry VIII's Dissolution. Nearly all of the region's important abbeys, including Glastonbury, Shaftesbury, Buckfast, Muchelney, Athelney, Cleeve, Bodmin and Glasney College in Penryn, were abolished; assets were stripped, buildings dismantled and most of the monks were forcibly retired, or in many cases, put to death. In the absence of the abbeys, the cathedrals of Exeter, Wells, Bath and Bristol flourished alongside a host of smaller chapels and churches.

» 939	» 1050	» 1201
Athelstan, king of Wessex and the first recognised king of a unified England, dies and is buried in Malmesbury Abbey.	Foundation of the first cathedral at Exeter, although the original building is substantially remodelled by successive bishops in the 12th and 13th centuries.	King John grants the first charter to the Stannaries (tin-mining districts) of Cornwall. Further charters are granted in the early 13th century by Edward I.

BACKGROUND

BRISTOL & THE SLAVE TRADE

As with many important British ports (including London and Liverpool) in the 17th and 18th centuries, Bristol's huge growth as a maritime city was due in no small part to the 'Triangle Trade'. This brutal trading arrangement ran as follows: munitions, textiles and manufactured goods were shipped to Africa, where they were sold for slaves; the slaves were transported to work in the booming colonies in the New World, principally in America and the Caribbean, and in exchange for the slaves, British merchants carried back luxury goods produced on the plantations (especially sugar, tobacco, rum, indigo and cotton) to the markets in England and Europe.

Needless to say, the conditions on the ships were horrific; it was routinely expected that more than 10% of the 'cargo' would be lost to disease or malnutrition on the 'Middle Passage' (transatlantic crossing), but the actual figure was often far higher. In the 100 or so years until slavery was abolished in Britain in 1807, it's estimated that more than 2100 slaving ships set sail from Bristol, transporting approximately 500,000 Africans to the New World – around one-fifth of the slaves transported by British vessels during the period.

The Reformation also abolished the use of Latin in church services and introduced a new all-English Book of Common Prayer. This was the final straw for many devout worshippers in Cornwall and Devon, but the so-called Prayer Book Rebellion of 1549 was put down in similarly bloody fashion to the An Gof rebellion 50 years before; the Westcountry armies were summarily crushed outside Exeter, and the leaders executed.

THE NEW WORLD

Religion was yet again the cause of troubles following the ascension of Elizabeth to the throne in 1558. Tensions between Protestant England and the mainly Catholic countries of southern Europe culminated in a series of skirmishes and battles, prompting Elizabeth to expand the navy's power to counter the increasing strength of Spanish fleets. The Queen also encouraged the practice of 'private enterprise' (otherwise known as piracy) on the open seas; many of her favourite sea captains were born in the southwest, including the Cornish nobleman Sir Richard Grenville (born at Buckland Abbey in Devon); his cousin, Sir Walter Raleigh (born in Hayes Barton, East Devon); Sir John Hawkins (Plymouth); and his cousin, Sir Francis Drake (Tavistock).

BACKGROUND

» 1348	» 1497	» 1549
The Black Death, a form of flea-borne bubonic plague spread by rats and other rodents, reaches the southwest. The epidemic kills an estimated one-third of the population.	The 'An Gof' rebellion against Henry VII marches on London, but is quashed and its leaders executed. A second Cornish rebellion under Perkin Warbeck fails later the same year.	Parliament passes the Act of Uniformity enforcing the use of an all-English Book of Common Prayer. A minor rebellion outside Exeter is quickly crushed.

In 1588 Philip II of Spain dispatched an armada of 130 warships to invade Britain and bring the island under Catholic rule. The Armada was sighted off the Lizard on 19 July, and the message was carried to London via a series of beacons along the south coast. Whether Drake was really bowling on Plymouth Hoe at the time of the invasion is unlikely, but he lost no time in organising his response: he set sail from Plymouth with a fleet of 55 ships. Over the next two weeks Drake fought a series of engagements against the Spanish fleet, culminating in the Battle of Gravelines on 29 July, in which 11 Spanish galleons were destroyed and the rest put to flight. Drake and Hawkins' subsequent exploits were rather less worthy of commendation: they were instrumental in establishing the first slave-trafficking routes with Africa, a trade that underpinned the growth of several southwest ports (especially Bristol and Plymouth) over the next two centuries.

The southwest also had a pivotal role to play in the move from Old to New World. Following Sir Francis Drake's circumnavigation of the globe from Plymouth in 1577 (a replica of his ship, the *Pelican,* renamed the *Golden Hind,* can be seen on Brixham Harbour, p146), the city of Plymouth also witnessed the first voyage of the Pilgrim Fathers, who set sail from the Barbican (p164) on 16 September 1620 aboard the *Mayflower*. The pilgrims landed at Provincetown Harbour in present-day Massachusetts and founded the colony of New Plymouth, effectively marking the start of modern America.

CIVIL WAR

As in many other areas, the Civil War from 1642 to 1646 resulted in massive turmoil throughout the Westcountry. Broadly speaking, Cornwall declared itself for the king, Charles I, while loyalties varied widely across the rest of the region with neighbouring villages often declaring contradictory allegiances. Key battles were fought at Braddock Down, Stratton, Lostwithiel, Lansdown (near Bristol) and Plymouth, but the tide of the war swept back and forth until a new commander, Oliver Cromwell, galvanised the Parliamentarian armies and led them towards a string of crushing victories, most notably at the Battle of Lostwithiel in 1644, which effectively ended Royalist control of the southwest. The Royalists eventually surrendered at Tresillian, 3 miles outside Truro, on 15 March 1646.

Forty years later, the Protestant Monmouth Rebellion broke out against the Catholic rule of James II, culminating in the last battle ever fought on English soil, at Sedgemoor in northern Somerset in 1646. The ringleaders of the rebellion were rounded up

» 1588	» 1620	» 1720
The Spanish Armada invasion fleet, first sighted off the Lizard Peninsula, is defeated by the Royal Navy fleet under the command of Sir Francis Drake, stationed at Plymouth.	The Pilgrim Fathers set sail from Plymouth aboard the *Mayflower,* founding the colony of New Plymouth in Massachusetts in November the same year.	Thomas Newcomen builds an 'atmospheric engine' at Wheal Fortune Mine, in the Gwennap mining district, heralding the arrival of mechanised mining.

SMUGGLING

In the late 18th century, rising customs duty on imported goods (especially luxury items such as brandy, gin and tea) led to a huge growth in smuggling along the southwest coastline. Cornwall's remote coves were perfect hideouts for the enterprising 'free traders', and the sight of government 'preventive' boats in pursuit of smuggling vessels off the southern Cornish coastline became commonplace.

But the government operatives were often fighting a losing battle; widespread opposition to the taxes, coupled with the lucrative returns that could be made from handling contraband goods, meant that collusion between the smugglers and onshore communities was widespread.

Smuggling rapidly became a hugely profitable industry – according to some estimates, as much as four-fifths of the tea drunk in England in the late 19th century had escaped official duty – and some smugglers, such as Harry Carter and Jack Rattenbury, became local celebrities. Harry Carter even published his own autobiography.

and tried in the 'Bloody Assizes' at Taunton Castle. Predictably, most of them ended up losing their heads.

THE AGE OF INDUSTRY

Following the upheavals of the Civil War, the southwest developed as an industrial and maritime powerhouse over the next century. The huge demand for metals during the Industrial Revolution (particularly tin, iron and copper) heralded the beginning of the golden age of mining in Cornwall and West Devon, and the advent of new technologies such as steam power, beam engines and 'blast' extraction enabled the region's miners to reach previously inaccessible lodes of high-quality metals.

Mining in Cornwall boomed: in 1800 the county boasted 75 mines employing 16,000 people, but by 1837 this had mushroomed to 200 mines employing some 30,000 workers. The industry flourished until the mid-19th century, when declining mineral yields and a crash in commodity prices led to the closure of huge numbers of mines. Entire communities upped sticks and emigrated to Australia, Mexico and the western United States (a phenomenon referred to as the 'Cornish Diaspora').

Meanwhile, maritime trade was expanding almost as rapidly as mining. Between 1730 and 1745, Bristol had effectively become Britain's second city and one of the country's busiest trading ports. The city established a network of trading links with

BACKGROUND

» 1729	» 1743	» 1768
John Wood the Elder constructs Bath's first great Georgian terrace on Queen Square, later followed by the Circus and Royal Crescent.	The preacher and theologian John Wesley delivers his first sermon in Cornwall, and begins the long process of Methodist conversion in the county.	James Cook sets out from Plymouth to record the transit of Venus across the Pacific Ocean, but inadvertently discovers Tahiti, New Zealand and Australia.

the New World, and grew rich on the proceeds of the 'Triangle Trade' (see box p260). Meanwhile Plymouth consolidated its status as a naval base, and Falmouth established itself as the home of the Falmouth Packet Service, which carried mail and goods around the Empire between 1689 and 1850.

Many of the Westcountry's newly rich industrial magnates lavished fortunes on grand country estates, or embarked on ambitious architectural projects designed to showcase the wealth and prestige of the English elite. Among the great architectural achievements of the period are Bath's celebrated streets, Royal Crescent and The Circus (p53), the remodelling of Ralph Allen's estate at Prior Park (p58), the redevelopment of Clifton in Bristol (p41) and the foundation of many of the southwest's finest landscaped gardens.

> *'maritime trade was expanding almost as rapidly as mining'*

As the Industrial Revolution rolled on, pioneering engineers set about reinventing Britain's infrastructure, constructing tunnels, canals and railways to link Britain's industrial bases. Foremost among them was Isambard Kingdom Brunel, one of England's brightest engineering minds, who built everything from groundbreaking bridges to the first great transatlantic steamers (such as the SS *Great Britain,* now moored on Bristol's dockside, p38).

Another of Brunel's great achievements was the development of the Great Western Railway, which provided the first rapid link between London and Bristol, one of Britain's booming provincial cities. Spurred on by Brunel's success, within a few decades the nation was criss-crossed by one of the world's finest railway systems, laying the foundations for the expansion of British industry and empire.

THE EARLY 20TH CENTURY

The railway also brought a new phenomenon to the southwest: tourism. Rising living standards and better wages, coupled with the expanding rail network, brought swathes of trippers from the region's smog-choked cities to the southwest's shores. Many towns were quick to seize on the opportunity: Torquay, Paignton, Ilfracombe, Weymouth and Weston-super-Mare grew rapidly to cater for the booming tourist trade, adding a plethora of posh promenades, piers and seaside villas. The wealthy landowner Louis Tregonwell even founded his own purpose-built resort in Bournemouth. Over a century later, tourism remains one of the southwest's biggest industries, accounting for around 20% of the region's total income.

» 1801	» 1833	» 1859
Redruth-born Richard Trevithick demonstrates his groundbreaking *Puffing Devil* steam locomotive on Fore St in Camborne.	Isambard Kingdom Brunel begins construction of the railway line from London to Bristol, and four years later launches the first transatlantic liner, the *Great Western.*	The Brunel-designed Royal Albert Bridge over the River Tamar connects Cornwall to Devon. Five years later, Brunel's Clifton Suspension Bridge over the Avon opens.

BACKGROUND

As with many corners of England, the southwest suffered heavily during the Great War. For many men, especially those employed in low-paying industrial and agricultural jobs, joining up was often seen as the means to a steady wage and a route out of menial labour. The devastating casualties that followed were often compounded by the fact that many rural regiments recruited their men en masse from local villages, which meant that entire populations could be wiped out in the space of just a few hours of fighting.

The region fared little better in WWII, when its ports and manufacturing bases became key targets for the Luftwaffe's bombing campaign. Bristol and Plymouth fared the worst, and by the end of the Blitz huge swathes of both city centres had been reduced to rubble. But they weren't the only cities to experience the horrors of the Blitz: during the Baedeker raids in 1942, the German High Command bombed culturally important British cities in an effort to sap morale (the commanders were said to have chosen their targets by consulting Baedeker tourist guides). Exeter and Bath were both severely damaged: Bath's historic Assembly Rooms were gutted by incendiary bombs, and several houses of the Royal Crescent and the Circus were hit.

'The railway also brought a new phenomenon to the southwest: tourism'

Later in the war, the deep-water harbours around Falmouth and the Carrick Roads played a pivotal role in the preparations for D-Day, and marked the embarkation point for millions of American troops setting sail for the Normandy beaches.

RECENT HISTORY

The last 50 years has been a period of fluctuating fortunes for the southwest. Traditional blue-collar industries such as farming, fishing and mining have almost completely disappeared over the last few decades; since the closure of South Crofty near Camborne in 1998, there are now no working mines in the southwest, and only Brixham and Newlyn retain sizeable fishing fleets.

In contrast, Bristol still has a strong manufacturing base – the major aeronautical firms of BAE Systems, Airbus and Rolls-Royce are all based in the Bristol suburb of Filton, where Concorde was developed in the 1970s. Devonport Dockyard in Plymouth is still an important shipyard and, with 15 dry-docks and 4 miles of waterfront, the largest naval base in Western Europe.

BACKGROUND

» 1940–42	» 1951	» 1998
Bristol and Plymouth experience heavy bombing raids by the Luftwaffe, and both sustain heavy damage. Bath and Exeter are later damaged during the Baedeker Blitz.	Dartmoor becomes the southwest's first designated national park, followed three years later by Exmoor.	The closure of South Crofty, the last working mine in Cornwall, results in thousands of job losses and an end to over 4000 years of metal mining in Cornwall.

But there's no doubt that the region's great growth industry over recent years has been tourism. Depending on which statistic you listen to, tourism adds between £4.5 and £8 billion to the region's coffers every year, and in some areas over half of all jobs are related to the wider tourist industry. In general terms the more regional areas are the poorer ones, with Cornwall the poorest; in the 1990s Cornwall qualified for a emergency £350 million aid package from the EU called Objective One, which ended in 2007.

But it's not all doom and gloom. With the decline in manual industries, the southwest has slowly made the transition towards a more knowledge-based economy, while exciting developments such as the Eden Project (p241) and the SS *Great Britain* (p38), plus Unesco World Heritage status for Bath, the Jurassic Coast, and the Cornwall and West Devon Mining Landscape, have helped refocus attention on the region's history, heritage and creativity.

» 2001	» 2006	» 2007
Foot and mouth strikes the southwest. The Eden Project opens in a disused Cornish clay pit. The Jurassic Coast becomes the UK's first natural World Heritage Site.	The Cornwall and West Devon Mining Landscape is recognised by Unesco for its cultural and historical importance.	The MSC *Napoli* is beached off Beer Head on the east Devon coast, shedding hundreds of containers and prompting a chaotic free-for-all claiming of the salvage.

BACKGROUND

CORNWALL & THE ARTS
· · · · · · ·

Whether it's the wild landscape, the craggy cliffs or simply the unique quality of light, there's something about Cornwall that has proved an irresistible attraction for successive waves of painters, artists and sculptors since the early 19th century.

THE EARLY YEARS

One of the first major artists to make an artistic pilgrimage to Cornwall was JMW Turner, who secured a commission to tour the southwest in 1811 to produce watercolours for a series of engravings entitled *Picturesque Views on the Southern Coast of England*. Throughout the summer of 1811, Turner travelled widely across the Westcountry, making stops across Dorset, Devon and Somerset, but it was under Cornwall's wide-open skies that his passion for dreamy, ethereal landscapes found fullest expression. It has been argued that Turner's Westcountry sojourn played an important part in his enduring fascination with light, colour and form; many of the sketchbooks and canvases he produced during this period provide tantalising glimpses of his later, quasi-abstract experiments.

But Turner wasn't only interested in Westcountry views. He was also a keen observer of contemporary society, and many of his paintings provide a fascinating insight into Cornish life in the early 1800s. His 1812 work *St Mawes at the Pilchard Season* depicts a chaotic harbour scene filled with pilchard boats, fishing smacks and bustling villagers, played out against the backdrop of St Mawes Castle bathed in typically Turneresque sunlight. With its moody contrast of social realism and romantic scenery, it is intriguing not just in terms of Turner's own body of work, but also when considered in relation to the next major artistic movement to develop in Cornwall.

IMPRESSIONISM & THE NEWLYN SCHOOL

It was the extension of the Great Western Railway west of the Tamar in 1877 that really put the region on the artistic map. For the first time, artists were able to enjoy relatively easy access to the region's scenery and landscapes, and they arrived in ever-increasing numbers as the century wore to its close.

The Impressionist movement, which had developed across the channel in Normandy and Brittany with artists such as Monet, Pissarro, Dégas and Eugène Boudin, was a major inspiration to many artists of the period. The movement's central doctrine of painting *en plein air* (on location, rather than working from sketches in a studio) in order to capture the immediacy of a scene encouraged many artists to travel to the southwest, among them the German-born artist Walter Sickert and the American James McNeill Whistler.

But while some artists dabbled with the colours and forms of Impressionism, others took a markedly more figurative approach. In the early 1880s, a loose group of artists settled around the fishing port of Newlyn, spearheaded by Birmingham-born Walter Langley, Dubliner Stanhope Forbes and the Lincolnshire artist Frank Bramley. Following in the footsteps of the Barbizon School, a group

KEY FIGURES: STANHOPE FORBES

The so-called 'father of the Newlyn School', **Stanhope Forbes** was born in Dublin in 1857, the son of an Irish father and a French mother. As a young man, he became interested in painting during a family holiday in the Ardennes and later studied at the Lambeth School of Art and the Royal Academy School, exhibiting for the first time at the Royal Academy in 1878. He later studied in Paris, and in 1880 travelled to Normandy with his fellow artist, Henry la Thangue, to work with artists of the Breton *plein-air* school, where he was profoundly influenced by the naturalistic depictions of real people and everyday scenes.

Seeking to establish his own movement along *plein-air* lines, Forbes arrived in Newlyn in 1884 with his wife-to-be Elizabeth, and immediately knew he had discovered the ideal home for his artistic colony. Within a year his landmark 1885 painting, *A Fish Sale on a Cornish Beach,* had established his style: powerfully painted, moodily lit and strongly representational, depicting the chaotic hubbub of a Cornish fish market in typically figurative style. It was exhibited at the Royal Academy, where it was bought by Henry Tate (whose collection later helped found the Tate Gallery) for the princely sum of £600.

Having founded his own painting school and been elected to the Royal Academy in 1910, Forbes continued to live and work in Cornwall for the rest of his life, even after the untimely deaths of his wife Elizabeth in 1915 and his son, Alec, in the trenches of northern France in August 1916. Forbes could still be seen painting *en plein air* around the quaysides and clifftops of west Cornwall well into the 1930s; he died in 1947, shortly before his 90th birthday.

of naturalistic French painters based on the Île-de-France, the Newlyn artists set out to depict the everyday reality of people's lives in a naturalistic and representational way.

They became particularly fascinated by Newlyn's fishermen, and documented their lives in closely observed detail. Some canvases depicted such everyday tasks as net repair, sail rigging or fish sales on the quayside, while others exploited the natural drama and pathos of the fishermen's lot: poverty, hardship, storms and the ever-present danger of shipwrecks.

'The Newlyn artists set out to depict the everyday reality of people's lives in a naturalistic and representational way'

Among the most characteristic paintings of the period are Forbes' *The Health of the Bride,* depicting the marriage of a young sailor and his wife in a Newlyn inn, and Bramley's *A Hopeless Dawn,* which shows a distraught wife receiving the news that her husband has been lost at sea. A lighter side of the Newlyn School is represented by artists such as Norman Garstin, whose *The Rain It Raineth Every Day* depicts a typically rainy scene on Penzance promenade and is now among the most prized possessions of the Penlee House Museum and Gallery in Penzance.

By 1884 there were at least 30 artists working either in Newlyn or the nearby towns of St Ives, Lelant and Falmouth. In 1889 Forbes and his wife Elizabeth formally established

BACKGROUND

the first Newlyn School of Artists; a second colony of artists later developed in the nearby cove of Lamorna, forming the Lamorna Group (often referred to as the later Newlyn School).

'By 1884 there were at least 30 artists working in New-lyn or the nearby towns'

The work of many of the key Newlyn and Lamorna artists – particularly Forbes, Bramley, Henry Scott-Tuke, Samuel John (Lamorna) Birch, Thomas Cooper Gotch and Walter Langley, as well as female artists Laura John-son, Dod Procter and Elizabeth Forbes – became both highly influential and highly prized, with many of the artists exhibiting their work in major London venues such as the Royal Academy and the National Gallery. Though the Newlyn artists have never quite attracted the same degree of fame and fortune as the Impressionists who inspired them, they collec-tively produced some of the Westcountry's best-known, and best-loved, works of art.

THE ST IVES SCHOOLS

The next generation of artists reacted powerfully against the figurative concerns of their predecessors. The advent of modernism in the 1920s opened up the canvas far beyond the confines of representational painting, and it wasn't too long before Corn-wall became identified with a much more radical style of art.

The association of St Ives with the avant-garde can be traced back to the mid-1920s, when the ground-breaking potter Bernard Leach established his first pottery in St Ives, in partnership with the Japanese ceramics artist Shoji Hamada. Born in Hong Kong, Leach later studied in Japan, where he became fascinated with the functions, shapes and forms of Oriental pottery. Having established his studio in St Ives, where he installed Europe's first Japanese wood-burning kiln, Leach went on to develop a highly influential style, fusing Eastern philosophies with Western materials.

KEY FIGURES: ALFRED WALLIS

For most of his life, Alfred Wallis (1855–1942) never even contemplated an artistic career: he worked variously as a merchant seaman, deep-sea fisherman, marine dealer and odd-job man, before eventually taking up painting at the age of 67 to distract himself from the recent death of his wife.

Completely self-taught, his paintings are beautiful examples of naive art – they dis-regard perspective and apportion scale in relation to the subject's importance to the scene. Despite his popularity with other artists of the St Ives School, Wallis found little success further afield: his poverty meant he often had to work on cardboard using chandlers' paints.

Sadly, Wallis sold only a handful of paintings during his lifetime, and he eventually died in poverty at the Barnoon Workhouse in 1942. His grave is in Barnoon Cemetery, overlooking Porthmeor Beach; it's now decorated with tiles designed by Bernard Leach depicting one of Wallis' recurrent motifs, a tiny fisherman dwarfed by a looming lighthouse.

BACKGROUND

In Leach's wake came the painters Cedric Morris, Christopher 'Kit' Wood and Ben Nicholson, who first visited St Ives around the mid-1920s. During one of their visits in 1928, Wood and Nicholson stumbled across the work of an entirely self-taught Cornish fisherman and painter, Alfred Wallis, whose naive style – which paid little heed to conventional rules of perspective, scale or composition – proved a powerful influence on the modernist artists, many of whom were seeking a return to the more primitive style of art that Wallis' work seemed to embody.

Within a few years Wallis found himself surrounded by a new artistic community that established itself in St Ives throughout the 1930s and early 1940s. At the forefront of this new movement were Nicholson and his wife, the young sculptor Barbara Hepworth, who moved to St Ives following the outbreak of WWII, where they were soon joined by their friend, the Russian sculptor Naum Gabo, a key figure of the Constructivist movement.

ARTISTIC INSTITUTIONS

* **Tate St Ives** // Cornwall's artistic mothership, with work by all the key artists of the St Ives School (p206)

* **Bernard Leach Pottery** // Leach's former studio has recently benefited from a multimillion-pound makeover (p207)

* **The Barbara Hepworth Museum** // Hepworth's studio and sculpture garden contain many examples of her work (p207)

* **Newlyn Art Gallery & The Exchange** // Cornwall's most exciting contemporary art galleries (p217)

* **Penlee House Gallery & Museum** // Top spot for viewing canvases by the Newlyn School (p218)

* **Royal West of England Academy** // Bristol's venerable art gallery has a notable collection of Newlyn and St Ives artists (p44)

Together, the three artists began to develop a wealth of experimental, abstract work that had much in common with the modernist movements that were flourishing in the post-war period. They also took inspiration from the shapes, light and landscapes with which they found themselves surrounded in west Cornwall. Hepworth, in particular, became fascinated with her adopted home, and her distinctive combination of stone, metal and sinuous forms was clearly influenced by the rugged Cornish landscape, along with its wealth of industrial remains and ancient monuments.

Predictably, their work met considerable resistance among the more traditional sectors of St Ives' artistic establishment. The conservative outlook of the town's main artistic umbrella, the St Ives Society of Artists, led Hepworth and Nicholson to found the rival Penwith Society of Artists in 1949, which was specifically established to provide creative support and much-needed gallery space for new and experimental artists.

Attracted by St Ives' burgeoning reputation as a centre for abstract art, a new wave of exciting young artists, including Wilhelmina Barns-Graham, Terry Frost, Patrick Heron, Roger Hilton and Peter Lanyon, helped consolidate the town's position as a hub of creativity and experimentation throughout the 1950s and '60s.

BACKGROUND

RECENT ARTISTS

Half a century on, west Cornwall remains an important hub for British artists: it's thought there is a higher concentration of artists living and working in and around Penwith than anywhere else in the UK, outside London's East End.

Although none of them have attained quite the same level of notoriety as Damien Hirst and the YBAs (Young British Artists), there are still several well-known names to look out for. Among the best-known is Kurt Jackson, who was born in Dorset in 1961 but has been based near St Just since the mid-1980s. Having studied zoology at Oxford, Jackson later developed his artistic career and is now well known for his expressive landscapes, many of which bear a strongly ecological or environmental theme. He has previously served as artist-in-residence at the Eden Project.

Meanwhile, the abstract experiments of Terry Frost, Roger Hilton, Patrick Heron and others continue to resonate through the work of many contemporary Cornish artists, including Trevor Bell, Noel Betowski and Jeremy Annear. Two of the area's artists bear an even closer connection with their predecessors: Terry Frost's son Luke has continued in his father's artistic footsteps, while Rose Hilton has developed her own distinctive style since the death of her husband Roger in 1975.

OUTDOORS
· · · · · ·

The southwest of England is like one giant natural adventure playground. The region's vital statistics are impressive: it's home to England's first natural World Heritage Site, two evocative national parks, 14 Areas of Outstanding Natural Beauty (AONB), vast empty beaches and hundreds of miles of remote cliffs. It's perfect for living life to the full in the great outdoors. Whether you're after exhilaration or relaxation, you'll find it here.

WALKING

THE SOUTH WEST COAST PATH

At 630 miles, Britain's longest national trail ought to be good – and it is. Winding from Minehead around the end of England to Poole, it takes in precipitous cliffs, sandy beaches, fishing ports, World Heritage Sites and kiss-me-quick resorts along the way.

While the modern path is awe-inspiring, its past is compelling too. Until 1913 coastguards and revenue men walked the cliffs daily looking out for smugglers. These foot patrols created today's path; clusters of coastguard cottages still dot the trail today.

> *'Whether you're after exhilaration or relaxation, you'll find it here'*

The path also winds through England's fist natural Unesco World Heritage Site, the Jurassic Coast (p115), where a 95-mile section of shore has geological features spanning 185 million years. Meanwhile the far west boasts the iconic clifftop engine houses of Cornwall's Mining Landscape World Heritage Site (p205).

Expect to see peregrine falcons, gannets, fulmars, kittiwakes and guillemots, while seals, dolphins and huge basking sharks are often spotted close to the shore. The

KEY INFORMATION SOURCES

* **Bodmin Moor** (www.visitbodminmoor.co.uk)
* **Cornwall AONB** (www.cornwall-aonb.gov.uk)
* **Dartmoor National Park Authority** (DNPA; www.dartmoor-npa.gov.uk)
* **Dorset AONB** (www.dorsetaonb.org.uk)
* **Exmoor National Park Authority** (ENPA; www.exmoor-nationalpark.gov.uk)
* **Mendip Hills AONB** (www.mendiphillsaonb.org.uk)
* **National Trust** (NT; www.nationaltrust.org.uk)
* **Quantock Hills AONB** (www.quantockhills.com)
* **South Devon AONB** (www.southdevonaonb.org.uk)
* **Southwest Tourism** (www.itsadventuresouthwest.co.uk; www.naturesouthwest.co.uk)
* **Torbay Coast and Countryside Trust** (www.countryside-trust.org.uk)

BACKGROUND

WALKING FESTIVALS

These concentrations of guided walks and events route you straight to the heart of an area. Walking festivals are also generally held at quieter times of the year.

* **Isles of Scilly** (www.walkscilly.co.uk; late Mar-early Apr)
* **Ivybridge and Dartmoor** (www.ivybridge-devon.co.uk; late Apr-early May)
* **North Devon and Exmoor** (www.walkingnorthdevon.co.uk; early May & early Oct)
* **South Devon** (www.southdevonwalking festival.co.uk; late Sep-early Oct)

region's wildflower extravaganza is outstanding in spring and summer; a palette of pink thrift, creamy bladder campion, purple heather and yellow gorse.

The South West Coast Path's official **website** (www.southwestcoastpath.com) has a handy distance calculator; the **South West Coast Path Association** (01392-383560; www.swcp.org.uk) produces the *South West Coast Path Guide* (£11). The trail is at its best from April to September, although in July and August beds and serenity can be at a premium. Few people tackle it all in one go; you'll need around eight weeks (56 consecutive walking days) if you do. Smaller sections can provide memorable day- or multiday trips; see p22 for suggestions.

DARTMOOR NATIONAL PARK

The 368 sq miles of Dartmoor are the emptiest, highest and wildest in southern England. Rounded hills, or tors, pepper a rolling, primitive landscape studded by stone circles and rows, burial mounds and massive Bronze Age settlements.

Delving into Dartmoor's culture and heritage really enhances a visit. The DNPA runs guided walks themed around history, legends and geology. Good bases for hikers are remote Princetown, rugged Okehampton and picturesque Widecombe-in-the-Moor.

EXMOOR NATIONAL PARK

While land-locked Dartmoor is bigger, the 267-sq-mile Exmoor National Park (p80) has 34 miles of jaw-dropping coastline. Add ancient woods, time-warp villages, red deer and Exmoor ponies and you have a winner.

The ENPA runs guided walks to help you explore the area. Good bases are the gorge-side villages of Lynton and Lynmouth, sleepy Dulverton (the start point for a superb 12-mile circular walk via Tarr Steps) and picturesque Exford.

BODMIN MOOR

On atmospheric Bodmin Moor (p247) old tin mines dot a mystical landscape of bogs, Stone Age sites and high tors. Walking highlights include the stone circle at the ancient mining village of Minions, and the high tors of Brown Willy and Rough Tor.

CYCLING

A wealth of traffic-free routes and varied landscapes make the southwest one of the best cycling regions in the country. The paths themselves speak eloquently of the

OTHER WALKING ROUTES

★ **Coleridge Way** (www.coleridgeway.co.uk) This 36-mile (three- to four-day) jaunt runs from the Quantocks to Exmoor, in the footsteps of the poet Samuel Taylor Coleridge.

★ **Cotswold Way** (www.nationaltrail.co.uk/cotswold) Meanders for 102 delightful miles (eight days) along a steep escarpment north from Bath, passing quintessential English villages crafted out of warm, honey-coloured stone.

★ **Saints' Way** A 30-mile (three- to four-day), cross-Cornwall, former pilgrims' route, from Padstow in the north to Fowey in the south.

★ **Templar Way** Leisurely stroll (18 miles, two days) from Haytor to seaside Teignmouth.

★ **The Quantocks** A 12-mile-long, 3-mile-wide ridge of russet hills that provides a couple of varied day hikes in north Somerset.

★ **Two Moors Way** (www.twomoorsway.org.uk) Coast-to-coast epic (117 miles, eight days) from Wembury, in south Devon, to Lynmouth on Exmoor.

past; many are on former railway or tram lines and snake from now-extinct mines or quarries.

Dartmoor has a superb selection of routes; the DNPA sells a comprehensive map (£13). Exmoor's exhilarating mountain-bike trails are graded, ski-run style, in *Exmoor for Off-Road Cyclists* (£9.95).

CYCLING ROUTES

Routes range from coast-to-coast uphill epics to level day rides. The biggest is the **West Country Way**, which runs for 250 miles from Bath or Bristol, via Exmoor and Bodmin, to Padstow on the north Cornwall coast. It's traffic free for 75 miles. The **Devon Coast to Coast** snakes from Ilfracombe to Plymouth; of its 102 miles, 71 are car free.

In north Devon, the **Tarka Trail** (p180) is a delightful, traffic-free, 30-mile loop through the county's lowlands. North Cornwall's **Camel Trail** (p194) is a 17-mile, car-free cycle from the heights of Bodmin Moor to the north Cornwall coast. The **Railway Path** (p45) links Bristol and Bath with a 16-mile cycle route, while in Devon the **Granite Way** (p175) is a superb, 11-mile, traffic-free route on a former Dartmoor railway line.

In Dorset the **Maiden Newton to Dorchester** route is an 8-mile meander along quiet roads and bridleways, while in south Devon the **Ply Valley Trail** winds from Plymouth to Dartmoor, for 7 car-free miles. In Cornwall the **Clay Trails** (p240) are 3- to 5-mile tracks amid St Austell's mining heritage – one even goes to the Eden Project (p241).

SURFING

The southwest's surf culture has helped drive its reinvention as a cool holiday hot spot. Surprisingly, the roots reach back more than a century – sepia archive images show people surfing in the region in 1904. The sport really took off in the 1950s, and now racks of wetsuits and boards tempt thousands into the waves. With good reason: local beaches get the full force of Atlantic line-ups, re-sulting in the most consistent quality surf conditions in England.

The self-styled surfing (and party) capital is Newquay (p199). More relaxed surf hubs include Polzeath (p197), Bude (p190) and Sennen Cove (p214) in Cornwall, and Woolacombe (p179), Croyde (p179) and Bantham (p161) in Devon. In Dorset, Bournemouth has created an ingenious artificial reef offshore that, despite teething problems, has increased wave size; see p90.

LEARNING TO SURF

The British Surfing Association runs courses from its **National Surfing Centre** (☎ 01637-850737; www.nationalsurfingcentre. com) in Newquay and accredits schools region wide; costs start from around £30 for 2½ hours. It costs around £10 to hire a wetsuit for a half-day; the same for surfboards or the easier-to-manage bodyboards.

> ### DON'T MISS...
>
> **OUTDOOR ADVENTURES**
>
> ★ **Fossil Hunting, Dorset** // Rummage for dinosaur remains near Lyme Regis (p117)
>
> ★ **Surfing, Cornwall** // Get churned by washing-machine waves at Newquay (p199)
>
> ★ **Sailing, Portland** // Beat the Olympians to the 2012 sailing course in Dorset (p113)
>
> ★ **Hiking past mining heritage** // See engine houses clinging to west Cornwall's cliffs (p211)
>
> ★ **Cycling the Camel Trail** // Freewheel beside an estuary of golden sands (p194)
>
> ★ **Swimming beneath Durdle Door** // Take a dip by this massive, natural stone arch (p102)

The north shores of Devon and Cornwall tend to enjoy better conditions, but wind and swell directions mean different beaches on either coast can be better on the day. Check the latest surf conditions at www.magicseaweed.com.

SAILING

The southwest's past is inextricably bound up with sail-power: Iron Age tin traders; 17th-century fishermen working the Newfoundland cod banks; an expansionist Royal Navy; fast fruit clippers racing to the Azores; fleets of boats fishing closer to home.

The tradition has come full circle. Weymouth and Portland are hosting the sailing events in the 2012 Olympics, resulting in multimillion-pound investments, a flurry of building work and improved facilities for athletes (and the rest of us).

LEARNING TO SAIL

The **Royal Yachting Association** (RYA; ☎ 023-8060 4100; www.rya.org.uk) lists approved schools. Many are in the region's traditional maritime centres, including Weymouth and Portland (p113) and Poole (p96) in Dorset; Salcombe (p159) in Devon; and Falmouth (p228) and Fowey (p242) in Cornwall.

Half-day sessions in smaller craft (eg a topper) cost about £35. A weekend, live-aboard course for an RYA qualification costs from £200 per person.

BACKGROUND

DIVING

The number of wrecks off the southwest coast makes sailors nervous. But couple them with reefs and crystal-clear waters and you have a great area to dive. Wrasse, conger eels and dogfish float past face masks in a watery world that drifts from shallow reefs to deeper waters.

The big dive attraction is the **Scylla** (www.national-aquarium.co.uk/scylla-reef). This gutted ex-warship was sunk near Plymouth by the National Marine Aquarium in 2004, to study how reefs form. Devon and Cornwall's coasts have more than 4600 wrecks; the Isles of Scilly alone have a remarkable 150 recognised dive sites.

The **British Sub Aqua Club** (☎ 0151-3506203; www.bsac.com) approves training centres. Weymouth and Portland (p113), Exmouth and the Isles of Scilly (p251) are popular dive bases.

A half-day taster is around £30; four-day training courses start at £340.

ROCK CLIMBING

Strings of fabulous crags stretch across Dorset, Somerset, Devon and Cornwall. Dartmoor, Portland, Swanage, Torbay, Bodmin and Cheddar make particularly good focus points. Dartmoor alone has scores of accessible climbs with multi- and single-pitch routes; the DNPA produces a free leaflet.

OTHER WATER SPORTS

KITESURFING & WINDSURFING

Kitesurfing's huge popularity sees fleets of brightly coloured canopies sweeping the southwest skies on windy days. The **British Kite Surfing Association** (☎ 01305-813555; www.britishkitesurfingassociation.co.uk) lists approved schools; prices start from around £80 for a half-day.

Windsurfing also remains popular; the **Royal Yachting Association** (RYA; ☎ 023-8060 4100; www.rya.org.uk) details courses. Taster sessions start from £45. Exmouth (p136), Poole (p96) and Weymouth (p113) are good bases for both sports.

WHITE WATER

Dartmoor's deep, steep gorges ensure heavy winter rains turn stretches of the River Dart into foaming, fast-flowing water. The rapids are only open between October and March. Winter kayaking also takes place on the Rivers Exe and Barle on Exmoor. The DNPA and ENPA can advise. The **British Canoe Union** (BCU; ☎ 0845 370 9500; www.bcu.org.uk) approves training centres; many require you to be BCU two-star standard. Prices start at £40 for a half-day.

SEA KAYAKING

The southwest's rugged coast makes paddling the shore tempting, as do regular sightings of seals, dolphins and basking sharks. Prices start at £40 for a half-day; north Devon–based **Sea Kayaking South West** (☎ 01271-813129; www.seakayakingsouthwest.co.uk) does a two-day beginners course for £150.

BACKGROUND

The **British Mountaineering Council** (☎ 0161-4456111; www.thebmc.co.uk) has a database of indoor and outdoor climbs. For tuition try the **Rock Centre** (☎ 01626-852717; www. rockcentre.co.uk; Rock House, Chudleigh) in Devon. Expect to pay around £20 per half-day.

HORSE RIDING

Many riders dream of cantering across open countryside and that dream can be realised in the southwest. Diverse environments include dappled bridleways, spectacular moorland or the ride-through-the-surf beloved of films.

The region's expansive moors are among the big draws, with many stables within easy reach of Exmoor (p80) and Dartmoor (p175). Other prime sites are the Mendips and the Dorset Downs. Prices start at £15 an hour.

In general, you're not allowed to ride horses on public footpaths, but you can ride on the vast network of bridleways – check the key of OS (Ordnance Survey) maps to see which routes are which. You can also ride on much of the common land on Dartmoor, and on some of the region's other trails, such as the Coleridge Way. Wherever you plan to head out, always check whether riding is permitted.

GARDENS
· · · · · · ·

If there's one season when the Westcountry really comes into its own it's spring, when the region's many famous gardens burst into colourful life with all manner of exotic blossoms and blooms. While the gardens themselves may be well known, it's useful to have a little bit of horticultural background to help you appreciate the sights.

MONASTERIES & KITCHEN GARDENS

While the Romans certainly knew the value of a good bit of landscaping, the concept of the garden as we know it today really began during the early Middle Ages, when many of Britain's monasteries and abbeys began developing small kitchen gardens and allotments as part of their estates. The value of these gardens was both practical and spiritual: they not only provided food, medicine and sustenance, but also offered spaces for contemplation, meditation and communion.

'monks were responsible for developing the art of brewing, and the concept of the lawn and the flowerbed'

Abbey gardens were generally divided into sections: herb gardens, kitchen gardens, 'physic' gardens for making medicines, cloister gardens for meditation and orchards for fruit cultivation. Many of the monasteries' early horticultural experiments continue to exert an influence: among other things, English monks were responsible for developing the art of brewing, and the concept of the lawn and the flowerbed.

Although all the southwest's great abbeys were dismantled during the Dissolution, they were often later redeveloped as stately homes or landscaped estates, for example at Hartland (p181), Buckland (p171) and Forde (p119).

Glastonbury Abbey (p70), Shaftesbury (p108), Muchelney (p72) and Cleeve (p83) provide a better insight into how the abbey grounds might have appeared during medieval times, although sadly little of their original monastic layout remains.

TUDOR GARDENS

The next change came during the Tudor era, when garden designers began to be heavily influenced by Renaissance fashions (particularly from Italy and France). Among the concepts introduced during this period were the use of garden 'rooms', which were often intentionally designed to mirror the architectural alignment or interior layout of the house. A key component of Tudor designs was the 'knot' garden, which usually featured small areas of lawn bordered by intricate patterns of box or laurel hedges, often viewed from raised walkways or ornamental terraces. The gaps between hedges were often filled with colourful flowers, herbs or shrubs, many of which had a hidden meaning to a Tudor audience (in a famous speech in *Hamlet,* Ophelia relates some of the secret symbolism of many flowers, including rosemary for remembrance, pansies for thoughts, columbine for ingratitude and fennel for regret).

Very few Tudor gardens have survived the centuries intact, although there is a superb example at Montacute House (p79), which, although heavily restored, is thought to resemble its original layout fairly closely. Another replica knot garden exists at the Red Lodge (p43), one of Bristol's only surviving Tudor houses.

LANDSCAPE GARDENS

Fashions changed again during the early 18th century, when the rigid, tightly controlled gardens of the Tudor era gave way to much bolder statements. Inspired by the lavish country parks of European chateaux, which many of them had visited on their 'grand tours', England's 18th-century aristocrats set out to use their gardens as a means of projecting their power, prestige and cultural sophistication.

This was the era of landscape gardening on an industrial scale. Lakes, woods, terraces, lawns and even entire hills were created from scratch to attain the desired aesthetic effect, leading the eye towards a perfectly aligned view, a shapely classical statue or a romantically positioned folly. Among the greatest exponents of 18th-century landscape gardening was Lancelot 'Capability' Brown (1716–83), who designed over 170 of Britain's greatest estates during his long career (his nickname apparently stemmed from his tendency to promise prospective clients that their gardens showed 'great capabilities').

Though the southwest has relatively few Brown-designed gardens, you can clearly see his influence at Prior Park (p58) near Bath, designed for the wealthy magnate and philanthropist Ralph Allen. From the lavish house itself, strategically positioned on the crest of the hill, the grounds of Prior Park sweep dramatically down through a series of winding walkways and terraced lakes to a Palladian bridge, one of only four such structures in the world. It's a classic example of Capability Brown's ostentatious,

PIONEER PLANTS

You don't have to look far to find evidence of the weird and wonderful things brought back by Victorian plant hunters. Consider the humble **Monterey pine**. It's a frequent sight in Cornwall, often planted along the county's shores as a windbreak or shelter tree and twisted into strange shapes by the winter gales which batter the Cornish coasts. It's so common that many people assume it's a native species. In fact, the Monterey pine was brought back to Britain from California in 1833 by the famous tree hunter David Douglas, and planted in huge numbers in Cornwall due to its tolerance of salty climates and rapid growth. The rest is horticultural history – the Monterey pine rapidly took root, and today the Cornish landscape would be almost unimaginable without it.

Similarly, the natural home of the **rhododendron** is in the Himalayas, usually at altitudes of more than 5000 feet, but the plant positively flourished once it was introduced to Cornwall's gardens. The world's largest rhododendron – measuring a mighty 82 feet from root to tip – lives not on some distant mountainside in the high Himalaya, but in the rather more pastoral location of Flora's Green, a grassy lawn in the middle of the Lost Gardens of Heligan (p239), near Pentewan. It comes as no surprise to discover that the man who brought back the plant to Heligan was one of the great British plant hunters of the 19th century, Sir Joseph Hooker, who went on to direct the Royal Botanical Gardens at Kew.

grandstanding style; one of his star pupils, Humphry Repton, is said to have remarked that Brown 'fancied himself an architect', and many of his greatest designs certainly feel closer to architectural statements than gardens.

Repton himself went on to enjoy a distinguished landscaping career, and was responsible for the landscaping of several Westcountry houses, notably Antony (p245) and Port Eliot (p245) in Cornwall and Ashton Court (p44) just outside Bristol.

VICTORIAN GARDENS

As Britain's empire flourished in the late 18th and early 19th centuries, a flood of exotic new plants began to find their way back to Britain's shores from the furthest reaches of the globe. Many of the plants we now take for granted in our own modern-day gardens were in fact brought back by the great Victorian plant hunters: men such as Frank Kingdon Ward, Sir Joseph Hooker, EH Wilson and the Lobb brothers, who braved treacherous seas, hostile natives and all manner of distasteful tropical diseases to discover new species with which to delight European gardeners at home.

Among these exotic imports were azaleas from Japan, rhododendrons, magnolia and camellias from the Himalayas, tree ferns from New Zealand and Australia, North American pines and sequoias, Canadian maples and South American monkey puzzles. Although there was more than a touch of Indiana Jones about these early explorers, they were far from happy-go-lucky adventurers – most were serious scientists, natural historians and botanists, with an insatiable passion for scientific discovery and an abiding fascination for the natural world.

With its sheltered valleys and subtropical climate, the southwest provided the perfect habitat for many exotic plants. Many of the region's landmark gardens were developed during this time, including Trebah and Glendurgan (p232), Heligan (p239), Caerhays Castle (p241), Trelissick (p233) and Abbotsbury (p115).

Perhaps the most spectacular example of all is the Tresco Abbey Garden (p252) on the Isles of Scilly, which was founded by ex-banker turned philanthropist Sir Augustus Smith, who also served as Scilly's governor for over 30 years. The island's temperate climate and sheltered aspect enable many exotic species, which would stand little chance of surviving anywhere else in the UK, to thrive.

It was also the philanthropic Victorians who established many of the southwest's finest public parks, designed for the education, enlightenment and general enjoyment of the masses. The elegant terraces of Bournemouth's Pleasure Gardens (p92) and

---

DON'T MISS...

SECRET GARDENS

* **Coleton Fishacre //** An Art Deco house with stunning subtropical gardens (p153)
* **Caerhays Castle //** A great Cornish estate which boasts the national magnolia collection (p241)
* **The Garden House //** This real-life secret garden near Yelverton is a riot of colourful blooms (p171)
* **Chygurno //** A cliffside wonder nestled above Lamorna Cove, near Penzance (p233)
* **Barley Wood Walled Garden //** Idyllic kitchen garden, artist's studios and a fantastic cafe near Wrington in Somerset (p68)

BACKGROUND

the grand lawns and stately trees of Royal Victoria Park in Bath (p53) are among the finest.

20TH-CENTURY GARDENS

The most influential garden designer of the early 20th century was Gertrude Jekyll, whose work in many ways harked back to garden concepts first developed during the Elizabethan era. For Jekyll, gardens were seen as an integral part of the house, rather than something separate to it; she became particularly renowned for her garden 'rooms' connected with formal pathways, arbours or hedges. She was also one of the first designers to make use of the herbaceous border, basing her planting schemes around harmonious colours and complementary plant species. Some of her best work can be seen at Hestercombe (p75) near Taunton and Barrington Court (p79), near Yeovil.

'With its sheltered valleys and sub-tropical climate, the southwest provided the perfect habitat for many exotic plants'

Other 20th-century gardens of particular note are the subtropical valley of Alum Chine (p92), the RHS gardens at Rosemoor (p181) and Agatha Christie's glorious riverside gardens at Greenway (p152).

Meanwhile, the giant greenhouses of the Eden Project (p241) have taken gardening in Cornwall to an entirely different level: if you're after a vision of what gardening might look like in the 22nd century, this might just be the place to find out.

FOOD & DRINK

The southwest's food scene marches at the vanguard of championing fresh, local produce, as today's society becomes increasingly aware of how what we eat was made, where it came from and how it got on our plate. The desire to overcome the gulf between those who produce food and those who eat it is strong. In the southwest you can bridge that gap. Fabulous eateries are springing up on farms and vineyards; fishermen sell you their catch beside the beach. Slow food is making fast progress. The region's impressive organic sector has pioneered whole eco-movements, and for some visitors the eateries encountered here inspire changes in how they dine at home.

CAMPAIGNING CHEFS

When Rick Stein opened a restaurant in the quaint Cornish fishing village of Padstow in 1975, few realised he was kick-starting a transformation of the region's culinary landscape. By 1995, Stein's *Taste of the Sea* TV series had placed Cornwall firmly in the foodie spotlight; his show *Food Heroes* went on to bring local food to mainstream attention.

'In the southwest, food is about much more than what you eat; it's also about how you live your life'

Others followed. Hugh Fearnley-Whittingstall set up **River Cottage** on the Devon–Dorset border in 1998; now you can dine at his **farm HQ** (p139), eat in his canteens in east Devon (p139) and Bath, and learn how to grow vegetables, make bread and butcher meat.

And Fearnley-Whittingstall hasn't just created a small-screen lifestyle idyll – his campaigns on sustainability have made a substantial impact on British awareness of mass-produced food. Meanwhile his national **Landshare project** (www.landshare.net) is forging links between 40,000 would-be vegetable growers and people with spare acres.

So, crucially, the region's celebrity chefs are also campaigning chefs. Jamie Oliver, who battled for quality school dinners, brought **Fifteen** (p201) to a beach near Newquay in 2006. This gourmet restaurant also teaches underprivileged youngsters how to cook, and batches of apprentice chefs graduate each year – this is cooking as a community project.

In the southwest, food is about much more than what you eat; it's also about how you live your life.

High-profile eateries have had a big impact on local towns. Some chefs' ubiquitous natures cause locals to roll their eyes; Stein has no fewer than four eateries, three shops and four B&Bs in Padstow, earning it the local nick-name 'Padstein'. Others point to the jobs these high-profile chefs bring to areas badly in need of them.

And then there are chefs who don't have blockbuster TV shows, but still dish up superb food: Michael Caines in Exeter (p131) and Gidleigh Park (p176); Nathan Outlaw at Rock (p197); and Paul Ainsworth in Padstow (p198).

LOCAL & ORGANIC PRODUCE

High-profile individuals may have helped reinvent the region's culinary scene, but it's the quality local produce that makes it possible. Geography helps hugely; few places are more than 30 miles from the sea, while rich farmland stretches between the shores.

Local producers have seized the chance to go organic. A whopping 25% of the UK's registered organic producers are based in the region, 9% more than the next biggest area, Wales.

The southwest is also home to early pioneers of the chemical-free movement. **Riverford Farm** (www.riverford.co.uk), near Totnes, has been growing organic food for more than 20 years and now runs one of the UK's biggest organic delivery schemes. It's also set up an innovative **field kitchen** (p151), where you eat food that's harvested to order from the furrows in front of you.

DON'T MISS...

LOW FOOD-MILE EATERIES

- ★ **Bordeaux Quay** // Top Bristol bistro which shrinks the food-miles map (p46)

- ★ **Fat Hen** // Gather your own grub – then cook it – on Cornish wild-food foraging expeditions (p215)

- ★ **Riverford Field Kitchen** // Exquisite meat and veg from the surrounding Devon fields (p151)

- ★ **Crab House Café** // A Dorset beachside eatery serving super-fresh fish (p116)

- ★ **River Cottage HQ** // Fearnley-Whittingstall's idyllic Devon farm (p139)

- ★ **Terra Madre** // They cure their own chorizo at this north Devon slow-food gem (p183)

Nearby, **Transition Town Totnes** (p149), with its emphasis on sustainability and local produce, became the first UK transition town in 2005. More than 180 have since sprung up nationwide.

The arbiters of all things organic, the **Soil Association** (www.whyorganic.org) is Bristol-based; its online directory has hundreds of listings. **Taste of the West** (www.tasteofthewest. co.uk) has an online, searchable database of local producers.

STAPLES & SPECIALITIES

Traditionally Cornwall has the pasty, Devon the cream tea, Dorset the fudge and Somerset the cider. While locals wince at the 'yokel chewing straw' stereotypes these foods conjure up, they're still firmly the focus of county pride.

CORNISH PASTIES

If you can capture the essence of a county in food, the Cornish have done it with the pasty. More than just pastry-wrapped meat and veg, its roots reach deep into the Cornish psyche and economy.

Dating back to the 13th century, this crinkly-edged, half-moon of carbohydrate consisted of vegetables (originally no meat) wrapped in pastry with a pocket of fruit or jam at one end   the result was a portable, durable two-course lunch. Over the centuries

BACKGROUND

meat was added when affordable, and pasties became a staple of tin-mining communities – those working underground in grim, arsenic-laced conditions didn't eat the crimped seam, instead it allowed them to hold their food without contaminating it.

When waves of impoverished Cornish miners emigrated in the mid-1800s, they took their food traditions with them, particularly to Australia and the USA – today you can pop out for a pasty in Adelaide and Arizona and across the UK.

The economic pasty factor is huge; production is worth a staggering £150 million to Cornwall each year; the industry directly employs around 1800 people and it's estimated another 11,000 are reliant on the trade. Yet the brand has suffered from copycat production, prompting the Cornish Pasty Association to bid for protected status, meaning only those pasties made in the county could have the title (think Champagne versus sparkling wine). At the time of going to print, the European Commission had not made a decision about the pasty's status.

For many, it's as much about identity as it is about lunch. A giant pasty is still hoisted over the crossbar at key Cornwall county rugby matches. Even the question of its invention stirs the blood, with rival claims from neighbouring Devon being fiercely rejected.

CREAM TEAS

If the Cornish can claim pasties as their own, Devonians can do the same for cream teas. Some historians date the sweet snack back to the 10th century, when monks fed bread, cream and jam to workers repairing a Devon abbey after a Viking raid.

REGIONAL ODDITIES & DELICACIES

Not one for the squeamish, **stargazy pie** features fish heads sticking out of the pastry. Why? Tradition has it that one Christmas, people in the fishing village of Mousehole (p220) were starving because fierce storms stopped them heading out to sea. One local man defied horrendous conditions and returned home a hero with a boat full of seven types of fish. Their heads were kept on in the resulting communal pie to show what was what.

Even now the events are re-enacted in Mousehole the day before Christmas Eve, with a huge pie baked and served up at the port's Ship Inn.

Other delicacies of the southwest:

* **Laverbread** Fried patties of boiled seaweed, oats and bacon, particularly popular in north Devon and Exmoor

* **Salcombe Smokies** A south Devon speciality of richly flavoured, smoked mackerel (p160)

* **Samphire** A traditional regional delicacy, this wild coastal plant has more than a hint of asparagus

* **Bath Oliver** A savoury biscuit from the city's days as a fashionable spa town

* **Saffron Buns** Yellow Cornish fruit cake; the spice may be a legacy of the early Phoenician tin trade

* **Luxury Ice Cream** Look out for Cornwall's Treleavens and Roskilly's Farm (p226), Devon's Salcombe Dairy, Dorset's Purbeck and Somerset's Lovington's

BACKGROUND

At its best a cream tea is a delightful combination of light scones, tasty homemade jam, a steaming brew and utterly gooey, stand-your-spoon-up-in-it clotted cream. At its worst it's more reminiscent of an in-flight meal – check what's coming out of the kitchen before ordering.

Locally there's often heated debate about which to spread first: the jam or the cream. In Cornwall traditionally it's the jam on first; in Devon it's the cream. A Cornish variation that's seeing a resurgence is Thunder and Lightning, with treacle, syrup or honey replacing the jam.

FISH

The fruits of the southwest's seas provide a tasty and tangible link between food and place. Eating fish that's been landed a few yards away is special – still in buckets, it's sometimes even carried past diners by waterproofs-clad fishermen.

Good places to rejoice in these negligible food miles include the ports of Newlyn, Falmouth, Padstow and Mevagissey in Cornwall; Brixham, Torquay and Dartmouth in Devon; and Lulworth Cove, Poole, Muddiford, Portland and Weymouth in Dorset.

Despite a decline in the fleet, restaurant tables still feature the 40-plus species hauled in locally. Highlights include superb oysters, mussels, crab and lobster, line-caught sea bass and mackerel, and the freshest monkfish, John Dory and Dover sole. Around Bath and Bristol look out too for River Severn salmon.

Then there's that great British staple: fish and chips. Wrapped in paper, dripping with vinegar and scattered with salt, it can be surprisingly good, especially in the region's fishing ports where the day's catch ends up in batter.

CHEESE

Creamy, tangy, soft and hard, the southwest offers cheese lovers countless slices of gourmet heaven. Fittingly for a region that's home to Cheddar (the place), there are some mouth-puckeringly strong traditional varieties. Try the Cheddar Gorge Cheese Company (p66), Green's of nearby Glastonbury or Quickes, near Exeter.

There's also the gentle, nettle-wrapped, semi-hard Cornish Yarg; melting, local brie-type cheeses (try Sharpham, p150); and full-bodied, vein-laced offerings. Traditionally a mouldy horse harness was dragged through leftover milk to induce the 'blue' of the Dorset Blue Vinny; that or storing it next to mouldy boots. Other pungent delights are the Exmoor (cow), Devon (cow), Harbourne (goat) and Beenleigh (sheep) Blues.

DRINKS

CIDER

The southwest is rightly famous for ciders that conjure images of russet summers and hazy days. Centuries ago no farm would have been without its orchard; apples were pressed and then fermented to form the 'scrumpy', which was often drunk instead of water, then the H_2O was more toxic than the alcohol. Dazed but delighted labourers were paid partly in this golden currency – an average 4-pint (2.25L) daily allowance increasing to 8 pints during hay-making.

This deeply flavoured elixir was evocatively dubbed 'wine of wild orchards' by the writer Laurie Lee and, mass-produced offerings aside, the survival of local makes provides a link to that past. The apple names alone are enough to give you a warm, fuzzy glow: Slack ma Girdle, Sops in Wine and Quench.

Excellent, small-scale producers include south Devon–based Luscombe and the Lyme Bay Winery. Somerset's Burrow Hill Cider comes in sparkling or scrumpy forms; it also makes the 'cousin of Calvados' Somerset Cider Brandy range, which retails at up to £39 a bottle. For more on cider, see p73.

SOUTHWEST BREWERIES

* **Abbey Ales** (www.abbeyales.co.uk) Look out for the award-winning Bellringer, a light, hoppy ale, at this Bath-based brewery.

* **Badger Ales** (www.hall-woodhouse.co.uk/beers/badgerales) Products include the evocatively named Tanglefoot, and the mellow Golden Champion. You can tour its Dorset brewery too.

* **Bath Ales** (www.bathales.com) Top tipples include Barnstormer and the limited-edition Rare Hare, best supped in their city-centre pub, the Salamander (p61).

* **Beer Engine** (www.thebeerengine.co.uk) This Devon microbrewery-cum-pub used to be a railway hotel, hence the brews: Rail Ale and Sleeper Heavy (p133).

* **Blue Anchor Inn** (☎ 01326-562821; www.spingoales.com; 50 Coinagehall St, Helston) This pub in Cornwall has been brewing its own Spingo ale for six centuries; ask behind the bar to see the vats.

* **Bristol Beer Factory** (www.bristolbeerfactory.co.uk) A microbrewery rustling up Sunrise (smooth and pale) and the full-bodied Red. They've even got their own pub-on-a-barge, the Grain Barge (p49).

* **Dartmoor Brewery** (www.dartmoorbrewery.co.uk) Set in Princetown, Devon, just yards from Dartmoor Prison, and famous for its sweet-finishing Jail Ale.

* **Keltek Brewery** (www.keltekbrewery.co.uk) Small, traditional Cornish brewer, with offerings from mild Even Keel (3.4%) to superstrong Beheaded (7.6%), as well as a new nettle cider, appropriately named Stingers.

* **Palmers** (www.palmersbrewery.com) A 200-year-old west Dorset brewery; look out for its fruity Dorset Gold, and the hefty Tally Ho! (5.5% ABV).

* **Sharp's** (www.sharpsbrewery.co.uk) Rock-based brewer whose best-known beers include its popular Doom Bar bitter and two ales inspired by Rick Stein's much-missed terrier, Chalky's Bark and Chalky's Bite.

* **Skinners** (www.skinnersbrewery.com) This small-scale Truro operation is known for its cheekily named brews: Betty Stogs, Cornish Knocker, Ginger Tosser and Keel Over.

* **St Austell Ales** (www.staustellbrewery.co.uk) The big boy's been around since 1851, and you'll find its ales including Tribute, Proper Job, HSD and Tinners all over Cornwall.

BACKGROUND

WINE

The mild southwest weather ensures good conditions for vineyards, and sipping a chilled glass of white on a sun-drenched terrace, overlooking neatly stacked rows of vines feels more like Chablis than the southwest. Set in 200 stunning hectares, Devon's Sharpham Vineyard (p150) produces highly acclaimed wines; prices range from £8.25 for a very decent off-dry white to £25 for its Beenleigh Red, a Cabernet Sauvignon–Merlot blend. Camel Valley Vineyard (p247), in north Cornwall, is another seriously good award winner. Look out for its aromatic and appropriately named Bacchus (£13). Polgoon Vineyard, near Penzance, produces award-winning still rosé and a champagne-style pear drink, while at Devon's Yearlstone Vineyard (p133) you can take a tour, then eat and drink beside the vines.

GIN

The city of Plymouth bears the tag line 'Spirit of Discovery'; apt, considering it's the home to Plymouth Gin (p165). For 200 years no British Royal Navy vessel left port without its own supply of the brand, helping it spread to drinking dens and the world's first cocktail bars; it's still a major global player. Distillery tours allow you to sniff botanicals (things that add flavour) and carry out your own taste tests.

ACCOMMODATION

FINDING ACCOMMODATION

These days the southwest is popular with everyone from family travellers to urbanites looking for a luxury seaside getaway, and there's accommodation to suit all comers. The region's hotels have come on leaps and bounds in recent years, and you'll find a plentiful supply of city, coastal and country-house places, as well as a fast-growing number of boutique options.

Even that great old British institution, the B&B, has started to haul itself into the 21st century; the days of late-night lockouts and bossy landladies are largely long gone, and the best B&Bs now match up very favourably against the region's fancier hotels. All but the most basic places are en suite these days. Some small places still don't take cheques or credit cards; rather cheekily, some have also started to add a surcharge to card transactions to cover bank costs.

Camping is also becoming increasingly trendy, and these days you're not just limited to basic tap-and-toilet sites in a farmer's field: luxurious options include everything from Mongolian yurts to eco-pods and retro caravans. We've picked out some of our favourite sites throughout the regional chapters: see p139 for Devon, p103 for Dorset, p67 for Somerset and p214 for Cornwall. Hostels can be a good way of cutting costs; the **YHA** (Youth Hostel Association; www.yha.org.uk) has some superb hostels, especially around Dartmoor, Exmoor and the coast.

Self-catering can be a good option, especially if you're travelling with kids. Across the southwest there are snazzy flats, fishermen's cottages and country retreats waiting to be booked, but self-catering's not without its drawbacks: many of the region's prettiest villages have been swamped by holiday lets, making that idyllic community atmosphere a little harder to find than you might have hoped.

PRICES & BOOKING

As with any holiday destination, prices take a hefty hike upwards in the high season, particularly from June to August. Especially if you're travelling as a family, it might be worth rescheduling your plans to take advantage of low-season deals. Prices also spike around Christmas, New Year, Easter and major bank holidays. Whenever you're travelling, booking ahead is pretty much essential.

Most B&Bs still include breakfast in their rates, but many still quote prices per person, rather than per room. Hotels tend to quote room rates but usually tack breakfast on top. Many places offer cheaper rates for online bookings.

BRISTOL, BATH & SOMERSET

BRISTOL

♨ FUTURE INN CABOT CIRCUS // ££
Map p40; ☎ 0845 094 5588; www.futureinns.co.uk; d £59-99; Ⓟ 🛜

This efficient mini-chain has outlets in Plymouth, Cardiff and Bristol. It's modern, functional and businessy, but the rooms are clean in beige, white and pine, and the rates are pretty fantastic this close to the centre – especially considering the free parking in Cabot Circus car park next door.

♨ HOTEL DU VIN // £££
Map p42; ☎ 0117-925 5577; www.hotelduvin.com; Narrow Lewins Mead; d £150-205, ste £225; Ⓟ

'Boutique' is bandied about too often these days, but this is the real deal. Huge open-plan rooms and split-level suites (all named after famous wines) with floating futon beds, claw-foot baths, frying-pan

showerheads and a mix of industrial trappings left over from the building's days as a sugar warehouse. Ooh la la.

♨ MERCURE BRIGSTOW HOTEL // ££
Map p42; ☎ 0117-929 1030; H6548@accor.com; Welsh Back; d £99-149; 🖥

The charmless concrete skin of this riverfront hotel conceals a surprisingly stylish heart: curving walls, trendy floating beds, mood lights, big river-view windows and tiny plasma TVs lodged in the bathroom tiles. Gimmicky, yes, but good fun.

♨ PREMIER TRAVEL INN, KING ST // £
Map p42; ☎ 0117-910 0619; www.premiertravelinn. com; The Haymarket; r £59-79; 🟢 🛜

Yes, we've noticed it's a Premier Inn, but without any decent B&Bs near Bristol's city centre, it's a find. It is just steps from the harbour and the Old Vic; the rooms have big beds and desks (and free wi-fi), and some even have harbour glimpses.

BATH

♨ 139 BATH // ££
Map p54; ☎ 01225-314769; www.139bath.co.uk; 139 Wells Rd; d £65-195; 🟢 🛜

Up in the B&B-heavy zone around Wells Rd, this is a standout. The proprietors have pulled out the luxury stops: Hypnos beds, huge flat-screen TVs, posh fabrics. The only downside is the summer price hike; visit during low season for a much better deal.

♨ BROOKS // ££
Map p54; ☎ 01225-425543; www.brooksguest house.com; 1 & 1a Crescent Gardens; d £69-175

On the west side of Bath, this hotel is another plush option, with heritage fixtures blending attractively with snazzy contemporary finishes. The owners of

Brooks have made an effort with the details: goose-down duvets, pocket-sprung mattresses, DAB radios and a thoughtful choice of breakfast spoils, including smoked-salmon brioche and homemade muesli.

❦ HALCYON // ££

Map p54; ☎ 01225-444100; 2/3 South Pde; www.thehalcyon.com; d £99-125

This new boy is rightly turning some heads. A shabby terrace of hotels has been knocked through, polished up and totally reinvented. It's style on a budget: the lobby is cool and monochrome; off-white rooms have splashes of colour, Philippe Starck bath fittings and White Company smellies; studio rooms have kitchens. We like it a lot.

❦ OLDFIELDS // ££

Map p54; ☎ 01225-317984; www.oldfields.co.uk; 102 Wells Rd; s £49-115, d £65-160; Ⓟ 🛜

A heritage honey. Spacious rooms and deep, soft beds for comfort; brass bedsteads and antique chairs for character, Laura Ashley fabrics and Molton Brown bathstuffs for luxury, all wrapped up in a lemon-stone house with views over Bath's rooftops.

❦ QUEENSBERRY HOTEL // £££

Map p54; ☎ 01225-447928; www.thequeensberry.co.uk; Russell St; d £185-280, ste from £410; Ⓟ

The city's coolest rooms, in a terrace of townhouses between George St and the Circus. Every room's different: some are all modern fabrics, muted colours and funky throws; others boast Zen-tinged furniture and feature fireplaces. The Queensberry is also home to a top contemporary restaurant, and the walled garden is a chilled asylum from the city fizz.

RENT YOUR OWN

Whether it's a cosy country cottage or a converted lighthouse you're after, these specialists can help you find your very own home away from home.

Beach Retreats (☎ 01637-861005; www.beachretreats.co.uk)

Classic Cottages (☎ 01326-555555; www.classic.co.uk)

National Trust (☎ 0870-458 4422; www.nationaltrustcottages.co.uk)

Rural Retreats (☎ 01386-701177; www.ruralretreats.co.uk)

Stilwell's (☎ 0870-197 6964; www.stilwell.co.uk)

Unique Homestays (☎ 01637-881942; www.uniquehomestays.com)

West Country Cottages (☎ 01803-814000; www.westcountrycottages.co.uk)

❦ THREE ABBEY GREEN // BATH ££

Map p54; ☎ 01225-428558; www.threeabbeygreen.com; 3 Abbey Green; d £85-135; 🛜

For location, you can't beat this place: the abbey and Roman baths are literally on your doorstep. The Grade-II Georgian house overlooks a tree-shaded green, and the rooms are simply and classically furnished. The Asher and Westwood Suites have adjoining singles, ideal for families.

WELLS & THE MENDIPS

❦ BERYL // WELLS ££

☎ 01225-678738; www.beryl-wells.co.uk; Hawkers Lane; d £75-130; Ⓟ 🐾

A country manor just a mile from Wells, full of ticking grandfather clocks, dolls' houses and walnut dressers, and run by an endearingly eccentric English family. The rooms spread out over several floors; some have four-posters, others upholstered sofas, most overlook acres of grounds.

ACCOMMODATION

❦ GLENCOT HOUSE //
NEAR WELLS £££
off Map p63; ☎ 01749-677160; www.glencothouse.
co.uk; Glencot Lane, Wookey Hole; r £165-295; Ⓟ ▣
This 19th-century manor is a jaw dropper. The house was built for paper
magnate William Hodgkinson, and it's
packed to the rafters with luxurious features. Rooms are opulent – canopy beds,
vintage rugs, antiques, leaded windows
– and outside there's a private park, a
croquet lawn and, of course, a helipad.

❦ HARPTREE COURT //
EAST HARPTREE ££
☎ 01761-221729; www.harptreecourt.co.uk; d £95; Ⓟ
This ab-fab manor is a Mendip gem,
ensconced down a private drive and surrounded by parkland. While the three
colour-coded rooms aren't particularly lavish, the country-house setting is
straight from *Brideshead Revisited*.

❦ CHALICE HILL //
GLASTONBURY ££
☎ 01458-838828; www.chalicehill.co.uk; Dod Lane;
d £100; Ⓟ
This grand Georgian B&B has been renovated with flair by its artistic owner Fay
Hutchcroft. A sweeping staircase circles
up through the house, leading to three
characterful rooms. Our pick is Phoenix,
with modern art, colourful fabrics and
garden views.

TAUNTON & AROUND

❦ FROG STREET FARMHOUSE //
HATCH BEAUCHAMP ££
☎ 01823-481883; www.frogstreet.co.uk; d £80;
Ⓟ ▨
According to the owners, the name derives from the Anglo-Saxon for 'meeting
place'. Frogs or no frogs, this amber-
stoned longhouse is a back-country
beauty, with three rooms mixing rustic

trappings (beams, stone, wonky doors)
with luxurious furnishings.

❦ FARMER'S INN // WEST HATCH ££
☎ 01823-480480; www.farmersinnwesthatch.co.uk;
d £125-150; Ⓟ
The country overcoat of this Somerset
inn conceals fancy undergarments. The
stunning rooms, all named after Somerset hills, are a wonder – our faves are the
Blackdown, with its elegant tub, mahogany furniture and exposed stone, and the
Quantock, with wet room, chaise longue
and Bergère bed.

YEOVIL & AROUND

❦ THE FARMYARD // YEOVIL ££
☎ 01935-426426; www.farmyardretreat.co.uk;
Longcroft House, Stone Lane; d £110, cottages £110-
240; Ⓟ
Funky split-level apartments glittering
with chrome and glass on the edge of a
Somerset farm. Wet rooms, wi-fi, roll-
top baths, dinky patios and rolling farm
views: what more could you wish for?

❦ LORD POULETT ARMS //
HINTON-ST-GEORGE ££
☎ 01460-73149; www.lordpoulettarms.com; s £60-65,
d £85-95; Ⓟ
It's mainly known for its fantastic food,
but Hinton-St-George's much-plaudited
pub has some wonderfully quirky upstairs rooms, where rough brick, bespoke
wallpapers, hefty dressers and cast-iron
beds blend into a satisfyingly chic whole.

EXMOOR

❦ TARR FARM // DULVERTON ££
☎ 01643-851507; www.tarrfarm.co.uk; s/d £90/150;
Ⓟ ▨
This valley getaway is hidden near the
Tarr Steps, 5 miles from Dulverton.
Despite the farmhouse appearance, it's
a top-class treat: nine rooms in rich

creams and yellows, with organic bath goodies and old-fashioned bath taps, plus spoils such as home-baked cookies, in-room fridges, DVD players and a fab country restaurant.

THREE ACRES // DULVERTON ££

☎ 01398-323730; www.threeacrescountryhouse.co.uk; Brushford; s £60-75, d £90-120; P wi-fi

A sweet retreat reached by narrow, twisty lanes from Dulverton. It has scooped lots of B&B awards, and with good reason: the six prim rooms overlook rolling Exmoor hills, and there's a different daily special for breakfast each day, from Exe trout to homemade bangers. Lovely.

ST VINCENT LODGE // LYNTON £

☎ 01598-752244; www.st-vincent-hotel.co.uk; Castle Hill; d £75-80; P

No sea view, but this classy lodge is still our favourite Lynton base. The house has history – it was built by a sea captain who sailed with Nelson – and the decor's full of cosy heritage. The Belgian owner is also a gifted chef: book for the downstairs bistro.

SEA VIEW VILLA // LYNMOUTH ££

☎ 01598-753460; www.seaviewvilla.co.uk; 6 Summer House Path; d £100-150

Georgian grandeur in seaside Lynmouth. This 1721 villa offers Egyptian cotton, Indian silk and suede fabrics gracing rooms done out in 'Champagne', 'ginger' and 'vanilla'. Eggs Benedict, smoked salmon and cafetière coffee ensure the breakfast is classy, and they'll even pack you a picnic.

DORSET

BOURNEMOUTH & AROUND

AMARILLO // BOURNEMOUTH £

off Map p91; ☎ 01202-553884; www.amarillohotel.co.uk; 52 Frances Rd; s £25-45, d £50-90, f £80; P wi-fi

A rarity: a budget Bournemouth B&B with style. Neutral tones are complemented by tweaks of minimalist chic: abstract paintings, beige throws and arrangements of willow. Rooms include two singles and a triple – some have shared bathrooms.

BALINCOURT HOTEL // BOURNEMOUTH ££

off Map p91; ☎ 01202-552962; www.balincourt.co.uk; 58 Christchurch Rd; s £40-70, d £75-120; P

Impeccable attention to detail sets this late Victorian B&B apart from the rest – even the china on the tea tray is hand-painted to match each room's colour scheme. The decor is bright and tasteful, respecting both the building's heritage and modern antifrill sensibilities.

LANGTRY MANOR // BOURNEMOUTH ££

off Map p91; ☎ 01202-553887; www.langtrymanor.com; Derby Rd; s from £100, d £105-200; P wi-fi

Your chance to sleep in a royal lovenest. Built by Edward VII for his mistress Lillie Langtry, this hotel overflows with opulent grandeur – from the red carpet in the entrance to the immense chandeliers inside. Rooms are named after Lillie's friends (Oscar Wilde, Ellen Terry, Sarah Bernhardt) and ooze Edwardian elegance; modern touches include recessed lights and jacuzzi baths. The King's Suite is a real jaw dropper: a monumental, climb-up-to-get-in four-poster bed and a wood-and-tile fireplace big enough to fit two seats inside.

URBAN BEACH // BOURNEMOUTH £££

off Map p91; ☎ 01202-301509; www.urbanbeachhotel.co.uk; 23 Argyll Rd; d £95-170; P internet wi-fi

Bournemouth's finest hipster hotel is packed with boutique flourishes: oatmeal, brown leather and rippling velvet define the rooms; the hall sports brightly coloured wellingtons for guests to borrow. There's a cool bistro downstairs and a heated deck for predinner cocktails. It's all just a 10-minute walk from Boscombe Pier.

❦ HOTEL DU VIN // POOLE £££

Map p95; ☎ 01202-665709; www.hotelduvin.com; Thames St; d £170-265, ste from £350; 🛜

Tucked away in an artfully converted Georgian merchant's house, this hotel is one to linger in. An impressive tartan-carpeted hallway leads to soothing bedrooms of subtle olives, creams and soft greys. Open-plan minisuites have a bath (or two baths) in the middle, plus two TVs thoughtfully positioned so you can watch them either from the bath or the bed.

❦ MILSOMS HOTEL // POOLE £

off Map p95; ☎ 01202-609000; www.milsomshotel. co.uk; 47 Haven Rd; d £60-75; 🅿 🛜

The eight supremely stylish rooms of this minihotel sport off-white fabrics, painted wood, purple throws and a restrained scattering of cushions; bathrooms are glam in chrome and cream. It's set above a Loch Fyne seafood restaurant, so smoked salmon features on a breakfast menu packed with treats.

❦ SALTINGS // POOLE ££

off Map p95; ☎ 01202-707349; www.the-saltings. com; 5 Salterns Way; d £80-90; 🅿

In this utterly delightful 1930s B&B, Art Deco charm is everywhere: expect curved windows, arched doorways and decorative uplights. Dazzling white rooms feature dashes of spearmint and pastel blue, as well as minifridges, digital radios and Lush toiletries.

❦ LORD BUTE // CHRISTCHURCH ££

☎ 01425-278884; www.lordbute.co.uk; 181 Lymington Rd; d £98-108, ste £140-225; 🅿 🏾

Classy name, classy place. Rooms range from contemporary (all oatmeal-coloured fabrics, slim leather sofas and ultramodern sinks) to traditional, plastered with plush drapes and peppered with antiques. Some of the suites even have their own garden areas. The Lord Bute is 3 miles east of Christchurch.

❦ OLD GEORGE // WIMBORNE MINSTER £

☎ 01202-888510; www.theoldgeorge.net; 2 Corn Market; s/d £40/70; 🅿

A charming 18th-century house on a tiny square right beside the minster. Chic rooms are done out in duck-egg blue and cream, the bathrooms are tasteful in blue and white.

❦ PERCY HOUSE // WIMBORNE MINSTER £

☎ 01202-881040; e_camp@sky.com; 4 East Borough; s/d/f £70/100/110; 🅿 🛜

A hot tub in the garden and a river to fish in set this Georgian B&B way above the rest. An impressive staircase sweeps up to rooms where the style is rustic meets elegant: raspberry-red walls, antique furniture and stripped woods.

ISLE OF PURBECK

❦ GOLD COURT HOUSE // WAREHAM £

☎ 01929-553320; www.goldcourthouse.co.uk; St John's Hill; s/d £50/75; 🅿

Airy rooms featuring lightwood beams, peach and aquamarine grace this Georgian B&B full of thoroughly civilised English charm. TVs are tucked away in cupboards, while magazines and board games (the owners are Scrabble addicts) lie scattered around.

❦ TRINITY // WAREHAM £

☎ 01929-556689; www.trinitybnb.co.uk; 32 South St; s/d/f £40/60/80

This 15th-century B&B oozes so much character, you half expect to bump into a chap in doublet and hose. The staircase is a swirl of ancient timber, floors creak under stately rugs; bedrooms feature fantastic brickwork and inglenook fireplaces. The bathrooms are reassuringly modern, all yellow and green tiles and smart shiny fittings.

❦ MORTONS HOUSE // CORFE CASTLE £££

☎ 01929-480988; www.mortonshouse.co.uk; East St; d £130-225; P 🛜

A place to break out the Bollinger: a romantic, luxurious 16th-century, mini-baronial pile. The rooms are festooned with red brocade and gold tassels – an occasional chaise longue adds to the effect.

❦ BEACH HOUSE // LULWORTH COVE ££

☎ 01929-400404; www.lulworthbeachhotel.com; Main St; d £90-120; P 🛜

At this oh-so-stylish hotel 200m from the beach, rooms feature blond woods, coconut matting and flashes of leather and lime – the best has its own private sea-view deck.

❦ BISHOPS COTTAGE // LULWORTH COVE ££

☎ 01929-400880; www.bishopscottage.co.uk; Main St; d £100; P 🛜

This shabby-chic, effortlessly cool B&B throws together antique furniture and sleek modern fabrics – and makes it work. Chill out on your own window seat or in the funky bar downstairs.

DORCHESTER & INLAND DORSET

❦ BEGGAR'S KNAP // DORCHESTER ££

Map p106; ☎ 01305-268191; www.beggarsknap. co.uk; 2 Weymouth Ave; s £45, d £70-90; P

Despite the name, this utterly fabulous, vaguely decadent guesthouse is far from impoverished. Opulent raspberry-red rooms drip with chandeliers and gold brocades; beds draped in fine cottons range from French sleigh to four-poster. The breakfast room, with its towering plants and a huge harp, is gorgeous. You could pay much, much more and get something half as nice.

❦ KINGS ARMS // DORCHESTER ££

Map p106; ☎ 01305-265353; www.kingsarms dorchester.com; 30 High East St; s £69, d £90-135; P

A huge heraldic crest and ceilings lined with elaborate plasterwork indicate this hotel's Georgian origins, while sleek armchairs and ultratrendy sinks bring the bedrooms up to date. The bar is definitely different: riding boots, stuffed fish and a ship's figurehead hang from the walls.

❦ WESTWOOD HOUSE // DORCHESTER £

Map p106; ☎ 01305-268018; www.westwoodhouse. co.uk; 29 High West St; s/d/f £60/80/90; 🛜

Lord Ilchester built this Regency town-house for his coachman – he'd marvel at today's tasteful furnishings: wicker chairs, cast-iron bedsteads and dinky cushions; colours range from cream and brown to lemon, sky blue or red.

❦ CROWN HOTEL // BLANDFORD FORUM ££

☎ 01258-456626; www.innforanight.co.uk; West St; s/d £80/120; P 🛜

Thick drapes hang the length of this Georgian hotel's tall ceilings, gold picture frames line the walls and brown leather armchairs sit beside brass beds. The hotel's bar is also a stylish spot to relax, surrounded by elegant wallpaper, burnished woods and leather-bound books.

☙ PORTMAN LODGE // BLANDFORD FORUM £
☎ 01258-453727; www.portmanlodge.co.uk; White Cliff Mill St; s/d £50/70; Ⓟ ☎
The perfect place to swap travellers' tales, this Victorian house overflows with souvenirs amassed during the owner's 40 years working abroad. Ask the owner to share the stories behind the Thai figurines, Egyptian bridal jewellery and huge Angolan masks (especially the one with the grass beard), and head off on a virtual world tour.

☙ FLEUR DE LYS // SHAFTESBURY ££
☎ 01747-853717; www.lafleurdelys.co.uk; Bleke St; s £80-90, d £110-135, f £175; Ⓟ ▢ ☎
For a dollop of luxury immerse yourself in the Fleur de Lys. The restrained decor is teamed with fluffy bathrobes, mini-fridges and laptop computers. Rooms are named after grape varieties, so you can sleep in Shiraz, Muscat or Pinot Noir, or sample them in the elegant restaurant (see p110) downstairs.

☙ CUMBERLAND HOUSE // SHERBORNE £
☎ 01935-817554; www.bandbdorset.co.uk; Green Hill; s £50-55, d £65-75; Ⓟ
In this 17th-century B&B there are few straight lines – instead walls undulate towards each other. Cumberland House's charming rooms are done out in white, beige and tiny bursts of vivid pink. Breakfast is either Continental (complete with chocolate croissants) or full English – either way there's freshly squeezed orange juice.

☙ SLADES FARM // CHARMINSTER £
Map p86; ☎ 01305-264032; www.bandbdorset.org.uk; s/d/f £50/70/110; Ⓟ
Barn conversions don't come much more subtle and airy than this – done out in oatmeal and cream, lit by tiny

skylights dotted across ceilings that meet walls in gentle curves. The riverside paddock (complete with grazing alpacas) is perfect to laze in. It's 2 miles north of Dorchester.

☙ STONELEIGH BARN // NORTH WOOTTON ££
Map p86; ☎ 01935-815964; www.stoneleighbarn.com; s £55, d £80-90, f £80-100; Ⓟ ☙
Outside, this gorgeous 18th-century barn delights the senses – it's smothered in bright, fragrant flowers. Inside, exposed trusses frame rooms calmly decorated in cream and gold and crammed with books and jigsaws. Three miles southeast of Sherborne.

WEYMOUTH & THE WEST COAST

☙ CHATSWORTH // WEYMOUTH ££
Map p112; ☎ 01305-785012; www.thechatsworth.co.uk; 14 The Esplanade; s £45, d £78-108
With big bay windows and squishy settees, this B&B boasts a great location that means you can choose to see the harbour or the seafront. The furnishings team leather armchairs, vanilla candles and worn wood with splashes of seaside chintz. There's also a lovely waterside terrace – watch yachts cast off just metres away as you breakfast.

☙ OLD HARBOUR VIEW // WEYMOUTH ££
Map p95; ☎ 01305-774633; www.oldharbourviewweymouth.co.uk; 12 Trinity Rd; d £80-88
Here you get boats right outside the front door and boating themes in the bedrooms – the headboards are in the tall, pared-down shape of a prow. It's set in a Georgian terrace and rooms are fresh with lots of white-painted wood; one overlooks the bustling harbour, the other faces the back.

LYME REGIS

❦ COOMBE HOUSE // £

Map p118; ☎ 01297-443849; www.coombe-house.
co.uk; 41 Coombe St; s/d £36/72; Ⓟ

Easygoing and stylish, this is a B&B of airy
rooms, sunny bay windows, wicker and
white wood. Breakfast is delivered to your
door on a trolley, complete with toaster,
allowing for perfectly lazy lie-ins in Lyme.

❦ HOTEL ALEXANDRA // £££

Map p118; ☎ 01297-442010; www.hotelalexandra.
co.uk; Pound St; s £75, d £120-190; Ⓟ

Walking in here feels like strolling into
an Agatha Christie film set. Built in 1735
for a countess, this venerable hotel is
all dignified calm, creaking floors and
murmured chatter. Rooms feature antique chairs and fine drapes or marble
bathrooms and bright, striped satin.
Most have captivating views of the Cobb;
the glorious terrace has a view of the
sparkling bay – ideal for perusing the
Telegraph in a panama hat.

❦ OLD LYME GUEST HOUSE // £

Map p118; ☎ 01297-442929; www.oldlymeguest
house.co.uk; 29 Coombe St; d £75; Ⓟ

This former post office – look out for the
wooden post box embedded in the front
wall – is now an award-winning B&B. It
provides ladylike rooms with plenty of
frills, power showers and free-range eggs
for breakfast.

DEVON

EXETER & AROUND

❦ ABODE, ROYAL CLARENCE HOTEL // EXETER ££

Map p128; ☎ 01392-319955; www.abodehotels.
co.uk/exeter; Cathedral Yard; r £115-135, ste £175-
260; 🛜

At ABode, Georgian grandeur meets
minimalist chic. Wonky floors and
stained glass combine with recessed
lighting, pared-down furniture and
neutral tones. The rooms range from
'comfortable' and 'enviable' to 'fabulous'.
The last is aptly named: bigger than most
people's flats, its slanted ceilings frame a
grandstand view of the cathedral. Prices
depend on availability; make sure you
book ahead to bag the bargains.

❦ RAFFLES // EXETER £

Map p128; ☎ 01392-270200; www.raffles-exeter.
co.uk; 11 Blackall Rd; s/d £42/72; Ⓟ

Creaking with antiques and awash with
Victoriana, this B&B is a lovely blend of
old woods and tasteful modern fabrics.
Plant stands, dado rails and Pear's Soap
adverts add to the turn-of-the-century
feel. Largely organic breakfasts, a walled
garden and much coveted parking seal
the deal.

❦ ST OLAVES // EXETER ££

Map p128; ☎ 01392-217736; www.olaves.co.uk;
Mary Arches St; d/ste/f £125/155/165; Ⓟ

This hotel's swirling spiral staircase is so
gorgeous it's tempting to sleep beside it.
But you better opt for the 18th-century-
with-contemporary-twists bedrooms:
expect rococo mirrors, brass bedsteads
and plush furnishings.

❦ COMBE HOUSE // GITTISHAM £££

off Map p128; ☎ 01404-540400; www.thishotel.com;
Gittisham; s £160-345, d £180-365, ste £344-400; Ⓟ

More like a National Trust property
than a hotel, this Elizabethan manor has
a great hall with floor-to-ceiling wood
panels, ancient oak furniture and original Tudor paintings. In the bedrooms,
indulge in crisp cottons, monogrammed
towels, rain showers and sumptuous
throws. One room even has a vast copper washtub for a bath. It all resides on a
massive estate near Gittisham, 14 miles
east of Exeter.

ACCOMMODATION

EAST DEVON

☙ DURHAM HOUSE // BEER £

☎ 01297-20449; www.durhamhouse.org; Fore St; s/d £40/70, f £75-80; Ⓟ

This laid-back, airy 1897 B&B is perfectly positioned in the centre of the appealing village of Beer. Rooms are a chilled combo of cream, light beams, wicker chairs and reclaimed pine. It's all topped off with dashes of period charm: an arched doorway, bright tiles and stained glass.

☙ SALTY MONK // SIDFORD ££

☎ 01395-513174; www.saltymonk.co.uk; Church St; s £80, d £110-120, ste £136-200; Ⓟ 🛜

A place to indulge all the senses, this 16th-century restaurant-with-rooms panders to your comfort zone. Sink into an exquisite pared-down pod of a bath, then doze off in a chic low-level bed surrounded by beams and antiques. Or book exclusive use of its sparkly new spa, complete with sauna, hot tub and outdoor shower. This little pamper palace is 2 miles out of Sidmouth in Sidford, on the A3052.

TORQUAY & AROUND

☙ CARY ARMS // TORQUAY £££

Map p142; ☎ 01803-327110; www.caryarms.co.uk; Babbacombe Beach; d £150-250, ste £200-350

The great British seaside has just gone seriously stylish. At this boutique bolt-hole neutral tones are jazzed up by candy-striped cushions; balconies directly overlook the beach and children are given a fishing net and bait on arrival. There's even a stick of rock with the hotel's name running through it on your pillow.

☙ HEADLAND VIEW // TORQUAY £

Map p142; ☎ 01803-312612; www.headlandview. com; Babbacombe Downs; s/d £45/70; Ⓟ

Set high on the cliffs at Babbacombe, this cheery B&B is awash with nauticalia, from boat motifs on the curtains to 'welcome' life belts and salty sayings on the walls. Four rooms have tiny flower-filled balconies overlooking a cracking stretch of sea.

☙ HILLCROFT // TORQUAY ££

Map p142; ☎ 01803-297247; www.thehillcroft. co.uk; 9 St Lukes Rd; s £65-110, d £75-85, ste £100-130; 🖥 🛜

This minihotel exudes chic. Rooms are either full of French antiques and crisp lines or Asian-themed furniture and exotic fabrics, while bathrooms range from the grotto-esque to the sleekly styled. The gorgeous top-floor suite has broad views over the town.

☙ LANSCOMBE HOUSE // TORQUAY ££

Map p142; ☎ 01803-606938; www.lanscombehouse. co.uk; Cockington Lane; d £80-100; Ⓟ

Laura Ashley herself would love this design: a 19th-century house filled with lashings of tasteful fabrics, four-poster beds and free-standing slipper baths. Set on the edge of Cockington Village, it has a lovely English cottage garden where you can hear owls hoot at night.

☙ OSBORNE // TORQUAY £££

Map p142; ☎ 01803-213311; www.osborne-torquay. co.uk; Hesketh Cres; d £130-230; Ⓟ 🛜 🏊

The terrace of this grand hotel is more St Tropez than Torquay: think palm trees, white parasols and utterly gorgeous sea views. The Osborne is built in the style of a Georgian crescent; plump for a bay-view room for period flourishes and binoculars to watch the boats go by.

☙ SAMPFORD HOUSE // BRIXHAM £

off Map p142; ☎ 01803-857761; www.sampford house.com; 57 King St; s £44-56, d £54-82; Ⓟ

Judging by the low ceilings in this delightful 18th-century fisherman's cottage, seafarers were much smaller 200 years

ACCOMMODATION

ago. The compact cream and peach bedrooms have little window seats and captivating views down onto the harbour.

BRITANNIA HOUSE //
TEIGNMOUTH £
off Map p142; ☎ 01626-770051; 26 Teign St; s/d
£55/75

This 17th-century B&B in the heart of town packs a few surprises. Old cutlasses meet abstract art, and the gorgeous blood-red lounge is lined with exotic curios. The soothing bedrooms have comfy chairs and swish bathrooms, breakfast is a feast of local food, while the walled garden is ideal for afternoon tea.

THOMAS LUNY HOUSE //
TEIGNMOUTH ££
off Map p142; ☎ 01626-772976; www.thomas-luny
-house.co.uk; Teign St; s/d £70/98; Ⓟ

The essence of refined, restrained luxury, this 200-year-old town house oozes quality and is graced by heavy fabrics, antiques, wooden trunks and old sailing prints. The patio garden is an oasis of quiet calm.

TOTNES & AROUND

OLD FORGE // TOTNES £
☎ 01803-862174; www.oldforgetotnes.com;
Seymour Pl; s £60, d £70-85, f £105; Ⓟ ☎

In this 600-year-old former jail, comfort has replaced incarceration: deep reds and sky-blue furnishings cosy up to bright throws and spa baths. The delightful family room even has its own decked sun terrace. It's a 10-minute walk to town.

ROYAL SEVEN STARS // TOTNES ££
☎ 01803-862125; www.royalsevenstars.co.uk; The
Plains; s £85-115, d £119-150; Ⓟ ☎

They've been putting up travellers here since Charles II's day, and this grand old coaching inn in the heart of Totnes is all 17th-century charm. Bay windows, bowed ceilings and slanting floors give it atmosphere, while rich throws, solid wood furniture and fancy bathrooms ensure modern comforts.

STEAM PACKET INN // TOTNES ££
☎ 01803-863880; www.steampacketinn.co.uk; St
Peters Quay; s/d/f £60/80/95; Ⓟ

It's almost as if this wharfside warehouse's minimalist rooms have been plucked from the pages of a design magazine, so exquisite are the painted wood panels, willow arrangements and neutral tones. Ask for a river-view room, then sit back in style and watch the world float by.

MALTSTERS ARMS //
TUCKENHAY ££
☎ 01803-732350; www.tuckenhay.com; d £75-115; Ⓟ

If you want something bland and conventional, don't stay here. The rooms in this old stone, creek-side pub blend silky fabrics and painted oil drums – there's even a ship's rudder in one room. The three with gorgeous river views are easily the best. The Malsters is in the hamlet of Tuckenhay, 4 miles south of Totnes.

DARTMOUTH & START BAY

BROWN'S HOTEL //
DARTMOUTH ££
Map p154; ☎ 01803-832572; www.browns
hoteldartmouth.co.uk; 29 Victoria Rd; s £70,
d £90-180; Ⓟ

Somehow this smoothly sumptuous hotel manages to combine leather curtains, pheasant-feather lampshades and animal-print chairs, and make it all look classy. Breakfasts are laid-back affairs: organic bread, freshly squeezed orange juice and homemade marmalade.

ACCOMMODATION

♥ ROYAL CASTLE HOTEL //
DARTMOUTH £££
Map p154; ☎ 01803-833033; www.royalcastle.co.uk;
The Quay; s £95, d £140-200; ☜
This exquisite hotel has stood plumb on
Dartmouth's waterfront for 500 years.
Expect a library full of battered leather-
bound books, timbers from a Spanish
man-o-war in the bar and antique chaises longues, massive carved chairs and
velvet curtains in the rooms. Pack a copy
of Agatha Christie's *Ordeal by Innocence*;
the crime writer used the hotel as inspiration for the Royal George in the novel.

♥ SEABREEZE //
TORCROSS, START BAY ££
off Map p154; ☎ 01548-580697; www.seabreeze
breaks.com; d £90-125; ℗
Fall asleep to a real-life soundtrack of the
waves at this funky former fisherman's
cottage. Just metres from the sea wall,
bedrooms have slanting ceilings, whitewashed walls and artfully arranged bits
of weathered driftwood. Candy-striped
window seats face directly onto the bay
and you can sip your breakfast cappuccino ensconced in a cane chair on the
terrace.

SALCOMBE TO BURGH ISLAND

♥ RIA VIEW // SALCOMBE ££
☎ 01548-842965; www.salcombebandb.co.uk;
Devon Rd; d £86; ℗ ☜
The panorama on offer at this B&B is
so scenic the rooms almost come as
an extra. Effortlessly stylishly decor
blends cream, peach and hints of dull
gold; wicker sofas are scattered around.
The front rooms and the flower-filled
deck have captivating views down onto
floating boats and a rising and falling
tide. It's a few minutes' steep walk into
town.

♥ TIDES REACH // SALCOMBE £££
☎ 01548-843466; www.tidesreach.com; South
Sands; d £200-260, f from £300; ℗ ☳
The tide doesn't quite (reach), but
South Sands does lie just across a lane.
All rooms have sight of the sea, many
have balconies, and the atmosphere is
countrified rather than superchic (think
cosy fabric armchairs not sleek leather).
Prices fall by up to £60 a room out of
high season.

♥ SLOOP INN // BANTHAM ££
☎ 01548-560489; www.sloopatbantham.co.uk; s/d
£50/84; ℗
Just a sandy stroll from the beach, this
14th-century inn makes a chilled-out
base. The stylish rooms are decked out
in neutral tones, suede headboards
and floaty curtains. Choose from views
over the rolling fields or the sand dunes
stretching to the sea.

♥ HENLEY HOTEL //
BIGBURY-ON-SEA ££
☎ 01548-810240; www.thehenleyhotel.co.uk; Folly
Hill; s £75, d £113-136; ℗
This charming Edwardian holiday cottage clings to the cliffs just inside the
Avon estuary. Lloyd Loom furniture,
leafy house plants and exotic rugs dot
the interior, and the views down onto
Bantham are extraordinary. Steps (150 of
them) lead to the beach below.

♥ THURLESTONE HOTEL //
THURLESTONE £££
☎ 01548-560382; www.thurlestone.co.uk; d £184-
340; ℗ ☳
Smart blue parasols dot the grounds,
glass screens shelter the almost-infinity
pool and luxury reigns in rooms with
superfluffy bathrobes, crisp linens and
balconies with sweeping sea views. Prices
drop by as much as £80 a room in low
season.

☙ BURGH ISLAND HOTEL //
BURGH ISLAND £££
☎ 01548-810514; www.burghisland.com; s/d £280/380, ste £440-600
Full of 1920s glamour, this gleaming-white Art Deco hotel sits gracefully on its own tidal island. Past guests include Agatha Christie (who wrote *And Then There Were None* here), Noel Coward, Prince Edward and Wallis Simpson. Jazz Age rooms merge flapper style and modern luxury: uplighters illuminate slipper baths; rich woods frame retro radios. It's perfect for cocktails and croquet, and the views are superb.

PLYMOUTH

☙ ASTOR // ££
Map p164; ☎ 01752-225511; www.astorhotel.co.uk; 22 Elliot St; s £45, d £60-150, f £100-200; ☎
This sumptuous Victorian hotel has a finish fit for film stars, with flouncy flourishes, four-poster beds and Jacuzzis in the suites. A place full of character, it's also run by one: Joseph, a charming, can-do guy who could write a handbook on customer service.

☙ BOWLING GREEN // £
Map p164; ☎ 01752-209090; www.bowlinggreen hotel.co.uk; 10 Osborne Pl; s/d/f £47/68/78; Ⓟ ☎
Some of the smart cream and white rooms in this family-run hotel look out onto the modern incarnation of Drake's famous bowling green. If you tire of watching people throw woods after jacks, you can play chess in the conservatory.

☙ ST ELIZABETH'S HOUSE // £££
off Map p164; ☎ 01752-344840; www.stelizabeths. co.uk; Longbrook St; d £140-160, ste £180-250; Ⓟ
A manor house in the 17th century, this minihotel now oozes boutique chic. Free-standing slipper baths, oak furniture and Egyptian cotton grace the rooms; the suites feature palatial bathrooms and private terraces. It's set in the suburb-cum-village of Plympton St Maurice, 5 miles east of Plymouth.

DARTMOOR NATIONAL PARK

☙ BROWN'S // TAVISTOCK ££
☎ 01822-618686; www.brownsdevon.co.uk; 80 West St; s from £80, d £120-230; Ⓟ ☎)
Bursts of boutique chic fill this 17th-century coaching inn. Beams and stone sit alongside stained glass and Egyptian motifs. Luxury flourishes include crisp sheets, Molton Brown toiletries and mineral water drawn from the hotel's Roman well.

☙ HORN OF PLENTY //
TAVISTOCK £££
☎ 01822-832528; www.thehornofplenty.co.uk; Gulworthy, near Tavistock; d £120-200; Ⓟ
The swish rooms at this sumptuous country-house hotel boast claw-foot baths, canopied beds, warm wooden floors and scattered antiques. Most have balconies or terraces from which to gaze out at rolling, tranquil countryside.

☙ TWO BRIDGES //
TWO BRIDGES £££
Map p169; ☎ 01822-890581; www.twobridges. co.uk; Two Bridges; s £95-125, d £140-190; Ⓟ
Walking into this classic moorland hotel feels like slipping on a favourite pair of shoes – everything fits, perfectly. It's a place to lounge in the gently elegant rooms, with their huge inglenook fireplaces and squishy leather sofas. Former guests Wallace Simpson, Winston Churchill and Vivien Leigh probably liked it too. Two Bridges is 1.5 miles northeast of Princetown.

ACCOMMODATION

🍴 22 MILL STREET // CHAGFORD ££

☎ 01647-432244; www.22millst.com; 22 Mill St; d £110-130; Ⓟ

The smoothly comfy rooms of this boutique oasis feature exposed stone walls, wooden floorboards and slatted blinds, tastefully offset by satin cushions and bursts of modern art. It's conveniently placed in the heart of Chagford's quiet, winding streets above a top-notch eatery (p176).

🍴 EASTON COURT // CHAGFORD £

Map p169; ☎ 01647-433369; www.easton.co.uk; Easton Cross; s £55-60, d £60-75; Ⓟ

It's worth staying here just for the breakfasts: choices include fresh fish or soufflé omelette. The rooms are lovely too, with their cast-iron beds, soft sofas and views of wooded hills. It's 1.5 miles from Chagford.

🍴 COLLAVEN MANOR // SOURTON ££

☎ 01837-861522; www.collavenmanor.co.uk; s £65, d £106-146; Ⓟ

At this delightful, clematis-clad mini-manor house a wooden chandelier crowns a 16th-century hall. Restful bedrooms are lined with tapestries and window seats – soothing places to enjoy tor-top views. Collaven Manor is 5 miles west of Okehampton.

🍴 GIDLEIGH PARK // GIDLEIGH £££

Map p169; ☎ 01647-432367; www.gidleigh.com; s £340, d £310-1155; Ⓟ 📶

A prestigious oasis of luxury, Gidleigh teams crests, crenellations and roaring fires with shimmering sanctuaries of blue marble, waterproof TVs and private saunas. Bowls of fruit and a decanter of port or Madeira help you feel at home. After breakfast in the double Michelin-starred restaurant, work it off at the tennis courts, bowling

green or croquet lawns. It's 2 miles from Chagford.

🍴 LYDGATE HOUSE // POSTBRIDGE ££

Map p169; ☎ 01822-880209; www.lydgatehouse. co.uk; s £50-55, d £110-140; Ⓟ

This beautifully furnished Victorian house oozes tranquillity and is hidden away at the end of a moss-lined track. There are rich tapestries, linens and antique furniture inside; birdsong and a rushing river outside. You can even feed the rescue sheep. It's a 10-minute walk from Postbridge.

NORTH DEVON

🍴 WESTWOOD // ILFRACOMBE ££

☎ 01271-867443; www.west-wood.co.uk; Torrs Park Rd; d £80-110; Ⓟ 📶

Modern, minimal and marvellous, this ultrachic B&B is a study of neutral tones and dashes of vivid colour. It's also graced by pony-skin chaises longues and stand-alone baths, while some rooms have sea glimpses.

🍴 BROOMHILL ART HOTEL // BARNSTAPLE £

☎ 01271-850262; www.broomhillart.co.uk; Muddiford Rd; s/d £50/75; Ⓟ

Funky, arty and very comfy, this innovative hotel cleverly combines contemporary design and antiques. A creaking, sweeping staircase leads to bedrooms packed with artwork and decked out with bursts of purple velvet. Broomhill Art is 3 miles north of Barnstaple on the B3230.

🍴 CHAPEL FARM // CROYDE £

☎ 01271-890429; www.chapelfarmcroyde.co.uk; Hobbs Hill; s/d £30/70; Ⓟ

Walls and ceilings shoot off at atmospherically random angles in this cosy, thatched cobb farmhouse, formerly a home to monks. Some of the light, pretty rooms share bathrooms. Self-catering is available too.

♥ SAUNTON SANDS HOTEL //
SAUNTON SANDS ££

☎ 01271-890212; www.brend-hotels.co.uk; d £95-200; Ⓟ 🛜 🖭

Dominating the cliff, this is a delightful Art Deco, wedding-cake-white creation – all clean lines and curves. The 1930s style doesn't extend to the slightly uniform bedrooms, but the pool and the mind-expanding beach views are superb.

♥ RED LION HOTEL // CLOVELLY ££

☎ 01237-431237; www.clovelly.co.uk; s from £60, d £120-136

Not so much a room with a view, more a view with a room. Set right on Clovelly Quay, the hardest choice here is whether to look out over the sea or the harbour – both are captivating – and the fresh rooms are dotted with Lloyd Loom-style furniture.

CORNWALL

BUDE & THE ATLANTIC HIGHWAY

♥ ELEMENTS HOTEL // BUDE ££

☎ 01288-275066; www.elements-life.co.uk; Marine Dr; s/d/f £70/105/160; Ⓟ

Eleven soothing rooms in whites and creams, with big views from the outdoor deck, a gym and Finholme sauna, and surf lessons courtesy of nearby Raven Surf School. It's in a great detached position on the cliffs above Bude.

♥ BOSCASTLE HOUSE //
BOSCASTLE ££

☎ 01840-250654; www.boscastlehouse.com; Tintagel Rd; d £120; Ⓟ 🛜

The fanciest of Boscastle B&Bs, this Victorian house overlooks the valley, with six rooms named after Cornish legends. Charlotte has bay-window views, Nine Windows has his-and-hers sinks and a freestanding bath, while Trelawney has space and its own sofa.

♥ MILL HOUSE INN //
TREBARWITH ££

☎ 01840-770200; www.themillhouseinn.co.uk; d £100-140; Ⓟ 🛜

There are eight elegant rooms in calming creams and dark wood at this converted corn mill. They're a little old-fashioned, with some old beams and poky corners, but the inn's pub and restaurant make up for any shortcomings.

♥ OLD RECTORY // ST JULIOT ££

☎ 01840-250225; www.stjuliot.com; d £95; 🗓 Mar-Nov; Ⓟ

This house, a short drive from Boscastle, was the home of St Juliot's parson and the place where Thomas Hardy wooed his wife-to-be. It's heavy on the Victoriana – upholstered furniture, thick drapes, sash windows – but the grounds are gorgeous. There's more space in the stable, with private entrance and woodburner.

♥ OLD SCHOOL HOTEL //
PORT ISAAC ££

☎ 01208-880721; www.theoldschoolhotel.co.uk; Fore St; d £107-147; Ⓟ 🛜

A sweet small hotel that was originally Port Isaac's schoolhouse. Appropriately, rooms are named after school subjects: top of the class are Latin with its sleigh-bed and cupboard bathroom, Biology with its sofa and church-style windows, and split-level Mathematics, with shared terrace and bunkbeds for the kids.

ACCOMMODATION

☙ CORNISH TIPI HOLIDAYS //
ST KEW ££
☎ 01208-880781; www.cornishtipiholidays.co.uk; Tregare, Pendoggett; med/large/extra large tipi per week £545/615/820

Camp Sioux-style in a wooded valley near St Kew. Tepees are in communal 'village' fields, or pay a premium for a private site. All come with coolboxes, stoves, cooking gear and camp lanterns. BYO sense of adventure.

PADSTOW

☙ TREANN HOUSE // ££
☎ 01841-553855; www.treannhousepadstow.co.uk; 24 Dennis Rd; £95-115; Ⓟ

Offering luxury that far outstrips its price point, this B&B shimmers with understated style. The three rooms (Cove, Bay and Estuary) are classic, with views over Padstow's rooftops, while the sitting room is blond wood and open plan. Breakfast's a treat: fresh berry pancakes, or poached eggs with asparagus and sweet potato hash.

☙ TREVERBYN HOUSE // ££
☎ 01841-532855; www.treverbynhouse.com; Station Rd; d £80-115; Ⓟ

Harry Potter would feel at home at this turreted villa, complete with four colour-coded rooms (lilac, pink, green, yellow) plus an ultra-romantic tower hideaway. It's beautifully decorated, and jams are homemade with fruit from the garden.

NEWQUAY & AROUND

☙ THE BEDRUTHAN STEPS //
MAWGAN PORTH £££
off Map p200; ☎ 01637-860555; www.bedruthan.com; d from £158; Ⓟ

Don't be put off by the boxy exterior: inside the Bedruthan Steps offers contemporary rooms in taupes and creams, plus spacious villas and apartments for longer stays. Several kids' clubs and lots of organised activities have earned it a reputation as one of Cornwall's top family hotels.

☙ THE SCARLET //
MAWGAN PORTH £££
off Map p200; ☎ 01637-861600; www.scarlethotel.co.uk; d £180-395; Ⓟ 🛜 🛋

Cornwall's sexiest hotel by a country mile, and it's ecofriendly to boot (recycled rainwater, biomass boiler, renewable energy supplier). On the bluffs above Mawgan Porth, the hotel's rooms all boast eye-popping ocean views and defiantly modern design: minimalist bathrooms, statement furniture, industrial-chic materials (plastic, fibreglass, concrete) and an infinity pool that'll blow your flip-flops off. Accommodation as art.

☙ GLENDORGAL HOTEL //
PORTH BEACH ££
off Map p200; ☎ 01637-874937; www.glendorgalhotel.co.uk; Lusty Glaze Rd; d £110-190; Ⓟ 🛜

Thoroughly decent hotel in a clifftop spot above Porth Beach. There are only 26 rooms, so it feels intimate. They're nicely finished, but a little on the small side and only a handful have proper sea views. The location's wonderful though, with headland and coves on your doorstep.

☙ HARBOUR HOTEL //
NEWQUAY £££
Map p200; ☎ 01637-873040; www.harbourhotel.co.uk; North Quay Hill; d £130-160; ▣

This small hotel is right in on the action in the centre of Newquay, but its hillside location feels far removed from the summer throngs. The plain bedrooms have great ocean views onto Newquay Bay, and a few have balconies.

☙ HEADLAND HOTEL //
NEWQUAY £££
Map p200; ☎ 01637-872211; www.headlandhotel.
co.uk; Fistral Beach; d £199-329; Ⓟ ▯ ⚥
Featured in the film of Roald Dahl's *The Witches*, this red-brick Victorian pile stands aloof on Fistral Headland. Old-style hotel pampering includes heated pools, tennis courts and a nine-hole golf course, and the rooms range from courtyard standards up to top-of-the-line 'Splendids'. Two tower rooms have their own staircases.

PERRANPORTH TO PORTREATH

☙ ARAMAY // ST AGNES ££
☎ 01872-553546; www.aramay.com; Quay Rd; d £95-105; Ⓟ ⌃
Not long on the scene, but with five fine rooms and a sweet St Agnes location, it won't stay secret for long. Try No 1, with contemporary crimson-and-cream decor, or swanky No 3, with silky throws and views of the Stippy Stappy.

ST IVES

☙ BLUE HAYES // £££
off Map p208; ☎ 01736-797129; www.bluehayes.
co.uk; Trelyon Ave; r £170-210; ⊗ closed Nov-Feb; Ⓟ
A favourite of the Sunday supplements, this hotel has a French Riviera flavour thanks to its manicured grounds, balustraded breakfast terrace and five supremely well-appointed rooms. The Trelyon Suite even has its own private roof terrace with wonderful views over St Ives Bay.

☙ BOSKERRIS // £££
off Map p208; ☎ 01736-795295; www.boskerris
hotel.co.uk; Boskerris Rd; d £130-195; Ⓟ ⌃
This 1930s guesthouse in Carbis Bay has had a swish makeover and, if you like your fabrics fancy, your materials modern and your colours cool and contem-

porary, you won't go far wrong. Big bay views, a soothing seaside ambience and plenty of classy touches make it popular: book well ahead.

☙ 11 SEA VIEW TERRACE // ££
Map p208; ☎ 01736-798440; www.11stives.co.uk; 11 Sea View Tce; d £100-120; Ⓟ
Creams, checks and cappuccino carpets distinguish this chic St Ives B&B. The two front rooms have lovely town and sea views, while the rear one overlooks a garden patio; for more space there's a smart holiday flat (£500 to £925 per week).

☙ ORGANIC PANDA // ££
Map p208; ☎ 01736-793890; www.organicpanda.
co.uk; 1 Pednolver Tce; d £100-130; Ⓟ
Food and art are the guiding principles of this Carbis Bay B&B. Spotty cushions, technicolour artwork and timber-salvage beds in the rooms, and the house is dotted with work by St Ives artists. Needless to say, the organic brekkie is a real spoil.

☙ PRIMROSE VALLEY // ££
☎ 01736-794939; www.primroseonline.co.uk; Porth-minster Beach; d £120-165, ste £160-225; Ⓟ ⌃
The boutique choice, with ecofriendly credentials and an eye for interior design to rival most big city hotels. The rooms are eclectic – exposed stone and retro lights in some, designer wallpaper, pale wood and keynote colours in others. Throw in the fab location near Porth-minster's sands, and you have one of Cornwall's best bolt-holes.

PENZANCE & AROUND

☙ ABBEY HOTEL // PENZANCE £££
Map p218; ☎ 01736-366906; www.theabbeyonline.
co.uk; Abbey St; d £150-210
A 17th-century sea-captain's house turned heritage hotel, off Chapel St. Its creaky rooms brim with burnished antiques, vintage rugs and Victoriana, and

there's a delicious secret garden hidden out back. Layouts are higgledy-piggledy: ask for Rooms One or Three, or the lovely book-lined suite for maximum space.

❦ SUMMER HOUSE // PENZANCE ££

Map p218; ☎ 01736-363744; www.summerhouse -cornwall.com; Cornwall Tce; d £120-150; ⊗ Apr-Oct; ℗

Just off the Penzance prom, this former artist's house is now a stylish hotel, blending Knightsbridge chic with seaside accents. Checks, pinstripes and cheery colours characterise the bedrooms, and downstairs there's a Mediterranean restaurant with alfresco terrace.

❦ BOUTIQUE RETREATS // MOUSEHOLE ££

off Map p218; ☎ 01872-270085; www.boutique- retreats.co.uk; per week £790-835; ℗ 🛜

Boutique retreats indeed, halfway between a holiday cottage and a high-class hotel. There are two Mousehole properties (an old fisherman's store and a cute skipper's cottage) plus a divine beach cabin at Porthkidney, near Hayle. All three ooze style – slate tiles, up-to-date kitchens, groovy furniture and modern art.

❦ THE COVE // LAMORNA £££

☎ 01736-731411; www.thecovecornwall.co.uk; apt per week £1158-2412; ℗ 🛋

If it's style you want, it's style you'll find at the Cove. These lavish apart-ments above Lamorna Cove are straight out of *Wallpaper:* glossy wood, clean lines, plasma TVs, minimalist bath-rooms and picture-window patios opening onto coastal views. Book early: this is fast becoming West Cornwall's des res.

THE LIZARD

❦ BEACON CRAG // PORTHLEVEN ££

☎ 01326-573690; www.beaconcrag.com; d £85-95; ℗ 🖥

Built for a local artist, this Victorian villa perched above Porthleven is now one of the Lizard's loveliest B&Bs. Rooms are plainly furnished to make the most of the house's grandstand position: craggy coastline unfurls in abundance all around the house.

❦ HALZEPHRON HOUSE // GUNWALLOE ££

☎ 07899-925816; www.halzephronhouse.co.uk; d £100; ℗

Upscale B&B near Gunwalloe Cove in an unusual crenellated house. It's often booked out as a package in summer, but off season you'll have the pick of five rooms and the 'Observatory' cottage. The Nigella Lawson crockery and Gaggia coffee-maker give you some idea of the style standard.

❦ LIZARD YHA // LIZARD POINT £

☎ 0870 770 6120; lizard@yha.org.uk; dm £14; ⊗ Apr-Oct

Even if you're not a habitual hosteller, this YHA hostel boasts the kind of loca-tion that might just convert you. It's in the old lighthouse-keeper's cottage above Lizard Point, so the coastal vistas are out of this world; summer BBQs and guided walks are a bonus.

❦ LANDEWEDNACK HOUSE // CHURCH COVE ££

☎ 01326-290877; www.landewednack.uniquehome stays.com; d £110-180; 🛋 ℗

A slice of Lizard luxury: a restored rec-tory surrounded by two green acres and a gorgeous pool. It's been carefully modernised while retaining the house's heritage: the big Cornish hearth is still in situ, while little windows peep out over the grounds and the house's private chef prepares yummy meals.

FALMOUTH, TRURO & THE ROSELAND

❦ BUDOCK VEAN HOTEL //
FALMOUTH £££

off Map p230; ☎ 01326-250288; www.budock.co.uk; Mawnan Smith; d £214-240; ℗ ◪ ▨

Another stalwart on Cornwall's luxury-hotel scene, this riverside beauty sits on the Helford's north bank, with country-chic rooms (some with sitting rooms), four lounges, a health spa, tennis courts, 13 hectares of parkland and even a private jetty.

❦ FALMOUTH TOWNHOUSE //
FALMOUTH ££

Map p230; ☎ 01326-312009; www.falmouth townhouse.co.uk; Grove Pl; d £85-120

The choice for the design-conscious, in an elegant mansion. Despite the heritage building, the feel is studiously modernist: slate greys, retro bits-and-bobs and funky scatter cushions throughout, plus walk-in showers and king-size tellies in top-of-the-line rooms.

❦ GREENBANK // FALMOUTH £££

Map p230; ☎ 01326-312440; www.greenbank-hotel. co.uk; Harbourside; d £145-185, ste £199; ℗

Ships in bottles and model boats cruise around Falmouth's original upmarket hotel. Rooms are 'Classic' (classic colours, pine furniture, quilted bedspreads) or 'Executive' (deluge showers, king-size beds, harbour views); the Sheldrake Suite even has its own telescope.

❦ HOTEL TRESANTON //
ST MAWES £££

☎ 01326-370055; www.tresanton.com; d £240-335, ste £315-360; ℗ ▨ ▨

Long the choice for sojourning celebs and film stars, Olga Polizzi's ritzy St Mawes establishment is still the queen of the castle. Chilled checks, sea stripes and deluxe fabrics in the bedrooms, plus little extras including a private cinema, motor launch and award-winning bistro. It's a wallet-buster, but definitely one to remember.

❦ THE ROSEVINE //
PORTSCATHO £££

☎ 01872-580206; www.rosevine.co.uk; apt £195-350; ℗ ▨

This country house outside Portscatho is one of Cornwall's finest family-friendly hotels, with 12 self-contained apartments, all named after local beauty spots. It's very stylish, and the kids are superbly well-catered for, with playhouses, trampolines and climbing frames dotted round the grounds.

❦ LUGGER HOTEL // PORTLOE £££

☎ 01872-501322; www.luggerhotel.co.uk; r £140-200; ▨

The consummate romantic hideaway, teetering on the harbour's edge in pretty Portloe. Sumptuous rooms dot the smugglers' inn and adjoining fishermen's cottages, with classy furnishings, decadent beds and the sound of waves breaking from your window; the restaurant's a spoil too. The Cornish seaside gone sexy.

❦ LOVELANE CARAVANS //
CONSTANTINE £

☎ 01326-340406; www.lovelanecaravans.com; Retallack Farm; caravan per week £340-435

Kitsch connoisseurs mustn't miss this place, with a collection of caravans tricked-out in retro designs – from a full-blown Gypsy wagon and an aluminium airstream to a 1950s relic complete with lino floor, charity-shop china and floral wallpaper.

SOUTHEAST CORNWALL

❦ TREVALSA COURT //
MEVAGISSEY ££
☎ 01726-842468; www.trevalsa-hotel.co.uk; School-Hill; d £125-225; Ⓟ

This Edwardian pile is one of the best places to stay on the south coast, but the word's out and prices have skyrocketed. Still, its restoration-meets-retro approach is persuasive: some rooms have sleigh beds and leather sofas, others funky fabrics and modernist lamps, while a mullion-windowed lounge opens onto coast views.

❦ CORIANDER COTTAGES //
FOWEY ££
☎ 01726-834998; www.foweyaccommodation. co.uk; Penventinue Lane; r £90-130, cottages £130-220; Ⓟ

This cottage complex has something to suit all tastes: garden-view B&B rooms and deluxe open-plan barns powered by underground heat pumps and rainwater harvesting. It feels countrified without being rustic, and the mix of old stone and contemporary fixtures is very convincing.

❦ OLD QUAY HOUSE // FOWEY £££
☎ 01726-833302; www.theoldquayhouse.com; 28 Fore St; d £180-250; 📶

Fowey's upmarket trend continues at this exclusive quayside hotel. Natural fabrics, rattan chairs and tasteful tones characterise the interior, and the rooms are a mix of estuary-view suites and attic penthouses. Very Kensington; not at all Cornish.

❦ TREDUDWELL MANOR //
FOWEY ££
☎ 01726-870226; www.tredudwellmanor.co.uk; Lanteglos-by-Fowey; r £84-104; Ⓟ

Old-fashioned it may be, but this Queen Anne manor is a wonderful retreat, lost deep in the countryside across the River Fowey. It boasts huge rooms full of an-tiques and oil paintings, a lavish spiral staircase and hectares of private grounds.

❦ BARCLAY HOUSE // LOOE ££
☎ 01503-262929; www.barclayhouse.co.uk; St Martins Rd, East Looe; d £115-145; Ⓟ 📶 🖥

By far and away Looe's best place to stay, perfectly positioned amongst terraced gardens above East Looe. The rooms are big and bold, finished in tones of aquamarine, gold and pistachio, and several have bay windows offering memorable twilight views over town. Cottages are available for longer stays.

❦ BOTELET // LOOE £
☎ 01503-220225; www.botelet.com; Herodsfoot; d £80, cottages per week £570-1200; Ⓟ

The farmstay you've been dreaming of. Lost in lush farmland between Fowey and Looe, the Tamblyn family have created a haven of Cornish quiet: soothing B&B rooms, a brace of cottages, a little campsite and even a yurt. You won't want to leave.

❦ WESTCROFT // KINGSAND ££
☎ 01752-823216; www.westcroftguesthouse.co.uk; d £90-110; 📶

Wildly extravagant guesthouse in button-cute Kingsand, offering three suites plastered in posh wallpaper and trendy fixtures: walk-in showers, clawfoot baths, iPod docks. Pick of the bunch is the Clocktower room, where the hot tub nestles under A-frame beams and you can hear the sea swash from your window. No parking is a pain.

BODMIN MOOR & AROUND

❦ SOUTH TREGLEATH FARM //
BODMIN ££
☎ 01208-72692; www.south-tregleath.co.uk; d from £80; Ⓟ 📶 ♿

The farmstay goes fancy at this fab nook on Bodmin Moor, where the three rooms are all silky wood, wet rooms and bamboo screens. Go for the Columbine Room if you can – it's got the most space and a patio – or book out the cottage, which sleeps six. South Tregleath is still a working farm: kids can help milk the cows and collect the eggs.

☙ TREVENNA // ST NEOT ££
☎ 07872-647730; www.trevenna.co.uk; d from £110; P ☎

Just because you're in the wilds of Bodmin Moor doesn't mean you have to sleep in a sack. These old farm buildings have been dialled up to the luxury maximum: rustic Cornish stone exteriors conceal designer log-burners, drench showers, underfloor heating and iPod docks.

☙ QUIRKY HOLIDAYS // LAUNCESTON ££
☎ 01579-370219; www.quirky-holidays-cornwall.co.uk; d £65-106; P

Quirky by name, quirky by nature. Three vintage carriages – a showman's wagon, a wood-panelled steamroller wagon and an old ale-wagon – plus an old potting shed have been lovingly renovated by enthusiast owners. Each has its own woodburner and is stuffed with period knick-knacks, and the country setting is to die for.

ISLES OF SCILLY

☙ BELMONT // ST MARY'S £
☎ 01720-423154; www.the-belmont.co.uk; Church Rd; s £28-65, d £56-80, f £90-120

Solid St Mary's guesthouse, in a double-fronted detached house 15 minutes' walk from the quay. The six rooms are clean and bright and the price is definitely right.

☙ ST MARY'S HALL HOTEL // ST MARY'S £££
☎ 01720-422316; www.stmaryshallhotel.co.uk; r £180-240

This Scilly mansion was originally built for a holidaying Italian nobleman. Grand staircases, *objets d'art* and wood-panelled walls give an upmarket feel, but the Godolphin and Count Leon rooms are standard considering the price; if you can, plump for one of the plush suites with their own sitting areas and a galley kitchen.

☙ STAR CASTLE HOTEL // ST MARY'S £££
☎ 01720-422317; www.star-castle.co.uk; The Garrison; r £188-312, ste £242-362; ☎

Shaped like an eight-pointed star, this former fort on Garrison Point is one of Scilly's star hotels, with a choice of heritage-style castle rooms or more modern garden suites. It's a bit stuffy, but prices include dinner at a choice of restaurants.

☙ THE NEW INN // TRESCO £££
☎ 01720-422844; d £140-230; ☎

Compared with Tresco's two wallet-shreddingly expensive hotels (the Island Hotel and The Flying Boat Club), the New Inn is a bargain. The rooms are soothingly finished in buttery yellows and pale blues, although you'll have to fork out for a view.

☙ HELL BAY HOTEL // BRYHER £££
☎ 01720-422947; hellbay@aol.com; d incl dinner £420-550; ☎

The poshest place to stay in Scilly – a lavish island getaway blending New England–style furnishings with sunny golds, sea blues and pale wood beams. Rooms have sitting rooms, private balconies, and, of course, stunning sea views.

☙ POLREATH // ST MARTIN'S ££
☎ 01720-422046; www.polreath.com; Higher Town; d £90-110, weekly stays only May-Sep

This friendly granite cottage is one of the only B&Bs on St Martin's – titchy and traditional, with a sunny conservatory serving cream teas, homemade lemonade and hearty evening meals.

DIRECTORY

BUSINESS HOURS

SHOPS, BANKS & OFFICES

Despite the occasional 'back in 10 minutes' that stretches to an hour, most shops have fairly regular hours: Monday to Saturday 9am to 5.30pm, with many in urban areas also open 10am to 4pm on Sunday. Those are the hours we use as standard; they're not specified unless they differ.

Convenience stores stay open into the evening; in bigger towns and cities some are 24 hours. But in the region's rural areas stores can shut at lunchtime and on Sunday, while sometimes whole streets full of shops close on Wednesday or Saturday afternoons.

Banks tend to open 9.30am to 5pm Monday to Friday, 9.30am to 1pm Saturday; we note where it's different. In big cities post offices keep normal shop hours, in rural areas it's much more sporadic.

SIGHTS & ATTRACTIONS

For attractions the maxim is bigger equals open more often – blockbuster sights have longer hours and fewer days when they're closed completely, the rest

PRACTICALITIES

- ★ The regional daily newspaper is the *Western Morning News.*
- ★ BBC local news is on the radio and online. See www.bbc.co.uk/(county name).
- ★ The regional TV news shows are *Spotlight* (BBC) and *The West Country Tonight* (ITV).
- ★ Miles are driven but map heights are in metres.
- ★ Order a pint (beer or cider) in a pub, but fill your car with litres of petrol.
- ★ Shop goods are labelled in kilograms, but people think in pounds and ounces.
- ★ Electricity is simple: three flat pins connect to the 240V (50Hz AC) power supply.

tend to target tourists peaks: between Easter (March/April) and October, often with longer hours in July and August. Some cut hours drastically or close completely between November and March.

PUBS, BARS & CLUBS

Many countryside pubs have stayed true to the traditional 11pm closing time. Those in more popular rural and coastal areas are often open all day in the summer, although some do still close midafternoon. Pubs and bars in larger towns and cities tend to pull pints all day and later into the night.

This book takes standard hours to be 11am to 11pm Sunday to Thursday and 11am to midnight or 1am Friday and Saturday. Hours are only detailed when they're different.

Clubs and bigger bars in the region's cities tend to be open until at least 3am, in towns they can close earlier – as it varies we outline what time they shut.

RESTAURANTS & CAFES

In general, places tend to be either open for lunch and /or dinner, while some serve breakfast too. We indicate which it is alongside each entry, taking standard hours to be noon to 2pm for lunch, and 6pm to 10pm for dinner. We specify where it's different.

CHILDREN

Packed with beaches, moors and bucket loads of attractions, the southwest is a delight for kids, and we detail options throughout the guide. The regional tourist board, **Visit South West** (www.visitsouth west.co.uk), has a section on family holidays on its website. Two other official websites are aimed at parents: www.easypreschool southwest.co.uk and www.familyholiday southwest.co.uk. They detail familyfriendly attractions and beaches that have lifeguards and toilets.

Tourist offices are rich sources of more localised information and advice. Look out too for events aimed at children organised by National Park Authorities (NPAs), local authorities, museums and heritage organisations; these are often great fun, educational and cheap too.

Some hotels, restaurants, pubs and attractions are equipped for and welcome children – others clearly aren't and don't. As elsewhere some people will frown on breastfeeding in public, while others will barely notice.

Most, but by no means all, of the key tourist beaches have lifeguards. Where it does exist, cover is seasonal (often Easter to September) and tends to finish at 6pm. The **Royal National Lifeboat Institution** (☎ 0845 045 6999; www.rnli.org. uk) lists where and when it provides lifeguards.

CUSTOMS REGULATIONS

What you can bring into the UK depends on where you set off from; a key distinction is normally whether you arrive from inside or outside the EU.

DUTY FREE

Limits on duty-free goods brought from *outside* the EU include 200 cigarettes, 4L of still wine and 16L of beer, plus 1L of spirits or 2L of fortified wine (such as port or sherry) and £390 worth of all other goods.

TAX & DUTY PAID

In many cases there's no limit to the goods you can bring from *within* the EU (if taxes have been paid), provided it's for your own use. Customs officials use the following guidelines to distinguish personal use from commercial imports: 3200 cigarettes, 200 cigars, 10L of spirits, 20L of fortified wine, 90L of wine and 110L of beer.

Be aware that if travelling from some EU countries (including Bulgaria, Czech Republic, Poland and Romania), at the time of writing some limits do apply. For more details see www.visitbritain.com (search for 'customs allowances').

DANGERS & ANNOYANCES

Compared to the world's trouble spots England is a safe place and the southwest corner of it particularly so; it has the second-lowest crime figures in the country. Crime can happen anywhere and in places you still need to be careful, especially at night. In particular where there are concentrations of bars and clubs, avoid walking alone and beware of becoming embroiled in a fight.

On the region's main city streets muggers, bag-snatchers and pickpockets are relatively rare, but money and important documents are best kept out of sight and reach rather than in hand or shoulder bags. If you're staying in hostels take a padlock for the lockers and keep stuff packed away.

Stash luggage and valuables out of sight in cars, even at remote moorland and coastal beauty spots, which are sometimes targeted by thieves.

BEACHES

The lifesaving charity, the RNLI has to rescue hundreds of people each year in the Westcountry. Its advice includes: use beaches with lifeguards; swim and bodyboard between red and yellow flags and surf in water marked by black-and-white chequered flags. It also advises parents not let children use inflatables – if they do an adult should attach a line and hold onto it.

Some of the biggest tidal ranges in the world occur in the southwest, and the clear, sandy route out of that secluded cove can soon disappear under feet of water – people having to be rescued after getting cut off isn't that uncommon.

Times of high and low water are often outlined at popular beaches, as well as on local BBC TV and radio, and in newspapers. Small yellow booklets of tide times are available from newsagents and local shops (£1.30).

'Blue Flags' are awarded to beaches with high water-quality standards, and good safety and environmental records. See the latest list at www.keepbritaintidy.org.

WALKING

While stunning to hike, the region's moors are also remote, so prepare for upland weather conditions. Warm, waterproof clothing, water, hats and sunscreen are essential; they'll make hiking coast paths more comfortable too. Parts of Dartmoor are used by the military for live-firing ranges, see p172.

DISCOUNT CARDS

Regional railcards are outlined in our Transport chapter (p323). Otherwise there are no regionwide discount cards for visitors. Sometimes two or more attractions team up with joint tickets; they're mentioned throughout the guide.

The Westcountry has a superb sprinkling of historic buildings and if you're visiting more than three or four, it's worth considering joining a heritage organisation for a year. The **National**

Trust (NT; ☎ 0844 800 1895; www.nationaltrust.org.
uk) has an excellent range of properties in
the region; members can park for free at
their car parks too. Annual membership
is from £36 for an adult, £60 for two and
£62 for families.

English Heritage (EH; ☎ 0870 333 1181;
www.english-heritage.org.uk) also has a good
selection of properties in the southwest.
Annual adult membership is £43 (over
60s £32) and allows up to six children
free entry; joint adult membership is £75
(joint senior £53).

Throughout this book, National Trust
and English Heritage sites are denoted by
the abbreviations NT and EH.

FOOD & DRINK

For an overview of Food & Drink in the
southwest, see p281. Opening hours are
outlined on p309.

Restaurant listings in this book are in
alphabetical order and feature a price
guide alongside the name. The price
guide indicates the cost of a main dish.
The categories:

£ (budget; under £10)
££ (midrange; £10-20)
£££ (top end; more than £20)

WHERE TO EAT & DRINK

Bigger towns and cities have the widest
variety of eateries and fly more diverse
culinary flags. Booking is recommended
at the more popular restaurants, especially at weekends in the summer – at
Rick Stein's Seafood Restaurant tables
are reserved a year in advance. Parents
with young children can expect menu
choices similar to the rest of the UK.

There's a vibrant nightlife scene in
Bristol, Bath, Bournemouth, Plymouth,
Newquay, Torquay and Exeter. While
some violence inevitably occurs, region-

SEAGULLS

Gulls are an evocative part of any southwest seaside break, but their insistent
demands to be fed mean many locals see
them as a pest. The birds are blamed for
scattering rubbish from bins, intimidat-
ing picnickers and sometimes plucking
food right out of your hand. The gulls'
defenders argue intensive fishing has
forced the birds inland. Either way, those
who do chuck a gull a chip become
the focus of a Hitchcockean swarm of
screeching birds and some very dirty
looks from the locals.

wide the picture is similar to the various
degrees of beery, leery rowdiness you
find all over the UK.

Pubs range from old-fashioned city
boozers to time-warp village locals where
the welcome is genuine, the fire is real and
that horse brass has hung on that hook
for centuries. Regional pub-grub encompasses the ubiquitous scampi and chips,
deeply satisfying cheese-rich ploughman's
lunches and fancier gastropub fare. Expect
to pay around £8 for standard bar food,
from £13 for fancier dishes.

By no means do all pubs have a children's menu but many have a family
room or are happy to allow children in
the bar until about 7.30pm.

VEGETARIANS & VEGANS

In general vegetarians should encounter
enough possibilities to make their stay
enjoyable, while judicious restaurant
selections will provide real menu options
rather than that infamous 'choice' of one
dish. As ever, the cities and bigger towns
will cater to your needs better; in some
rural and coastal areas meat and fish
dominate menus.

DIRECTORY

Predictably vegans fare worse except in larger towns and cities, but ethnic restaurants and counterculture hubs such as Glastonbury, Totnes and Falmouth boost prospects considerably.

GAY & LESBIAN TRAVELLERS

The southwest generally mirrors the UK's relatively tolerant attitude to lesbians and gay men. Bristol has a fairly vibrant gay scene and Bournemouth has a cluster of venues in the central Triangle area.

Gay (and gay-friendly) clubs and bars can also be found in the other cities and bigger towns (such as Exeter, Torquay, Truro and Plymouth), although there's often not a huge range and sometimes gay venues don't exist at all.

The usual instincts about how open you want to be about your sexuality are the best guide; you can be the victim of homophobia, or not, in the most surprising places.

Even in the southwest's deepest rural areas individual gay businesses, be they lesbian owned B&Bs or exclusively gay hotels, are thriving – see the wittily titled www.queery.org.uk, which has a good searchable database, and www.ukgayguides.co.uk, which details the southwest's lesbian and gay bars, clubs, B&Bs and hotels. The region also crops up quite often in adverts in *Gay Times* (www.gaytimes.co.uk) and *Diva* (www.divamag.co.uk).

The **Intercom Trust** (☎ 0845 6020 818; www.intercomtrust.org.uk) runs a lesbian and gay switchboard for Cornwall, Devon, Plymouth and Torbay.

HOLIDAYS

As a tourist hot spot, the southwest can get very crowded at peak holiday times, especially during the school summer holidays. Easter can be busy too. Bank holidays, especially the summer ones, can get very overcrowded and there are minipeaks around Christmas, New Year and Valentine's Day (mid-February).

SCHOOL HOLIDAYS

Easter Holiday The week before and the week after Easter (March/April)
Summer Holiday The third week of July to the first week of September
Christmas Holiday Mid-December to the first week of January
There are also three week-long 'half-term' school holidays – usually late February (or early March), late May and late October.

PUBLIC HOLIDAYS

Bank (or public) holidays see the southwest's nontourism-related business close, but attractions, hotels, B&Bs, and eateries gear up for their busiest times. Christmas and New Year are exceptions and many southwest attractions close.
New Year's Day 1 January
Easter (Good Friday to Easter Monday inclusive) March/April
May Day First Monday in May
Spring Bank Holiday Last Monday in May
Summer Bank Holiday Last Monday in August
Christmas Day 25 December
Boxing Day 26 December

Throughout the summer, the increase in traffic can cause delays around popular tourist areas. For more on driving to the region see p318; for driving around it see p322.

In peak season hotels and B&Bs can get booked out quickly and prices also rise, often by as much as £15 to £20 for a double room, sometimes much more. In Bath it also costs more to stay at the weekends.

The shoulder seasons (Easter to late July and September to October) can be great times to visit. Many attractions are still open, the roads and restaurants are less crowded and accommodation is cheaper. Perversely, the weather might even be better too.

INSURANCE

Worldwide travel insurance is available at www.lonelyplanet.com/travel_serv ices. You can buy, extend and claim on-line any time, even if you're already on the road.

MEDICAL INSURANCE

A European Health Insurance Card (EHIC) covers EU citizens for most medical care, but not non-emergencies or emergency repatriation. The cards has to be obtained in your own country before travelling. Non-EU citizens should check if there are reciprocal arrangements for free medical care between their country and the UK, and what its precise terms are; see www.dh.gov.uk (search for 'overseas visitors').

Everyone, regardless of nationality, is entitled to free treatment at NHS Accident and Emergency (A&E) departments but, crucially, charges may apply once that care transfers to another department.

TRAVEL INSURANCE

Even if you're covered by a reciprocal health agreement, or are a UK national, travel insurance can be advisable, as it can offer greater flexibility over how and where you are treated, and cover any additional costs incurred.

It also compensates for the loss of bags and valuable items, such as cameras. UK nationals may be covered for their trip to the southwest by their household insurance.

INTERNET ACCESS

While not packed with wi-fi zones, most towns and cities have fair-to-good provision. Many hotels and a reasonable number of B&Bs also have wi-fi access; cafes are another good option, there the charges range from nothing to £5 per hour.

Many hotels and hostels have internet access and there are internet cafes in the cities and main towns. Prices range from around £1.50 to £3 per hour. Public libraries often have free access but sometimes run booking systems and limit sessions to half an hour.

This book uses an internet icon (🖳) if a venue has PCs for public use and a wi-fi icon (🛜) in accommodation and eating reviews.

LEGAL MATTERS

The UK's emergency number is 999. Call this if life is threatened, people are injured and / or offenders are nearby. The text number for those with hearing or speech impairments is 80999.

If you're the victim of petty crime, report this to the nearest police station. Locations are marked on maps in this book; locals can also advise.

These are non-emergency police numbers:

Avon and Somerset (includes Bath and Bristol) ☎ 0845 456 7000

Devon and Cornwall ☎ 08452 777 444

Dorset ☎ 01305 222222

Drink-driving is treated as a serious offence and can result in imprisonment or a driving ban. The legal limit is 80mg of alcohol for every 100ml of blood in your body.

On buses and trains, people without a valid ticket may be fined on the spot, usually around £20, or required to pay the full fare.

MAPS

If you're heading onto the region's smaller roads, a good regional atlas will save you frustration and 'interesting' diversions; in remote areas you can't rely on signposts, or them mentioning places you're familiar with.

The most useful maps have a scale of about 1:200,000 (three miles to one inch). The region's cities have their own A-Zs; look out too for county-specific map books. Most road atlases cost £7 to £10 and can be bought at petrol stations and bookshops.

For walkers and cyclists the **Ordnance Survey** (OS; www.ordnancesurvey.co.uk) *Landranger* (1:50,000) series (£7) can be ideal, although many prefer the greater detail of the *Explorer* (1:25,000) range (£14).

MONEY

ATMS

ATMs (or cash machines) pepper cities and towns, but some smaller communities simply don't have them, so a cheque book or small emergency stash of cash is a good idea. Alternatives can be the stand-alone cash machines in convenience stores (charges may apply) or 'cash back'; see Credit & Debit Cards below.

CREDIT & DEBIT CARDS

Visa and MasterCard credit cards, and debit cards such as Switch and Maestro, are widely accepted, but some of the region's smaller businesses, such as B&Bs or pubs, only take cash or cheque.

Most supermarkets and village shops have a 'cash back' system: if you spend more than £5 on your debit card, they also allow you to withdraw a relatively small amount of cash, which is added to your bill.

POST

The recent post-office-closure program saw more than 100 outlets disappear from the southwest, but in theory there should be one within 3 miles of the vast majority of rural areas. Stamps can be bought at many village stores.

Towns and cities are still well served and hours mirror normal shop hours; in the countryside it's much harder to predict. Post boxes are widespread even in remote villages.

A first-class letter (36p) posted from the southwest to within the UK often arrives the next day (or the one after); second class (25p) tends to take around three working days.

A letter to an EU country costs from 56p; the wider world can be reached from 62p; postcards overseas are also 62p. Prices rise periodically, see www. royalmail.com.

TELEPHONE

Mobile-phone coverage in the southwest's towns, cities and urban areas is good, as are signals in many rural and coastal areas. But the geography means different networks have different zones where they provide only poor or no reception. Some moorland or coastal areas have no signal at all. Payphones are common in towns and cities, with a reasonable number in rural areas.

Phones in the UK use GSM 900/1800, which is compatible with Europe and Australia but not with North America or Japan, although phones that work globally are increasingly common.

USEFUL NUMBERS & CODES

In this book, the usual area codes (eg ☎01752 for Plymouth) are separated from the local number by a hyphen; only the local number needs to be dialled from the same area.

Useful numbers follow:

International access code ☎ 00 to dial out of the UK (see below)

International direct dial code ☎ 44 to dial into the UK (see below)

International directory enquiries ☎ 118 505

Local directory enquiries ☎ 118 118, 118 500

Operator ☎ 100

To call somewhere outside the UK, dial ☎00, then the country code (☎1 for USA, ☎61 for Australia etc), the area code (you usually drop the initial zero) and then the number.

To call England from abroad, dial your country's international access code, then ☎44 (the UK country code), then the area code (dropping the first 0) and then the rest of the number.

TIME

Wherever you are time is measured relative to GMT or Greenwich Mean Time (also known as Universal Time Coordinated – UTC). British Summer Time (BST) is Britain's daylight saving; one hour ahead of GMT from late March to late October.

TOILETS

Public toilets tend to be relatively clean and plentiful, although sometimes they are a little unsavoury. Even rural petrol stations are likely to have a customer loo. In some seasonal tourist areas the toilets are shut in the winter. Charges are rare, around 20p where they exist.

TOURIST INFORMATION

Universally helpful and brimming with local knowledge – staff at tourist offices are an invaluable holiday resource. There are offices throughout the southwest; some information centres are also run by national parks. Predictably, tourist offices in the bigger cities are busier, larger and open for longer; we specify opening hours throughout the book.

Many hand out free town maps and are crammed with leaflets. Some sell a good selection of walking maps and local books and can help with booking accommodation (sometimes for a fee). Staff that are fluent in other languages aren't that common; French and to a lesser extent Spanish are the most likely specialities.

The regional tourist board, **Visit South West** (www.visitsouthwest.co.uk), has a wealth of info on the region, and links through to county-specific websites. County, city and district organisations are detailed throughout this guide.

TRAVELLERS WITH DISABILITIES

Conditions in the southwest, like elsewhere in the country, are patchy. In places genuine and successful efforts have been made to make things accessible, in others they haven't and the situation is woeful. Sometimes best intentions are defeated by heritage and geography, in others quite simply more needs to be done.

Modern developments are required to have wheelchair access and in some places ramps, lifts and other facilities have been put into to existing properties, but again it's by no means universal. You might also find it's inconsistent within a building: a posh restaurant might have ramps and excellent wheelchair-access loos, but tables 10in apart.

For long-distance travel, coaches can present problems but staff will help where possible. On trains there's often more room and good facilities; in some modern carriages all the signs are repeated in Braille. If the train proves difficult to access there's normally a phone and a sign detailing how to request help. In the region's cities and towns you may find buses with lower floors, but it's unlikely in rural areas. Some firms have taxis that take wheelchairs.

Exploring the region's wilder spaces can present obvious challenges, but real efforts have been made. These include on the **South West Coast Path** (☎ 01392-383560; www.southwestcoastpath.com) where some of the more remote parts (as well as resort sections) have been made more accessible. You can search for easier-access options on the trail's website.

The **Dartmoor National Park Authority** (DNPA; ☎ 01822-890414; www.dartmoor-npa.gov.uk) produces the *Easy Going Dartmoor* booklet for less-mobile visitors – this outlines facilities and has a good range of accessible routes to explore. The DNPA also has a regular minibus tour for those with disabilities.

Visit South West runs www.accessible southwest.co.uk, a searchable direc-tory that includes accommodation, attractions, beaches and toilets. In some categories it doesn't feature a wealth of options, but reviews are detailed and it makes a good starting point. Another useful site is the Good Access Guide (www.goodaccessguide.co.uk).

VISAS

If you're a European Economic Area (EEA) national, you don't need a visa to visit (or work in) England. Citizens of Australia, Canada, New Zealand, South Africa and the USA are given leave to enter the UK at their point of arrival for up to six months (three for some nationalities), but are prohibited from working without a permit.

UK immigration authorities are tough, and if they suspect you're here for more than a holiday, you may need to prove you have enough funds to support yourself, or provide details of hotels, local tours booked, or personal letters from people you'll be visiting. Having a return ticket helps.

Visa and entry regulations are always subject to change, so it's vital to check before leaving home. See www.ukvisas.gov.uk or www.ukba.homeoffice.gov.uk. If you still have questions, see your local British embassy, high commission or consulate.

TRANSPORT

ARRIVAL & DEPARTURE

AIR

The southwest's position at the far end of England makes arriving by air tempting. Costs vary insanely depending on when you book and when you want to fly, with some prices rising at peak holiday times. Once tax has been added, a return flight to the region from within the British Isles is around £60 to £120 for an adult. Going onto the Isles of Scilly (see p249) costs more. If travelling from outside the UK, you'll often need to come via one of the country's key international airports.

Airlines operating in the southwest:

Air Southwest (☎ 0870 241 6830; www.airsouthwest.com) Mainly UK destinations including Bristol, Leeds, Manchester, Newquay, Plymouth and Jersey.

BMI Baby (www.bmibaby.com) UK and European destinations.

easyJet (☎ 0870 600 0000; www.easyjet.com) UK and European destinations.

FlyBe (☎ 0871 5226100; www.flybe.com) UK and European destinations.

Ryanair (☎ 0871 246 0000; www.ryanair.com) Belfast, Dublin and European destinations.

Skybus (☎ 0845 710 5555; www.ios-travel.co.uk) Flights to the Isles of Scilly.

AIRPORTS

Ryanair, easyJet and Flybe operate out of the region's biggest airport, **Bristol International Airport** (BRS; ☎ 0871-3344344; www.bristolairport.co.uk). It combines transatlantic connections with a full range of European and UK flights.

At **Exeter International Airport** (EXT; ☎ 01392-367433; www.exeter-airport.co.uk), Flybe provides extensive routes

THINGS CHANGE...

The information in this chapter is particularly vulnerable to change. Check directly with the airline or a travel agent to make sure you understand how a fare (and ticket you may buy) works and be aware of the security requirements for international travel. Shop carefully. The details given in this chapter should be regarded as pointers and are not a substitute for your own careful, up-to-date research.

within the British Isles, and links to the continent.

Newquay Cornwall Airport (NQY; ☎ 01637-860600; www.newquaycornwallairport. com) has a good range of flights to mainly UK and Ireland destinations (beware the £5 per person departure tax). Air Southwest's services out of **Plymouth City Airport** (PLH; ☎ 01752-204090; www. plymouthairport.com) are less extensive but cover similar territory.

Bournemouth Airport (BOH; ☎ 01202-364000; www.bournemouthairport.com) links the city with Dublin, Edinburgh, Jersey and a range of European cities.

The main gateway to the Isles of Scilly is **St Mary's Airport** (ISC; ☎ 01720-424330; www.scilly.gov.uk). Flights are Monday to Saturday only.

BUS

Travelling by bus to the southwest is cheap and reliable, but normally takes longer than the train. **National Express** (☎ 08717 81 81 78; www.nationalexpress.com) has a comprehensive network of services, running between four and 15 direct departures daily from London to the main cities in the region. Some adult return-journeys are London to Bath (£35, 3½ hours), Bournemouth (£27, two to three hours), Exeter (£42, 4½ hours) and Newquay (£52, seven hours).

There are also regular National Express routes from the midlands and the north: adult return Birmingham to Exeter (£43, 4½ hours). Special deals ('fun fares') can be a real bargain.

CAR & MOTORCYCLE

The vast majority of visitors to the southwest come by car, resulting in some serious traffic jams at peak times – try to avoid obvious Bank Holiday and school holiday travel periods.

London's circular M25 leads onto the M4; it links into the M5 around Bristol. The M5 winds south to Exeter, passing Bath, Somerset and Exmoor on the way. From the midlands and the north, the M6 links up with the M5 at Birmingham.

Dorset is reached via the M3 that ends near Southampton – an alternative route west is the A303, which heads from the

CLIMATE CHANGE & TRAVEL

Every form of transport that relies on carbon-based fuel generates CO_2, the main cause of human-induced climate change. Modern travel is dependent on aeroplanes and while they might use less fuel per kilometre per person than most cars, they travel much greater distances. It's not just CO_2 emissions from aircraft that are the problem. The altitude at which aircraft emit gases (including CO_2) and particles contributes significantly to their total climate-change impact. The Intergovernmental Panel on Climate Change believes aviation is responsible for 4.9% of climate change – double the effect of its CO_2 emissions alone.

Lonely Planet regards travel as a global benefit. We encourage the use of more climate-friendly travel modes where possible and, together with other concerned partners across many industries, we support the carbon-offset scheme run by ClimateCare. Websites such as climatecare.org use 'carbon calculators' that allow people to offset the greenhouse gases they are responsible for with contributions to portfolios of climate-friendly initiatives throughout the developing world. Lonely Planet offsets the carbon footprint of all staff and author travel.

M3 towards Somerset via Stonehenge. It has some quite prolonged single-lane stretches.

The 190-mile London-to-Exeter drive should take around 3½ hours; Birmingham to Newquay is 240 miles (five hours); Leeds to Bath is 220 miles (four hours). Expect to add anything from half-an-hour to two hours (and beyond) for summer delays.

For driving within the region see Getting Around, p322.

TRAIN

Services between the major cities and the southwest tend to run at least hourly. **National Rail Enquiries** (☎ 08457 48 49 50; www.nationalrail.co.uk) has information on times and fares.

Routes run by **First Great Western** (☎ 08457 000 125; www.firstgreatwestern.co.uk) include those from London Paddington to Bath, Bristol, Exeter, Penzance, Plymouth, Taunton and Truro. It also runs routes to Gatwick airport and branch lines to Dorchester, Exmouth, Falmouth, Newquay, St Ives, Torquay and Weymouth.

CrossCountry (☎ 08447 369 123; www.crosscountrytrains.co.uk) links the southwest with the midlands, the north of England and Scotland. Stations served include Aberdeen, Birmingham, Edinburgh, Glasgow, Leeds, Newcastle, Cardiff and the main southwest stations between Bristol and Penzance, as well as the Reading–Bournemouth link.

South West Trains (☎ 0845 6000 650; www.southwesttrains.co.uk) runs services between London Waterloo and Axminster, Exeter, Salisbury and Yeovil. It also links Waterloo with Bournemouth, Christchurch, Dorchester, Poole and Weymouth.

Travel times and costs vary; the later wildly; advance booking and travelling off-peak cuts costs dramatically. Some

TICKET WEBSITES

Sites selling tickets from all train companies to all national destinations:

★ www.thetrainline.com

★ www.qjump.co.uk

★ www.raileasy.co.uk

off-peak adult returns include London to Bath (£35, 1½ hours), Glasgow to Penzance (£140, 10 hours) and Birmingham to Plymouth (£85, 3½ hours).

SEA

Brittany Ferries (☎ 0871 244 0744; www.brittany-ferries.com) sails between Plymouth and Roscoff in France (nine to 9½ hours, four per week to two daily) and Santander in northern Spain (20 hours, one per week). It also links Poole with Cherbourg in France (2½ to 6½ hours, one to three daily).

Prices vary dramatically; for cheap fares book early and take nonpeak, nonweekend crossings. A 10-day, mid-week return in mid-August between Poole and Cherbourg is £90 for foot passengers; £400 for a car and two adults.

Condor Ferries (☎ 01202-207216; www.condorferries.co.uk) runs daily services between Poole and Weymouth and the Channel Islands (two to three hours). A return fare for a car and two adults is £315 and it's also possible to go onto St Malo.

GETTING AROUND

The southwest is a relatively compact destination, with good concentrations of attractions and environments. The vast majority of people drive – and then complain about the traffic. If you're planning to leave the cities and tour rural areas, the car is the quickest way to get around, but for

TRANSPORT

trips to relatively compact or urban areas, public transport could meet your needs.

The regional **Traveline** (☎ 0871 200 22 33; www.travelinesw.com) is a one-stop shop for all local bus, coach and train timetables. Calls from a landline cost 10p per minute.

AIR

Air Southwest (☎ 0870 241 8202; www.airsouthwest.com) flies from Bristol to Newquay (single £29, 45 minutes, one or two daily except Saturday) and Plymouth (single £29, 35 minutes, one or two daily). Air Southwest's parent company put the airline up for sale in May 2010, but at time of writing services were unaffected.

Isles of Scilly Skybus and British International run plane and helicopter trips to the Isles of Scilly (see p249).

For flights to Lundy Island, see p178.

BICYCLE

The southwest has a good network of car-free or cyclist-friendly routes – for some highlights, see p21. The most enjoyable cycling weather tends to fall between spring and autumn; because July and August are busy months, May, June and September make attractive alternatives.

You can take a bike, for free, on all the national train routes in the southwest, but booking can be required and restrictions often apply at peak times. Make reservations via the following numbers:

CrossCountry (☎ 0844 811 0124; www.crosscountrytrains.co.uk)

First Great Western (☎ 08457 000 125; www.firstgreatwestern.co.uk)

South West Trains (☎ 0845 6000 650; www.southwesttrains.co.uk)

Some basic rules cover where you can cycle. Bicycles are banned from motorways, but are allowed on other public roads. Pedaling the region's 'A' roads, though, can be both dangerous and frightening; some of the busier 'B' roads are also unappealing. Cyclists can use public bridleways but must give way to other users. Be aware you can't cycle on footpaths, something that's a particular bone of contention on the southwest's moors and coast paths.

Hundreds of miles of National Cycle Network routes cross the southwest. For info and maps try the sustainable transport charity, **Sustrans** (www.sustrans.org.uk).

HIRE

We specify bike-hire places throughout the guide. In general where there are well-used cycle paths, a good cycle-hire shop is often nearby. Expect to pay around £10 for a half-day rental.

BOAT

The Isles of Scilly (see p320) and Lundy Island (p178) aside, you don't have to get on a boat to get around the southwest, but it can be more fun if you do. The deep rivers and wide estuaries that cut into the landscape sometimes make ferries the fastest, most scenic, route from A to B. At others times peak-period ferry queues make that 20-mile road detour seem a better idea.

Some ferries take cars, people and bikes but some only carry foot passengers; we specify throughout the guide. The key car ferries run all year; some other routes are seasonal. If you miss the boat you can go by road (or sometimes path), although the detour can be significant, especially for cyclists and walkers.

For information on car-ferry charges, see p322.

Isles of Scilly Travel (☎ 0845 710 5555; www.islesofscilly-travel.co.uk) operates the archipelago's emblematic ferry (the *Scillonian*) between Penzance and the main island, St Mary's (adult return £80 to £95 and child £40 to £47, two hours 40 minutes). The service is for foot passengers only, with between one and two sailings, Monday to Saturday, between late April and early October. From late March to mid-April and in October there are four sailings a week.

Once in the Isles of Scilly, a fleet of ferries shuttles between St Mary's and the smaller islands that surround it. Services are operated by the **St Mary's Boatmen's Association** (☎ 01720-423999; www.scillyboating.co.uk) and run at least daily in the summer, leaving St Mary's in the morning and returning in the afternoon. Adult/child returns cost £8/£4.

BUS

REGIONAL TRAVEL
National Express (☎ 08717 81 81 78; www.nationalexpress.com) runs frequent services between the region's cities, major towns and resorts. Sample fares include Bristol to Exeter (£14, two hours, four daily), Bristol to Plymouth (£29, 2½ to three hours, four daily) and Bristol to Newquay (£37, five hours, one per day). For shorter trips buses may meet your needs, especially in cities and holiday hot spots, but services in some rural areas can be as infrequent as one a day, or even a week.

First (☎ timetable information 0871 200 22 33, general information 01224 650100; www.firstgroup.com) is a key operator in Bath, Bristol, Cornwall, north, south, east Devon and Dartmoor, Dorset and Somerset.

In Cornwall **Western Greyhound** (☎ 01637-871871; www.westerngreyhound.com) serves the north coast (covering Bude, Newquay, Padstow, St Ives and Tintagel), Bodmin Moor, St Austell and the far west (including Penzance, Porthcurno, Land's End and Sennen).

Stagecoach Devon (☎ 01392-427711; www.stagecoachbus.com) runs local services in Torbay, Exeter and east, south and north Devon, as well as buses between Plymouth and Exeter. **Wilts & Dorset** (☎ timetable information 0871 200 22 33, general information 01983-827005; www.wdbus.co.uk) connects Dorset's rural and urban areas.

WITHIN CITIES
The region's cities normally have good bus networks, although some wind down at about 11pm. City day passes (with names like Day Rover, Wayfarer or Explorer) can be good value. Expect to pay around £1.60 to £2 for a single fare.

BUS PASSES
The Firstday Southwest ticket (adult/child/family £7/5.70/17.20) buys a day's unlimited bus travel on First buses in Devon and Cornwall. There's also a seven-day equivalent (adult/family £32.50/49). Cheaper day and weekly passes are available for smaller zones within the region.

The **PlusBus** (☎ 08457 000 125; www.plusbus.info) scheme adds bus travel around towns to your train ticket from around £1.60 per day. Places covered include Bath, Bournemouth, Bristol, Bodmin, Exeter, Falmouth, Penzance, Plymouth and Truro. Tickets can be bought at any train station.

GREAT FERRY ROUTES

Bodinnick–Fowey Atmospheric crossing to a pretty Cornish port (p242).

Dartmouth–Kingswear Chugs across a stunning South Devon estuary (p158).

Falmouth–St Mawes Exhilarating route across the fringes of the sea (p232).

Mudeford Ferry A trip to a strip of sand near Christchurch in Dorset (p97).

Salcombe–East Portlemouth From a Devon yachting haven to golden sands (p159).

TRANSPORT

Stagecoach's Explorer tickets (adult/child/family £6.50/4/16) allow one day's travel on its southwest network.

CAR & MOTORCYCLE

The southwest doesn't have an extensive motorway network – there are none west of Exeter and none cross Dorset. While many stretches of the region's key 'A' roads are dual carriageway, some aren't, while the lesser 'A' roads are rarely so.

Sometimes the sheer volume of traffic overwhelms the road network. Be aware: in the southwest in the summer, even on a clear road, when the sign before a bend says 'traffic queuing ahead' – it's probably going to be true.

The region's cities feature the usual ring roads, traffic jams and sometimes confusing one-way systems – Bristol, Bath, Torquay and Exeter can be particularly bad. Many towns and cities have pedestrian-only central zones.

'A' roads and many 'B' roads have plenty of petrol and service stations. But it's worth filling up before heading off these main routes into rural areas, onto the moors or lesser used coastal routes. In the towns and cities fuel prices mirror those nationwide, but rise as you head into the countryside.

BRIDGE TOLLS

There is a bridge toll for drivers leaving Cornwall on the A38 via the Tamar Bridge, near Plymouth. Rates are £1.50 for a car and £3.70 for touring vans over 3.5 tonnes; motorcycles cross the bridge for free. Charges apply eastbound only; you can pay by cash at the booths. Motorists pay 50p to cross the Clifton Suspension Bridge (p41) in Bristol. Both bridges are free for pedestrians and cyclists.

CAR FERRIES

Car ferries shuttle across some of the region's key estuaries (see p320). Queues for these can be long at peak holiday and commuter times. The following are one-way, combined car and passenger fares; unless specified, charges apply when travelling in both directions.

Dartmouth Higher/Lower Ferry Across the River Dart in Devon; £3.50/£3.20.

King Harry Ferry Links St Mawes and the Roseland Peninsula in Cornwall; £4.50.

Sandbanks Ferry Between Poole and Swanage in Dorset; £3.

Torpoint Ferry Between Devon and Cornwall at Plymouth; £1.50; eastbound only.

HIRE

Rates echo those charged nationwide. The region's airports and cities, and many major towns, have car-hire outlets. Firms with a good presence in the region include the following:

Avis (☎ 0844 581 0147; www.avis.co.uk)

Europcar (☎ 08713 849 847; www.europcar.co.uk)

Hertz (☎ 020 7026 0077; www.hertz.co.uk)

National (☎ 0871 384 11 40; www.nationalcar.co.uk)

PARKING

Expect to pay from £1 to £1.60 for an hour and around £7 to £12 for the day. Sometimes a minimum two-hour rate is charged, while maximum durations are from 30 minutes onwards. Sometimes you won't have to buy a ticket to park overnight on one road, but will on a neighbouring one.

Charges at beaches, even remote ones, can also mount up; some cost £2.50/3.70 per two/three hours and £7 a day.

Parking can also be at a premium amid the winding, cobbled streets of the region's fishing villages and tourist hot spots. Many have park-and-ride systems, with costs ranging from around £2.50 to £5. Details are outlined throughout the guide.

We identify hotels and B&Bs that have parking spaces by using a parking icon: Ⓟ; when booking check if any spaces remain and if there's a charge.

TAXI

The southwest's towns and cities are well served by taxis, with ranks to be found near shopping centres, train stations and popular nightlife zones. In many rural areas there's also a reasonable network – partly because public transport is scarce and a taxi for four people often provides a fairly cost-effective means of getting around.

In the region's cities taxis cost around £2.50 to £3.50 per mile; in rural areas, it can be about half this. Taxi ranks are marked on maps throughout the guide; phone numbers for local firms are also given.

TRAIN

Services between cities and main towns on the Bristol to Penzance, the London to Penzance and the Waterloo to Weymouth line are good, as are those between Bristol and Bath. Trains on these routes normally run at least hourly; sometimes more frequently. Some sample trips include Bristol to Bath (£6, 11 minutes, three to five per hour), Plymouth to Exeter (£8, one hour, three per hour) and Exeter to Truro (£16, 2½ hours, three per hour).

Getting to Devon and Cornwall from the south coast of Dorset by train is harder. For example, the Weymouth to Exeter journey (£15 to £54) takes 2¼ to 4½ hours, with one or two changes.

Branch lines fan out from the main intercity routes. Key ones are Castle Cary to Weymouth, Exeter to Barnstaple, Exeter to Exmouth, Liskeard to Looe, New-

RAIL VIEWS

Some of the region's train routes offer superb coastal and estuary views. It's definitely worth looking out the window between the following places:

★ Exeter and Newton Abbot

★ Plymouth and Gunnislake

★ Plymouth and Liskeard

★ St Erth and St Ives

★ St Erth and Penzance

The website **Great Scenic Railways of Devon and Cornwall** (www.carfreedaysout. com) has a wealth of information, plus details of local walks.

ton Abbot to Torquay and Paignton, Par to Newquay, Plymouth to Gunnislake, St Erth to St Ives and Truro to Falmouth.

Privately operated steam trains include those linking Paignton with Kingswear (p145); the nearby **South Devon Railway** (www.southdevonrailway.org), which shuttles between Totnes and Buckfastleigh; the West Somerset Railway (p75); and the Swanage Railway (p104) in south Dorset.

TRAIN PASSES

The Freedom of the SouthWest Rover covers an area west of (and including) Bath, Bristol, Sherborne and Bournemouth. It allows an adult eight days' unlimited, off-peak travel in a 15-day period for £95, or three days' travel in a week for £70.

The Devon and Cornwall Rover allows you unlimited, off-peak train trips across Devon and Cornwall. Eight days' travel in 15 days costs an adult £60; three days' travel in one week is £40.

The passes are accepted by all the national (but not private) train companies and can be bought either from them or at staffed stations.

TRANSPORT

GLOSSARY

AONB – Area of Outstanding Natural Beauty

Brizzle– Bristol

BSA – British Surfing Association

bucca – a type of spirit or sprite, usually living in mines

CAMRA – Campaign for Real Ale

chine – a narrow river valley in Dorset

cist – half buried stone box originally covered in granite slabs

coombe – a narrow river valley in Cornwall

Dartmoor NPA – Dartmoor National Park Authority

day-mark – an onshore landmark used as a navigational aid by fishermen and sailors

EH – English Heritage

emmet – Cornish word for tourist

Exmoor NPA – Exmoor National Park Authority

firkin – type of barrel traditionally used to carry beer or cider

flicks – the movies

flip-flops – casual beach sandals (called thongs in the USA and Australasia)

gert lush – Bristolian for very nice

grockle – common word for tourist in Devon, Dorset and Somerset

Kernow – traditional name for Cornwall in the Cornish language

menhir – standing stone

minster – cathedral or large church; originally connected to a monastery

NT – National Trust

ope – narrow alleyway in Cornwall and Devon

pilchard – an immature sardine

quoit – a circle of stone pillars topped by a flat capstone, thought to mark an ancient burial site

RNLI – Royal National Lifeboat Institution, a charity that saves lives at sea

sarnie – slang for sandwich

scrumpy – traditional term for cider made from scrumped (stolen) apples

SSSI – Site of Special Scientific Interest

tor – hill or pillar made of rock or granite

towan – Cornish word for sand dune

wheal – Cornish word for tin or copper mine

withy – dialect word for willow

yarg – type of Cornish cheese, traditionally wrapped in nettles

BEHIND THE SCENES

THIS BOOK

This 2nd edition of *Devon, Cornwall & Southwest England* was updated by Oliver Berry and Belinda Dixon, who both also wrote the 1st edition. This guidebook was commissioned in Lonely Planet's London office, and produced by the following:

Commissioning Editor Clifton Wilkinson
Coordinating Editors Erin Richards & Louisa Syme
Coordinating Cartographer Andy Rojas
Coordinating Layout Designer Yvonne Bischofberger
Managing Editors Imogen Bannister, Brigitte Ellemor

Managing Cartographers Alison Lyall, Herman So
Managing Layout Designer Indra Kilfoyle
Assisting Editors Janet Austin, Jackey Coyle, Helen Yeates
Cover & Internal Image Research Aude Vauconsant
Thanks to Ryan Evans, Mark Griffiths, Imogen Hall, Lisa Knights, Susan Paterson, Raphael Richards, Celia Wood

THANKS

OLIVER BERRY

There are lots of people to thank for their sage advice and assistance on this book. Thanks to everyone who suggested new

THE LONELY PLANET STORY

Fresh from an epic journey across Europe, Asia and Australia in 1972, Tony and Maureen Wheeler sat at their kitchen table stapling together notes. The first Lonely Planet guidebook, *Across Asia on the Cheap,* was born.

Travellers snapped up the guides. Inspired by their success, the Wheelers began publishing books to Southeast Asia, India and beyond. Demand was prodigious, and the Wheelers expanded the business rapidly to keep up. Over the years, Lonely Planet extended its coverage to every country and into the virtual world via lonelyplanet.com and the Thorn Tree message board.

As Lonely Planet became a globally loved brand, Tony and Maureen received several offers for the company. But it wasn't until 2007 that they found a partner whom they trusted to remain true to the company's principles of travelling widely, treading lightly and giving sustainably. In October of that year, BBC Worldwide acquired a 75% share in the company, pledging to uphold Lonely Planet's commitment to independent travel, trustworthy advice and editorial independence.

Today, Lonely Planet has offices in Melbourne, London and Oakland, with over 500 staff members and 300 authors. Tony and Maureen are still actively involved with Lonely Planet. They're travelling more often than ever, and they're devoting their spare time to charitable projects. And the company is still driven by the philosophy of *Across Asia on the Cheap*: 'All you've got to do is decide to go and the hardest part is over. So go!'

SEND US YOUR FEEDBACK

We love to hear from travellers – your comments keep us on our toes and help make our books better. Our well-travelled team reads every word on what you loved or loathed about this book. Although we cannot reply individually to postal submissions, we always guarantee that your feedback goes straight to the appropriate authors, in time for the next edition. Each person who sends us information is thanked in the next edition – and the most useful submissions are rewarded with a free book.

To send us your updates – and find out about Lonely Planet events, newsletters and travel news – visit our award-winning website: **lonelyplanet.com/contact**.

Note: We may edit, reproduce and incorporate your comments in Lonely Planet products such as guidebooks, websites and digital products, so let us know if you don't want your comments reproduced or your name acknowledged. For a copy of our privacy policy visit lonelyplanet.com/privacy.

additions: Laura Bower, David Brittain, Lisa Cain, Zoey Cotton, Rhona Gardiner, Simon Harvey, Helen Harvey-Tiplady, Adam Laity, Dan and Tamsin Mallett, Claire Marshall, Alice Marston, Laura Martin, Louise McDonagh, Jack Morrison, Annamaria Murphy, Taylor-Sian Paciuszko, Charlie Riley, Gabby Rogers, Lee Trewhela, Sarah Walsh, Sally Williams and Jo Woodcock. Special thanks as always to Susie Berry and to everyone at LP, especially Erin Richards and Louisa Syme for judicious editing, Andy Rojas for making sense of the maps and Cliff Wilkinson for steering the ship. Last of all big thanks to Belinda for bridging the old Cornwall–Devon divide. The next pasty's on me.

BELINDA DIXON

A huge thank you to all who've advised along the way, including all at LP, from editors to cartos and everyone in between. Cliff: I value this opportunity; coordinating author Oliver Berry: your calm advice has, again, been invaluable – may your favourite beaches never be crowded, may your glass always be full. And warm thoughts and big smiles to my occasional travelling companion: here's to more Dorset day trips – perhaps without the rain?

OUR READERS

Many thanks to the travellers who used the last edition and wrote to us with helpful hints, useful advice and interesting anecdotes:

Linzi Banks, Chas Bayfield, Claudia Canevari, Alessio Cazzola, John David, Ilona Elias, Sean Everett, Barbara Helm, Michael Hornickel, Jay Howard, Alistair Hunter, Robert Kettle, Julia Knight, Ina Meyerhof, Andrea Mikleova, Dirk Nehls, Paul & Kumari Pease, Alberto Santangelo, Thu Trang, Michelle Udry, Angela Valente

ACKNOWLEDGMENTS

All images are the copyright of the photographers unless otherwise indicated. Many of the images in this guide are available for licensing from Lonely Planet Images: www.lonelyplanetimages.com.

INDEX

INDEX

INDEX

INDEX

000 MAP PAGES
000 PHOTOGRAPH PAGES

MAP LEGEND

Note *Not all symbols displayed below appear in this guide.*

ROUTES

- Tollway
- Freeway
- Primary Road
- Secondary Road
- Tertiary Road
- Lane
- Unsealed Road
- Under Construction
- Tunnel
- Pedestrian Mall
- Steps
- Walking Track
- Walking Path
- Walking Tour
- Walking Tour Detour
- Pedestrian Overpass

TRANSPORT

- Ferry Route & Terminal
- Metro Line & Station
- Monorail & Stop
- Bus Route & Stop
- Train Line & Station
- Underground Rail Line
- Tram Line & Stop
- Cable Car, Funicular

AREA FEATURES

- Airport
- Beach
- Building
- Campus
- Cemetery, Christian
- Cemetery, Other
- Land
- Mall, Plaza
- Market
- Park
- Sportsground
- Urban

HYDROGRAPHY

- River, Creek
- Canal
- Water
- Swamp
- Lake (Dry)

BOUNDARIES

- International
- State, Provincial
- Suburb
- City Wall
- Cliff

SYMBOLS IN THE KEY

Essential Information
- Tourist Office
- Police Station

Exploring
- Beach
- Buddhist
- Castle, Fort
- Christian
- Diving, Snorkelling
- Garden
- Hindu
- Islamic
- Jewish
- Monument
- Museum, Gallery
- Place of Interest
- Snow Skiing
- Swimming Pool
- Ruin
- Tomb
- Winery, Vineyard
- Zoo, Bird Sanctuary

Gastronomic Highlights
- Eating
- Cafe

Nightlife
- Drinking
- Entertainment

Recommended Shops
- Shopping

Accommodation
- Sleeping
- Camping

Transport
- Airport, Airfield
- Cycling, Bicycle Path
- Border Crossing
- Bus Station
- Ferry
- General Transport
- Train Station
- Taxi Rank

Parking
- Parking

OTHER MAP SYMBOLS

Information
- Bank, ATM
- Embassy, Consulate
- Hospital, Medical
- Internet Facilities
- Post Office
- Telephone

Geographic
- Cave
- Lighthouse
- Lookout
- Mountain, Volcano
- National Park
- Picnic Area

LONELY PLANET OFFICES

AUSTRALIA
Head Office
Locked Bag 1, Footscray, Victoria 3011
☎ 03 8379 8000, fax 03 8379 8111
talk2us@lonelyplanet.com.au

USA
150 Linden St, Oakland, CA 94607
☎ 510 250 6400, toll free 800 275 8555
fax 510 893 8572
info@lonelyplanet.com

UK
2nd fl, 186 City Road, London EC1V 2NT
☎ 020 7106 2100, fax 020 7106 2101
go@lonelyplanet.co.uk

Published by Lonely Planet Publications Pty Ltd
ABN 36 005 607 983
© Lonely Planet 2010
© photographers as indicated 2010
Cover photograph Shingle beach at Clovelly, Devon,
Holger Leue/Lonely Planet Images.
Internal title-page photograph St Mawes, Cornwall,
Christine Osborne/Lonely Planet Images. Many of
the images in this guide are available for licensing